BEYOND THE DOCTRINE OF MAN

Beyond the Doctrine of Man

Decolonial Visions of the Human

Joseph Drexler-Dreis

AND

Kristien Justaert

Editors

FORDHAM UNIVERSITY PRESS

New York 2020

Fordham University Press has no responsibility for the persistence or accuracy of URLs for external or third-party Internet websites referred to in this publication and does not guarantee that any content on such websites is, or will remain, accurate or appropriate.

Fordham University Press also publishes its books in a variety of electronic formats. Some content that appears in print may not be available in electronic books. Visit us online at www.fordhampress.com.

Library of Congress Cataloging-in-Publication Data

Names: Drexler-Dreis, Joseph, editor.
Title: Beyond the doctrine of man : decolonial visions of the human / Joseph Drexler-Dreis and Kristien Justaert, editors.
Description: First edition. | New York, NY : Fordham University Press, 2020. | Includes bibliographical references and index.
Identifiers: LCCN 2019015944 | ISBN 9780823286898 (cloth : alk. paper) | ISBN 9780823285860 (pbk. : alk. paper)
Subjects: LCSH: Philosophical anthropology. | Decolonization. | Postcolonialism.
Classification: LCC BD450 .B4456 2020 | DDC 128—dc23
LC record available at https://lccn.loc.gov/2019015944

Printed in the United States of America

22 21 20   5 4 3 2 1
First edition

CONTENTS

BEYOND THE DOCTRINE OF MAN

The Projects of Unsettling Man

Joseph Drexler-Dreis and Kristien Justaert

We have lived the millennium of Man in the last five hundred years;
and as the West is inventing Man, the slave-population is a central
part of the entire mechanism by means of which that logic is working
its way out. But that logic is total now, because to be not-Man is to be
not-quite-human. Yet that plot, that slave plot on which the slave
grew food for his/her subsistence, carried over a millennially *other*
conception of the human to that of Man's. . . . So that plot exists
as a threat. It speaks to other possibilities. And it is out
of that plot that the new and now planetary-wide and
popular musical humanism of our times is emerging.

—SYLVIA WYNTER, in an interview with David Scott, "The
Re-Enchantment of Humanism: An Interview with Sylvia Wynter"

Being human as a praxis, as the Jamaican novelist, dramatic critic, and essayist Sylvia Wynter conceives of it,[1] goes through the flesh. Against the
annihilating theories that construct Man as a doctrine, there is the slave's
plot, where the slave grows food, there is the strengthening flesh of the
person who is not permitted within the historical structures and parameters
of understanding within Western modernity to be human, but who nevertheless concretely lives an alternative. The question of living out humanity within European modernity entails what Aimé Césaire calls a "science
of the Word."[2] That is, it entails a praxis of reimagining ways of being and
knowing, beyond those codified by the modern world-system. An analysis
of the understanding of a specific genre of the human person that emerged
in the North Atlantic trade circuits in the fifteenth century, which Wynter
refers to as "Man," uncovers the importance of rewriting knowledge and
inventing new practices as a way of contesting dominant definitions of the
human through the creative act of expressing and presenting alternatives.
This is precisely what the essays in this volume strive to do.

These essays engage how thinkers have taken up the half-millennium
struggle for decoloniality in relation to the question of being—that is, in

relation to how the human person is constructed within colonial modernity.[3] The essays particularly grapple with the ways an interdisciplinary set of thinkers since the mid-twentieth century have struggled to articulate the problem of modern/colonial delineations of being with greater precision. The specific contribution that the essays as a whole make is to further interrogate the problem and to call attention to constructive responses.

Decolonial thinkers have pointed to how the being and rationality of the White Euro/US American subject is defined against others who are constructed as not thinking and not inhabiting being. Decolonial thinkers have further shown how the idea of race has played a specific role in legitimizing this process in Western modernity.[4] Frantz Fanon articulates this reality by describing Black humanity as humanity forced to live in relation to ways the specific genre of the human constructed as White has come to stand in for the human person as such: "As painful as it is for us to have to say this: there is but one destiny for the black man. And it is white."[5]

In their analysis of the construction of the idea of the human in Western modernity, decolonial theorists have demonstrated how the New World provided a space for very different relations between "Men" and "Women" than those that were the norm in Europe. María Lugones and Hortense J. Spillers show, for example, that gender was a category attached to European bodies, not to objects of property that could be located below the category of being.[6] Within colonial modernity and into the contemporary context, gender comes to indicate much more than a way to understand the relation between men and women; colonization and labor processes within colonization have given gender categories meaning, such that a gender system and colonial modernity are mutually constitutive.[7] Like race, Lugones shows how gender was created within the process in which Europe became a colonial power and came to see itself as the epistemological center of the world in the fifteenth century. Gender is constructed within the modern European project in order to serve the interests of modern capitalism.[8] The definition of the human person, Aníbal Quijano argues, is constructed within the processes by which modern/colonial interests structure sex, labor, collective authority, and subjectivity and intersubjectivity.[9]

By articulating how the description of the human person from the perspective of Western modernity becomes a problem, the contributors to this volume already initiate responses to how this description plays out in lived experiences of colonial modernity. The contributors do this by turning to the lived experiences and responses present within the underside of modernity, as a way to uncover alternative ways of being human and to open up a space for creating new ways of life. While this project transcends any absolute categorization, we have organized the essays into three parts as a way to indicate the main locus for decolonial creativity in the contributions. The volume begins with essays that explicitly engage the work of Sylvia Wynter within the project of unsettling Man, moves to essays that focus on ways religious cosmologies can contribute to the project of unsettling Man, and ends with a set of essays that seek to unsettle Man via critical reflections from perspectives shaped by biopolitics.

Sylvia Wynter and the Project of Unsettling Man

Sylvia Wynter has, at least since the late 1970s, worked to respond to Western modernity from the particular locus of the Caribbean (and specifically Jamaica). Her response to the ways the human person has been signified within European modernity comes out of a specific experience of European modernity as coloniality within the Caribbean. In her analysis of the historical matrix of modernity, Wynter describes herself as moving "beyond *resentment*, beyond a feeling of anger at the thought of how much the population to which you belong has been made to pay for their rise to world dominance," and instead asking, "How did they do it?"[10] In raising this question of "how," Wynter goes to the causes of the modern/colonial world-system in order to open up the possibility of unsettling and countering its hegemony in radical ways. This is a key move that Fanon also makes. On the first pages of his first book, Fanon describes his own move from a cry or shout (*le crí*) to discourse.[11] When Fanon moves to discourse, he searches for that which produces the coloniality that constitutes modernity—that is, he searches for causes of the modern/colonial world-system in order to pose an alternative, a new humanity. In centralizing an analysis of modernity/coloniality by drawing on thinkers like Fanon, Wynter introduces significant conceptual categories into decolonial ways of thinking that can open up possibilities for decolonial futures. Contributors to this collection follow in this move—sometimes in direct reference to Wynter's work and sometimes primarily focusing on the work of others—of asking the question of *how* the modern world-system has naturalized itself through a discourse on the human. The analytical work taken up by the contributors is at the service of unsettling and countering this naturalization.

One of the crucial categories that Wynter brings to the analysis of the modern/colonial world-system is the overrepresentation of White, bourgeois, heterosexual males as the human, which she argues is an overrepresentation foundational to Western modernity. Wynter calls this overrepresentation "Man." She presents the historical development of Man by describing a move from the theocentric Christian descriptive statement of the human as Man to an invention of Man as political subject (a shift occurring between the fifteenth and eighteenth centuries) and then to an invention of Man based on biological sciences and racializing discourses (beginning in the eighteenth century).[12] Part of the tactics of the affirmation of Man is the "blocking out" of any "counter-voice" and, in the contemporary context, particularly a "Black counter-voice."[13] Because the persistence of Man is "the foundational basis of modernity," and a general problem that creates subsets of problems, Wynter describes the central struggle of the contemporary context as taking place on the level of either securing the well-being of Man or of the Human.[14] As a decolonial task, this struggle requires "unsettling" Man by imagining the human outside of Man.

The analytic dimension of Wynter's project leads to a guiding constructive question, already suggested by Wynter herself, of how to reimagine the human person beyond the confines of Man or beyond what we call the "doctrine of Man." This process of reimagining the human person can uncover forms of life that emerge in epistemic sites that Walter D. Mignolo describes as "the moments in which the imaginary of the modern world system cracks."[15] Wynter frames the question as such: "How can *we*, the non-West, the always native Other to the true human of their Man, set out to transform, in our turn, a world in which we must all remain always somewhat Other to the 'true' human in their terms?"[16] Wynter describes this as a process of taking back the "Word."[17] This is a world-making process. It creates new social worlds, or reveals already existing alternative social worlds, that people inhabit and in which they actualize their humanity beyond the doctrine of Man. In taking back the Word, in creating a "science of the Word," Wynter values the intellectual production of those relegated below being and outside of rationality within the modern/colonial description of the human person as Man. She brings forth ways communities in the "cracks" of the modern world-system have lived out their humanity as viable contestations of Man.

The first essay in the volume, Mayra Rivera's "Where Life Itself Lives," provides a close reading of Wynter's 1962 novel, *Hills of Hebron*. It draws out the persistent theme in Wynter's work of the connection between the imaginative, cultural, and material elements of being human. The novel focuses on religion as an integral part of a community's life. Rivera particularly draws out how Wynter narrates "the importance of local histories, the specificities of landscape, religious visions, and creative practices in the invention of particular ways of being human." Theological visions materialize in history, and the capacity to create theological visions beyond the contours of Man is central within the praxis of living out humanity beyond the genre of Man. Rivera demonstrates how Wynter's work opens up a call to move beyond the modern European "degodding" of being, which was essential to the invention of Man insofar as it allowed the conquering European Man to take ownership of the world. In doing so, Rivera calls attention to ways Wynter might open up the possibility for religious cosmologies to be a part of the project of unsettling Man. Rituals that hold together the material dimensions of being with deep imaginaries—imaged in the novel in the practice of carving, which brings together the transformation of matter, dreams, and acts—constitute a project of unsettling Man.

Like Rivera's contribution, Rufus Burnett Jr.'s "Unsettling Blues" opens up the possibility of decoloniality within a religious cosmology. Burnett specifically takes up Wynter's insight, in both *Hills of Hebron* and in her theoretical and critical essays, that the option for life is located in a rootedness in the land or in space. Burnett reads the blues as presenting an alternative option to the Afro-Christian adoption of Judeo-Christian traditions within the praxis of being human. As an episteme that contrasts with Afro-Christian episteme, in the post-Reconstruction historical context the blues episteme offered an-other relation to European modernity. Rather than abandoning that which Christianity has represented as the abject flesh for the Spirit, the blues episteme resides in the flesh, without conceptualizing the flesh as shaped by a lack of humanity in need of redemption. Burnett then shifts to the work of Mississippi rap artist Justin Scott (Big K.R.I.T.) in order to show how the blues episteme is sustained in music and poetry that "breaks the epistemic hegemony that binds the oppressed to a constant state of adapting to life on the terms of the coloniality enforced by the doctrine of Man." Burnett's work opens up a fundamental question regarding the possibility of the joining of decolonial and theological projects by moving beyond the abject status of the flesh in Christian thought and what epistemic shifts are necessary for theologians if they seek to join decolonial projects.

The final essay in the first part, by Xhercis Méndez and Yomaira C. Figueroa, investigates the praxis of "taking back the Word." Méndez and

Figueroa link women of color feminisms to Wynter's call to take back the Word and her call for a new humanism. By highlighting the resonances between women of color feminisms and Wynter's project, Méndez and Figueroa call into question ways scholars identifying as decolonial theorists have used Wynter's critiques of feminism to legitimize their own critiques of, or lack of engagement with, women of color and decolonial feminists. Méndez and Figueroa take their cue from Wynter's project while pushing it further by drawing out how women of color feminisms are committed to reimagining "all types of relations, including the *relationships between those racialized*, from 'outside' the epistemic universe that has given Western 'Man' its power, ontological weight, and value." Drawing on the Combahee River Collective, Wendy Rose, and Toni Morrison, among others, Méndez and Figueroa demonstrate that women of color have consistently built relations and value systems beyond those established through colonization and slavery and beyond those that serve to bolster "Man."

Rather than solely being a book on the work of Wynter herself, the goal of this volume is to wrestle with this question of the construction of the human person within Western modernity and to provide constructive responses in line with the way Wynter makes a turn to the intellectual production of those exiled, on the epistemological level, from Western modernity. Taking on this goal also means uncovering new questions, and all three of the essays in the first part of the book open up such questions. Whereas the logics that maintain and legitimize colonial modernity suggest that conceptions of the human orbit around Man and define themselves in relation to Man, most often as assimilation or opposition, there are alternative perspectives that emerge from the undersides of modern/colonial definitions of the human person. How might these perspectives challenge Man? How might academic disciplines emerging in the 1960s out of political movements—for example, Black studies, Latina/o studies, Native studies, women and gender studies, queer theory—help to draw out how new modes of humanity are already being lived out? Wynter describes the process of the solidification of Man as a definition of the human person as such as developing in ways entangled with a Christian theological understanding of the human person in the fifteenth century, centralized in the person of Christopher Columbus.[18] Might religious thought, and even Christian theology, provide decolonial openings despite ways it has historically legitimized colonial modernity? What would that look like? In the second part of this book, the questions posed by the essays in the first part that directly engage Wynter's work are further explored in relation to religion.

Religious Cosmologies and the Project of Unsettling Man

The contributions in this volume as a whole dive into what we call "the doctrine of Man." The subdiscipline within theology that explores what it means to be human, and particularly what it means to be human in relation to God, is referred to as "theological anthropology." Historically this field of study was labeled the "doctrine of man." Michelle A. Gonzalez, a theologian focusing on theological anthropology, notes ways the discursive move from "the doctrine of man" to "theological anthropology" to signal inclusivity can actually conceal the ways men have in fact served as paradigmatic for the study of the human as such. Thus, Gonzalez contends, the "doctrine of man" may often be a more accurate description of this field of study.[19] The four essays in Part II begin to conceptualize what shape a theological anthropology that ceases to take Man as its point of reference that then gets generalized might take.

Wynter identifies a shift from a theocentric or Christian-centric descriptive statement of the human person to a Man-centric statement of the human beginning in the European Renaissance.[20] Some Christian theologians, most prominently J. Kameron Carter and Willie James Jennings, have approached a similar analysis, though not directly in reference to Wynter's work. They argue that Whiteness replaced or superseded the Jewish Jesus of Nazareth within Christianity at the dawn of Western modernity in the fifteenth century.[21] This analysis leads these theologians to argue for a return to a Christian form of identity before this "supersessionistic mistake."

Wynter does not advocate for such a move, as she does not push for Christian theology as any sort of solution. For her, the shift from a theocentric to a Man-centric anthropology began with Christopher Columbus's assertion that "creation had indeed been made by God *on behalf of* and for *the sake of* human kind *(propter nos homines)*."[22] Columbus introduced a new "poetics of the *propter nos*" based on the humanistic principle that the whole earth needed Christian redemption in the particular form in which he conceptualized redemption. Wynter sees theology to have canonized a doctrine of Man that liberation movements in the 1960s have begun to undo.[23] She argues that the deconstruction of Man as a model of being "is to be found not in the neoliberal humanist piety of *multiculturalism* of the 1980s, but in the poetics of a new *propter nos* that began with the 'general upheaval' of the 1960s."[24] Conceptualizing this "new *propter nos*"—that is, a new humanism, premised on the well-being of humanity in general rather than on the well-being of Man—within a theological lens moves against

the general trajectory of Wynter's work. In this respect, it would be paradoxical to turn toward religious—and especially Christian—cosmologies
as a way to counter Man.

David Scott argues that Wynter uncovers the ways Europe's humanism depends on its discovery of its Others. Yet, Wynter does not want to
give up on humanism; she wants to find a way to correct it and, as Scott
puts it, "re-enchant" humanism."[25] The essays in Part II from M. Shawn
Copeland, Joseph Drexler-Dreis, and Andrew Prevot "enchant" understandings of the human person with recourse to Christian thought, and
thus in different ways than Wynter suggests, but nonetheless in ways
guided by her identification of the problem of Man. Copeland, Drexler-
Dreis, and Prevot each see possibilities to recalibrate being beyond the
parameters of understanding within the modern world-system precisely
by drawing on Christian thought. Patrice Haynes's essay enchants humanism with reference to a Yoruba religious cosmology. All four of the
essays draw on a religious cosmology in order to envision the human outside
of Man.

M. Shawn Copeland proposes a decolonial way of thinking and loving—a project that connects knowing and doing—as a form of what Walter Mignolo refers to as "epistemic disobedience." Liberation entails
delinking from Eurocentric forms of thinking and the construction of
other options. In bringing a decolonial episteme into conversation with
Christian theology, Copeland recognizes two aspects of Christianity that
must be interrogated, on which the contributions from Drexler-Dreis and
Prevot each follow up in different ways. On the one hand, Christianity has
a long-established entanglement with the construction of what Wynter
terms "Man" that has not ended. On the other hand, Christianity rests on
the subversive memory of Jesus of Nazareth and a social praxis guided by
this memory. Copeland reads Toni Morrison's novel *Beloved* through a decolonial theological lens in order to unearth how *Beloved* might offer a
decolonial and theological episteme. How, Copeland asks, might *Beloved*
offer an episteme that unsettles the way flesh was constrained with Christian and ontological categories that operated within European colonialism and slave trading?

Copeland is careful to read Morrison's text without "subordinating" her
work to a Christian interpretation. Rather, *Beloved* can, in Copeland's reading, indicate a "reception of the grace through which a future might be
imagined." That is, Copeland allows *Beloved* to speak theologically, or to
say something about God and God's presence in the world, without forcing it to conform to Christian theological boundaries. She allows, to quote

Alexander G. Weheliye, "freedom and humanity [to be] conjured from the vantage point of the flesh and not based on its abrogation."[26] Copeland opens up a possibility for *Beloved* to speak theologically in a way that counters how theologians have often employed Christian categories to support ontological misconstructions. In doing so, Copeland poses questions that focus on how freedom, which she understands as the basis of liberation, relates to the conundrum of God's relation to the world, particularly as this relation is articulated within Christian tradition as love.

Like Copeland's contribution, Drexler-Dreis's essay questions how Christian tradition has been used in ways that might counter the reification of Man. Drexler-Dreis specifically considers how Nat Turner, a leader of the 1831 Southampton slave rebellion, lived out his Christian faith in response to the dominance of modern/colonial significations of the human. In unsettling Man through a specific religious orientation that included but was not limited to his participation in the 1831 Southampton slave rebellion, Drexler-Dreis sees Nat Turner as offering a path for unsettling Man in present contexts. Like the other essays in this section, "Nat Turner's Orientation beyond the Doctrine of Man" develops a constructive option for contesting Man and an alternative to Man. Nat Turner's religious practices—and Drexler-Dreis largely focuses on those Nat Turner explained as taking place before the rebellion that made him famous—provide the framework for this constructive option.

While also working within the dual process of decolonizing Christian thought and holding up decolonial possibilities within Christianity, Prevot's "Mystical Bodies of Christ: Human, Crucified, and Beloved" much more strongly suggests an implicit decolonial track within European Christian traditions. The Christian theological understanding of the human person rooted in the faith claim of the incarnation of God in Jesus Christ and its implications for all bodies, Prevot demonstrates, allows for a stronger decolonial vision of the human person than do secular options. Prevot thus argues for a wider anthropological use of the Christian idea of the "mystical body of Christ." Prevot specifically turns to ways the practice of actively following Jesus's life centered on the Reign of God (that is, discipleship) is coupled with a Christian anthropology that particularly sees the bodies of those who suffer to be united to divinity. Christian faith recognizes a real presence of Christ in the victims of a social order and motivates martyrial and prophetic action. These Christian claims ground a "decolonially significant" image of the human and praxis of solidarity.

While Haynes also responds to Man through a religious cosmology, and like Copeland, Drexler-Dreis, and Prevot sees ways of conceiving of the body within religious cosmologies to be significant, she opens up modern African humanism as a response to Man. The modern African humanism that Haynes uncovers is one grounded in principles from African indigenous religions underpinning precolonial African societies and cultures rather than a humanism imported from Europe. Specifically, Haynes draws on a Yoruba cosmology in order to understand an anthropocentrism within an African indigenous framework that allows for an alternative conception of the human to what Wynter describes as Man. Haynes significantly draws out what she terms an "animist humanism," retrieving animism from the ways anthropologists have previously linked it to the signification of primitiveness.

These four moves—allowing *Beloved* to speak theologically, uncovering ways Nat Turner's life may show how religious orientations can transcend Man, retrieving decolonially significant elements of European theological traditions and how liberation theologians have drawn on such traditions, and turning to Yoruba animist humanism—all show how a conception of the human person can be "enchanted" in ways that unsettle Man. Assuming the persistence of the problem of Man, each essay searches for a constructive path forward by positively drawing from religious cosmologies. Thus, while the problem Wynter articulates provides a starting point, the essays in this section move in different directions than Wynter's constructive project.

Biopolitics and the Project of Unsettling Man

The way in which power structures increase to control the concrete lives of human beings has become an object of attention in analyses of our late capitalist society. The essays in the third part of this book approach Wynter's project of "unsettling Man" from this "biopolitical" perspective. All three essays start from the effects of exclusion and oppression on concrete human bodies that have, through this oppressive logic, been reduced to bare flesh: bodies that are being deprived of a place in "the world"— that is, of meaning, of representation. Bodies that only need to be obedient and useful, whose only task is to produce capital and enable its flow. The essays from Linn Marie Tonstad and Kristien Justaert connect biopolitical oppression to the logic of global capitalism, while Alexander G. Weheliye's essay starts from the oppression of Black flesh as the core of biopolitics. All three essays locate an alternative way of life in concrete flesh. Thus, the essays in this part reveal the transformative power of flesh, its ability to "reorder the world," as Tonstad puts it. In line with the tensions in Wynter's work, the essays in this part struggle in their articulation of the relation between "flesh" and "world": How to create a space for flesh that has been denied the possibility "to be"? Does one create a space *in* the world, does one create *another* world, or does one *disconnect* world and flesh entirely? At stake, in the task of responding to each of these questions, is the development of a strategy that makes life possible for those who are being denied humanity in the world of Man.

Gender and sexuality are paramount themes in all three essays. Being tightly connected to body and flesh, a creative or queer approach to flesh that refuses to pin down norms concerning gender and sexuality opens the door to liberation. Linn Marie Tonstad puts forward the queer prophet as the excluded body that cannot be categorized and that as such is able to lead "the pursuit of liberation" from global capitalist logics. The transformations embodied by the queer prophet can be perceived through the prophet's performance, or agency—not through its identity, as there is no fixed identity. The figure of the queer prophet is the result of what Tonstad calls a "collision between biblical stories and contemporary performance art." The queer prophet's bodily agency—which Tonstad recognizes, for example, in the bodies of queer performance artists or the Black Lives Matter movement—enables the reshaping of space and reconfiguring of time, the restructuring of relations, and the emergence of a collective subject that demands change and that believes in another future, however impossible and unimaginable that future may be in times of global capitalism.

Unsettling Man is not enough to end global capitalism, Tonstad contends. Indeed, the versatility of capitalism has already accounted for a dissolved modern subject, and capitalism makes use of constructed, colonial divisions as different spaces that carry out its different "functions." Moving beyond the doctrine of Man requires a restructuring of space and time, the possibility of which is shown to us by the queer prophet's body, and the body's mediation by a "becoming collective" that is not per se permanent but that forms an alliance and demands change.

While Tonstad focuses on bodily agency as a strategy to induce transformation, Kristien Justaert reflects on the conditions for transformation on an ontological level (though this level too may function strategically). In her essay on the connection between life and flesh, Justaert brings together negative queer theory with the French philosopher Michel Henry's understanding of flesh. In a way, Justaert pushes the dualism between life, situated in the abject flesh, and death, situated in the worldly logic of capitalism, to its extremes by denouncing—in line with queer thinkers such as Lee Edelman and Leo Bersani—all hope for a future of this world. Henry's articulation of the way in which life resides in the flesh—which remains outside of the confines of representation—pushes Justaert in an almost gnostic fashion to reject the search for transformation and redemption "from within" and to seek liberation and life in the flesh, or in that part of the material world that remains unnamed and ungraspable. From this perspective, there is no room for a narrative of inclusion after the unsettling of Man. The alternative, then, consists of continuously creating space for the negative, for that which escapes all forms of control. In this "negative" resides the flesh as the seat of life itself. So however negative this view of the world might be, it does not give up on life. To the contrary, it attempts to make room for a life that is not controlled or disciplined, that is not defined or categorized, and that therefore necessarily remains out of the reach of representation and language.

To this Henrian analysis of unworldly Life, Alexander G. Weheliye demands that "Black" be added. Black Life is the negative ontological ground for the modern world. It is the negative for the being of the white Western Man. Indeed, in order to understand and transform the conditions of Black Life, it should be considered as more than an ontic situation of oppression: Black Life is a structural force, it is the ontological condition of possibility for the ontic existence of Black people, as well as for whiteness. In his essay, Weheliye searches for ways in which Black people have inhabited and embraced Black Flesh, even if as an ontological reality created by violence. Weheliye focuses on the themes of gender and sexuality, among others, in Jackie Kay's literary character Joss Moody from the novel *Trumpet*, and on Sun Ra's musical ways of articulating Black Life. The ungendering of Black subjects is put forward as the condition of possibility for different ways of living in the world. Gender and sexuality have always played an important role in the racist structuring of the world: Black people have been and are being denied sexuality or have been/are being hypersexualized. According to Hortense Spillers, these are two sides of the same coin, eventually expressing that Black gender and sexuality do not belong in the world of Man. Both Joss Moody and Sun Ra have invented themselves—they have created different places of belonging in which their gender and sexuality could not be defined. They reshaped their "unbelonging" in this world into a belonging in the flesh. Black Flesh thus becomes a space where Black Life can be recreated as more than a negative to whiteness.

In the words of Jackie Kay, when asked, "Where do you come from?," a question Black people in the world of Man are continuously required to respond to and unable to answer by referring to generations and blood-lines, one can say, "Here. These parts."[27] In the flesh.

Coda: Taking Back the Word, beyond the Doctrine of Man

Wynter argues that Caribbean authors—particularly Aimé Césaire, Édouard Glissant, and Frantz Fanon—made a particular intervention starting in the mid-twentieth century: They developed a discourse that went "'beyond the Word of Man' in that it is impelled to replace the latter's postulate of 'man as Man.'"[28] The revolt explicitly taken up by Caribbean thinkers in the mid-twentieth century was a fundamental revolt, directed at the Word of Man, or the regulatory discourse of the modern/colonial world, but also at the "tradition of discourse" developing since the inception of the modern/colonial world-system in 1492.[29] The authors in this volume follow in the tradition that Wynter unpacks by continuing a praxis of "taking charge of the Word."[30]

This project of taking charge of the Word in ways that move beyond the postulate of Man is, of course, multifaceted and in many ways exceeds the possibilities of categorization. This volume is intended to be neither exhaustive nor a typology of viable avenues of response. Rather, our intention is to bring together contributions to a tradition of responding to how the modern/colonial world-system has regulated being and knowing that continue to develop what Wynter calls "a new theoretical attitude"[31] that conceptualizes modes of being and knowing that exist beyond the doctrine of Man.

NOTES

1. See Katherine McKittrick, ed., *Sylvia Wynter: On Being Human as Praxis* (Durham, N.C.: Duke University Press, 2015).

2. See Aimé Césaire, "Poetry and Knowledge," trans. Krzystof Fijlkowski and Michael Richardson, in *Refusal of the Shadow: Surrealism and the Caribbean*, ed. Michael Richardson (London: Verso, 1996); and Sylvia Wynter, "Beyond the Word of Man: Glissant and the New Discourse of the Antilles," *World Literature Today* 63, no. 4 (Autumn 1989).

3. We refer to colonial modernity to describe the historical situation since the European discovery and conquest at the end of the fifteenth century to acknowledge that Western civilization is experienced as modernity by those on the side of domination and as coloniality by those on the side of subjugation.

4. See, for example, Nelson Maldonado-Torres, "On the Coloniality of Being: Contributions to the Development of a Concept," *Cultural Studies* 21, no. 2–3 (March/May 2007).

5. Frantz Fanon, *Black Skin, White Masks*, trans. Richard Philcox (New York: Grove Press, 2008), xiv.

6. See María Lugones, "Heterosexualism and the Colonial/Modern Gender System," *Hypatia* 22, no. 1 (Winter 2007); and Hortense J. Spillers, "Mama's Baby, Papa's Maybe: An American Grammar Book," in *Black, White, and in Color: Essays on American Literature and Culture* (Chicago: University of Chicago Press, 2003).

7. See Xhercis Mendez, "Notes toward a Decolonial Feminist Methodology: Revisiting the Race/Gender Matrix," *Trans-Scripts* 5 (2015); Lugones, "Heterosexualism and the Colonial/Modern Gender System"; and Spillers, "Mama's Baby, Papa's Maybe."

8. See Lugones, "Heterosexualism and the Colonial/Modern Gender System," 202–3.

9. See Aníbal Quijano, "Coloniality of Power, Eurocentrism, and Latin America," *Nepantla: Views from South* 1, no. 3 (2000): 544–45; and Aníbal Quijano, "Colonialidad del poder y clasificación social," *Journal of World-Systems Research* 6, no. 2 (Summer/Fall 2000): 345.

10. David Scott, "The Re-Enchantment of Humanism: An Interview with Sylvia Wynter," *Small Axe* 8 (September 2000): 175.

11. See Fanon, *Black Skin, White Masks*, xi.

12. See, for example, Sylvia Wynter, "Unsettling the Coloniality of Being/Power/Truth/Freedom: Towards the Human, after Man, Its Over-representation—An Argument," *CR: The New Centennial Review* 3, no. 3 (Fall 2003); and Sylvia Wynter, "1492: A New World View," in *Race, Discourse, and the Origin of the Americas: A New World View*, ed. Vera Lawrence Hyatt and Rex Nettleford (Washington, D.C.: Smithsonian Institution Press, 1995).

13. Wynter, "Unsettling the Coloniality of Being/Power/Truth/Freedom," 268.

14. Wynter, 288.

15. Walter D. Mignolo, *Local Histories/Global Designs: Coloniality, Subaltern Knowledges, and Border Thinking* (Princeton, N.J.: Princeton University Press, 2000), 23.

16. Scott, "Re-Enchantment of Humanism," 175.

17. See Wynter, "Unsettling the Coloniality of Being/Power/Truth/Freedom," 329.

18. See Wynter, "1492."

19. See Michelle A. Gonzalez, "Who We Are: A Latino/a Constructive Anthropology," in *In Our Own Voices: Latino/a Renditions of Theology*, ed. Benjamín Valentín (Maryknoll, N.Y.: Orbis Books, 2010), 65. To develop this point, Gonzalez draws significantly on Kristien E. Kvam, "Anthropol-

ogy, Theological," in *Dictionary of Feminist Theologies*, ed. Letty M. Russel and J. Shannon Clarkson (Louisville, Ky.: Westminster John Knox Press, 1996), 10.

20. Wynter, "Unsettling the Coloniality of Being/Power/Truth/ Freedom," 276–80.

21. See J. Kameron Carter, *Race: A Theological Account* (New York: Oxford University Press, 2008); and Willie James Jennings, *The Christian Imagination: Theology and the Origins of Race* (New Haven, Conn.: Yale University Press, 2010).

22. Wynter, "1492," 27.

23. See Wynter, "Unsettling the Coloniality of Being/Power/Truth/ Freedom," 311–13.

24. Wynter, "1492," 41.

25. Scott, "Re-Enchantment of Humanism," 120.

26. Alexander G. Weheliye, *Habeas Viscus: Racializing Assemblages, Biopolitics, and Black Feminist Theories of the Human* (Durham, N.C.: Duke University Press, 2014), 131.

27. Jackie Kay, *Other Lovers* (Newcastle, England: Bloodaxe Books, 1993), 24.

28. Wynter, "Beyond the Word of Man," 645.

29. See Wynter, 639.

30. See Wynter, 639.

31. Wynter, 643.

PART I

Sylvia Wynter and the Project of Unsettling Man

CHAPTER I

Where Life Itself Lives

Mayra Rivera

The story begins on Saturday. Holy Saturday, I presume, for their prophet is dead. Moses had inspired them to build a new community, to create a new life. He had promised them "those things that had been lost in their trespass across the seas, across the centuries": "gods and devils that were their own . . . familiar trees and hills and huts and spears and cooking pots . . . their own land in which to see some image of themselves."[1] Now even the land is dead and "a strange lassitude" affects the bodies of the New Believers (40). Having lost hope, they have become like petrified beings. It was as if "life itself had died" (79).

Life itself is woven out of seemingly disparate things—gods, trees, cooking pots, and dreams; its patterns unique and evolving. But we tend not to treat trees or hopes as constitutive of life, for we have inherited modern conceptions of "Man" that reduce the human being to a natural organism. These conceptions occlude how cultural and social forces shape life itself—and thus the historical specificity of any given view of humanity. Sylvia Wynter's work seeks to expose Man as an arbitrary and local conception inherently linked to racism. She also offers a more capacious model for being human—one that is culturally specific, relational, and dynamic.

Wynter presents this view lucidly and empathically in *The Hills of Hebron*, her only novel. While her essays take a broad historical view, *The Hills of Hebron* zooms in to observe the dynamics of life from the perspective of a Jamaican community, thus highlighting the importance of local histories, the specificities of landscape, religious visions, and creative practices in the invention of particular ways of being human.

Writing the Past, Reinventing Being

Published early in Wynter's career, *The Hills of Hebron* is marked by the urgency of questions of self-definition that occupied Jamaican intellectuals in the decades leading to independence. The novel offers a deep examination of how social/religious ideas shape life materially and thus implicitly challenges the avowed universality of European notions of the human, as well as reductionist biological views, which ignore history, landscape, and culture as inherent dimensions of what it means to be human. The novel is an example of what Wynter describes as the work of a "specific intellectual," one who does not trade in universal categories but rather works "on the terrain and in the mode of struggle provided by the existential conditions of her or his life to which she or he bears witness."[2]

Wynter relates the novel to the world of her grandparents, peasants who owned land. She explains that *The Hills of Hebron* was written out of her memories of that "self-contained peasant world."[3] "Even today," Wynter explains, "the memory of that gives me a sense of grounding in an existential sense of justice, not as grim redistribution but as shared happiness."[4] The novel also gives witness to the memories of religious movements in the Caribbean; the legendary prophets Bedward in Jamaica and Jordan in Guyana serve as its main inspiration.

Prophet Bedward was a grassroots religious leader who worked mostly in Kingston at the beginning of the twentieth century. He identified with the Baptist leader of the Morant Bay rebellion of 1865, Paul Bogle. Bedward's message emphasized "the need for land and justice, the injustices associated with White rule, and the necessity of setting up social welfare schemes that addressed the needs of the aged, infants, sick, and illiterate."[5] His congregation of up to thirty-six thousand members provided for its poor members. Bedward performed healing ceremonies at a time when the economic crisis in Jamaica affected medical services.[6] Around 1920, he claimed that he would fly to heaven—evoking both the Caribbean legends of enslaved peoples flying back to Africa and the biblical story of Elijah riding in a chariot of fire. Bedward asked his followers to sell their possessions in preparation for departing with him. There are different versions of what Bedward meant and what transpired on the day of the flight. Folk stories and songs relate that Bedward put on his white clothes and climbed a tree, telling the crowd gathered around him that he would fly and take them with him—only to crash.[7] But even after his dramatic fall, Bedward continued to exercise influence on his remaining followers. In April 1921, in response to conflicts between his followers and the colonial authorities, he planned a march from August Town to Kingston, which resulted in his arrest for sedition.[8] He was committed to a mental asylum, where he died. Bedward is remembered as a lunatic by some and as a political leader feared for his power to galvanize marginalized people into action by others.[9]

Prophet Jordan was a shoemaker who lived in Agricola, Guyana. Jan Carew describes him as an "extraordinary prophet-storyteller" who "never hesitated to bring biblical characters into his pagan mytho-poetic folk legends."[10] "Jordan spun tales of redemption and escape. . . . The reality he invented became more palpable, more real than the tawdry reality of Agricola itself."[11] In his 1958 novel *Black Midas*, Carew gives an account of prophet Jordan's ministry.[12] Jordan knows about farming, it explains, and thus he rented land where his followers worked. The farm prospered. When his enemies questioned "his right to the gift of prophecy," he decides to make a strong statement on the day of his birthday. At the churchyard where they had gathered, he commands some of his followers to crucify him.

Moses, the main character in Wynter's story, integrates traits of both Bedward and Jordan. Like Jordan, he is a storyteller who brings biblical stories to life and planned his own crucifixion. Like Bedward, Moses is a leader who promised he could fly and who was confined to a mental hospital. It would be easy to mock Jordan and Bedward for their extravagant promises. But Wynter refers to these prophetic movements as "precursors of the anticolonial movement that had opened onto [her] own political horizon."[13] Indeed, she points to the connection between the movements and the philosophical questions that occupy her. They "raised a specific political issue . . . a question of being"—not as an individual but as a collective one.[14] Wynter draws on these histories creatively, seeking to illuminate the challenges of seeking new ways of being in a context shaped by the legacies of colonialism and slavery. As Wynter describes it, her aim was to think through alternative models of being human beyond its prevalent conceptions, beginning with the lives of the "wretched of the earth" (Fanon).

The Hills of Hebron highlights the significance of the question of being by treating the emergence of a religious movement among the disenfranchised as an assertion of their dignity against a world that denied their humanity. As she argues in her theoretical essays, our very conception of the human is founded on the definition of indigenous peoples and those of African descent as lacking in being. Modernity defined Man in terms of the capacity for Reason, and it presupposed that only some men have the required rationality while others remained captive of their bodily senses. "Ontological Lack," which medieval Christianity had attributed to all fallen humanity, "was now embodied, outside of Europe, in the binary opposition between the European settlers and the New World peoples (Indios) and the enslaved peoples of Africa (Negroes)."[15] She calls this logic the "Word of Man."

Those who are marked as lacking in true being experience the effects of this conception of the human externally—as social, political, and economic forces. But we also experience it internally—as self-abjection. Wynter notes the similarities between this self-abjection and Original Sin. "Like the lay man of medieval-Christian Europe who could realize optimal being as a baptized, redeemed feudal Christian subject *only* through his or her autophobic aversion to prebaptismal being as the embodiment of 'fallen natural humanity' enslaved to Original Sin," Wynter observes, "the Antillean subject had to become reflexively autophobic to its own specific physiognomic being as the condition" of becoming Man.[16]

Even aspiring to be *accepted* as Man is a trap—for it mistakes a Modern European "local culture" conception of Man for humanity as a whole. "This conflation of Man/human then enables the well-being of this specific category of the human to be represented as if its well-being, too, were isomorphic with the well-being of the human species as a whole."[17] These cultural conceptions of the human continue to shape our desires, our behavior, our being. We are enchanted by Man, as if our well-being depended on it, and we accept carrying the burden of Original Sin. Uncovering this view of Man and its Others as arbitrary—as historically and culturally contingent—is a step in breaking our enchantment with Man. It implies a recognition that visions of Man cannot support the flourishing of those marked as others. New understandings of humanity must be invented, moving beyond Man and renouncing the very project of defining humanity in abstraction from culture in order to see human beings as always constituted by their sociomaterial environment. *The Hills of Hebron* offers glimpses of the emergence of culturally grounded, life-sustaining forms of being.

Transforming Religion

Religion is part of the cultural fabric that shapes communal and individual perceptions of the world, and thus their actions and their being. Yet religion is not adopted passively. It is transformed in radical ways by those who live by it. *The Hills of Hebron* conveys the constitutive power of religion through its content and its style. The novel does not offer the reader a spectator's position; instead, the author guides us to see the world through the eyes of the characters. The use of biblical names for the characters—Moses, Aaron, Isaac, and Obadiah—accentuates the significance of Christian stories in the novel. The names evoke specific biblical stories and thus also draw attention to the discontinuities between the expectations created by the biblical names and the realities of the twentieth-century story. Through the consistent use of biblical language and names, the novel explores the creation of unofficial religious visions through the transformation of received imaginaries in relation to the geographical, historical, and social contexts. By reinventing religion, the characters are reinventing themselves.[18]

The whole story unfolds in a time shaped by the Christian story of the death of Jesus. This is accentuated by the novel's organization in four parts, entitled "Saturday," "Friday," "Night," and "Morning." "Night" is the time of the crucifixion. The focus on a community at the margins of society and on the everyday struggles of its characters—for food, water, and belonging—implicitly places the lives of ordinary peoples in a complex and ambivalent relation to the Christian narrative of salvation. The first-century Christian story is not the only narrative of the past at work in the life of the community. Stories of colonialism in Africa and in the Caribbean, accounts of slavery and rumors of revolt, and reports of ancient African ontologies are also constitutive of their lives.

The prophet's appearance is a poignant example of the transformation of a biblical story to a new soil. His past is not revealed. He offers only a past recast in the likeness of the biblical patriarch. Moses claims to have been adopted by the reincarnated daughter of Pharaohs. He encountered God in a burning rhododendron bush, though, unlike the patriarch, he had no shoes to take off.

The specificity of the epiphany—a rhododendron, not just a "bush," a prophet too poor to worry about sandals—shows not only the creativity of the prophet's reinterpretation but also the significance of the revelation linked to the particularities of its time and place. Here and throughout the novel, the particularities of the geography, climate, and vegetation of the island, as well as the most ordinary phenomena, acquire theological significance. "A single drop of water trickled into the dry soil, was quickly absorbed, 'like water spilt on the ground and never to be gathered up . . .!' Where had she heard that? It must have come from the Bible. Everything came from the Bible" (279).[19]

The words shape their world—their social world as well as the landscape around them and even their bodies. Their anger, hopelessness, or forgiveness bring about analogous responses from the air, the trees, the ground on which they stand; intangible feelings could call forth tangible ecological effects. This intertwining of the social and ecological is exemplified in Obadiah's expressions of anger at being misjudged and isolated from the community: "He would show them, would hurl down hail and thunder and lightning, and a black rain to flatten trees, sweep away the soil, cut deep wounds and crevasses in their slopes as a reminder of his fury" (65). But his relationship to the land did not imply control over it. Obadiah could not stop what he initiated.

> And yet, days after his initial rage had subsided, his rain still cursed [*sic*] through secret channels of the hills to feed the roots of living things, to send the sap pulsing through branches which sprouted green leaves that sparkled as they caught the sun and breathed in moisture that would one day renew his anger, would one day force open the bowels of his wrath, his business always theirs, theirs, his. . . .(65)

The stories, the land, and the individuals' affective relationships to one another constituted the community of Hebron.

Choosing Life

Hopes and desires for a new life are expressed in the community's relentless search for God's embrace. The narrative unfolds as an account of this search, its triumphs and disappointments. The members of the community live by different visions of God. The worldviews are religious and also cultural and ontological; each reflects a specific relationship to the Word of Man. These different communal visions become actualized in the life of the community of Hebron. Their theological visions influence the way men relate to women, how the community relates to the land, what they cultivate and eat, how they dress, and the rituals that they practice. "Beliefs materialized in deeds."[20]

Moses first appears in Cockpit Centre as "a prophet of the castaways, a cavalier of the impossible, seeing visions, dreaming dreams." Like the people of Cockpit Centre, God was wearied of waiting and commissions Moses to stir people "out of their waiting on faith, hope, and charity under the sun" (135). He preaches a "Kingdom of Heaven Now"; his church is oriented toward escaping the intolerable conditions of their existence. In heaven, rather than in Kingston or in Africa, they would be able to experience their full humanity.

Moses's message was an alternative to that of the white Baptist church, as well as to the African traditions that flourished in Kingston. The Pocomania rituals associated with African traditions openly rejected the white God and offered exaltation and abandon to the spirits. Its followers were sure that the white God would eventually betray Moses. The God of the Baptist church demanded respectability, that is, conforming to the colonial elite's rules of social propriety; his followers were called to conform to the Word of Man. Aloysius, a deacon in the Baptist church, embodies the traps of becoming enchanted by the Word of Man and caught in its autophobic demands. Aloysius's participation in church is premised on his ownership of a suit, as if it could cover over his lack in relation to Man. He is deeply embarrassed by the New Believers, for they threaten the fragile acceptance that he had worked so hard to earn. However, the narrator's harshest description of autophobic behavior is reserved for the officials of the court. "They were all black clowns striking postures in a circus of civilization." They too saw Moses's rejection of the Word of Man as a threat. And thus the "barristers worked out their frustrations on the prisoner, attacking him for being black and stupid and not knowing the white man's ways, not talking like him, not hiding his black madness under a wig and gown, as they had done" (135). The conflict depicted in the courthouse is between those who accept the mode of rationality and of being human imposed by colonial authorities and those who attempt to live otherwise. A bourgeois European definition of humanity can only regard the refusal of Man as madness.

Escaping the enchantment of the Word of Man is never easy. Wynter articulates the need for, and the great difficulties of discarding "a stereotyped view of yourself that you yourself have been socialized to accept."[21] Aloysius represents the painful and doomed project of becoming Man, which is expressed as both self-hatred and resentment against those who, like Moses, reject the path of respectability. But even as Moses and his followers seem to reject the externally imposed definitions of Man, they struggle with its persistence in their own being—reflected most clearly in their gender relations. They would have to reorient their relationships inside as well as outside their community.

Moses's followers imagine salvation as an escape from the world. Still their otherworldly visions filled them with productive hope. They were able to dream of abandoning the "circus of destitution" into which they were born. They gave their possessions to the prophet, who made sure all were fed. They dressed and acted differently. Their lives were "touched by the magic of new hope" (122). They became a community. They placed their trust in Moses, just as Moses placed his in a God who would rescue him, enabling him to rescue his followers. But on the appointed day, when all had gathered to witness Moses's flight to heaven in anticipation of their own escape, Moses falls. His failure—interpreted by some as God's betrayal—sent most of his followers back into hopelessness.

The prophet's conversion to the black God is, ironically, inspired by learning (from the Irish superintendent of the mental hospital) about the practices of the Englishman who had stolen away Africa in exchange for a God created in the Englishman's own image—"a wise and holy *father*-figure who never existed" (142, emphasis added). Moses never says that he will create a God who never existed; instead, he speaks about turning toward him. The question of the ontological reality of this God is thus marked but suspended—or at least deferred. Still Moses recreated himself in the image of his God—"a man with all the craftiness and the cunning of the deity he was to serve," a black God partial to black men (146). This God would be on their side. He used deception to get the land of Hebron, their redeemed land. "After all," Moses argued, "in this *life itself* it is only the right to squat that the Lord hath granted unto us, the right to dwell upon the face of the earth for three-score years and ten which is the life of a man" (201). They would move to Hebron, where they would all work and build houses; they would be fed and clothed.

The land of Hebron now replaces heaven as a site of hope. Rather than taking leave from the world, they would abandon their past. To mark their break with their previous life, Moses made a bonfire of all the belongings they had brought. "And their past vanished, like Elijah, riding in his chariot of fire, a conqueror in an empty sky" (5). Or so they thought.

Miss Gatha held on to an apron that had belonged to her grandmother as a quiet rebellion against the new order under her husband's leadership. The seemingly simple action "marked her first impulse to withdraw a part of herself from Moses" (87). The object became her tangible connection to the past and to the life of other women, lives too often sacrificed to the community and its male leaders. Indeed, it is Miss Gatha who sees the hidden truth behind Moses's call for purification. "She could see that when Moses made the bonfire that night, claiming that he wanted to destroy the symbols of their past sufferings, what he had really planned to do was to leave them all like the naked clay to be shaped into an image of his making" (87). For Miss Gatha, the absolute separation from the past was not a liberation but a subjection to a new master. Moses "created this community in his own image," for which he secretly depended on the sacrifice of women. He demanded Miss Gatha's financial resources. He told Sue that "the sacrifice of her virginity was necessary to their successful exodus into the land of Hebron" (11). Patriarchy undermines the vision of dignity that was supposed to guide Hebron; it tears the fabric of the community from the inside.

Moses's dramatic end, however, is brought about by his own desire to prove himself worthy to those outside the community, who reject the uniqueness of his project and his position. He encounters a political activist proclaiming the social principles on which Hebron was built, the dreams that were, in Moses's view, realized in Hebron. Yet the speaker has not heard about Hebron and ridicules Moses's religious speech. For those aspiring liberators, the longings of the New Believers were merely a failure of rationality, a delusion. Their political ideology was modeled after Western ontologies that relegate religious visions to the realm of irreality.

The crowd contests Moses's claims to be the Son of a black God, demanding that he prove it by crucifying himself. Moses decided to end his life. "The market-place had become his Golgotha, his place of skulls; and God had manifested His Presence, not in anger against the unbelievers, but in the sacrifice of His Son" (227). Moses's God appears to be no different from the God of the white church, whose embrace depended on self-negation. Moses subordinates the life-giving impulse at the heart of the constitution of Hebron to his desire to be the only Son of God and to prove his Sonship to others. He asks Aloysius and Obadiah to bind him to a cross of their own making. In his agony on the cross, Moses cries out, "God is white after all. . . . God is white!" (243).

The crucifixion had been a betrayal—Moses's betrayal of life.

And thus, with his death, Prophet Moses made all the New Believers accomplices in his legend. Their belief became a necessity, was magnified into myth. . . . Moses alone had died, but Hebron, its past, present, and future were entombed with him, awaiting his resurrection. The life led by the New Believers after his death was an epilogue, a ritual dance, *ossified by repetition now that its original impulse had been forgotten.* (243–44)

This is Obadiah's retrospective account of the community's demise. The original impulse behind the creation of the New Believers, the vision and hope that had guided them, was replaced by a myth that could not sustain life. It was as if "life itself had died." The long, detailed description of the drought that follows conveys the sense that this was at the same time the death of the leader, their hopes, and the material elements needed for their survival. "Now that the land was dying they were careless of themselves. They sprawled on the benches, their dresses crumpled and soiled, their bare toes indolent on the earthen floor, the nails invisible under layers of dirt. The reddish dust of Hebron had powdered their faces and necks, settled into seams and wrinkles, gathered in secret whorls of unkempt hair" (57).

The nature of God and the fate of the leader are linked to the whole community. This is clear after Moses's death but had been the case all along. Moses's vision of God shaped the type of power he exercised in the community. His widow, Miss Gatha, has a very different vision of God: "Anonymous and not to be depended upon. For he might turn out to be white after all, and harsh." Miss Gatha was similarly addressed as "a blind and merciless God" (46). Her leadership was harsh. Her contempt for what she sees as the submissiveness of the people bears a certain similarity to the attitude of her grandfather, who had betrayed other slaves in order to gain the favor of his master. Miss Gatha does not envision a revitalized community but a new order under the leadership of her son Isaac who was sent to get an education and is expected to return and rule the community in Hebron. Ultimately, she placed her trust in the very patriarchal order that had consistently used and betrayed her. Despite their starkly different visions of the world, neither Moses nor Miss Gatha escape the grip of the colonial/patriarchal order.

Given the novel's critiques of colonialism and its racial ideology, the reader might expect the black God to be presented as the solution to the problems of the white God. Or she might, alternatively, anticipate an argument about the delusions of religion and an appeal to a secular liberation project. And those opinions are voiced by some of the characters. But Wynter does not advocate such stock solutions. Wynter's critiques of modern understandings of Man and his Others include its secular forms as much as its Christian antecedents. Wynter locates "secularism" or "de-godding" as part of the local culture of Europe, the universalization of which should be seen as part of the project of modernity, which "made the 'real real' and the 'normal normal'"[22] for the conquerors. This de-godding is a step toward a merely biological understanding of human, which bolsters the assumed universality of Man. The dismissal of religion as irrational is often a veiled call to conform to Man. Wynter exposes the hidden investments of secularism and has also written insightfully about the role of the religion of the formerly enslaved in the Caribbean in resisting their dehumanization. This is not the official religion, she argues, but a religion reinvented in new soil. "Their recreation of a culture and a religion in which their gods could sustain and affirm their humanity was a central moment in their struggle to rehumanize themselves."[23] The humanizing impulse, what appears in the novel as the "original impulse" of Hebron, is an affective orientation structured by ritual, song, and ceremony.[24] Rituals can harbor and structure longings with the power to stir new life. But they can also cease to be effective. When the humanizing impulse is lost or forgotten, rituals become ossified.

The Hills of Hebron represents religious rituals as arising from the strivings that animate human life. Moses had stirred the people out of waiting and inspired them to create a new world for themselves. But after Moses's crucifixion, Obadiah had treated "the ritual of existence" as if it were "immutable" and "sealed" (13). Obadiah performed the same rites that had animated their lives. When he preached, his voice, gestures, and the inflection of his words merely repeated Moses's masterful performance.[25] Similarly, Aunt Kate recognized that the rites assured the community of the reality of their world, but the "madwoman" wanted only to escape that world and thus she simply repeated them.

Obadiah's path toward the revitalization of a belief that is no longer a repetition of an ossified ritual starts with his rejection of the patriarchal rules that demanded that he curse and cast away his wife for conceiving a child that was not his. After months of madness, after finding out Isaac had raped his wife, after losing even his anger toward Isaac, Obadiah reached out to console his wife. In doing so, he "stumbled upon himself." After finding himself, Obadiah begins carving—a return to what had been his trade before he joined the New Believers. His initial intention is to make a crib for the baby, but he finds himself carving a figure. What began as an almost unconscious task evolves into an intentional act. "For the first time in his life he created consciously, trying to embody in his carving his new awareness of himself and of Hebron" (28). The simple creative act of shaping wood brings about what they had been longing for: "In carving the doll, Obadiah had stumbled upon God" (28).

Creativity

The Hills of Hebron treats creativity as a necessary element for the vitality of religious beliefs and practices, and thus also for the transformation of life itself. Moses recreated himself in the image of a biblical patriarch and then in the image of a black God as he imagined him. He had a performer's "ability to lift the magic of words from the printed pages of the Bible" (82). Obadiah had different skills. His craft was the slow, laborious art of carving. Obadiah's metamorphosis was a similarly gradual and deliberate process.

At the beginning of the novel, when Obadiah is still just trying to repeat Moses's gestures and rituals, he is described as a "rough-hewn unfinished carving." His becoming would require both rejecting the patriarchal mode of being human and emancipating his creativity to invent himself anew. Through the act of carving, "something that had long been pent up inside him, crying out to be released, had been set free" (298).

The act of self-expression is, however, not merely an individual act. Obadiah learns from a traveler that his carving was similar to those made in Africa,

> where your ancestors came from. And there they carve from father to son, and they carve out of the stories of their tribe, and their beliefs, their gods and devils. I bought a carving once that was made by the Dahomey. . . . They made this out of a belief that each man has four souls, one given to him by an ancestor . . . one, his own, the third, the small bit of the Creator that lives in each man, the last one, that which joins him to the others in his group. (300)

Obadiah's carvings, like Miss Gatha's hidden apron, link him to his ancestors. But they represent contrasting attitudes toward the past. For Miss Gatha, keeping the apron was an act of rebellion against Moses but also a reminder of the relative wealth and status of her family and thus a symbol of superiority in relation to others in the community. The apron was a given thing that had to be kept hidden and intact. Obadiah's carving was created out of the materials available to him—the history of his people and their hopes, the craft that the elder had taught him, the wood that he carefully chose from the land of Hebron. It is a model for and an expression of the transformation of his being and that of his community. Obadiah had carved the doll out of "the story of Hebron, of their search for God . . . out of this, the dream and the reality" (300). And the object itself becomes part of the new reality being born of his labor. The object is also a commercial good that allows him to buy food and water for the community. "This object which had been dredged out of his anguish, his search for a sense of being, had become an extension, not only of his living body, but of Hebron" (300). After Moses, the world of Hebron had felt dead and life itself was escaping their bodies. Obadiah's carving was the materialization of revitalized belief.

Obadiah's model of creativity stands in stark contrast to Moses's self-centered charisma and ingenuity. It is also different from Isaac's cultivated, but self-conscious and anxious, intellect. Isaac tries writing as a creative activity and finds himself struggling with its meaning. He wanted to write the history of Hebron. But he doubts, "For whom am I writing? And why?" (266). Those in his community cannot read. Those outside the community cannot understand the longings that animate it. Isaac knew that even those outsiders who espoused anticolonial views had been seduced by "the false coin of shallow dreams" (266).

> Unlike their illiterate would-be followers, they were spiritually and emotionally emasculated. In exploring the symbols of power that their rulers had trapped in books, they had become enmeshed in their complexities, had fallen victims to a servitude more absolute than the one imposed by guns, whips, chains, and hunger. . . . They had surrendered even the right to dream their own dreams. (257)

To "explain his present" to those distant from the community would require telling them "of the submerged past." But what language could he use? If he adopted their language, he "would be seduced into distortions, and the bare truth that might have spanned the centuries and the differences would vanish, leaving only lost echoes" (266). How then to tell the story of the community? The task was too threatening for Isaac's wounded soul. Like those seduced by shallow dreams, Isaac became a "shadow-man" who seeks security in a violent manhood (261). In the end, Isaac is also seduced by and becomes enslaved to the prescriptions of Man.

The encounter with the traveler reveals to Obadiah hidden connections to distant communities. It represents what Wynter calls, in a different context, "a transfer of empathy"—the possibility of connecting with the experiences of different subordinated groups.[26] There are hints of this possibility in Moses's relationship with the Irish doctor, who also saw himself as a colonized subject. But the Irishman's view of freedom was still mired in racism. "Only Moses, through his madness, had begun to liberate himself from the spiritual shackles which held the Irishman in their grip" (138). In contrast to the Irishman, the unnamed traveler finds in the story of Hebron a source for renewing his own hopes after a catastrophe. The traveler tells Obadiah that he comes from Germany, where a group of people had sought to create a "Promised Land." But others had taken over; he had lost his family and everything he owned. Now he had stopped in "Paradise Bay" on his way to exile. And there the fortuitous encounter with Obadiah made the traveler believe that "man's attempts to create Hebrons would continue forever" (301). Creating out of culturally specific stories and styles of craftsmanship allows Obadiah to begin to question the isolation under which they had lived since Moses led them to Hebron. Why were they "shut amidst these arid, thorny, almost inaccessible hills, straining for the embrace of God?," he had asked himself (22). With a new consciousness of himself as part of the world, Obadiah became a different type of leader. "His own moment of vision had been brief, like a rainbow reflected in water. To explain it to [the people of Hebron] he would need the words and the rhythms, not of a sermon, but a song" (305). The songs were the appropriate vehicle to convey truths of their past and a new vision for their future. As Wynter argues, in oral cultures, memory is "maintained, reconstructed, represented, and in essence, reinvented in the very flesh of each generation," not least through song and dance.[27] Rather than seeking to create a community in his own image, Obadiah would guide the community to reclaim the right to dream their own dreams and reassert their humanity.

Conclusion

> Human beings are magical. Bios and Logos. Words made flesh, muscle
> and bone animated by hope and desire, belief materialized in deeds.
>   SYLVIA WYNTER, "The Pope Must Have Been Drunk,
>   the King of Castile a Madman"

Words, rituals, and hope shape the social and material dimensions of being.[28] Belief materialized in deeds. The reinvention of beliefs, including our understandings of what it means to be human, is a crucial political practice. It is also an aesthetic endeavor.

The use of the metaphor of carving in *The Hills of Hebron* conveys the conjunction of materiality, dreams, and acts by suggesting intentional processes of re-creating society by giving shape to received materials through embodied creative labor—and in the process reshaping oneself. The invention of alternative forms of being human implies also perceiving and describing the ongoing interweaving of dreams and flesh.

These are the themes of Wynter's novel and also the traits of her practice as a writer. The novel is the product of a creative process through which she invokes a submerged past in order to help explain the present and transform it. The novel's story explicitly reworks materials received from Caribbean history and geographic context. The writing is also indebted to Caribbean intellectual and aesthetic traditions. Antillean intellectuals of Wynter's generation saw themselves as creating a new postindependence collective identity. Wynter describes the context of the anticolonial movement as one in which "everything Caribbean was still new, still to be done." Then "all of a sudden, writers began writing, painters began painting . . . people who had been silent for so long now 'found their voices.'"[29] This historical context marks Wynter's theorizations of the human. Understanding the human as a culturally grounded praxis was a political necessity. That praxis is conceptualized as analogous to artistic creation. Wynter's consistent use of artistic metaphors is far from incidental. Wynter the playwright speaks about inventing new selves as roles in a dramatic reality. And it is Wynter, the literary scholar, who writes about the need to invent "new genres of being" or new "figurations of the human."[30]

The works of intellectuals like Fanon and Glissant are a "continuation of the act of poetic uprising" started by their predecessors, Wynter argues.[31] The "mode of revolt" of the Antillean intellectual "is one against the very roots of our present mode of conventional reason and therefore of the order of discourse and its Word of Man," Wynter argues.[32] This rebellion entails denouncing the fallacy of abstract conceptions of being, refusing to perform the role assigned to the Caribbean subject as its Other, and offering their own imaginaries of being. This project is aesthetic and political.

The fictional prophets in the novel are artists of sorts, inasmuch as they transform the symbols of the religious traditions they have received to stir hope and desire in a disenfranchised community. They abandon the white colonial churches—disenchanted with the roles those churches prescribed them. But the story is not about secularization in the Western modern sense of the term. To the contrary, religion expressed their particular longings, coded their ethical values, and concretized their claims to full humanity. Religion shaped their story, and their experiences changed their religion. As Wynter argues in an essay about C. L. R. James, "The novel, in its true pedagogical function . . . is not the product of a doctrine, not the formgiving mechanism to an already preestablished content. It is rather, the condition of possibility of the emergence of a new doctrine."[33] Words that constitute acts.[34]

NOTES

1. Sylvia Wynter, *The Hills of Hebron* (Kingston, Jamaica: Ian Randle Publishers, 2010), 52. Originally published in 1962. All future page citations to this work will appear in parentheses in the text.

2. Sylvia Wynter, "Beyond the Word of Man: Glissant and the New Discourse of the Antilles," *World Literature Today* 63, no. 4 (Autumn 1989): 640.

3. David Scott, "The Re-Enchantment of Humanism: An Interview with Sylvia Wynter," *Small Axe* 8 (September 2000): 124.

4. Scott, "Re-Enchantment of Humanism," 124.

5. Charles Reavies Price, "'Cleave to the Black': Expressions of Ethiopianism in Jamaica," *New West Indian Guide* 77, no. 1/2 (2003): 46.

6. *Encyclopedia of the African and African American Experience*, ed. Kwame Anthony Appiah and Henry Louis Gates, s.v. "Bedward, Alexander," www.oxfordaasc.com.

7. Daryl C. Dance, *Folklore from Contemporary Jamaicans* (Knoxville: University of Tennessee Press, 1985), 72–76.

8. Price, "'Cleave to the Black,'" 47.

9. See Roxane Watson, "The Native Baptist Church's Political Role in Jamaica: Alexander Bedward's Trial for Sedition," *Journal of Caribbean History* 42, no. 2 (2008); and Price, "'Cleave to the Black.'" For the folktales based on Bedward, see Dance, *Folklore from Contemporary Jamaicans*, 72–77.

10. Jan Carew, "The Fusion of African and Amerindian Folk Tales," *Caribbean Quarterly* 23, no. 1 (1977): 7.

11. Carew, "Fusion of African and Amerindian Folk Tales," 7.

12. Jan Carew, *Black Midas* (London: Secker and Warburg, 1958), 60.

13. Scott, "Re-Enchantment of Humanism," 137.

14. Scott, 137.

15. Wynter, "Beyond the Word of Man," 641.

16. Wynter, 643 (emphasis added).

17. Sylvia Wynter, "The Pope Must Have Been Drunk, the King of Castile a Madman: Culture as Actuality, and the Caribbean Rethinking of Modernity," in *The Reordering of Culture: Latin America, the Caribbean and Canada in the Hood*, ed. Alvina Ruprecht and Cecilia Taiana (Ottawa: Carleton University Press, 1995), 29.

18. In her study of Jamaican religions, Wynter argues that "the pattern of religious creativity begun under slavery—the slaves reinvented themselves through their reinvention of religion—continued in the cities." Sylvia Wynter, "Black Metamorphosis: New Natives in a New World" (unpublished manuscript), 201.

19. Wynter quotes 2 Samuel 14:14.

20. "Human beings are magical. Bios and Logos. Words made flesh, muscle and bone animated by hope and desire, belief materialized in deeds, deeds which crystallize our actualities" Wynter, "Pope Must Have Been Drunk," 35.

21. Scott, "Re-Enchantment of Humanism," 131.

22. Wynter, "Pope Must Have Been Drunk," 19.

23. Wynter, "Black Metamorphosis," 74.

24. Wynter, 180.

25. When Obadiah "spoke and was caught up in the rhythm of words," however, "his body flowed like water. His face, with its high sloping forehead, fleshly nose, drooping lips, and heavy jowls, was like some rough-hewn and unfinished carving. A perpetual self-doubt lurked in his eyes." Wynter, 9.

26. Scott, "Re-Enchantment of Humanism," 131.

27. Wynter, "Black Metamorphosis," 140.

28. "It is man who brings society into being" is a quote from Frantz Fanon, *Black Skin, White Masks* (New York: Grove Press, 1967), 11. "The maps of spring always have to be redrawn again" evokes a verse from Aimé Césaire's "Notebook of a Return to the Native Land": "Calm and lull oh my voice the child who does not know / that the map of spring is always to be drawn again." Aimé Césaire, "Notebook on a Return to the Native Land," trans. Clayton Eshleman and Annette Smith, *Montemora* 6 (1979): 39.

29. Scott, "Re-Enchantment of Humanism," 128.

30. This is the case even in her novel, *The Hills of Hebron*, where the main metaphor for the new being and thus the survival of the community is wood carving.

31. Wynter, "Beyond the Word of Man," 641.

32. Wynter, 639.

33. Cited in Kelly Baker Josephs, "The Necessity for Madness: Negotiating Nation in Sylvia Wynter's *The Hills of Hebron*," in *Disturbers of the Peace: Representations of Madness in Anglophone Caribbean Literature*, ed. Kelly Baker Josephs (Charlottesville: University of Virginia Press, 2013), 46.

34. Wynter uses the phase "themes-that-constitute acts" repeatedly in Wynter, "Beyond the Word of Man."

CHAPTER 2

Unsettling Blues: A Decolonial Reading of the Blues Episteme

Rufus Burnett Jr.

Sylvia Wynter's work and the broader movement, known to some as the decolonial turn, present a challenge to theologians and other intellectuals who seek to interpret the modern/colonial world. This turn in thought opens the possibility for theological intellectuals to "take a second look" at those perspectives that are repressed by the modern project.[1] A crucial part of theological perspectives that seek to take a second look at worldviews repressed by Western modernity is a process of reinterpreting indigenous cosmovisions with an eye toward how they might inform Christian praxis in the context of European expansion and the makings of the modern/colonial world.

Wynter's insights on the makings of modern Eurocentric modes of being offer a helpful analysis of the decolonial turn and the way in which subaltern voices assert ontologies and epistemologies that have the potential for providing options for human living. Wynter's analysis of the emergence of the modern Eurocentric idea of "Man" and its various modalities of human being, during and after colonialism, is a significant addition to the decolonial canon in that it further treats the problem of colonial ontology and how it works to deny the autonomy needed for humans to articulate themselves in the world. Her critique begins with a critical view of the Christian epistemological underpinnings of coloniality and ends with an analysis of the more secular underpinnings that undergird the idea of Man. Of particular note is Wynter's notion of the Spirit/Flesh, which has roots in the Judeo/Christian (ethnocentric) representation of humanity as Spirit/Flesh.[2] According to Wynter, "Spirit" and "Flesh" represent the redeemed and fallen nature of humanity, respectively.[3] Spirit/Flesh representations of the human, Wynter argues, provide a foundational ethnocentrism or bias that has not yet been abandoned—even in more secular representations of the human (in fact, the bias has most likely only globalized itself).[4] For Wynter, a decolonial option is a vision of humanity that is unbound from ethnocentrism. It is important to note that, for Wynter, ethnocentric cosmology or ethnocosmologies are not unique to Judeo-Christian cultures but are integral to all human cosmologies. As such, cosmological understandings of the world and the universe are locally situated despite their function as universals in the minds of their adherents. Most striking about Wynter's work is her ability to expose the provincial nature of cosmologies and how this provinciality reaches a globally oppressive form in the makings of the modern/colonial world-system.

With a focus on Wynter's analysis of ethnocentric cosmologies, the Spirit/Flesh binary, and the doctrine of Man, I want to consider a cultural production that emerges from the post-Reconstruction era in the US South, namely the blues. The blues acts as starting point for considering the theological dynamics of the doctrine of Man mainly because of its distinguishability from the modern/colonial imagination. The blues emerges at a time when Americans living in the post-Reconstruction era were solidifying theological visions for human life under the massive weight of racial ideology. The blues and its treatment in black American cultural and theological thought presents an alternative option by which black Americans dislocated what Wynter identifies as Man_1 and Man_2. The blues option is not lost within Wynter's consideration of decolonial or anticolonial options for life. In her assessment of the thought of Amiri Baraka, she recognizes the blues as a subaltern option for reimagining a human mode of being. Drawing on LeRoi Jones (now Amiri Imamu Baraka), Wynter communicates, via Baraka, that the blues is a cultural production that emerges from a "frontier zone."[5] By frontier zone, Baraka identifies the obscurity and invisibility of the context from which the blues emerges. Further,

Wynter connects the blues and jazz to the syncretic strand of black American culture that worked to refashion humanity by standards set by black Americans. To this point she writes:

> There were two streams of African survivals in the New World, the stream which retreated and preserved themselves with minor changes in the Maroon areas; and the stream which, in a great syncretic process re-established itself as the cultural subsoil of the peasant relation to the new land; which reinvented religion, folksongs, folklore, folk beliefs, peopled innumerable "duppy plants" with the spirits of ancestors, with old and new gods. It was this stream which fed the roots of culture. Out of this stream, for example there came the spirituals, the urban blues and the still more urban jazz. This stream has been at once a "black" stream and a "native" stream.[6]

Wynter's reading of Baraka, who was writing in the 1970s, lays some of the foundation of her anticolonial framework that came together in both her analysis of modernity and her creative imagination of the characters in her novel, *The Hills of Hebron*. *The Hills of Hebron* captures some of Wynter's life experiences in Jamaica and her sentiments about the multiple modes of anticolonial struggle.[7] Similar to the peoples of Jamaica and the peoples depicted in the fictional tale of Hebron, the blues can also be considered for its epistemic contributions to the dislodging of the colonial episteme and its legacy. Following insights from blues commentators such as Amiri Baraka, Albert Murray, Daphne Duval Harrison, Angela Davis, Clyde Woods, and others, I will argue that the blues presents an option for human *being* that primarily asserts itself as a counter to the Afro-Christian adoption of Judeo-Christian perspectives on being.[8] The goal here is to read the blues at the border of Afro-Christianity, which operates as a discursive understanding of the material and immaterial worlds. Previous theological considerations of the blues, particularly from James Cone, Jon Michael Spencer, and Kelly Brown Douglas, have interpreted the blues not as a decolonial option but as an underrepresented voice in the pantheon of black American identity, culture, and worldview.[9] In distinction from these approaches, this brief essay will attempt to recover the blues as a moment of decolonial activity. As such, the aim is to dislocate racial oppression and racial identity as the primary basis by which to distinguish the blues representation of humanity. I argue that a decolonial turn in theological thought, as it pertains to the struggle for the liberation from antiblack racism, requires not only an end to the ideology of race and the violence of systemic racism but an end to the colonial cosmology that requires their continuance. The blues moment in black American cultural production offers options for living that dislocate race by working toward an emergent indigeneity. As such, Blues People enact their own epistemic and cosmological difference. Wynter's call for the end of the doctrine of Man has much to offer in recovering the indigeneity and epistemic difference of the blues. Let us turn now to her insights, particularly her analysis of the makings of the colonial cosmology.

A Prelude to the Blues: Modernity/Coloniality and the "Man" That Blues Forgot

The title of this section refers to the blues as a moment in which "Man" is forgotten. By this I mean to suggest the "Man" that was internalized as an expression of black American humanity. Most crucial to "taking a second look" at the blues is Wynter's analysis of the epistemic foundation of Man_1 and Man_2.[10] Man_1 has a theocentric and ethnocentric foundation and Man_2 has a biologically based foundation. Within the modern/colonial world that emerges in 1492, these foundations would take on racial and gendered notions.[11] Modernity's white heterosexual male, in Wynter's thought, is the humanity that bares the highest value because it is both more rational and selected by natural occurrences in line with Darwinian notions of evolution.[12] Wynter's analysis of Man_1 and Man_2 is helpful in that it provides a way of reading the blues epistemically rather than racially. With Man_1 and Man_2 in mind, one can see how the blues episteme contrasts with the Afro-Christian episteme, particularly in relation to how both engage Man and its overrepresentation as Spirit/Flesh, Rational/Irrational, and Selected/Dis-selected.[13] When Wynter's thought is mobilized for reading black American cultural production, the systemic effects of antiblackness are exposed with an eye toward a new way of "being" human. Rather than reading the blues as an articulation of racial being in counterdistinction from white being, the blues can be recovered as an episteme/ontology that belies the colonial representation of blackness.[14]

Blues People and the Autonomy of Being

Peoplehood is understood here as a phenomenon engaged in by human groups to orient and establish their place within the space that they perceive as the reality. The above discussion about episteme and ontology indicates how both are involved in the dynamics of human groups and how they represent themselves within time and space. In the 1960s, Amiri

Baraka used a similar understanding of peoplehood to distinguish black Americans as "Blues Peoples." "Blues People," for Baraka, signified a people that emerged from beyond the boundary of peoplehood set by modernity.[15] There is a great challenge to reading this history because in many ways the reader is often already given over to the facticity of race and racial oppression as defining characteristics of time and space. Under the weight of the lens of race and racial oppression, a human group built a blues vision for life that dislocated the ideology of race and the systemic oppression of racism. However, this activity worked to dislocate not through a one-to-one ratio of insurgence and counterinsurgence but through the creative production of culture that worked to inspire decolonial activities of mind, body, and soul.

The blues read from this perspective represents the emergence of a way of being a people rather than a way of being a race. Race, as Aníbal Quijano argues, is woven within the coloniality of power, which begins with the racialization of humanity under Eurocentric frameworks of peoplehood, economics, and politics.[16] When modernity is understood in this way, the blues difference speaks to more than what it means to be black. It also tells us something about what it means to be a human in relation to modernity and how it is manifesting itself within the post-Reconstruction world. Similar to the peoples that Wynter brings to life in her novel *The Hills of Hebron*, the Blues Peoples are one of the many groups that have worked to "unsettle"[17] the dominance of the colonial imagination that rendered the peoples of Africa as cosmologically and geographically inferior. In the world of Hebron, those living under the imposition of the modern/colonial world assert their peoplehood in the spiritualism of pocomania, maroon culture, Afro-Christian faiths, and the political hopes of organized labor.

Wynter's articulation of the world of the colonial subalterns, however, is wanting in regards to the specific treatment of religion. Oftentimes, similar to the perspective of many other decolonial theorists, Wynter sees religion as *in the way* of human groups that are looking to delink from modernity. Because of this, some further treatment of faith and religion is needed to help flesh out decolonial options that work in and through a people's faith. Religious scholars Albert Raboteau, Joseph Washington, and, more recently, Tracey Hucks, John Giggie, and William David Hart argue that slave religion and its ambiguities faced the scrutiny of black American conceptions of orthodoxy, which begin to emerge prior to and after the emancipation of enslaved black Americans in 1865.[18] As such, 1865 and the coming years of the Reconstruction placed an enormous amount of pressure on the cultural world of the formerly enslaved as they attempted to articulate themselves as citizens of a very broken and uncertain American Union.[19] Internally, during the Reconstruction era black Americans made sense of their past in light of a very volatile and uncertain future as a people engaging the idea of citizenship. The cultural underpinnings of slave religion and the newfound, yet severely limited, postemancipation life greatly affected this process, which led to multiple options for peoplehood. As Raboteau notes, slave religion with its rituals of the ring shout and ecstatic expression, often understood as retentions from African faiths, were overtly and covertly oppressed by the emerging orthodoxies of Afro-Christian communities.[20] In an attempt to interpret the theological significance of the rise of Afro-Christian communities and their relative autonomy from Euro-American protestant communities, Joseph Washington raises a question that has since been undertreated in the disciplines of Black, Womanist, and black feminist theologies in particular. In effect, Washington asks, "What is the theological content of black churches that distinguishes them from Euro-American Christian communities?"[21] In Washington's own answer to his question, he suggests that the primary motivation of Afro-Christian autonomy from Euro-Christian churches was their emphasis on communal solidarity as a tactic against systemic racism and the denial of civil rights. Christianity, in Washington's estimation, required more than just the following of Christian principles. Faith, in Washington's estimation, was not about following principles but a response to God who is "Creator, Judge, and Redeemer of the Universe."[22] However, Washington underestimated how the response to God is also entangled with ethnocentric visions of the world. Wynter's analysis of the ethnocentric bias is helpful in that it exposes the provinciality of a Christian cosmovision that would divide the cosmos into the fallen realm of humanity governed by the "Fallen Flesh" and the perfected realm of God to which all humans should strive to achieve spiritual redemption.

Drawing on David Bohm, Wynter argues that the Spirit/Flesh dynamic is based on a cosmological mapping that discursively works to disassociate humans from the rest of the natural world.[23] Through the inheritance of original sin, the human predicament of Christians and non-Christians alike is already represented as a problem of sin and flesh that only the institution of the church can remedy. The blues, when read epistemically and ontologically, reveals another way of thinking about the reality that works to dislocate the nonhomogeneity within the Christian imagination.[24]

The Blues as Episteme and Counterstatement

In his text *Development Arrested*, Clyde Woods indicates that the blues is a representation of an episteme that is distinguishable from the Afro-Christian episteme or, as James Cone would argue, the episteme of the spirituals.[25] Woods contends that the blues episteme is also the underpinning that produces blues music. For Woods, the blues is a repository for a vision of human development that can be read in the self-organizing activity of black Americans living in the Yazoo River Valley located in the state of Mississippi (known locally as the Delta).[26] Woods reads the history of the Delta Region through a geographical lens—that is, he employs a way of reading that privileges human visions for the land and the material and cultural artifacts of such visions. The blues then, as the title of his text communicates, is a land development vision that is arrested. The arrest of the blues vision results from the imposition of the Mississippi Plan of development implemented by the landowning elite White Male Planters and their supporters. It is important to remember here that the first vision or "cosmovision" lived out in the Delta was that of the Mississippian indigenous peoples.[27] The violent removal of the Mississippian peoples in Woods's critical geography was the first mobilization of the Mississippi Plan of Development, which eventually also arrested the blues episteme.[28] Thinking through Woods's assessment with Wynter's analysis of the modern/colonial world-system in mind, we can see that the Mississippi Plan is the vision for the land that makes modernity possible in the Delta. Recalling Wynter's assessment, the Mississippi Plan was a plan informed by a zeal that looked to bring the fallen nature of the Delta lands under a more perfected order of the Spirit realm. What Woods explicates as the "arrested" visions of the Mississippian peoples, the enslaved black and the subsequent black Americans, is parallel to Wynter's critical assessment of the Christian cosmovision that is based on a binary understanding of the earthly realm and the heavenly realm. The degree to which the cosmovisions of the Mississippian and black American peoples were dislocated is associated with how damaging they were to the Eurocentric Christian cosmovision and its secular analogue.

Man and its overrepresentation cannot persist without also representing its respective liminal genre of the human that produces the need for paternalistic oversight or the annihilation of other human groups. Hence, Wynter's reflections on Sambo and Nat Turner. These two figures, she contends, are like the Janus face and are representative of the liminal genre of black nonhumanity that props up the representation of the human as white heterosexual male.[29] The suppression of the blues epistemology occurs in part because of the way in which Afro-Christianity negotiated its proximity to Sambo and Turner. This conception of liminal culture was influenced in Wynter's thought by Amiri Baraka, then LeRoi Jones, who referred to a "frontier zone" as a space from which the black oppressed articulated their own cultural order.[30] In reading blues commentators and historians of the blues, several things remain consistent. Many blues commentators and historians of the blues agree that the themes within blues indicate a vision for human life that is distinguishable from Afro-Christian visions of humanity. Afro-Christian readings of humanity often read black experience through the liberation themes of the Exodus narrative and the salvation motif of the Gospels. As James Cone notes in *Spirituals and the Blues*, the spirituals are marked by the hope in God's activity in human history on the side of the oppressed. The vision for human life in the spirituals is oriented toward the hope of God's activity of liberation in history. In Cone's insights, there is a recognition of the cosmological difference between the blues and the spirituals, but he still understands the experience of white supremacy as the unifying experience of black Americans in a prescriptive way. The blues, Cone argues, deals head on with the "absurdity of black life in a white supremacist world."[31] However, as much as Cone recognizes the contributions of the blues, his view does not seek to distinguish the epistemic difference between the blues and the spirituals. Both the blues and the spirituals are signifiers of "black experience." As such, Cone's analysis of cultural production is not delinked entirely from the coloniality in which racial and cosmological distinctions are rooted. While some of this is indeed because of the time in which Cone is thinking about the blues, his adherence to the descriptive categories of the modern world, such as sacred and secular, indicate a peculiar allegiance to the modern/ colonial episteme. The spirituals, for Cone, are expressions of a people oriented toward the sacred act of God acting in history to redeem the oppressed. However, the blues in Cone's thought is the expression of a people who lift the matters of secular life to the level of the ultimate. Within the blues perspective, secular activity, especially with regard to sex, dance, and music, is looked to with the same hope as those who live in hopes of Christian spiritual redemption. Cone's emphasis on hope and liberation is not yet dealing with Wynter's decolonial option of "unsettling the doctrine of Man" as it relates to the epistemic underpinnings of the Judeo-Christian world. For instance, Cone recognizes that the spirituals move from the more fluid setting of slave religion to the orthodoxy and orthopraxis of Afro-Christian congregations in which Afro-Christian practitioners look to solidify systems of authority in order that they might replicate the liberationist spirit of the spirituals.[32] However, Cone's focus on racial oppression and how resistance to racial oppression worked to establish Afro-Christian orthodoxy is less critical of the ways in which Afro-Christian religious outlooks engage in epistemic repression. While Cone lauds the ways in which Afro-Christian practitioners deemed the blues to be worldly and not concerned with the matters of the sacred, he does not analyze the sacred and the secular as extensions of modernity and the colonial matrix of power.[33] Cone is right to assert that the repression of the blues by Afro-Christian practitioners was unfortunate; however, my endeavor is to push his assertion further and highlight how the episteme of the blues is asserting its own cosmovision that dislocates the binary Christocentric cosmology of the sacred/secular.[34] This brief treatment of Cone's theological/philosophical commentary on the blues is meant to clarify the intraracial depth at which I make use of Wynter's analysis. If the doctrine of Man is to be critiqued, it should be critiqued in all of its manifestations, even those manifestations perpetrated by those who are distinguished as the subaltern or the oppressed.

Wynter warns about the internalization of colonial reasoning most viscerally in *The Hills of Hebron*, where she presents the Prophet Moses's proclamation of the black God that ultimately fails to deliver a viable option for human life.[35] Moses's character is contrasted to the revelation of the hero character, Obadiah, who finds that the option for life did not lie in the color of God but in the activity of one's hands. Similar to the revelation of Obadiah, Blues People saw the sonic as the moment of realization that they themselves were sources for representation.

Albert Murray on the Blues as Counterstatement

Blues commentator Albert Murray gives some further insight into the blues vision by distinguishing the blues as a signifier of three separate phenomena: music, low-spirits, and counterstatement.[36] The first of these phenomena, music, recognizes the communal-based naming of the sonic production. This has much to do with both the sound of blues music as well as the lyrics that accompany the sonic output of guitars, voices, and other instruments. The second phenomenon is low-spirits,[37] or what was often articulated as having or seeing the blues. To have the blues is a feeling of being outdone by the circumstances of life. It is not always related to the oppression of race and racism but also articulates general misfortune. For instance, Whiskey Blues is a type of "low-spirit" associated with running out of the coveted distilled spirit of corn and grain. Blues as low-spirits is the condition that brings on the moments of sonic production and dance that work to both name and resist, or "stomp,"[38] the everyday sufferings of life. Finally, Murray observes that the blues is counterstatement. Murray's emphasis on counterstatement is primarily exacted against the theological revelation heralded by Afro-Christian churches, which have adopted the Spirit/Flesh as an adequate description and representation of black American humanity. Murray's point on this is significant and worth quoting at some length:

> The church is not concerned with the affirmation of life as such, which in its view is only a matter of feeble flesh to begin with. . . . Unlike the revelers of the Saturday Night Dance Function [where blues music is played] the worshipers attending the Sunday morning Service are very concerned with guilt and seeking forgiveness for their trespasses. . . . What each [worshiper] expresses is not affirmation of life as such but rather his determination not to yield to the entice-ments of the fleshpots of Baal.[39]

For Murray, the Saturday Night Dance Function, a blues ritual, coun-terstates the Afro-Christian ritual that reorients the Flesh toward the Spirit. What is affirmed in the Afro-Christian ritual, according to Murray, is the idolatry and temptations that proceed from the desires of the flesh. Coping with the blues, "the low-spirits," requires more than "walking after the Spirit." For Murray, it requires an embrace of the flesh and, with it, all that makes the flesh stomp the blues. The blues is not only naming the reality and experience of "low-spirits" but also providing a response that is sonic, vocal, and sensual. This is not to say that the Sunday morn-ing worship within black churches did not include sonic, vocal, and sen-sual activity. However, it is to say that the Sunday morning rituals were aimed at the affirmation of life that is oriented toward the Spirit and the eschaton of Christian salvation. Blues People reject the idea of relegating the sonic, vocal, and physical activity of music and dance as only being ap-propriate when it is oriented toward the expiation of sin. Further, Blues People affirm and create their own struggle with "low-spirits" through sonic stylization, performance, dance, sensuality, sex, and sexuality. Blues life, in Murray's interpretation, is lived after *the spirit*(s) that are present and represented in the sonic production of blues music, blues dance, and the episteme that wrests the sensual from the strictures of the modern theological outlook. Among Blues People, the body is redeemed in those activities that resituate Blues People in relation to the land, the sonic, and the sensual.

Similar to Murray's interpretation of the blues episteme as a dislocation of the Afro-Christian interpretation of black flesh as feeble, Wynter argues that the measure of a new or anticolonial approach to reality requires a shift in how reality is understood. In her reflection on Édouard Glissant, Wynter articulates that an anticolonial approach to reality is distinguished by a shift from a loss of trust in "physical nature" to a loss of trust in the "modes of subjectivity."[40] For Wynter, the shift unsettles the modern/colonial imaginary and exposes it as an imposition—a discursive production that can be countered by other representations of subjectivity. This is especially the case in relation to the colonial imposition of Christian cosmology. To this point Wynter writes:

> All humans were now made the recipient of this Adamic negative inheritance and were therefore bearers of this universal mode of the Abject. Redemption from this legacy, for the layman, could only be obtained through the ritual processes of baptism into orthodox feudal-Christian identity. Because the original ritual construct of the Abject or of Pariah Otherness had been translated into the concept of Ontological Lack, the order of knowledge of scholastic theology had been elaborated, as the Word of the Christian, upon the a priori premise of an Ontological Lack of being as that of human enslavement to Original Sin.[41]

In this Wynterian analysis, suffering, temptation, and struggles with the desires of the flesh begin in this Judeo-Christian cosmological assessment of the separation between the earthly order and the transcendent order. Similar to Murray's assessment of the Sunday morning worship services of black churches, Wynter recognizes how the Judeo-Christian cosmology of flesh relegates human sensuality to a natural state of lack that can only be remedied by God. Further, the modern church as the steward of God's activity then recasts the representation of humanity through its discourse of the saved and the unsaved, the Christian and the non-Christian. In the Judeo-Christian representation, the human is determined by the cosmological binary and, as such, the clergy and its ascetic practices, especially that of celibacy—resistance to the "abject" desires of the flesh—is representative of optimal humanity. The clergy's ontological difference serves as a basis for their authority over laypeople. Moreover, the clerical "nature" is one of perfection that makes them natural resources for matters of spiritual discipline, reason, and knowledge.

Wynter's work praises the Renaissance and the Copernican Revolution for the ways in which they exposed the "false" universality of the cosmological and ontological authority of the church. Nevertheless, and this is a poignant assessment in Wynter's work, the shift from clerically justified theological reason to secular scientific reason keeps in place the denial of the provincial and ethnocentric nature of European reason. Wynter is convinced that the provinciality of human representation can be avoided as more human groups agree upon a "nonadaptive" mode of representation that mimics the objectivity of science.[42] The current writer is unconvinced that Wynter's alternative of a new humanism, when implemented as a revision of the former universality of the Renaissance humanism, will be devoid of the coloniality of being and the need to remain adaptive to the Eurocentric forms of being human.[43] When Wynter argues, in light of Aimé Césaire, that what the world needs is a "science of the word," she is arguing that the poetic imagination of the human, reflected in subaltern cultural productions, is inventing a new mode of human subjectivity that should be universalized as a new representation of humanity.[44] This new humanism then is oriented toward a decolonized universal representation of humanity. This hope seems to jettison in one stroke those indigenous forms of human representation that have little desire for newness or revising Eurocentric notions of humanness. Nevertheless, Wynter's point still articulates the coloniality present in both an imposed universality of Christian revelation and an imposed universality of objective reason. With this insight we can see that the blues articulates a peoplehood that begins to dislocate the "masquerade" of universality in both its modern secular and Judeo-Christian forms. Blues artist Mississippi Marvel gives us a picture into the blues episteme and the way it confronted the Afro-Christian mode of subjectivity in an interview where he laments the bifurcation of black music into the categories of sacred and secular.

> Now a lot of Churches don't want you to bring a guitar in there but they've got a piano. What's the difference, its music? But, the Bible tells you to make a joyful noise with your instrument. When God said make a loud noise with your instrument he did not tell you not to sing "Baby, please don't go" or nothing like that. He just said make a loud noise with your instrument and the Bible says when they're making a loud noise with their instrument they are singing Hallelujah. . . . It did not say what instrument.[45]

Mississippi Marvel's sentiments indicate an understanding of the sonic reality that is not easily divisible into sacred and profane sound. For Marvel, the significance of sonic production does not rest in its orientation toward the Afro-Christian representation of righteousness. Instead, the sonic production of blues guitarists who sometimes sing "Baby please don't go" are sounds that point to the significance of life and living. Marvel's sentiments are affirmed in the extensive research done on the blues by Daphne Duval Harrison.[46] Harrison notes the implications of the struggle against the restrictive notion of the Afro-Christian idea of humanity when she references the lyrics to a song by Clara Smith entitled "Every Woman's Blues."

> You can read your hymnbook, read your Bible read your history
>   and spell on down,
> You can read my letters, but you sho' can't read my mind.
> When you think I'm crazy about you, I'm leaving you all the time.[47]

Commenting on this and other songs by blues women, Harrison argues that the vision of the women that sang and found meaning in "Every Woman's Blues" was one that affirmed a woman's control of her mind in the face of women and men who were supposedly trained in the clerical matters of the church and formal education. As the lyrics of "Every Woman's Blues" suggest, Blues People engaged in a rigorous trust in their ability to assert themselves as epistemically and politically viable. As Harrison goes on to note, songs like "Every Woman's Blues" recovered the grassroots wisdoms that were forged in everyday engagement with the conditions of one's context.[48] The blues, then, created an option for those black women and men who were looking for a new idea of the human on which to base their visions for community. In reference to blues singer Ida Cox, for example, Harrison contends:

> Her advice is counter to the prevailing norms in the black
> community—monogamous relationships, fidelity, temperance, family,
> home and health—yet it illustrates the urge for self-determination and
> expression. . . .
>   They [Blues Women] introduced a new, different model of black
> women—more assertive, sexy, sexually aware, independent, realistic,
> complex, *alive*.[49]

Harrison's insights on what it meant for blues women to be "alive" echoes what Wynter often refers to as Frantz Fanon's idea of the "inventive."[50] The blues is "inventive" as sonic activity and in its political activity, which suggests that alternative visions of life are possible and worthwhile. It is this activity of living life in counterdistinction from the modern/colonial imaginary of reality that moves beyond reaction and into the realm of the Fanonian "invention."[51] What is significant about the blues difference in its projected genre of being human is its ability to articulate its own representation of human struggle. Blues People struggled not against the temptations of the flesh but with those "low-spirits" that threatened to enclose them in a world of despair. The blues episteme is distinct from the one promulgated by Western Christian pietism and its adoption within Afro-Christian communities. The adoption of pietism reinforced a theological version of what Wynter identified as the Sambo image. Blues Peoples affirm the Nat Turner image, which articulates that there is no lack of humanity in the subaltern that awaits a requisite redemption. The theological anthropology of Spirit/Flesh and its mobilization in pietism restricts the flesh into the ideology of lack. As such, human life is relegated to a feebleness, a *Sambo-ness*, which can only be remedied by adherence to those authoritative bodies that determine whether one's human flesh is oriented toward the Spirit. As alluded to above, conversion is understood as spiritual and moral change that is visible through one's actions. Further, the activity that indicates conversion is the sign of moral goodness for morality's sake as well as the physical presence of the Spirit working within the flesh to bring it to the promise of salvation. Under this Afro-Christian anthropology, the revelation of salvation, communicated through the reception of Jesus, is a revelation about the natural lack in human life and the salvation that retains the promise of perfection. Under this anthropology, the activity of the body and sonic production are restricted in ways that reinforce the ideal of ontological lack in dubious ways. As one blues singer sings,

I must be serving the devil, I can't be serving Jesus Christ
Because, I asked the Lord to save me and look like he trying to take
    my life.[52]

The blues is not alone in its recognition of the ways in which Afro-Christian modes of orthodoxy reinforced the colonial ideal of physical lack onto the human body in ways that were repressive. Some contemporary music artists living in the US South are regenerating and continuing the blues episteme within what can be loosely associated with the genre of rap music. The remainder of this discussion will read Justin Scott (Big K.R.I.T.) as one example of this blues legacy.

Southern Rap and Its Inheritance of the Blues Episteme

Thinking about the blues as an epistemic turn toward a "non-adaptive mode of being human"[53] demands a reorientation toward black cultural production in general. This reorientation calls into question the blues as well as other black American cultural products. My articulation of a call for reorientation, through Wynter, is not entirely unique. Reiland Rabaka, in his text *Hip-Hop's Inheritance*, suggests that interpretations of black cultural production are too often restricted to theories that are epistemically closed to the multiple ways in which black Americans have interpreted themselves in relation to Eurocentric modernity.[54] As such, the epistemic quality of black American cultural production is often undertreated. To this point, Rabaka argues:

> Hip hop culture can be said to be squarely situated within the stream of historic African American cultural aesthetic traditions and movements when and where its schizophrenic embrace and rejection of both black and white conservatism, liberalism, radicalism, and revolutionism is taken into consideration. . . . Instead of representing a completely new black youth culture, in many ways rap music and hip hop culture have, however unwittingly, recycled several racial, sexual and cultural myths and motifs bequeathed by antecedent African American youth inspired cultural aesthetic traditions and sociopolitical movements.[55]

Similar to Rabaka, I want to point to an inheritance particularly in the rap music of people raised in the space that helped give rise to the blues episteme, namely the US South. In contrast to Rabaka's articulation of the inheritance in hip-hop via the Harlem Renaissance, the civil rights movement, the Black Power movement and the Black Arts movement, I want to focus on a notion of inheritance that takes into consideration the geography of southern rap music. Rap artists that come of age in the southeastern part of the United States, the lands from which the blues emerge, have often described themselves in relation to the aesthetics of black Americans whose culture is situated in the ongoing struggle against what critical geographer Clyde Woods has articulated as the Mississippi Plan of Development. This forced plan of development moves to continuously reinscribe the lands and peoples of the Mississippi Delta under a Plantation regime of power.[56] The point here is that the Plantation and its relative modes of human being forcibly orient the South. One poignant example of an alternative to the cosmological and ontological dynamics of the Plantation regime resonates in the sonic and lyrical art of Justin Scott.

Justin Scott, known by his stage name Big K.R.I.T. (King Remembered in Time), is a music producer and rap artist who was born and raised in Meridian, Mississippi. I evoke his work here because of the stark ways in which the blues idiom and episteme is present in his art, especially in one of his most recent albums entitled *Cadillactica* (2014). The album is a sonic representation of Big K.R.I.T.'s adventures on a planet that he describes as Cadillactica. Justin Scott self-describes the planet as his subconscious and creative mind that is associated with one of the symbols of southern rap culture, the Cadillac.[57] On a previous album, entitled *Live from the Underground*, the album art depicts a purple Cadillac that has crash-landed onto the planet Earth. However, Earth within Scott's poetry is representative of the mainstream music industry, which under his assessment continues to alienate the lyricism and sonic creativity of southern rap artists. Scott's alter ego, Big K.R.I.T., is represented as an alien trying to make the best of life away from the sonic and creative world of Cadillactica. Scott's lyrics represent Cadillactica as a planet born from a cosmic sonic explosion, *a big bang*, associated with the sound output of audio speakers that *bang* with the music technology of the Roland TR-808 synthetic sound machine.[58] The influence of Scott's southern context bleeds through as many of the themes in Cadillactica connect with the Mississippi Blues themes of dislocation, sonic difference, and the desire for autonomy. The first song on the album, entitled "Creation," speaks to the longing of a new way to imagine the cosmos that is relevant to the present reality.[59] As Rabaka's interpretation of hip-hop suggests, Scott inherits vernacular, idiom, and an epistemic imagination that is not unique to the art form of rap. Scott's art inherits a blues sensibility that is expressed sonically and lyrically. Verse by verse Scott, through his stage character Big K.R.I.T., makes sense of epistemic dissonance between his subconscious and the mainstream stereotypes, which demean the lyrical creativity of southern rap artists. "Creation" displays the epistemic dissonance through several different images. The first and most stark image is the planetary image. As a whole, the song describes the birth of a planet, Cadillactica, which is born through the creative activity of Big K.R.I.T. and an unnamed female character. The beginning of the song opens with a female voice awakening Big K.R.I.T. by whispering the words, "Let's create." Big K.R.I.T. responds back begrudgingly, "Nah not yet . . . hold on." The voice whispers back slightly more forcefully, "No, let's create now." Finally, Big K.R.I.T. responds in the affirmative, "Aight." The voices sound of intimacy, a quiet dialogue in the

early hours of the morning or in a moment where Big K.R.I.T. is looking
to rest rather than create. Musically, there are sounds that reflect twilight.
High-pitched notes intermittently break into an ambiguous melody as if
to suggest moments of brilliant sparkle followed by moments of dim glow.
The early parts of the song long for a more distinct rhythmic form. It is
not yet dance music in the Albert Murrian sense. Rather, it is conversation
music on the cusp of the sensual moment of dance. As the conversation
fades, the sounds of bass-laden drums, a tightly tuned snare, and a more
rhythmic melody enter the score. When the rhythm and melody form
song, Big K.R.I.T. narrates the creation of the planet, dubbed Cadillactica,
that results from the creative activity of two intimately related partners.

As referred to above, one of the unifying characteristics of the blues
episteme is a longing for an autonomous mode of life and living. *Cadillactica* represents this longing through the character of Big K.R.I.T., who is
attempting to affirm his sonic dissonance from the predetermined aesthetics and sonic categories that exist beyond the world of Cadillactica. Similar to blues artists of the 1920s and 1930s, Scott's persona, Big K.R.I.T., is
the representation of a life born from the creative potential of ordinary
people. In alignment with Wynter's reflections on the poiesis of C. L. R.
James—especially his writings on cricket player Matthew Bondsman—
Justin Scott's poetry breaks the epistemic hegemony that binds the oppressed to a constant state of adapting to life on the terms of the coloniality
enforced by the doctrine of Man.[60] Big K.R.I.T., as a persona, unsettles
the confinement of black American life to the Eurocentric construction of
a "subrational" state of "otherness." In Scott's case, this is linked to the stereotypes concerning the lyrical and sonic dearth of southern rap artists.
Like Bondsman's creative athleticism, Big K.R.I.T.'s wit and sonic wisdom
are a representation of humanity that belies the preordained ontological
destiny projected by the humanism of the modern/colonial world. As such,
Big K.R.I.T. unsettles the anthropology of Man_2 and the ways it is internalized by some black Americans who adopt the hegemonic representations
of humanity that relegate human difference to degrees of ontological lack.

Justin Scott's poetry, in light of Rabaka's and Wynter's insights, is further illumined as a creative activity that "unsettles" the doctrine of Man
and its overrepresentation through a particular understanding of tradition
or, as Rabaka articulates, "inheritance." Reading Scott's poetry in this way,
we can delink hip-hop from a postmodern reading that might define
Big K.R.I.T.'s cosmic imagery as a break from the Afro-Christian metanarrative of Spirit/Flesh, on one hand, and a secular/sacred binary of the
postmodern humanist moment, on the other. Such a delinking from the

postmodern reading unsettles an interpretation of history that universally claims the death of metanarratives, once and for all, across all time and space. As Rabaka suggests, hip-hop and rap inherit the blues and continue the distinguishing characteristics of the episteme while adding their own concerns. They are not, in the postmodern sense, "new." Further, in light of Wynter, the inheritance of the blues that is incarnate in the character of Big K.R.I.T. reveals a "nonadaptive" mode of existence that is distinct from Eurocentric modernity and its adaptive mode of subjectivity. To say it another way, one does not need to claim the end of metanarratives in order to claim the end of the "doctrine of Man." As Wynter suggests, those who are ontologically and epistemologically subjugated by Eurocentrism have the power to project their own notions of subjectivity.

The art of southern rap at its best—of course many artists are still heavily beholden to themes of misogynoir, machismo, and conspicuous consumption—manages to break open inventive modes of being that continue in the spirit of the blues episteme. This episteme is distinguishable and has more to add than simply a darkening of the modern worldview. As one southern rap artist once proclaimed, "The South got something to say, and that's all I got to say." [61] Justin Scott makes this emphatically known in his blistering critique of the hip-hop consumers and their refusal to regard the lyricism and poetic genius of southern rap artists. In one of the other songs on the *Cadillactica* album, entitled "Mount Olympus," Big K.R.I.T. proclaims:

> You tellin' me I can't be King of Hip-Hop
> And they wouldn't give it to Andre 3000?
> Nigga please, this award ain't got shit to do with us
> God could physically come down and say "he the greatest
> My favorite, y'all should listen, he have potential
> To outlive the heatwave I'ma send through this motherfucker
> And rebuild for a whole 'nother other culture"
> And that wouldn't be enough

With these words, Scott articulates how his geographical location, and possibly his vernacular culture, land him into the intraracial reification of subrationality. André 3000, André Benjamin, another highly talented rap artist who was underappreciated as a result of his geographic location, is used as a pivot for Big K.R.I.T. to express the difficulty of dislocating the representation of southern black American cultural production as an indicator of subrationality. My argument here is that Scott's words are more than a response to a matter of taste or musical preference. More poignantly,

Justin Scott has identified his inheritance of the blues struggle and its confrontation with the colonial imagination of subrationality. Southern black
American artistry has long been represented as an archaic past incapable
of achieving the aesthetic heights of a supposed northern-born progres-
sivism. Just as black American country blues artists became the representation of an archaic essence among northern-born black Americans, so too
does the vocal and sonic delivery of many southern rap artists. As Justin
Scott's words indicate, not even an endorsement from God could save him
from being denied access to the normative designation of artistic great-
ness within the rap genre. Elsewhere in the song, Big K.R.I.T. also bemoans
the fact that the sonic creativity of southern rap is often borrowed and pop-
ularized by rap artists living outside the South.

> And it was easy for you to move through
> English class with your own thesaurus
> Like one of these days I'm gonna be a rapper
> But all my verses gonna be borrowed
> So I'ma take from all these southern artists
> That mainstream never heard of
> Recycle all of they lingo
> And make sure I screw my words up[62]

In Scott's poetry, we see the many social, ontological, and aesthetic layers
onto which the othering logics of coloniality are internalized and projected
at the intraracial level. With this recognition in mind, this brief excursion
into Big K.R.I.T. makes known the dynamics of contemporary black American cultural production and the ways in which it inherits the blues struggle for epistemic and ontological autonomy.

Conclusion

Inside of this limited space, the aim has been to articulate how Wynter's
analysis of the doctrine of Man indicates new challenges to faith, especially
the Christian faith. Both the blues and the continuation of its episteme/
ontology in southern rap, albeit from a new perspective, reveal how the
doctrine of Man is resisted and unsettled from within the creative and in-
novative capacity of ordinary people. Unsettling is exacted not only at the
border of blackness and whiteness but, as seen here, at the border of the
blues and blackness. Attention to the multiple ways in which the coloniality
of being is unsettled requires a new way of reading cultural production
and the intricacies of everyday life. It is within these geographical and cos-

mological nuances that the doctrine of Man, or the coloniality of being, restricts epistemic difference and "overrepresents" the diverse modes of subjectivity that emerge among black Americans.

While this discussion has been limited to cultural production as an expression of the dynamics of coloniality, one must remember that autonomy from the colonial imagination must also be clearly linked to political options. Unsettling projects cannot end when the music stops. As Clyde Woods indicates, the political legacy of the blues remains "arrested" and has not yet been fully engaged as a viable option for the establishment of autonomy from the politics that are constitutive with what Wynter identifies as Man$_1$ and Man$_2$. Overcoming Man is not only the creation of new aesthetics or ontologies; it is also about producing options for living them out. Such an option is actualized in political arrangements that dislocate the authoritative bodies that enforce epistemic hegemony through the practice of religion and the nation-state. This point about politics is not absent in Wynter's thought. As her articulation of a new humanism continues to gain traction, one must be mindful of the way in which such a project might overstate the possibility of a decolonial *and* universal representation of the human. Decolonial representations of the human must continue to be held in tension with Wynter's insights on political theorist C. L. R. James. Political activity, while necessary, cannot stand alone; rather, it must be integrally related to the life, culture, hopes, and dreams of a people. Similarly, human representation, while necessary, must also be integrally related to the life, culture, hopes, and struggles of everyday people—those Blues People who, as James Baldwin once wrote, possess "the toughness that manages to make this experience articulate."[63]

NOTES

1. The idea of "taking a second look" is drawn from the theological hermeneutics of Elochukwu Uzukwu, who attempts to rethink the contributions of Igbo epistemology—especially those captured in the work of Chinua Achebe—and how it might be used to arrive at an indigenous understanding of God and Spirit. My recovery of the blues, as an epistemic perspective, draws upon Uzukwu's emphasis of engaging the "dynamism and openness" living within indigenous perspectives. Such a move requires bracketing commonly held assumptions, especially those forged within the wound of colonialism. For more on this, see Elochukwu Uzukwu, *God, Spirit, and Human Wholeness: Appropriating Faith and Culture in West African Style* (Eugene, Ore.: Wipf and Stock Publishers, 2012), 8, 20–21.

2. Sylvia Wynter, "Unsettling the Coloniality of Being/Power/Truth/ Freedom: Towards the Human, after Man, Its Overrepresentation—An Argument," *CR: The New Centennial Review* 3, no. 3 (Fall 2003): 278.

3. Wynter, "Unsettling the Coloniality of Being/Power/Truth/ Freedom," 278.

4. Wynter, 322.

5. Sylvia Wynter, "One Love—Rhetoric or Reality?—Aspects of Afro-Jamaicanism," *Caribbean Studies* 12, no. 3 (1972): 66.

6. Wynter, "One Love," 65.

7. Sylvia Wynter, *The Hills of Hebron* (Kingston, Jamaica: Ian Randle Publishers, 2010).

8. For the purposes of this discussion, *Afro-Christian* refers to those black Americans that organized themselves into autonomous Christian churches and groups during and after enslavement.

9. For more on these perspectives, see James H. Cone, *The Spirituals and the Blues: An Interpretation* (Maryknoll, N.Y.: Orbis Books, 1992); Kelly Brown Douglas, *Black Bodies and the Black Church: A Blues Slant* (New York: Palgrave Macmillan, 2012); and Jon Michael Spencer, *Blues and Evil* (Knoxville: University of Tennessee Press, 1993).

10. Wynter's treatment of the doctrine of man is too broad to be included in this brief reflection. Readers looking for a more thorough treatment should see Sylvia Wynter, "Beyond the Word of Man: Glissant and the New Discourse of the Antilles," *World Literature Today* 63, no. 4 (Autumn 1989); and Wynter, "Unsettling the Coloniality of Being/Power/Truth/Freedom."

11. Wynter, "Unsettling the Coloniality of Being/Power/Truth/ Freedom," 260.

12. Wynter, "Beyond the Word of Man," 644; and Wynter, "Unsettling the Coloniality of Being/Power/Truth/Freedom," 272–312.

13. Wynter, "Beyond the Word of Man," 642; and Wynter, "Unsettling the Coloniality of Being/Power/Truth/Freedom," 324.

14. Catholic theologian Phillip Linden describes this process as "letting go of race." For more on this idea, see Phillip J. Linden, "Letting Go of Race: Reflections from a Historical Theological View," *Voices* 36, no. 1 (January–March 2013).

15. Leroi Jones, *Blues People: Negro Music in White America* (New York: Harper Collins, 1999).

16. Aníbal Quijano, "Coloniality of Power, Eurocentrism and Social Classification," in *Coloniality at Large: Latin America and the Postcolonial Debate* (Durham, N.C.: Duke University Press, 2008).

17. Wynter, "Unsettling the Coloniality of Being/Power/Truth/ Freedom," 260.

18. See Tracey E. Hucks, *Yoruba Traditions and African American Religious Nationalism* (Albuquerque: University of New Mexico Press, 2012); William David Hart, *Afro-Eccentricity: Beyond the Standard Narrative of Black Religion* (New York: Palgrave MacMillan, 2011); and John M. Giggie, *After Redemption: Jim Crow and the Transformation of African American Religion in the Delta, 1875–1915* (New York: Oxford University Press, 2007).

19. Albert J. Raboteau, *Canaan Land: A Religious History of African Americans* (New York: Oxford University Press, 2001), 69–71; and Albert J. Raboteau, *A Fire in the Bones* (Boston: Beacon Press, 1996), 53–56.

20. Raboteau, *Canaan Land*, 69–70.

21. Joseph R. Washington, "Are American Negro Churches Christian?," *Theology Today* 20, no. 1 (April 1, 1963).

22. Washington, "Are American Negro Churches Christian?," 86.

23. Wynter, "Unsettling the Coloniality of Being/Power/Truth/Freedom," 269–70.

24. More could be said here about how Wynter's analysis of the Spirit/Flesh pushes recent articulations of the problem of Race and the theological imagination, such as in the work of Willie James Jennings and J. Kameron Carter. The nonhomogenous cosmic imagination is seen as the fundamental dislocation of the human rather than the projection of racial inferiority.

25. Clyde Adrian Woods, *Development Arrested: The Blues and Plantation Power in the Mississippi Delta*, Haymarket Series (New York: Verso, 1998).

26. Woods, *Development Arrested*, 29–39.

27. Woods, *Development Arrested*.

28. Woods, 40.

29. Sylvia Wynter, "Sambos and Minstrels," *Social Text* 1 (1979): 150.

30. Wynter, "One Love," 5.

31. James H. Cone, *The Cross and the Lynching Tree* (Maryknoll, N.Y.: Orbis Books, 2011), 28. Cone thinks through the blues with Camus's idea of the absurd. For Cone, the blues singers recognize the absurdity of the black condition. Cone's option for finding meaning in absurdity ultimately rests in Christology: The cross of Jesus, an absurd event, becomes a symbol of God's activity in historical liberation. For this reason, Cone argues that the Spirituals and the Church had more to offer black struggles for freedom. My argument here is that Cone's move to the cross is uncritically engaged with a Christian cosmology that provides the basis for the epistemic repression of the blues.

32. Cone, *Spirituals and the Blues*, 46.

33. Cone, 97.

34. For more on Cone's take on the repression of the blues by black American Christians see Cone, *Spirituals and the Blues*, 111.

35. Wynter, *Hills of Hebron.*

36. Albert Murray, *Stomping the Blues* (Cambridge, Mass.: Da Capo Press, 1976), 23, 38, 57, 68–69, 250.

37. Murray, *Stomping the Blues*, 45.

38. In Murray's work on the blues "stomping" signifies the physical activity of dance that literally stomps the blues away.

39. Murray, *Stomping the Blues*, 38.

40. Wynter, "Beyond the Word of Man," 640.

41. Wynter, 641.

42. Wynter, "Unsettling the Coloniality of Being/Power/Truth/ Freedom," 275.

43. Wynter, 329.

44. Wynter, 331.

45. Roger Stolle, *Hidden History of Mississippi Blues* (Charleston, S.C.: History Press, 2011), 103–4.

46. Daphne Duval Harrison, *Black Pearls: Blues Queens of the 1920s* (New Brunswick, N.J.: Rutgers University Press, 1988).

47. Harrison, *Black Pearls*, 110.

48. This is also reinforced by Angela Davis and Kelly Brown Douglas. For more on their interpretations of blues women, see Angela Y. Davis, *Blues Legacies and Black Feminism: Gertrude Ma Rainey, Bessie Smith, and Billie Holiday* (New York: Knopf Doubleday Publishing Group), 2011, 42–65; and Douglas, *Black Bodies and the Black Church*, 13–20, 76, 96.

49. Harrison, *Black Pearls*, 111. Emphasis added.

50. Wynter, "Unsettling the Coloniality of Being/Power/Truth/ Freedom," 331.

51. Frantz Fanon, *Black Skin, White Masks*, trans. Richard Philcox (New York: Grove Press, 2008), 204.

52. As found in Paul Oliver, *Blues Fell This Morning: Meaning in the Blues* (New York: Cambridge University Press, 1990), 118. For the complete song, see "Fool's Blues," J. T. "Funny Paper" Smith, track 19 on *Complete Recorded Works in Chronological Order (1930–1931)*, Document Records (2), BDCD-6016, 1991, compact disc.

53. Wynter, "Unsettling the Coloniality of Being/Power/Truth/ Freedom," 275, 281, 331.

54. Reiland Rabaka, *Hip Hop's Inheritance: From the Harlem Renaissance to the Hip Hop Feminist Movement* (Lanham, Md.: Lexington Books, 2011), 32.

55. Rabaka, *Hip Hop's Inheritance*, xiii.

56. Woods, *Development Arrested*, 40–58. Here Woods gives an overview of some of the activity of the landowning planters who ensured the centrality of the plantation as a lifeway through the threat of violence, disenfran-

chisement of black labor, forced migration, entrapment, and a host of other activities that countered the Blues Peoples and their collective efforts at securing a plan for life during and after the Reconstruction. Woods indicates the long duration of the Mississippi plan and traces its effects from the Reconstruction to present-day federal and state government policies. Prior to his death, he used his analysis of the Mississippi Delta Plan to explain the deleterious act that disenfranchised the peoples of New Orleans during Hurricane Katrina.

57. WatchLOUD, "CRWN w/Elliott Wilson Ep. 13 Pt. 2 of 2: Big K.R.I.T.," YouTube video, 30:03, October 8, 2014, https://www.youtube .com/watch?v=7YDEL7miJok.

58. The Roland TR-808 is a drum machine that is preloaded with synthesized sounds that mimic live percussion and stringed instruments. Rap and hip-hop music producers have used the machine to replace the recording of live percussionists. For more on the history of the Roland TR-808 in southern rap and hip-hop, see Roni Sarig, *Third Coast: OutKast, Timbaland, and How Hip-Hop Became a Southern Thing* (Boston: Da Capo Press, 2007).

59. Big K.R.I.T., *Cadillactica*, Def Jam Recordings, B0021368-02, 2014, compact disc.

60. Sylvia Wynter, "Beyond the Categories of the Master Conception: The Counterdoctrine of the Jamesian Poiesis," in *C. L. R. James's Caribbean*, ed. Paget Henry and Paul Buhle (Durham, N.C.: Duke University Press, 1992).

61. OutKast, "Chonkyfire," track 16 on *Aquemini*, LaFace Records, 73008-26053-2, compact disc. Originally stated by André Benjamin at the 1995 Source Awards in an acceptance speech for best new rap group.

62. Big K.R.I.T., "Mt. Olympus (Reprise)," track 16 on *Cadillactica (Deluxe Edition)*, Def Jam Recordings, B0021368-02, 2014, compact disc.

63. James Baldwin, "Uses of the Blues," in *The Cross of Redemption: Uncollected Writings* (New York: Knopf Doubleday Publishing Group, 2010).

CHAPTER 3

Not Your Papa's Wynter: Women of Color Contributions toward Decolonial Futures

Xhercis Méndez and Yomaira C. Figueroa

These women poets have scrutinized their lives,

wrestled with their different inheritances of geography, of place;

with race, class, sexuality, body, nationality and belonging,

And molded it all into sources of insight and wisdom.

Among them they have lived three hundred and sixty-three years,

spanning continents, threading dreams, holding visions.

—M. JACQUI ALEXANDER, "Remembering *This Bridge Called My Back*, Remembering Ourselves"

An Introduction

Sylvia Wynter's decades-long project on the creation of a new human and human sciences, which challenges and defeats the overrepresentation of Western Man as the human, is one that spans thousands of pages and has been the subject of study for Caribbean philosophers and postcolonial, de-colonial, and feminist thinkers, to name a few. As an essayist, playwright, novelist, and critical theorist, Wynter has crossed disciplinary boundaries and created new ways of mapping human and Man's ontological narratives. We look to Wynter's work for both its historical and transdisciplinary breadth and the possibilities of articulating a decolonial politic grounded in the contributions of women of color feminists, activists, and writers toward the making of fully realized and complex human futures.

In this essay we aim to engage two important contentions in the work of/on Wynter: her understandings of feminism, gender, and patriarchy as they pertain to the overrepresentation of Man and in their relation to women of color and decolonial feminisms, as well as her articulation of the *studia humanitatis* and, by extension, literature as a fundamental site for radical transformation and liberatory imagination. Given that we have seen firsthand how her critique of mainstream liberal feminism has provided a language to dismiss the concerns articulated and work produced by women of color, we thought it important to first detail what we find suggestive in Wynter's project. We highlight where we see resonances between the substantive contributions of women of color and decolonial feminisms and Wynter's overall project. For instance, women of color feminists articulated similar and complementary critiques of mainstream liberal feminisms, and within this heterogeneous body of activism and political thought there has been a long history of taking back the "Word," specifically through a poetics and politics that seek to create new value systems beyond those established through colonization and slavery, and beyond those that serve to bolster "Man."

We argue that women of color and decolonial feminists, activists, and writers have, over time, contributed greatly to the making of a communal[1] and decolonial politics that seeks to bolster, strengthen, heal, and transform the relationships among those racialized, as opposed to primarily and/or solely concentrating on our relationship to "Man." To that end, we will underscore not only women of color's and decolonial feminists' attentiveness to and political organizing around the systematic oppression of men of color, but also their/our efforts to (re)value women of color's lives beyond a decontextualized "patriarchal discourse." Finally, we conclude with a reframing of women of color and decolonial feminisms and practice as complementary to Wynter's project and, more importantly, necessary for and indispensable to, the making of decolonial futures.

An Entry: On Wynter's Project

In her interview with David Allen Scott, we gain insight into the twofold nature of Wynter's decolonial humanist project. Scott summarizes the first part of this project as "the effort to track the 'codes' and 'genres' through which understanding, and especially self-understanding, is constituted."[2] According to Wynter, each culture establishes their own Norm of what it means to be human, which is then narratively described as well as mapped onto the various systems of symbolic representations. For Wynter, these descriptive statements of what the human Norm is within each culture function as an a priori definition that gives rise to ways of knowing and modalities of adaptive cultural truths. As such, descriptive statements govern the social order and hierarchies within a culture, orient the behavior of individuals and groups, and form part of the code of symbolic life and death.³ In other words, these codes give us an insight into which bodies have power and which bodies should and do matter within a given culture. However, modernity/coloniality established one and only one definition of the human that was supposed to represent all of humanity—that is, modernity/coloniality created "Man," which overrepresents himself as the human and dysselects all other living beings (the nonbourgeoisie, non-Western, racialized, nonheterosexual, etc.) from possible entrance into humanity.⁴

Since for Wynter colonizers were unable to conceive of the possibility that the human could be anything other than their conception of it, she argues that other ways of being human were fundamentally viewed as a lack.⁵ In her work she traces the Western colonial redescription of the human in its transition toward a pseudo-secularized and ultimately bio-economic form and tells us that these redefinitions gain legitimacy with the introduction of and in relation to physiognomically distinct Others, whose bodies were ideologically transformed into a departure, a deviation, and a degeneration away from the idealized human norm. Wynter's deco-lonial project and central problematic thus departs from what she defines as the overrepresentation of Western "Man" as the Human and the havoc that this overrepresentation has wreaked onto the world. As a result, she argues that the overrepresentation of "Man" is the problem of our time. Moreover, all of our contemporary struggles, such as "race," class, "gen-der," sexuality, the uneven distribution of wealth, global warming, etc., have their roots in/are differing aspects of the struggle against the over-representation of "Man" as the human.⁶

These categories are part and parcel of the human/subhuman distinc-tion that is essential to maintaining the overrepresentation's existence, and all knowledge, power, and economic systems have been organized in a way that continues to represent the existential interests of its benefactors, namely Europeans, Euroamericans, and their descendants.⁷ Wynter explains:

> The discursive and institutional re-elaboration of the central
> overrepresentation . . . enables the interests, reality, and well-being of
> the empirical human world to continue to be imperatively subordi-
> nated to those of the now globally hegemonic ethnoclass world of
> "Man."⁸

Her concern is that without a recognition and an unsettling of the eth-noracial and class specificity of this conception of the human, the bodies of those that fall outside of that description will continue to be sacrificed on its behalf.[9] At the forefront of these sacrificial liminal bodies are those that have been racialized and dehumanized in the colonial encounter and its "postcolonial" legacies.

Indeed, the severe global contraction of what it means to be human and the doing away with alternative models for and of humanity leads Wynter to claim that "the struggle of the new millennium will be one between the ongoing imperative of securing the well-being of our present ethnoclass (i.e., Western bourgeois) conception of the human . . . and that of securing the well-being of the human species itself/ourselves."[10] Thus, she calls for a new brand of humanism, one that would aspire to the well-being of humanity writ large.

Suggestive for us is the large percentage of her phenomenal oeuvre spent tracking the colonial processes and epistemic maneuvers through which the codes used to determine the "human/nonhuman" distinction have been produced and instituted. Namely, she highlights the relationship between the instituting of these codes and cognitive brain function by tracking the opiate release one affectively receives for realizing oneself within a positively marked code that then shapes how one gets to experience one's reality.[11] As Scott points out, "It is not the body's materiality itself that interests her so much as the ideological hegemonies—race principal among them[12]—that come to be imprinted on it in such a way that we live their inscriptions as the historically varying modes of our truth."[13] From this understanding of the ways in which the codes become imprinted on one's body, and the power they have to alter one's self-understanding, including a sense of one's value, she arrives at the more difficult, transformative, and hopeful component of her decolonial project. The second prominent line of her thinking includes a taking back of the "Word" in order to make possible new codes, in particular to form a new definition of the human that centers ontological sovereignty and being human as praxis. We understand her call for a new humanism as a politics of possibility that deeply resonates with the work of decolonial and women of color feminists, in that it opens up all forms of being human to revision and re(vision)ing.

What is most suggestive about this second prong of her work, and significantly in line with the work of women of color feminists, activists, and writers, is that the redefining of the Human requires a concomitant redefining of all subsequent relations. If taking back the "Word" is part of a "world-making" process, then her project includes the possibility of making a world where those relegated to the liminal get to (re-)emerge as complexly whole and human. For us, one of the goals of decolonial feminism is to make a world that does not reproduce or aspire to the oppressive relation that "Man"[14] has to others, but one that rewrites and reimagines relations beyond Western Man and moves us away from the violences produced by and in relation to his overrepresentation. The draw for us, which is in line with the politics of women of color and decolonial feminists, activists, and writers, is the potential to think and create a new world that ultimately seeks to thicken, strengthen, rebuild, or build anew all types of relations, including the relationships between those racialized,[15] from "outside" the epistemic universe that has given Western "Man" its power, ontological weight, and value.

Critiques of Feminism and the Persistence of Patriarchy

"Sylvia Wynter is my favorite kind of feminist."

However, in the effort to think outside of, or rather beyond, the epistemic universe that makes "Man" possible, Wynter develops a critique of feminism that in many ways serves to undermine the positive contributions of women of color and decolonial feminists, activists, and writers. Our concern is that her comments on feminism have provided a language for dismissing women of color feminisms and their poetics as potentially "Eurocentric" and/or "Western" and on the whole not worthy of serious engagement. For instance, the above is a quote from a well-established academic of color who made a point of sharing that Wynter was his favorite kind of feminist precisely because she has gone on record as saying she is not a feminist. And while we do not need Wynter to identify as a feminist, this is an example of how her work/words are used to articulate a dismissal of women of color and decolonial feminisms as a whole. As a result, it has become necessary to identify the imbrication and resonances between our political projects, as well as the places where we part ways. We want to argue that these political projects are far from mutually exclusive and that women of color have made substantive contributions toward making real her decolonial aspirations for a new kind of humanity.

What seems to have complicated Wynter's relationship to feminism is her own political desire to locate new models for the human informed by "native" standpoints.[16] In other words, Wynter underscores models of humanity that exist outside of and beyond European and Euroamerican ontology and epistemology. For instance, in the afterword to *Out of the Kumbla* (1990), an edited collection of Caribbean women writers compiled in an effort to define and inaugurate a Caribbean feminist critical literary tradition,[17] it is this political orientation that leads Wynter to argue for a shift away from feminism's "patriarchal discourse" toward a focus on the human/nonhuman distinction.

In the afterword, Wynter uses Shakespeare's *The Tempest* as a metaphor and symbolic representation to suggest that relations of subordination and domination are no longer "patriarchal," because Miranda has power over Caliban and not vice versa. She argues that they have instead been replaced by a secular racism and process of racialization that are monarchical (in that Miranda inherits power over Caliban through her proximity to her father/king Prospero and through her being canonized as the only rational object of desire for all males). Notably, this is one example where women of color and some decolonial feminists might part ways with Wynter, because while it is the case that Caliban's relationship to Miranda, specifically, is not one characterized by Patriarchy with a capital P, it is also true that this literary example does not help us better understand the relationship between Caliban and any racialized women. Women of color are precisely the bodies that are absented from the play.[18] If for women of color and decolonial feminists one key area of reflection and (re)visioning has been the complicated relationship *between* racialized men and women, and not only in heterosexist terms, then we cannot make sense of this relation using *The Tempest* as an example because women of color are completely invisible in Shakespeare's imaginary. As a result, we cannot know from here whether Caliban is capable of patriarchy with a lowercase "p" because his relationship to racialized women is never explored beyond filial memory.

And while we understand the liberatory impulse behind her effort to rethink patriarchy from a complicated history of colonization, we would argue that there are several reasons why completely excluding an analysis of patriarchy by women of color or taking "patriarchal discourse" off the table as an operative system that negatively affects the lives of women of color and our communities does not (yet) make political sense. First and foremost, Europe did not corner the market on patriarchy. There have been non-Western cultural systems that have systematically devalued cisgender women and nonnormative sexualities, outside of a Western epistemic cultural frame. While patriarchy is not reducible to these particular aspects they do give us insight into the larger point.

For example, we see evidence of this in the work of lesbian Aymara feminist Julieta Paredes who describes the *entronque patriarchal* as the historical convergence and interlocking of Western and Indigenous patriarchies that have negatively affected the lives of her communities' grandmothers and great-grandmothers.[19] For Paredes, decolonizing gender means recognizing the extent to which unjust relationships between community members existed long before colonization, and are not simply an inheritance of the colonial encounter. Paredes's claim is important because it challenges the implicit assumption that all "traditional" or "non-Western" models for being human are necessarily resistant or decolonial. It also challenges the assumption that any and all demands to revise practices that structurally, culturally, and systemically devalue some members of the community merely for existing, such as female, "queer," and gender nonconforming community members, is somehow necessarily Eurocentric.

The position that all "feminism" is Western or Eurocentric is a position that, on the one hand, refuses to acknowledge and take accountability for the harmful relations of power that pre-existed colonization and, on the other hand, refuses to recognize the violent modes and understandings of gender that were universalized through colonial relations.[20] So even if you are of the mind that gender is colonial imposition, then we still cannot take "patriarchal discourse" off the table, because that is exactly what racialized communities have imbibed through the coloniality of gender, power, knowledge, and being. In other words, we have to contend with the consequences of those legacies and the negative impact they have had on our communities and relations.

Second, if the argument for shifting the focus away from "patriarchal discourse" or a critique of patriarchy is based on the idea that men of color have been systematically denied access to it through violent historical processes that effectively "feminized" them, such as enslavement and colonialism, then we would like to take a moment to think through this claim from a decolonial feminist perspective. For the purposes of brevity, we will focus on the particular articulation of this trope by Nelson Maldonado-Torres. Notably, he is not by any means the only one to frame colonization/coloniality as a process that "feminized" men of color but rather the product of a long history and network of scholarship that has produced and naturalized this claim. In fact, one of the authors here recalls listening to a well-established historian who, during the question and answer period of a panel at the Association for the Study of the Worldwide African Diaspora, stated that "it has been proven that men of color were feminized during slavery and colonization." Taking a cue from Michel-Rolph Trouillot, and his brilliant text on the making of "history," it is not clear to us what would constitute such a proof. In fact, he tells us that what comes to be understood as "official history," or in this case what has been "proven," more often than not requires that a history of conflicts over such narratives/claims be obscured.[21]

Before returning to some of the ways in which coloniality/colonization is understood as a process that "feminizes" men of color, we want to point out that we are engaging Nelson Maldonado-Torres's work here for two reasons. First, we admire him, his work, and his deep commitment to decolonial transformation. There is a politics to who one cites and, rather than keep those without a commitment to decolonial transformation in circulation, we believe it important to cite those whom you want others to read. Second, he is an exception in that he is interpersonally committed to incorporating the thinking done by women of color feminists and engaging that work in thoughtful and meaningful ways. It is for these reasons that it is important to name the potentially harmful readings of this trope in his work. We are particularly attuned to how such readings pose challenges to the practices and approaches that would allow us to disrupt the coloniality in its many manifestations and move toward Wynter's hope of a new humanism.

In his article entitled "On the Coloniality of Being: Contributions to the Development of a Concept," Maldonado-Torres writes that coloniality

> can be understood as a radicalization of the non-ethics of war. This non-ethics included the practices of eliminating and slaving certain subjects e.g., indigenous and black as part of the enterprise of colonization. . . . War includes a particular treatment of sexuality and of femininity: rape. Coloniality is an order of things that put people of color under the murderous and rapist sight of a vigilant ego. And the primary targets of rape are women. But men of color are also seen through these lenses. *Men of color are feminized and become for the ego conquiro [a] fundamentally penetrable subject.*[22]

Here we draw your attention to the link between "feminization," penetration, and a violent process of dehumanization within the description of the coloniality at work. Feminization, and thus dehumanization, in this instance is coded as penetrability.[23] As a result, dehumanization here is (over)coded as the "humiliating" possibility of being penetrated, a condition that has been "naturalized" as permanently attached to female bodies. Indeed, it is the "naturalized" penetrability of female bodies that supposedly makes our bodies more susceptible to rape.

Implicit here is the notion that real "Men" or, rather, human men should be impenetrable. The meanings of "Man" hinge on it, since "feminization" as symbolic "penetrability" signals the historical dehumanization of colonized males. As such "feminization" as penetrability implicitly marks a condition that racialized males must not succumb to, a condition that racialized males must reject at all costs. The rejection of "feminization," and by extension all things "feminine," can be coded as a resistant (perhaps even decolonial) move that at its worst serves and has served to justify all kinds of harm against cisgender women, femmes, and queer, trans, gender nonconforming, and nonbinary folks within our communities.[24]

To be fair and clear, Maldonado-Torres is attempting to illustrate the role that the "feminization of enemies" played in the symbolic codes of conquest. However, centering the symbolic codes of those colonizing can also function to negatively affect the making of a new humanity and what we subsequently name as essential projects and ingredients for decoloniality. It is important to make a distinction between what colonizers projected onto the bodies of those they sought to colonize and what those under that gaze may have thought of themselves. Even if many of these projections have become internalized to different degrees over time, conflating the two unwittingly presupposes that there were no alternative frames of reference available to or operative among those enslaved to challenge these Eurocentric formulations of their Otherness.

In his efforts to indict the logics of the coloniality of being, and the *longue durée* of its impact, Maldonado-Torres writes that "lacking real authority, colonized men are permanently feminized."[25] While that may be true from the standpoint of the colonizer, where "Men" (think: White Bourgeois Heterosexual males) are the only ones empowered to occupy a position of "real authority," we cannot know that "lacking" authority was synonymous with "being feminized" for all those enslaved or that "masculinity" was predicated on or contingent upon "having authority." Beyond a question of intentionality, and in the case of Maldonado-Torres we do not assume this to be his intention, "feminization" in this instance assumes authority to be the "exclusive right" of males. However, this assertion can only hold true if we assume and represent "men" to be ahistorical, transhistorical, biological, and/or supracultural beings.[26]

More important, this conceptualization of what it means to be "feminized" lays the ground, again beyond a question of intentionality, for a competition between White Bourgeois Heterosexual "Men" (those who have authority) and males of color (those whose authority was "stolen") from within the terms and perspectives of those colonizing. This framing unwittingly paves the way for a desiring of the *wages of gender*;[27] in this instance patriarchy (the effort to achieve the status of authority granted to "Man") that then gets enacted within communities of color. In other words, this framing of men of color as "permanently feminized" functions to center the competition between White Bourgeois Heterosexual Males

("Men") and colonized/formerly colonized males (those constituted as not "Men") in a way that sacrifices the relationship between racialized males and females to the achievement of equality between "Men" and those aspiring to be recognized as "(hu)men."

Far from deconstructing the code, and thus moving beyond the Doctrine of Man, the trope actually functions to reinstate a version of patriarchy within communities of color while also functioning to obscure alternative coeval, non-Western, and non-Eurocentric formations of power. Indeed, what we do not see, what we cannot see in these accounts, is whether those colonized males understood themselves as "feminized" or if they had alternative frames of reference from which to evaluate themselves, their relations, bodies, and relative worth. Notably, it is here where women of color and decolonial feminists have substantively contributed to expanding our understanding of alternative modes of being human, in particular by expanding the scholarship on more egalitarian modes of relating and determining value.

For example, by the time of Wynter's interview with David Scott (2000), where she states that "the difference between [feminists and herself] is that they would continue to see *gender* as a supracultural phenomenon, and therefore as a universal whose terms could be the same for all human groups,"[28] women of color had already begun the work of documenting alternative modes of being human that included more egalitarian arrangements of the social and positive valuations of racialized women and "nonnormative"[29] sexualities and ways of being. At least fourteen years prior, Paula Gunn Allen had given us an account of the expansive role "women" played in communal governance, the sacred role two-spirit people held, and the deep value for "mothers" (a term for creators and not necessarily women who had reproduced offspring) within Indigenous communities in her book *The Sacred Hoop: Recovering the Feminine in American Indian Traditions* (1986).[30]

Another example is Oyèrónkẹ̀ Oyěwùmí's book *The Invention of Women: Making an African Sense of Western Gender Discourses* (1997), where she argues that in Yorubaland the social was primarily organized around seniority and not gender. Far from reducing gender, and by extension patriarchy, to a supracultural phenomenon Oyěwùmí tracks some of the power distortions that are enabled by this assumption. She goes on to suggest that the assumption that gender is a supracultural phenomenon has done the work of creating sexual hierarchies where there were none before.[31]

In addition to Oyěwùmí, the examination of alternative modes of being human has been followed up by Sylvia Marcos in her book *Taken from*

the Lips: Gender and Eros in Mesoamerican Religions (2006), where she examines the more fluid and egalitarian conceptions of gender, the body, and
the cosmos at play in the healing and ritual practices of *curanderas* in Me-
soamerica.[32] Gloria Wekker's book, *The Politics of Passion: Women's Sexual
Culture in the Afro-Surinamese Diaspora* (2006), echoes Wynter's critique
of gender and explores alternative sexual arrangements made possible
through an engagement with Winti, an Afro-diasporic religion and set of
ritual practices in Suriname.[33] In her article "Transcending Dimorphism:
Afro-Cuban Ritual Praxis and the Rematerialization of the Body," author
Xhercis Méndez troubles the way gender is deployed as a cross-cultural
category of analysis and explores how racialized women, as well as "queer"
and gender nonconforming folks of color, come to be valued and human-
ized through the more fluid and egalitarian arrangements of bodies and
power available in Ocha (more popularly known as Afro-Cuban Santería).[34]

For instance, Méndez tracks how spiritual seniority in Ocha constitutes
an alternative mode of empowerment and valuation wherein power is determined by a combination of one's time within the practice, accumula-
tion of specialized ritual knowledge, and the degree to which one expands
the spiritual lineage.[35] Those who do the work to attain specialized ritual
knowledge, expand the spiritual lineage, and are recognized by the community as knowledgeable are understood to be elders and given deference
regardless of body type, sexual preferences, or actual age. These ritual
practices illustrate some of the ways in which power and "authority" was
not the "exclusive right" of cisgender men.

Thus, if we center Ocha's alternative grid of intelligibility, valuation, and
power vis-à-vis spiritual seniority, then we can productively challenge the
feminization narrative and raise the following questions: First, if we think
of dehumanization as a process that for all intents and purposes "feminized" males of color, then to what extent are we internalizing and reinscribing the colonial gaze and logic? Second, in what ways does this kind
of narrative justify a contemporary urgency to "man up" and to reclaim
"Man"-hood on colonial terms? Finally, to what extent do these tropes re-
frame and center the relationship/competition between White Men and
males of color as the collective political project of undoing Race—and now
the collective political project of undoing coloniality—while simultaneously obscuring the violence of the light side gender dynamics they (re)
produce as a result?

These questions reveal how a resignation to the realm of "Man" enables
an equally violent reclamation of "gender" in its most colonizing form. Beyond a question of historicizing the world of "Man," engaging in this

trope serves to undermine Wynter's call for a new humanism, particularly one that urges the well-being of the collective. Important for our discussion are the ways in which women of color and decolonial feminists have done and continue to do the work of nuancing under what conditions it makes sense for us to use the category of gender and an understanding of patriarchy, particularly as they pertain to racialized bodies.

Finally, the uses of "patriarchal discourse" and critiques of patriarchy by women of color and decolonial feminists have not and are not articulated in the abstract, but instead firmly grounded in our very real lived experiences with it, both from outside as well as within our communities. If the concern is the use of this particular terminology, then we are open to the idea of seeking another term for it as long as we do not lose the possibility of naming and transforming behavior, logics, and modes of being that become destructive to our lives and our communities, whether chosen or inherited. We would argue that whatever concept/terminology emerges next needs to be able to account for the simultaneously operative forms of violence in our lives, such as the state-sanctioned institutions and racist structures that have Black and Brown women being imprisoned at record rates and disappeared at borders, and Indigenous women being raped and murdered with impunity, as well as the sexism, homophobia, misogyny, and assaults we face at the hands of our own communities. This sentiment is poignantly captured by the Combahee River Collective, a group of Black feminist activists and scholars who wrote:

> Although we are feminists and lesbians, we feel solidarity with progressive black men and do not advocate the fractionalization that white women who are separatists demand. *Our situation as black people necessitates that we have solidarity around the fact of race*, which white women of course do not need to have with white men, unless it is their negative solidarity as racial oppressors. *We struggle together with black men against racism, while we also struggle with black men about sexism.*[36]

Indeed, it is the need to find a way to name and talk about this double-edged sword and existence that we hear reflected in their words.

And yet, to dismiss the critique of patriarchy out of hand as "Western" means leaving women of color bereft of tools for talking about and dealing with their very real lived experiences with patriarchy coming from both "Man" and men of color. Any version of decoloniality or decolonization should not demand that we prioritize the embattled relationship to "Man" if it means we have to bypass the work of becoming accountable and responsible to and for each other. For those of us invested in healing, strengthening, and thickening the relationships between racialized folks, this means sitting in the complexity of this nuance and finding ways to do better for the next generation. That is the work we have done and continue to do as women of color and decolonial feminists.

For example, Wendy Rose's (Miwok/Hopi) 1993 poetry collection, *Going to War with All My Relations*, is a text that mourns the ongoing violence of settler colonialism while simultaneously offering ways of resisting the normalization of violence.[37] Throughout the text, Rose maintains a sustained critique of the forms of intimate and sexual violence enacted by her beloved brothers. In her poem, "men talking in the donut shop," Rose recounts overhearing three men excitedly discussing the brutal murder of a woman over a meal of coffee and donut holes, "an army of them/against the native earth of her."[38] This poem, a reflection of an actual conversation Rose overheard in passing, marks the quotidian nature of a conversation on the shooting death of a woman by her husband. In documenting this as a poem, she offers the possibility to continually hold space for the forms of violence wielded against Indigenous women's bodies. Rose's collection calls for a new mode of relating by refusing to allow the kinds of foundational violence that targeted and continually targets Indigenous communities for demise to serve as a justification for the sexual degradation and violence against her sisters. For Rose, as for many women of color feminist thinkers, activists, and writers, the only way to wage a battle against these oppressions is to foreground our responsibility to and for each other and to challenge all of one's relations to resist being complicit in perpetuating future harm. This is part of a poetic and political practice fueled by love and fury.

Moreover, as so many women of color have already argued, the naming of harmful behavior as enacted by racialized men over and against women of color, our lives, and our communities is not about undermining or being destructive to men of color for the sake of it. On the contrary, it is about finding ways to name the harmful behaviors that negatively affect our chosen and inherited communities in order to lay the ground for transformation. It is important to note that the naming of harm as enacted by men of color does not presume that women of color are incapable of violence and harm. Nor does it assume that the battle for racial justice will necessarily address or heal the broken relationships and harmful modes of relating between us. It also does not presume that violence and harm make up the totality of our relationships. As Kristie Dotson reminds us, these are part of the ongoing distortions and recalcitrant manifestations of ignorance to which Black feminist thought particularly, and women of color feminist thought more generally, are consistently subjected.[39]

Even in the midst of these distortions and manifestations of ignorance as well as the various forms of harm we experience at the hands of our communities, women of color do not make the mistake of naturalizing patriarchal behavior as a function of some type of essential maleness. Indeed, within this heterogeneous body of activism, theorizing, and poetics one will more often than not encounter efforts to develop nuanced understandings of racialized masculinity, complex analyses of the intersections between race, gender, sexuality, and class, and calls to alter the value systems that produce all members of our communities, albeit differently, as less worthy of a full humanity. And yet there has been an insistence that women of color primarily center our own individual lives at the expense of the collective.

For instance, in her interview with David Scott, Wynter distances herself from feminism writ large by suggesting that its vision is too myopic (in that it is primarily and or solely concerned with the plight of particular women) and therefore not sufficiently attentive to the concerns of the larger collective. She states, "Where I think there is a great distance between today's feminists and myself is that then we knew *that it was as a population—* men, women and children—that we had thought we could not do anything."[40] We respond to this by reminding folks, yet again, that women of color and decolonial feminists have never advocated for leaving the community or whole of the population behind in the name of some intangible individual freedom.

The suggestion that women of color are solely concerned with our own lives, at the expense of the communal, can only exist in a vacuum. In order to stand, this claim has to completely overlook the extent to which even in their critical confrontation with racialized men over the violences being enacted by them, women of color have rarely articulated a liberation model that would completely absent out or leave men of color behind. Nor have women of color been indifferent to the matrices of power in which men of color find themselves and the network of oppressive forces that negatively affect their lives, even when the same could not be said in reverse.[41] One explicit example of this, which was already in circulation at the time of her interview, can again be found in the Combahee River Collective Statement. They write:

> As we have already stated, we reject the stance of lesbian separatism because it is not a viable political analysis or strategy for us. *It leaves out*

far too much and far too many people, particularly black men, women, and children. We have a great deal of criticism and loathing for what men *have been socialized* to be in this society: what they support, how they act, and how they oppress. But *we do not have the misguided notion that it is their maleness,* per se i.e., their biological maleness—*that makes them what they are.* As black women we find any type of biological determinism a particularly dangerous and reactionary basis upon which to build a politic.[42]

Rather than buying into an oversimplified conceptualization of patriarchy as synonymous with maleness, a move they describe as "dangerous and reactionary," they exercise the same kind of skepticism that Wynter later expresses by rejecting facile notions of manhood and womanhood. This willingness to think through the complexities of racialized masculinity in an effort to push for a liberation model that will not leave "too many people behind" is an example of what it means to enact complex coalitions toward decolonizing oppressed and systematically dehumanized communities.[43]

Moreover, other women of color have echoed this call to think beyond the individual and build coalitions in complex ways. For instance, when Gloria Anzaldúa argues that in order for us to transform the world we have to develop a "tolerance for ambiguity" and open ourselves to the lessons proffered by the *atravesados,* she is arguing for the making of complex coalition between those who have been systematically dehumanized.[44] This is not an individualized feminist politic but one that reaches for the "squint-eyed, the perverse, the queer, the troublesome, the mongrel, the mulatto, the half-breed, the half dead, in short, those who cross over, pass over or go through the confines of the 'normal.'"[45]

This coalitional orientation is also echoed by the literary works of women of color feminist writers who refuse to imagine liberation struggles in separatist terms. This includes writers like Maxine Hong Kingston, Audre Lorde, Leanne Betasamosake Simpson, Mayra Santos-Febres, and Helena María Viramontes, to name a few.[46] Their work, spanning decades, imagines and reimagines what it means to work at a crossroads of relationality. For instance, taking seriously the plight of women, men, and children who suffer injustices under the heel of coloniality, Aurora Levins Morales, in *Medicine Stories: History, Culture and the Politics of Integrity,* argues that solidarity comes from the intolerance of collaborating in the oppression of others. She writes, "Like it or not, our liberation is bound up with that of every other being on the planet," anything else "is unaffordable."[47] Indeed, both women of color feminist politics and decolonial feminisms are deeply imbued with and inseparable from this radical relational paradigm.

Taking Back the "Word"

In her formative essay, "The Ceremony Must Be Found: After Humanism," Wynter argues that the development of a science of humanities in the fifteenth century was the methodology through which a new world was made. According to Wynter, the shift away from the religiosity that ruled "Man 1," an older and differently repressed form of humanity, toward the reasoning bio-ontological Man ("Man 2") that now represents what it means to be human, was achieved and instituted through a word-making process. It was this process, which she later refers to as "taking the Word," that produced

> an utterly new way of feeling, of imagining Self and World, and a mode of imagination that would no longer find its referential figurative *auctoritas* in the great religious schemas and symbols, but rather in a new referential figurative *auctoritas*, that of the fictional poetic/dramatic schemas of the phenomena we call "literature." Literature in its new role/ordering function, and the Studia were, therefore, to be twin forms of each other, forms through whose internal meditation, the human, who had hitherto imagined its mode of being through mythic/theological figurative schemas, would now come to imagine itself—and to act upon the world in the mode of that imagination—through the great poetic schemas which refigured and configured the first form of the secularly charted human being: the world of its order of things.[48]

Notably Wynter proclaims the literary humanities as a critical site through which we take back the "Word" and make possible a new human system of sciences, and ultimately a new humanity. She notes that "far from 'literature having no function,' as it is assumed, it is we who are the function. It is as specific modes of imagining subjects of the aesthetic orders which literature's figuration-Word weaves in great feats of rhetorical engineering that we come to imagine/experience ourselves, our modes of being."[49] For Wynter, that heretical practice of the late Middle Ages, of bringing poetic schemas into existence that reimagined the world, can and must be matched by a new form of heretical practice, "which takes the human rather than any one of its variations as Subject."[50] Wynter argues that it is "the literary humanities which should be the umbrella site for the trans-disciplinary realization of a science of human systems."[51] Thus, we, the bodies made liminal to Western Man, are tasked with creating a new literary humanities that allows us to imagine decolonial human futures. Wynter contributes to this future through her transdisciplinary historicism and critical texts as well as through her own poetic/dramatic productions, which punctuate the last five and a half decades of her work.[52]

Similar to Wynter, women of color and decolonial feminists' theoretical projects, activism, and creative productions are a reflection of our human experiences, concerns, and aspirations in and beyond the liminal space to which we have been relegated in the Word/world of "Man."[53] It is here where Wynter's work and women of color and decolonial feminists most closely and politically align. We see this political alignment reflected in the words of the Combahee River Collective when they write that "our politics initially sprang from the shared belief that black women are inherently valuable, that *our liberation is a necessity not as an adjunct to somebody else's but because of our need as human persons for autonomy.* We realize that the only people who care enough about us to work consistently for our liberation is us. *Our politics evolve from a healthy love for ourselves, our sisters, and our community,* which allows us to continue our struggle and work. We reject pedestals, queenhood, and walking ten paces behind. *To be recognized as human, levelly human, is enough.*"[54] This declaration of self-worth does not seek to displace the struggle against racism nor does it seek to undermine men of color. On the contrary, in this reclamation of worth we see the effort to take back the "Word" in order to challenge the deep and systemic/systematic devaluation of Black women's lives and bodies. Is this not a refusal of the genre of Man? Is this not the heresy of which Wynter speaks?

Women of color and decolonial feminists have substantively contributed to Wynter's political goal of moving beyond the genre of "Man," even when their/our access to an alternative epistemic universe was limited. Even without a clear "outside," women of color have crafted pluriverses through poetry, creative fiction, and through activism and relations that made room for an expansive sense of our own and our communities' value. They have enacted being human as praxis through the (re)building of relations that needed to be healed and transformed in order to emerge stronger. Women of color and decolonial feminists have produced visions for human futures that operate from palimpsestic notions of time, which includes what has happened before, the here and now, and the not yet here.[55] They are consistently creating worlds where more community members (chosen and inherited) are valued and of value, while also recognizing that there is still so much more left to do.

For instance, Rose's *Going to War with All My Relations* is an example of how that world-making happens in the battle against colonization and coloniality and across temporal and spatial locales.[56] In the preface of the collection she notes that while the book is a reflection of her experiences in the Indigenous Fourth World movement, the titular "war" that she refers to is "everyone's war" and the "relations" indicates a relation to one another.[57] Throughout the book, Rose makes connections to Indigenous peoples in what is now the United States, Canada, and the Caribbean, to the long legacies of slavery, settler colonialism, global warfare, and intimate and domestic violence. These gestures toward a relation to and with peoples in other temporal or spatial contexts, even when not materially accessible to Rose, are her attempt to bridge multiple struggles in order to create a more expansive sense of what constitutes a resisting community.

Instead of ascribing to the categorical fracturing purported by the world of Man, Rose's poetics represent a reclaiming of the Word and world-making process that sees the need for building bridges to each other's histories as a means for liberation. To this end, Rose opens the collection with a poem titled "Auction," which brings us to an auction block where bodies are sold "with the grace of death."[58] The poem is ambiguous about whether the bodies being sold are Indigenous or Black. Instead the reader is tasked with meditating on the institution of chattel slavery and how the histories of Indigenous and Black enslavement and dispossession are so deeply entangled that they cannot be extricated.

In "Song for the Warriors Taken Away," written in remembrance of the Anishinabek Occupation of 1975, she asks the warriors to "let [her] tongue lick/your bones back together."[59] Through her grief, she gives herself to her "Brothers Sisters," telling them how her heart hears the "man-dust . . . woman-dust" of their falling and that she "borrows for her battles/the copper of [you]."[60] Here Rose reads these warriors' struggles against the grain of powers that would render them successfully defeated or dead. Instead she recognizes that through her song and remembrance she can conjure their spirits, which were "never in danger" of being completely annihilated.[61]

In addition to conjuring bridges to each other's histories and narrating resistant histories, women of color have enacted being human as praxis through their persistent commitment to becoming faithful witnesses to others' trauma, including that of men of color.[62] For instance, in Toni

Morrison's *Beloved* (1987), a novel acclaimed as one of the most significant contributions to American literature in the twentieth century, Morrison uses the story of Margaret Garner as a point of departure to discuss the intergenerational and hauntological effects of chattel slavery.[63] In the novel, Morrison expands what we know about the emotional lives of the enslaved through an exploration of the unsaid and the extended relations of the protagonist Sethe. Even as the novel seemingly centers Sethe and her daughters Denver and Beloved, Morrison refuses to be indifferent to the unspeakable pain of Paul D and the traumas that he piled into the "tobacco tin lodged in his chest."[64] Morrison brings to life Paul D's experience and affectively takes us into to the dehumanizing labor of the chain gang, as well as the humiliation and the smiting of lives at the hands of the overseers. Through her fictional accounting we are made witness to the rape, terror, and humiliation to which Paul D and the forty-six men of the chain gang were subjected. She writes:

> Chain-up completed, they knelt down. . . . Kneeling in the mist they waited for the whim of the guard, or two, or three. Or maybe all of them wanted it. Wanted it from one prisoner in particular or none—or all. . . . Occasionally a kneeling man chose gunshot to his head as the price, maybe, of taking a bit of foreskin with him to Jesus.[65]

By centering Paul D's trauma alongside Sethe's, Morrison magnifies what we understand and feel about the pain of racialized men under the conditions of slavery. Indeed, her commitment to showing what is rarely documented—the rape and sexual degradation of Black men—reaches beyond the limits of material history and adds to an archive of the unseen. Morrison narrates Paul D's pain alongside Sethe's and many others. As a result, *Beloved* engages in the creation of an archive within the literary that presents the pain of men of color alongside that of Sethe's.

Rather than write Paul D as a character that has been "feminized" and who needs to recuperate a sense of masculinity over and against Sethe's trauma, Morrison's poetic universe does not center the world in which sexual violence would reduce them to nonhuman status. Nor does Morrison make of them characters that reveal their physical and psychological wounds as an effort to create a hierarchy of their traumas. Instead, she offers us a glimpse into a new mode of being human, one in which the mutual recognition of these acts against them allows Sethe and Paul D to radically reimagine what it means to love each other and be responsible to and for each other in the face of intense violence. For example, one of the fundamental metaphors for the lasting and haunting legacy of slavery is the "chokecherry tree" whipped onto Sethe's back. Paul D's reaction to Sethe's scars is one of the most affecting moments in the narrative, one that lingers in our imaginations long after.

> Behind her, bending down, his body an arc of kindness, he held her breasts in the palms of his hands. He rubbed his cheek on her back and learned that way her sorrow, the roots of it; its wide trunk and intricate branches. Raising his fingers to the hooks of her dress, he knew without seeing them or hearing any sigh that the tears were coming fast. And when the top of her dress was around her hips and he saw the sculpture her back had become, like the decorative work of an ironsmith too passionate for display, he could think but not say, "Aw, Lord, girl." *And he would tolerate no peace until he had touched every ridge and leaf of it with his mouth,* none of which Sethe could feel because her back skin had been dead for years.[66]

In this passage Morrison shows us the tangible remnants of slavery but she also does the work of reconfiguring these wounds from ugly scars to a tree that is lovingly tended to by Paul D, who has also suffered the lash. Though Sethe cannot feel Paul D's tracing of the scars with his mouth, she is moved to tears by the possibility of having the weight of her pain "in somebody else's hands."[67] Morrison's literary imagination maps new relations or reveals the kinds of potential for healing between racialized and often dehumanized subjects. Morrison takes this instance of the destruction of the body, keloid growths over scars inflicted as a way to annihilate resistance and desirability, to offer us one way to (re)imagine their humanity and a collective liberation that must include healing from trauma.

This moment is not made less powerful by the fact of its ephemerality or seeming intangibility. We can read this moment as a way through which peoples subjected to unspeakable violence are able to bear witness to each other's pain without erasing their own experiences. In other words, it is not a zero-sum game. Morrison gives us a glimpse of one way we could hold each other and each other's pain. This moment between Sethe and Paul D reimagines their humanity through a lens of mutual (re)valuation and a desire to be tender with the most pained and "ugly" parts of ourselves and one another. As they relate to one another's pain they attempt to make meaning out of the senseless violence to which they have been subjected. In crafting moments such as these, Morrison weaves for us a world where decolonial love becomes necessary for our moving toward a collective healing.[68]

A Decolonial Feminist Politic

There is no decoloniality without a decoloniality of gender!
MARIA LUGONES, Decolonial Feminism Workgroup,
Binghamton University

When Wynter asks us to consider "how can we come to know social reality outside the terms of the *sociogenic* code of symbolic life and death?,"[69] she is asking us to do the work of reimaging/reimagining ourselves and our communities. This proposition is about getting us to begin to identify, even in the midst of violence, the "who" and "what" we want to become. It is here where we see women of color and decolonial feminist projects and creative productions as gender/genre denunciations that move us toward a set of intimate and exponentially complicated questions and that resonate with Wynter's larger project—namely, that of locating ingredients for the "who" and "what" we want to become.[70]

While we recognize the epistemological and ontological limits of concepts like patriarchy and gender when deployed in decontextualized universalist terms, this does not mean that women of color who continue to use these concepts and categories have necessarily been duped by a Eurocentric liberal feminist politics. On the contrary, the dismissal of patriarchy and gender as useless categories for a decolonial turn has come all too facile. The reason for this contention is that although we are invested in moving toward a world beyond "Man," *we are not yet there!* So while one could argue that patriarchy and even gender are concepts that continue to respond to the epistemic universe and gender arrangements of "Man" and are therefore not worthy of our attention, women of color and decolonial feminists continue to do the work of clarifying when and under what conditions the concepts remain useful.

As it were, we are concerned with how the dismissal of women of color and decolonial feminisms, in all of their iterations, derail us from the possibility of developing new/alternative understandings of humanity (more complex, multiplicitous, and pluralistic conceptualizations). For us this includes developing modes of being that do not require women of color, queer, gender nonconforming, and trans folks of color to put our/their concerns to the side. Freedom cannot be understood solely as that which disrupts the violence between the *damnés* and the systems that oppress us in the service of "Man",[71] it must also work to develop strategies for dis-identifying with the very opiate nuggets that make that mode of being human attractive, so attractive as to make the *damné* aspire to it even when it harms their racialized counterparts.[72]

We are clear that Wynter's decolonial humanism is a project of justice and liberation for those embodied by the "liminal," that is, invested in re-defining freedom, truth, and being beyond mainstream paradigms. Fur-thermore, it is clear that Wynter's position on feminism does not propose or uphold a decolonization project that would have racialized females sac-rifice their bodies and reproductive labor so that men of color can emerge as (hu)"Men." Given that freedom for Wynter, as Neil Roberts points out, is a *practice* and not an ideal, then how can we call any project decolonial if *in practice* it requires that more than half of its population be sacrificed for the well-being of the rest?[73] What decolonial project would seek to atten-uate the ontological autonomy of a large percentage of its people in the name of freedom? We propose that women of color and decolonial femi-nists are offering some of the ingredients that are necessary for human freedom rather than attending or aspiring to the freedom of "Man."

More importantly, we are invested in tending to and developing the tools already available to us for moving toward a collective and communal liberation. As Wynter proposes, the practice of taking the "Word" is one such tool that allows us to reimagine and write ourselves alternatives to the epistemic universe of Man. As we have illustrated thus far, the work pro-duced by women of color feminists, activists, and writers has centered re-lationality and complex coalition building by expanding the sets of bodies and histories to be included in the project of liberation. These are critical aspects of a decolonial feminist politics of liberation. This political ges-ture refuses to imagine liberation as an individual or particularistic free-dom but rather recognizes the inseparable links between oppressions. Far from situating the experiences of women as the primary or singular foun-dational violence, this feminist politic has practiced bearing witness to others' trauma and has more oft than not organized in favor of a larger collective well-being, without losing sight of what we also need to be well. It is a both/and approach that we would like to see more broadly and fre-quently reciprocated on behalf of women of color.

The writing and activism of women of color and decolonial feminists reminds us that, in addition to nuanced analyses, decoloniality demands that we continue to develop not just concepts but *actual practices* (new ways of moving and being) that address sexual assault, domestic violence, ho-mophobia, transphobia, and other interpersonal violences within our com-munities of color. In other words, we cannot just think decoloniality, especially a decoloniality that does not demand that we live or act any differently than we do now. Decoloniality for us must contend with the violences and harms being enacted on our communities as well as within our communities. We must address the impact of contemporary harm as well as the intergenerational impact of violences, such as slavery, colonialism, and settler colonialism.[74] Because we have not yet arrived at a world beyond "Man," a world that has been thoroughly organized by gender, even if as a genre of the human, we are left to echo Lugones's claim that "there is no decoloniality without a decoloniality of gender!" And for those self-identified "decolonial" thinkers that continue to dismiss the indispensable contributions made by women of color, we continue to take back the "Word" through critical creative and political practices. In addition to responding to the larger structural forces that harm our communities, women of color and decolonial feminist politics have consistently and substantively contributed to the efforts to *strengthen, heal, transform, and/or build anew the relationships between those racialized*. In so doing, they/we have practiced a form of "loving big" that includes developing some of the very methods, approaches, and tools we deem necessary for decolonization, decoloniality, and the making of "other than this and better than this"[75] human futures.

NOTES

1. We want to be clear here that we do not believe that all communal projects are necessarily decolonial or devoid of violent relations. We know that our communities are not perfect and that there are long-standing practices that need to be revised and transformed if they are to ensure the well-being of all community members.

2. David Scott, "The Re-Enchantment of Humanism: An Interview with Sylvia Wynter," *Small Axe* 8 (September 2000): 121.

3. Sylvia Wynter, "Unsettling the Coloniality of Being/Power/Truth/Freedom: Towards the Human, after Man, Its Overrepresentation—An Argument," *CR: The New Centennial Review* 3, no. 3 (Fall 2003): 269–70, 328.

4. Wynter, "Unsettling the Coloniality of Being/Power/Truth/Freedom." See also Sylvia Wynter and Katherine McKittrick, "Unparalleled Catastrophe for Our Species? Or, To Give Humanness a Different Future: Conversations," in *Sylvia Wynter: On Being Human as Praxis*, ed. Katherine McKittrick (Durham, N.C.: Duke University Press, 2015).

5. Wynter, "Unsettling the Coloniality of Being/Power/Truth/Freedom," 282. For instance, if being human meant *having reason*, then other modes of being human were viewed as *lacking reason*. Indeed, other modes of being human were also represented as lacking control over one's passions, lacking culture, order and civilization, lacking language, and the list goes on.

6. Wynter, 260.

7. Sylvia Wynter, "Beyond Miranda's Meanings: Un/silencing the 'Demonic Ground' of Caliban's 'Woman,'" in *Out of the Kumbla: Caribbean Women and Literature*, ed. Carole B. Davies and Elaine S. Fido (Trenton, N.J.: Africa World Press, 1990), 363. Notably, white supremacists often deploy slogans that demand the securing of a "future for white children." "14 Words," ADL: Fighting Hate for Good, https://www.adl.org/education /references/hate-symbols/14-words.

8. Wynter, "Unsettling the Coloniality of Being/Power/Truth/ Freedom," 262.

9. And here we would add the heterosexist, gendered, and ableist specificity of this conception of the human.

10. Wynter, "Unsettling the Coloniality of Being/Power/Truth/ Freedom," 260.

11. What Wynter highlights for us is the power that these codes have in enticing our complicity with oppressive/oppressing regimes. Her work reorients us to consider the privileges/benefits we gain when we are in a position to align ourselves with these codes and the psychological harm we experience when we cannot. This "opiate" release is tied to how we understand our worth in relation to fitting the code, striving to achieve success in the code's terms, and or the pleasure gained from pointing out how others fail within the parameters of the code. Here we see the potential of the literary to undermine this power to entice complicity by rewriting or, rather, introducing alternative codes against and through which we can measure our worth.

12. We would add that the ideological hegemonies that do this work are not reducible to race alone. Many women of color and decolonial feminists contend that there are simultaneously operative and mutually constitutive hegemonies that work together to dysselect some from emerging as wholly human, and that one is not more foundational than the other.

13. Scott, "Re-Enchantment of Humanism," 121.

14. This aspirational phenomenon is what Xhercis Méndez refers to as the "wages of gender." See Xhercis Méndez, "Notes Toward a Decolonial Feminist Methodology: Revisiting the Race/Gender Matrix," *Trans-Scripts* 5 (2015); and Xhercis Méndez, "Decolonial Feminist *Movidas*: A *Caribeña* (Re) thinks 'Privilege,' the Wages of Gender, and Building Complex Coalitions," in *Theories of the Flesh: Latinx and Latin American Feminisms, Transformation, and Resistance*, ed. José Medina, Mariana Ortega, and Andrea Pitts. (New York: Oxford University Press, forthcoming).

15. Notably, racial justice work does not primarily center the relationship between those racialized; it is more oft than not focused on the oppressive forces and structures being enacted from outside of the "community." We

are clear that transformation demands that we attend to both types of relationships, not just one or the other.

16. Wynter uses the term *native* in ways that conjure up a notion of peoples who are understood as original to a land or space and include non-Western cultural practices, rituals, and ways of being, as well as to peoples that have in their encounter with colonizers been labeled as such as a result. For a discussion that can productively complicate Wynter's usage of the category "native," see Joanne Barker's edited volume, *Critically Sovereign: Indigenous Gender, Sexuality, and Feminist Studies* (Durham, N.C.: Duke University Press, 2017).

17. Natasha Barnes, "Reluctant Matriarch: Sylvia Wynter and the Problematics of Caribbean Feminism," *Small Axe* no. 5 (March 1999).

18. For more on the absence of women of color in *The Tempest*, see Abena Busia's "Silencing Sycorax: On African Colonial Discourse and the Unvoiced Female," *Cultural Critique* 14 (Winter 1989–1990); and Irene Lara's "Beyond Caliban's Curses: The Decolonial Feminist Literacy of Sycorax," *Journal of International Women's Studies* 9, no. 1 (2007).

19. See Julieta Paredes, *Hilando Fino: Desde el feminismo comunitario* (La Paz: Comunidad Mujeres Creando Comunidad, 2010).

20. We see this tension in Wynter's account of female circumcision. While we can appreciate the significance of tracking some of the more troubling assumptions embedded in Alice Walker's critique of the practice, we are also of the mind that not all critiques of the practice stem from a colonial rereading of them. We believe there should be some room left for those whose lives are directly affected by practices, "traditional" or otherwise, to critique them. This follows from the recognition that our communities and practices are not perfect and that there are, in fact, precolonial practices that can be and have also been harmful. Sylvia Wynter, "'Genital Mutilation' or 'Symbolic Birth'? Female Circumcision, Lost Origins, and the Aculturalism of Feminist/Western Thought," *Case Western Reserve Law Review* 47, no. 2 (1997): 501.

21. See Michel-Rolph Trouillot, *Silencing the Past: Power and the Production of History* (Boston: Beacon Press, 1995).

22. Nelson Maldonado-Torres, "On the Coloniality of Being: Contributions to the Development of a Concept," *Cultural Studies* 21, no. 2–3 (March/ May 2007): 247–48, emphasis added.

23. While this is not the only way in which men of color have been cast as historically feminized, this is one modern-day conception of it. Other narratives have included: 1) "Feminization" as a reduction to a permanent childlike status, a condition that was also attached to white women, and 2) Within the context of the United States, the feminization of men of color

has also been a reference to temperament, in the sense that African American men have been viewed as having a predisposition for emotion rather than reason, and a particular affinity to culture, hence the reference by sociologists Robert Park and Ernest Burgess in 1921 to "Negroes" as the "Lady Among the Races." See Roderick A. Ferguson, *Aberrations in Black: Toward a Queer of Color Critique* (Minneapolis: University of Minnesota Press, 2003), 58. A parallel and interrelated claim is the assertion that racism "emasculates" men of color. However, that assertion entails a more thorough discussion. In the interest of being ethically engaged we will not address that assertion within the context of this essay.

24. To complicate this point further, the rejection of "feminization" can also include justifying violence against cisgender women, femmes, queer, trans, and gender nonconforming people from other communities as well. For instance, there is an exchange between Prospero and Caliban where Prospero accuses Caliban of trying to "violate the honour" of his daughter. Caliban's response is "Would't had been done! Thou didst prevent me; I had peopled else this isle with Calibans." And while we are clear that there is a colonial logic at play here that casts Caliban as a sexual predator, we are also concerned with the seductiveness of casting a retributive violence that includes sexual assault as a form of anticolonial resistance.

25. Maldonado-Torres, "On the Coloniality of Being," 255.

26. Tonya Haynes notes this in her terrific article, "Sylvia Wynter's Theory of the Human and the Crisis School of Caribbean Heteromasculinity Studies," *Small Axe* 20, no. 1 (49) (2016): 103.

27. See Méndez, "Notes Toward a Decolonial Feminist Methodology."

28. Scott, "Re-Enchantment of Humanism," 185.

29. It is important to note that *nonnormative* here is referring to what is nonnormative in a Western/ized universe and not necessarily to whether these modes of being would have been considered nonnormative within their own cosmologies.

30. Paula Gunn Allen, *The Sacred Hoop: Recovering the Feminine in American Indian Traditions* (Boston: Beacon Press, 1986).

31. Oyèrónké Oyěwùmí, *The Invention of Women: Making an African Sense of Western Gender Discourses* (Minneapolis: University of Minnesota Press, 1997).

32. Sylvia Marcos, *Taken from the Lips: Gender and Eros in Mesoamerican Religions*, vol. 5 (Leiden, Netherlands: Brill Academic Publishers, 2006).

33. Gloria Wekker, *The Politics of Passion: Women's Sexual Culture in the Afro-Surinamese Diaspora* (New York: Columbia University Press, 2006).

34. Xhercis Méndez, "Transcending Dimorphism: Afro-Cuban Ritual Praxis and the Rematerialization of the Body," *Power* 3, no. 3 (2003).

35. This alternative arrangement of bodies and power is further fleshed out in Xhercis Méndez, "Decolonizing Feminist Methodologies from the Dark Side" (manuscript in progress).

36. Combahee River Collective, *The Combahee River Collective Statement: Black Feminist Organizing in the Seventies and Eighties* (New York: Kitchen Table: Women of Color Press, 1977), 235 (emphasis added).

37. Wendy Rose, *Going to War with All My Relations: New and Selected Poems* (Flagstaff, Ariz.: Entrada, 1993).

38. Rose, *Going to War*, 40–44.

39. Kristie Dotson, "Between Rocks and Hard Places," *Black Scholar* 46, vol. 2 (2016).

40. Scott, "Re-Enchantment of Humanism," 138, emphasis added.

41. Women of color organizing around prisons and police brutality is one great example of that. This is also visible in the women of color and queer, trans, and gender nonconforming organizing around transformative justice.

42. Combahee River Collective, *Combahee River Collective Statement*, 235–36 (emphasis added).

43. A contemporary example of feminist organizing that refuses to leave "too many people behind" is the Black Lives Matter movement created by three queer women of color: Opal Tometi, Patrisse Cullors and Alicia Garza. Even as it emerged in response to Black male death (Trayvon Martin), it articulated a corrective to previous liberation models that centered Black male leadership while leaving women of color, queer, gender-nonconforming, trans, disabled folks, and others outside of the vision and collective hope for the Black community. We include their words as a reminder to all those who continue to misappropriate and distort their more expansive decolonial vision for a future that includes the heterogeneity of Black life and lives. Black Lives Matter describes themselves as follows: "We are expansive. We are a collective of liberators who believe in an inclusive and spacious movement. We also believe that in order to win and bring as many people with us along the way, we must move beyond the narrow nationalism that is all too prevalent in Black communities. We must ensure we are building a movement that brings all of us to the front. We affirm the lives of Black queer and trans folks, disabled folks, undocumented folks, folks with records, women, and all Black lives along the gender spectrum. Our network centers those who have been marginalized within Black liberation movements." See "About," Black Lives Matter, http://blacklivesmatter.com/about/.

44. Gloria Anzaldúa, *Borderlands: la frontera*, 3rd ed. (San Francisco: Aunt Lute, 1987). This "tolerance for ambiguity" includes contending with all of the ways in which none of us neatly fit into the categories and roles that have been laid out for us, even as we try to do so.

45. Anzaldúa, *Borderlands*, 3.

46. Maxine Hong Kingston, *China Men* (New York: Vintage, 1980); Leanne Betasamosake Simpson, *Islands of Decolonial Love: Stories & Songs* (Winnipeg: Arp Books, 2015); Helena María Viramontes, *Their Dogs Came with Them: A Novel* (New York: Simon and Schuster, 2007); Mayra Santos-Febres, *Sirena: A Novel* (Basingstoke, England: Macmillan, 2000), and *Sobre piel y papel* (San Juan: Ediciones Callejon Incorporated, 2000); and Audre Lorde, *Sister Outsider: Essays and Speeches* (New York: Crossing Press, 2002).

47. Aurora Levins Morales, *Medicine Stories: History, Culture and the Politics of Integrity* (New York: South End Press, 1998).

48. Sylvia Wynter, "The Ceremony Must Be Found: After Humanism," *boundary 2* 12/13 (1984): 33.

49. Wynter, "Ceremony Must Be Found," 50.

50. Wynter, 56.

51. Wynter, 45.

52. Her first play, "Shh . . . It's a Wedding," was written/shown in 1961.

53. Scott, "Re-Enchantment of Humanism," 187.

54. Combahee River Collective, *Combahee River Collective Statement*, 234 (emphasis added).

55. M. Jacqui Alexander, *Pedagogies of Crossing: Meditations on Feminism, Sexual Politics, Memory, and the Sacred* (Durham, N.C.: Duke University Press, 2006).

56. Gratitude goes to Dr. Beth Piatote for introducing Figueroa to the work of Wendy Rose in 2008 at UC Berkeley.

57. Rose, *Going to War*, vii.

58. Rose, 1.

59. Rose, 30–31.

60. Rose, 30–31.

61. Rose, 30–31.

62. For more on decolonial and faithful witnessing, see María Lugones, *Peregrinajes/Pilgrimages: Theorizing Coalitions Against Multiple Oppressions* (Lanham, Maryland: Rowman and Littlefield, 2003); Yomaira Figueroa, "Reparation as Transformation: Radical Literary (Re) Imaginings of Futurities through Decolonial Love," *Decolonization: Indigeneity, Education & Society* 4, no. 1 (2015): 41–58; and Yomaira Figueroa's *Decolonizing Diasporas: Radical Mappings of Afro-Atlantic Literature* (Evanston, Ill.: Northwestern University Press, forthcoming).

63. Margaret "Peggy" Garner was an enslaved woman who in 1856 escaped with her family to freedom in Ohio. Upon the threat of capture, Garner killed her infant daughter rather than see her returned to slavery.

64. Toni Morrison, *Beloved* (New York: Alfred Knopf, 1987), 113.

65. Morrison, *Beloved*, 107–8.

66. Morrison, 17–18, emphasis added.

67. Morrison, 18.

68. For more on decolonial love, see Chela Sandoval, *Methodology of the Oppressed* (Minneapolis: University of Minnesota Press, 2000); Simpson, *Islands of Decolonial Love*; and Figueroa, "Reparation as Transformation."

69. Sylvia Wynter, "Human Being as Noun? Or *Being Human* as Praxis? Towards the Autopoetic Turn/Overturn: A Manifesto," *The Frantz Fanon Blog*, October 27, 2014, http://readingfanon.blogspot.be/2014/10/sylvia -wynter-human-being-as-noun-or.html, 17–18.

70. In her book *Hilando Fino*, Julieta Paredes argues that class and gender are useful concepts only to the extent to which they serve to *denounce* and ultimately *transform* oppressive (neo)colonial relations of power. We are applying this concept to Wynter's understanding of gender as a genre of the human to echo Paredes's claim that these categories are useful only to the extent to which they assist us in denouncing and transforming the oppressive relations that affect our lives.

71. The term *damné* comes from Fanon's 1963 *The Wretched of the Earth* and refers to those peoples condemned to liminality by "Man." See Maldonado-Torres, "On the Coloniality of Being."

72. José Esteban Muñoz, *Disidentifications: Queers of Color and the Performance of Politics* (Minneapolis: University of Minnesota Press, 1999).

73. Neil Roberts, "Sylvia Wynter's Hedgehogs: The Challenge for Intellectuals to Create New 'Forms of Life' in Pursuit of Freedom," in *After Man, towards the Human: Critical Essays on Sylvia Wynter*, ed. Anthony Bogues (Kingston, Jamaica: Ian Randle Publishers, 2006).

74. See Mia Mingus's and the Bay Area Transformative Justice Collective's work on transformative justice and the need to develop new strategies for addressing the multigenerational and intergenerational impact of violence, particularly as it relates to child sexual abuse. "About," *Leaving Evidence*, https://leavingevidence.wordpress.com/about-2/.

75. This particular usage of "other than this and better than this" emerges from the conversations author Méndez has had with Kristie Dotson in the writing of their/our decolonial feminist manifesto to talk about a future that is not predicated on the notion of a linear progression. We are clear that things do not always or necessarily get better over time, so we use this phrasing to name our aspiration for a world that is not organized in these colonial ways ("other than this") and can hold down more of us ("better than this").

PART II

Religious Cosmologies and the Project of Unsettling Man

CHAPTER 4

Enfleshing Love: A Decolonial Theological Reading of *Beloved*

M. Shawn Copeland

The being of slavery, its soul and body, lives and moves in the chattel
principle, the property principle, the bill of sale principle. . . . Talk not
then about kind and Christian masters. They are not masters
of the system. The system is master of them.

—JAMES W. C. PENNINGTON, *The Fugitive Blacksmith*

I, too, live in the time of slavery, by which I mean I am living
in the future created by it. It is the ongoing crisis of citizenship.

—SAIDIYA HARTMAN, *Lose Your Mother: A Journey along
the Atlantic Slave Route*

Toni Morrison's great novel *Beloved*[1] opens somber space in which to rethink the linkages between history and place, body and gender, power and
race and to theologize what it might mean to enflesh freedom within existential, intersubjective, intersectional, intercultural, and societal contexts
of human relations. "Fine writers," Emilie Townes reminds us, "help us
'see' things in tangible ways and 'feel' things through intangible means.
Their ability to turn the world at a tilt, to explore our humanity and inhu-
manity challenges."[2] As a neo-slave narrative, *Beloved* draws back the veil
on the depth of the interior suffering of women and men who have lived
their lives under slavery,[3] unsettling meanings of freedom, love, and subjectivity. If, as Chela Sandoval argues, freedom is the ground of love, enfleshing freedom enfleshes "de-colonial [and] prophetic love,"[4] and
enfleshing love realizes "decolonial being"[5] or decolonial subjectivity.
Moreover, decolonial and prophetic love, Sandoval declares, realizes itself
in the "hermeneutics of social change, a decolonizing *movida*."[6] Decolonial prophetic love rebuffs those cloying sentimentalities so typical of
Westernized notions of love and discloses itself concretely in option and
action for social (i.e., political, economic, technological) transformation.

Thus, love "break[s] through" whatever dominates or oppresses or controls in order to reach authentic understanding and community, to cultivate hope and faith in the potential of goodness,[7] to affirm the subjectivity of societally marginalized and excluded persons in their movement toward decolonized subjectivity. Such love calls for critical self-transcendence in *act*—i.e., a radical concrete *living out* and *living from out of* meanings and values that affirm the life and lives of subjugated or marginalized or excluded others. As Katherine McKittrick succinctly puts it: "Being human . . . signals not a noun but a verb. Being human is a praxis of humanness."[8]

In the effort to theologize what it might mean to enflesh love, this essay reads *Beloved* from a framework of political theology engaged with decolonial thought.[9] This interpretation takes seriously the concerns of Sylvia Wynter[10] and Walter Mignolo,[11] among other decolonial thinkers, to (re)connect knowing and doing and to repudiate the bioeconomic conception of being human, whereby, the "self" needs an "other" for its definition.[12]

The decolonial political theological perspective developed here pivots on two paradoxical aspects of Christianity: (1) its deep, pervasive, and continuing engagement with the global, colonial anthropological deformation that has resulted in what Wynter aptly names the "Doctrine of Man"[13] and (2) its commitment to justice as social transformation in situations of oppression inspired by critical recovery of the memory of the life, death, and resurrection of the Jewish rabbi, Jesus of Nazareth.[14]

A decolonial political theological interpretation brings to light some of the ways in which colonized (i.e., subjugated and putatively degraded) human persons seek to exercise freedom, power, and love in "undoing the logic of coloniality."[15] On the one hand, this reading protests the intentional "corrosion of [the] freedom, dignity, life, and culture[s]" of subjugated and marginalized peoples and supports their agency, creativity, and resourcefulness.[16] On the other hand, it contests all forms of ideologization that disguise themselves as theory or as disengaged (pseudo)objectivity; instead, it insists upon critical cognitive and social analysis, and concrete, action-oriented solidarity attuned to those coordinates set by the justice and equality, freedom and love, peace and joy promised by the Reign of God. From such a theological perspective, *Beloved* brings into relief an episteme—a decolonial episteme—that promotes the enfleshing of love. For like a parasite, the blasphemy of enslavement nests in and feeds on psychic flourishing, on life—consuming, despoiling, polluting—so, that for black human persons *made* slave, *made* marginal, the act of black self-love, love of black flesh, veers close to impossibility. Yet possibilities of resurrection of soul—individual or personal, communal or collective—lie in self-knowledge, self-affirmation, and love—daring to love self, to love others selflessly. For, the most radical, the most sacred act of subjectivity—divine or human—is enfleshing love.

Christianity and Black Flesh

Even as it remains deeply suspicious of flesh, of the body, Christianity always has made room for flesh and fleshly difference, for the body. Recall the second century Christian writer Irenaeus of Lyon, who situated the notion of *imago Dei in* the *body.* Christ, he tells us, is the very visible image of the invisible God. Further, the "perfect" human being is "the commingling and the union of the soul receiving the Spirit of God and joined to the flesh which was molded after the image of God."[17] But in fearful suppression of the body, in eagerness to constrain flesh, Christianity colluded in the disastrous dynamics of domination expressed in encounter, conquest, colonization, and enslavement. Because of the color of their skin, black peoples were forced to undergo a stigmatization freighted with ontological implications.

In their initial encounter with Africans, Europeans observed and remarked on differences in physical appearance, in religion, and in manner of living, but "the most arresting characteristic" was the color of the Africans' skin.[18] Researching the reactions of sixteenth-century English explorers, Winthrop Jordan analyzes the impact that difference in skin color effected: "Long before they found some men were black, Englishmen found in the idea of blackness a way of expressing some of their most ingrained values. No other color except white conveyed so much emotional impact."[19] The sixteenth-century meaning of the word *black* included "deeply stained with dirt; soiled, foul. . . . Having dark or deadly purposes, malignant; disastrous, sinister. . . . Foul, iniquitous, atrocious, horrible, wicked. . . . Indicating disgrace, censure, liability to punishment."[20] Jordan concludes that, for the English in particular, "white and black connoted purity and filthiness, virginity and sin, virtue and baseness, beauty and ugliness, beneficence and evil, God and the devil."[21]

Eulalio Baltazar argues that when European cultural color symbolism came into intense contact with a Christian theological and philosophical anthropology deeply influenced by Platonic and Aristotelian metaphysics, greater value was accorded to the "spiritual and transcendental [rather] than the material and the temporal."[22]

> The soul was the form of the body. As form was superior to matter, giving it its essence or meaning, so the soul was superior to the body. Because of this orientation toward the soul as opposed to that of the body, the symbolism of black and white was . . . related to the soul and its condition. Thus, the soul was spoken of as white when it was in a state of grace and spoke of as black when it was in a state of moral or grievous sin.[23]

European economic avarice and dominance combined with technological superiority reinforced the "positive theological values attached to white skin and, conversely, the negative theological values attached to peoples with dark[er] skins."[24] During the more than three hundred years of the Atlantic slave trade, negatory and debased meanings of blackness were transferred onto and attached to black flesh, black bodies, black peoples. At the same time, the philosophical move from the metaphysical to the empirical shifted epistemological concerns about the object of knowledge from substances, universals, and essences to phenomena, images, and sense impressions. It was but a short step to saying that the human being is her or his appearance or the human being is as she or he appears.[25] Black flesh, black bodies, black peoples quite literally *became* the embodiment of the sinister, the dangerous, the wicked, of evil and sin.

Wynter uncovers this racial or color differential as the "purely invented construct" that enabled the West's transmutation of the indigenous peoples of "militarily expropriated New World territories" as well as the enslaved peoples of Black Africa into occupants of "the matrix slot of Otherness—to be made into the physical referent of the idea of the irrational /subrational Human Other."[26] To borrow a phrase from Katherine McKittrick, the eruption of colonialism/modernity threw "humanness into crisis."[27] Being human *came to be* isomorphic with physical appearance or, more precisely, with white racial appearance, with whiteness.[28] In the highly profitable circumstances of the slave trade, Christianity and Christian theology scarcely protested this specious ontologization. The very meaning of being human was "defined continually against black people and blackness."[29] The terms and meanings, values and practices of human relations and engagement were reshaped by subtle and perverse "anti-Black logics"[30] deeply embedded in Scriptural interpretations, in religious and cultural symbols; moreover, these logics proved resistant both to intelligibility and to critique. *Being human* came to be defined as *white*, although concretely expressed as *being white male*.

On the theological account advanced here, the metaphysical constitutes the most comprehensive context; thus, all assaults aimed to degrade and destroy human beings are seeded in blasphemy, for human persons are made in the image and likeness of God. Such assaults insult the truth that human beings are social beings and are embedded in "biological, genetic, neurological, and psychic sets of schemes of recurrence relating us unconsciously and consciously to others."[31] The contemporary and ongoing antiblack assaults, shootings, and murders in the United States, in particular, ought to be understood as in "continuity [with] the enslavist white Euro-American abjectorship of the sixteenth to the nineteenth century."[32] Contemporary practices of antiblack racism uncover how black bodies, black flesh are at stake in forging not merely an *authentic* social (or national or global) future but an eschatological one. *All* human persons of good will have confronted these tragic events with condemnation and protest, but we seem not to grasp adequately why these events have occurred with such impunity and such frequency. Bigotry, speech acts of racial hatred, and physical acts of racial violence expose just how damaged our collective intersubjective spontaneity and human affectivity have become. These behaviors signal irruptions of the personal, structural, and social sin racism is and the vile ways in which that sin distorts life, spoils the spirit, and corrupts love.

Passing on a Story That Is Not *a Story to Pass On*

In the United States, chattel slavery confounds our national memory and troubles our national history. Chattel slavery is "the tough stuff"[33] *we, the people*, cannot face. With the twenty-first century, we have reached that historical juncture where there is no living person with personal experience or personal memory of chattel slavery—neither slaves nor slaveholders. Yet, the specter of slavery lingers, haunts our very modern nation despite repeated, even frenzied, attempts to suppress consciousness of the scope and depth of our national entanglement. We consign chattel slavery to a misbegotten past and conceal our ambiguous confession in shuttered archives. The national public narrative of compact, covenant, and immigration obscures the murderous undertow: the complex, angular, and expanding spatial, religious, economic, and cultural instantiation of power that *is* the United States of America. To our peril we forget the seizure of land and genocide through war and disease of indigenous peoples,[34] the "soul murdering"[35] enslavement of African peoples, whose stolen labor extracted the staple crops of tobacco, rice, sugar, and cotton, along with the "contracted" and conscripted "many," whose sweat and toil altered a continent and produced the infrastructure of one of the largest and most successful global economies.[36]

It is against this attempt to erase and sanitize our national history that Morrison excavates and narrates the sufferings and joys of enslaved peoples that were "systematically submerged, ignored, mistrusted, or superseded by 'historians' of the era,"[37] probes trauma and loss, recollection and resolution, past and future. Despite the novel's insistent and ambiguous refrain, *this is not a story to pass on*, Morrison prods the reader to consider how much it costs to cognitively, morally, and spiritually reclaim and re-member the past.

Beloved admits no easy summary. Adopting a nonlinear plot line, Morrison develops a "multidirectional narrative into which the past breaks unexpectedly to disrupt the movement forward in time."[38] An omniscient narrator opens *Beloved* with a cryptic judgment about the Cincinnati, Ohio, house on Bluestone Road: "124 was spiteful."[39] The year is 1873, a full decade following legal emancipation of black bodies, but the plans and policies of Reconstruction are being forced into retreat. For the past eighteen years, Sethe, a formerly enslaved woman, and her daughter Denver have lived in the house with the angry, venomous ghostly presence of Sethe's dead infant daughter. Sethe's sons Howard and Buglar also lived there until the strange occurrences became too much for them to endure. Not long after the boys run away, two years after formal Emancipation (1863) and just as the Civil War (1865) concludes, Baby Suggs, Sethe's mother-in-law, takes to her bed and dies.

The haunting of 124 rises from the rememory of the psychological, physical, and spiritual devastation of enslavement that Sethe tries hard to forget and to repress.[40] The novel unfolds in flashbacks of events on a Kentucky plantation named "Sweet Home," but as Paul D remarks, "It wasn't sweet and it sure wasn't home." The Garners maintain a patronizing system that crafts an illusion of collaboration between slaveholder and enslaved. Mr. Garner calls his so-called (human) property "men" and upholds this attribution against the scorn of his neighbors. Yet, he ignores the stark reality that his own liberty depends upon chattel slavery and its reduction of these men (and women) to talking work animals. Garner's fabrication may masquerade as human development, but the bitter truth of Sweet Home materializes in the calculation of profit and loss and in ontological legerdemain.

Mr. Garner's death brings his brother-in-law to the plantation as the overseer. He is known as "schoolteacher" and is accompanied by two younger adult men, perhaps sons or nephews, their relationship is not precisely clear. Almost immediately, the sour reality of the plantation boils up in schoolteacher's cruel exercises and harsh treatment that assault the enslaved people in mind, in body, and in spirit. They plan escape. Sethe continues to care for the gravely ill Mrs. Garner. She clings to what "good" and "love" she had known before schoolteacher's arrival, until he "broke three more Sweet Home men and punched the glittering iron out of [her] eyes, leaving two open wells that did not reflect firelight." [41]

As quickly as she can arrange it, Sethe sends her sons and the infant girl to the hoped-for safety of Baby Suggs. But, mammary rape, a vicious beating, the disappearance of her husband, Halle, and the grotesque humiliation of friends drive Sethe to leave—despite the impending birth of her fourth child. In the midst of her desperate escape, Sethe gives birth to a second daughter, Denver, with unexpected help from a young white girl, Amy. Stamp Paid ferries her across the Ohio River and, barely alive, she arrives at 124 Bluestone Road.

Reunited with her children, Sethe begins a fitful recovery from the traumatic assault. A few weeks into her new life, "four horsemen—schoolteacher, one nephew, one slave catcher, and a sheriff" arrive to claim her and her children. [42] Sethe resists; she will not hand over her children to the degradation of chattel slavery. She takes a loving and dreadful decision: Grabbing a handsaw, she slices the throats of her little ones, the crawling-already? girl and sons; then, Sethe attempts to swing her infant Denver's head against the wall planks of the shed. Sethe has chosen to murder her children in order to save them. Baby Suggs and Stamp Paid rescue the boys and the infant, but the beloved crawling-already? girl bleeds to death. [43] Sethe is arrested and confined in the jail, until Mr. Bodwin and the Colored Ladies of Delaware, Ohio, negotiate, petition, and obtain her release. Some years afterward, "a fully dressed woman walked out of the water." [44] New and more pain, trouble, and loss begin for the occupants of 124 Bluestone Road.

A Decolonial Episteme

The narrator presents Baby Suggs as determined and self-possessed: The sales ticket around her neck may have read "Jenny Whitlow," but she insisted that her name was Baby Suggs. That name was "all she had left of the 'husband' she claimed, . . . a serious and melancholy man who taught her how to make shoes."[45] Manumitted through the labor of her youngest and eighth son, Halle, Baby Suggs established 124 Bluestone Road as a way station for fugitive, emancipated, and free-born blackfolk. There they might pause to replenish supplies, leave messages, care for their children, share food, rest their bodies, catch up on and share news, refresh their hearts, and restore their spirits for whatever life journey that lay ahead.[46]

In her very person, in her great heart, Baby Suggs enfleshed a *praxis* of love. She was an "unchurched preacher, one who visited pulpits and opened her great heart to those who could use it."[47] Her "sole qualification" for claiming responsibility and authority for this leadership was "the vision of grace that came with the recognition that her heart was already beating. Despite a lifetime of enslavement by Whites, her humanity was intact, her life holy, and wholly hers."[48]

Every Saturday afternoon, Baby Suggs, holy, led black children, men, and women to the "Clearing—a wide-open place cut deep in the woods nobody knew for what at the end of a path." There she would sit on a "huge flat-sided rock," gather herself, and silently pray; the people would wait and watch from among the trees.[49] When she was ready she put down her stick and called them forth. She invited the children to laugh and, thus, give joy to the mothers from whom they had been separated by slavery's pernicious economics. Children who had picked cotton and plowed fields and cut cane, children who had never *been* children were called *to be* children. She summoned the men to dance and, thus, display their shrouded elegance and beauty to their wives and lovers and children. Men, from whom slavery had usurped the power to love and protect their wives and children, were called to be husbands, lovers, and fathers. She enjoined the women to cry for the living and the dead and, thus, disclose the depth and breadth of their sorrow. Women, who had built walls around their hearts to keep them from exploding at the pain of loss and the anguish of terror, are released to weep, to mourn. Baby Suggs preached:

> "Here," she said, "in this here place, we flesh; flesh that weeps, laughs; flesh that dances on bare feet in the grass. Love it. Love it hard. Yonder they do not love your flesh. They despise it. They don't love your eyes; they'd just as soon pick em out. No more do they love the skin on your back. Yonder they flay it. And, O my people they do not love your hands. Those they only use, tie, bond, chop off and leave empty. Love your hands! Love them . . . and the beat and beating heart, love that too. More than eyes or feet. More than lungs that have

yet to draw free air. More than your life-holding womb and your live-giving private parts, hear me now, love your heart. For this is the prize."[50]

Perhaps it is risky to suggest that Baby Suggs's sermon in the Clearing advances a decolonial episteme, yet the novel offers evidence that such an interpretation is plausible and without subordinating literary production to facile religious (read: Christian) interpretation. Certainly, Morrison upends the conventional view of sermons (of sermonizing or preaching) as moralistic and didactic and complicit in reinscribing asymmetrical power relations. To support and sustain realization of decolonized subjectivity, Baby Suggs's sermon functions to emancipate understanding, to heal psychic wounds, to rupture the hegemony of the (white) social imaginary.[51] "The being of slavery, its soul and body," James Pennington writes, "lives and moves in the chattel principle, the property principle, the bill of sale principle."[52] The specious reality of slavery depended not only upon physical constraint but, and chiefly, upon mental subjugation: If enslaved people were handled and constrained as nonhuman, controlled and oppressed in mind and person as nonhuman, then the specious reality of slavery might penetrate to the very marrow of being human.[53]

The sermon's command of love—*to love what you have been taught not to love*—lays the groundwork for a decolonial episteme—that is, new knowledge (understanding), new self-knowledge (restoring wounded subjectivity), and action (enfleshing love). Only through enfleshing love can the colonized subject move *away from* and *move out of* the social imaginary synonymous with the matrix of domination, affirm self-love, nurture and sustain community through a new freed-black social imaginary.

Through ritualized (dance and recitation or litany) actuation of decolonized subjectivity, Baby Suggs and the people sacralize the Clearing and counter the caricatures that slavery made. Here dominant (white) meanings and values of the concretized social imaginary that blackfolk were forced to endure, but within which they neither belonged nor inhabited, are ruptured and displaced. Preacher and people create a "commons," shared sacred black space, within which each child, woman, and man belongs and is made whole.[54] They create a generative patterning of reality that intends personal and communal flourishing, transformation, and "(re)construction of cultural and spiritual kinship."[55] Interconnectedness, recovery, and sharing of roles and responsibilities becomes not only crucial but part of the fabric of a new and black social imaginary: "Women stopped crying and danced; men sat down and cried; children danced, women laughed, children cried until, exhausted and riven, all and each lay about the Clearing damp and gasping for breath."[56]

Love what you have been taught not to love. Baby Suggs's preaching protests the capture and overrepresentation of humanness in Wynter's definition of Man (Man$_1$ and Man$_2$).[57] The sermon promotes and sustains transformative human *praxis* in *cognitive, psychic, aesthetic, moral,* and *practical* dimensions. The sermon's *cognitive* function emancipates understanding and self-understanding. Baby Suggs challenges the people to *un*learn, to "de-link"[58] from slavocracy's lingering power, to understand themselves as conscious and critical subjects of their own lives and relationships. The *psychic* and *aesthetic* functions of the sermon are realized in the black human subject's new vision, esteem, and love of self, in healed subjectivity. The people are called to love black flesh, to love themselves, and through that love to (re)member and caress all the torn and wounded body parts that slaveholders and whites despise, parts they would pluck out, flay, chop off, break, lynch, and destroy. The recitation of these offenses against black flesh and psyche conjures pain and recommends the soothing balm of touch, caress, kiss, and pat, of self-love.[59] Sermon and ritual revel in and prescribe joy in the sensuous and in sense experience (seeing, hearing, touching, smelling, tasting). Expressions of dance and rest, song and shout, tears and laughter contrast this decolonial episteme with eurologocentric fixity and dichotomous logic, on the one hand, and dominative and instrumental rationality, on the other.[60]

Through its *moral* and *practical* functions, the sermon supports and sustains the healed black subject in acting, in doing. And "doing . . . affects, modifies, changes the world of objects. But even more it affects the subject. For human doing is free and responsible."[61] At the same time, the subject's doing affects others. The subject consciously perceives herself or himself as *in* relation *to* and *with* others, hence, her or his "subjectivity is an involved-with-others subjectivity."[62] The subject involved-with-others is a subject prepared to enflesh love as transformative human *praxis*.

In the Clearing, Baby Suggs called black children, women, and men to new life *as a people*, to new identity-in-community, to love of their own and others' black flesh, black bodies, black selves. Colonialism, slavery, and their various iterations demanded "that all relations be accidental."[63] Any relationships between and among enslaved and/or free black peoples were deemed expendable and insignificant. Moreover, the dominative, antihuman culture of the plantation "demand[ed] self-negation."[64] In calling the people to love their black flesh, Baby Suggs conjures children, men, and women *anew*—makes them *whole* again. This love of black flesh upends the equation of whiteness with goodness and dominance, of blackness with evil and subservience.[65]

Through "the Word" she received and preached, Baby Suggs brought children, women, and men to new life. She led bodies and souls, hearts and minds damaged by slavery's cruelty beyond the sour wine of hatred, revenge, and resentment to openness and reception of the grace through which a future might be imagined and realized. Thus, she pled, "Love your heart. For this is the prize."[66] To spoil one's heart is to spoil all generative possibility of life, of love, of freedom, of being human. In Baby Suggs's sermon, the heart resonates as a sacred place, a sanctuary for the protection of what no one can take away: the *whole self.* The heart (symbol of love) is the seat of one's self-dispossession, of one's freedom and humanity. Here "freedom and humanity [are] conjured from the vantage point of the flesh and not based on its abrogation."[67]

Beloved *and the "Doctrine of Man"*

Morrison drew inspiration for *Beloved* from the dreadful and widely publicized case of Margaret Garner, whose escape from slavery in Boone County, Kentucky, stands as "one of the most shocking of all fugitive slave cases."[68] From a literary critical perspective, *Beloved* engages what Northrop Frye named "high mimetic tragedy."[69] Sethe may be perceived as a tragic heroine, yet she possesses neither that personal inherent nor ascribed flaw (*hamartia*) that drives the Aristotelian conception of tragedy. Sethe commands an "exposed position" and, as such, stands as "exceptional and isolated"; she fuses "the inevitable and the incongruous which is peculiar to tragedy."[70] Her act confounds most readers: Sethe's escape evokes admiration, her murder of her crawling-already? girl bewilders. Readers find themselves uncertain or hesitant to judge her action. Baby Suggs is quick to judge and judge comprehensively—the pain, who breathed and who did not. In sorrow and fury, she physically battles with Sethe for the body of the crawling-already? girl and tries to prevent Sethe from giving her "bloody nipple" to the infant Denver who would have drunk "her mother's milk right along with the blood of her [murdered] sister."[71]

Baby Suggs has defended black flesh, denounced its violation and disrespect; she has preached, commanded black self-love, love of black flesh. Deep in the woods, in the Clearing, deep in black people's hearts Baby Suggs planted, cultivated, pruned, and watered a garden of black-flesh-love and worship.[72] This was a place undefiled, black holy, out of harm's way: Here men were husbands and fathers, here women were wives and mothers, here children were children—treasured and precious. But Baby Suggs could only read "a toddler's dead body as failed mothering."[73] Because of her devotion to black flesh, Baby Suggs "cannot see Sethe's bloody nipple as the ultimate gift of a supreme sacrifice. For her, it can never be the chalice of a Passover meal paying homage to a 'passing' that promises the liberation of Denver's flesh—a commemorative last supper offered in a mixture of milk and blood, nurture and life."[74] Sethe cannot *re-member* the joys of the black body; her body memory roils from terror and trauma, the pornographic, pseudo-scientific, commodifying power of "Man" (or Man_2) as Wynter explicates *his* overrepresentation.[75] For Sethe "the truth was simple. . . . When she saw them coming and recognized school-teacher's hat . . .[she] carried, pushed, dragged [her children] through the veil, out, away, over there where no one could hurt them."[76] She resolves to kill her children rather than surrender them, her daughters in particular, to slavery's degrading soul murder. Schoolteacher's "measuring string" signals the crude power of phrenology, physiognomy, and pseudo-anthropological observations about the enslaved people's "human and animal characteristics"—all of which are to be written down in a notebook.[77] The so-called knowledge and judgments these observations produce derive from Western European (read: Greek) aesthetics and culture and function to define, to analyze, and to categorize in order to subjugate black mind, black body, and black soul.[78] Sethe declares: "No notebook for my babies and no measuring string neither."[79] Enslaved people also deployed a measuring string. Slavocracy's brutality and sexual depravity set the criteria by which Sixo and Ella measured all atrocities—kidnap, rape, beating, iron muzzles, burning, lynching, killing.

Sethe *acts from within* and *from out* of a critical *episteme* that projects a quality of life quite unthinkable in the social imaginary of the plantation. Intellectually, morally, practically, existentially Sethe *knows* that no other option is tenable: The laws and condition of enslavement *position* her and her children as objects of property, *isolate* her and her children, in particular, her female children from slavocracy's notions of humanity, and *expose* enslaved females to sexual assault.[80] Sethe defies the "necropolitics"[81] of the plantation; through murder she affirms, preserves, and acts for the sacredness of life, she acts for the beloved.

In the shed, behind 124 Bluestone Road, Sethe faces down "Man" (Man_2). The sight of the bleeding boys in sawdust and dirt, Sethe holding the blood-soaked crawling-already? girl, while swinging the infant by her heels confounds. Spitting his annoyance, schoolteacher concludes, "There was nothing there to claim." Sethe's action has upended his plans for productive labor and the labor of reproduction. Schoolteacher backs out of the shed; the slavecatcher and his nephew follow. The latter man shakes with a confusion rooted, perhaps, in his recall of schoolteacher's warning: Beware of "overbeating[ing] and mishandling" horses, hounds, and slaves. Or perhaps, for a fleeting moment he senses just how radically Sethe has unsettled the coloniality of being/power/truth/freedom. The black woman *knows* that neither she nor her children are "creatures" divinely ordained to slavery and the power of Man (Man$_2$).[82] Sethe overturns the power of Man (Man$_2$); she dares enflesh love.

Yet only one of her children, the beloved crawling-already? girl, is liberated "from the physical and psychological consequences of captivity . . . . The liberatory intent of Sethe's act of love collapses beneath the weight of social mandates defining 'good' mothering."[83] Debra Walker King cautions us not to read the death of the body in *Beloved* in the same way as does Baby Suggs: "If we read the idea of flesh metaphysically," Walker King writes, "we understand Sethe's decision to kill—for she kills only that which holds the spirit of black subjectivity captive. She kills only the body. . . . We should read the flesh and live the hope of its liberatory offering."[84]

The beloved crawling-already? baby girl rises in spiteful ghostly presence to trouble the house and occupants at 124 Bluestone Road. Paul D's arrival puts an end to her childish disruptions, and his love and touch change life for Sethe and for Denver. Then, just as these three set out tentatively on a new path, a tired and thirsty young woman confronts them. Her name, she says, is Beloved. Initially, Sethe welcomes the young woman's attention, her questions, and her companionship. She is mother hungry and Sethe feeds her, but Beloved grows greedy, her increasing demands pull Sethe away from the new life she attempts. Sethe offers reassurance and appeasement and begs for forgiveness, her harsh and dreadful act of love has generated a "cycle" from which neither mother nor daughter may easily escape.[85] *As* ghostly presence, perhaps Beloved exposes the pain enslaved mothers endured at the loss/sale/death of their children or perhaps she signifies the hunger and yearning of children under slavery for maternal milk, love, and intimacy or perhaps she projects the sixty million and more of the Middle Passage. Perhaps, the apparition *is* a phantasm of a mother's shattered heart and fevered agony or perhaps the apparition is real. The determined, defiant communal singing of black women exorcises the ghost, freeing and restoring Sethe to claim herself as her own best thing.

Conclusion

In *Beloved* a decolonial episteme, self-love, and love of others unite in powerful realized anticipation of new and authentic transformation of the black self and the black lifeworld. The epistemology that undergirds the novel counters racist stereotypes and "debunks 'master narratives' about enslaved Africans, their enslavers, and both their descendants that continue to (mis)inform public discourse."[86] Decolonial resistance to deforming knowledge constitutes relentless psychological and spiritual resistance to the lingering impacts of slavery on body and mind. Still, Cynthia Wallace cautions: "The challenge of ethical thought offered by *Beloved* as a whole, as a work of narrative fiction, is much broader, much more difficult than the inspiring speech of one of its characters. Its tone is more wary: it emphasizes more strongly the dangers of paradoxes, the struggle and difficulty, rather than naming them and moving on."[87]

Some interpreters suggest that Baby Suggs, after "witnessing the consequences of Sethe's choice, repudiates her own message, finding it inadequate to express or explain,"[88] and collapses in "marrow weariness."[89] Recall that the novel opens with Baby Suggs lying (dying) in bed: "Suspended between the nastiness of life and meanness of the dead, she couldn't get interested in leaving life or living it. Her past had been like her present—intolerable—and since she knew death was anything but forgetfulness, she used the little energy left her for pondering color."[90] Much earlier, when Stamp Paid fumed against her absences from the Clearing, Baby Suggs had shrugged and threatened to take to her bed. Now, with her death, he finally considers the pain of the truth: "The heart that pumped out love, the mouth that spoke the Word, didn't count. [Whitefolks] came in her yard anyway and she could not approve or condemn Sethe's rough choice."[91]

The narrator tells us "God puzzled [Baby Suggs] and she was too ashamed of Him to say so."[92] Whether Baby Suggs has lost faith with the God who sends her the Word and holds her heart, we do not know. But we do know she came again face-to-face with the painful conundrum of love. Unable to parse its mystery, she withdraws into a deep silent "fixing" on "harmless" color.[93] Much later, feeling his own marrow weariness and ashamed of having upbraided Baby Suggs, Stamp Paid acknowledges that in this world additional help is needed from other spiritual sources to deal with things "older, but not stronger than [Jesus] Himself was."[94]

Morrison offers us no comfortable conclusion, no pious affirmation of faith, no simplistic dismissal of grotesque suffering. *Beloved* is a work of fiction, but fiction that rises to the level of historical remembrance and that possesses "the capacity to teach us something about experience outside the diegetic level of narration."[95] Thick and familiarly strange evil batters 124 Bluestone Road—the same thick familiarly strange evil that ostracizes and assaults black children, women, and men, that drives them out of towns, that lynches them, that assaults and rapes them, that burns the churches in which they worship, that acquits the police officers who shoot them, that overlooks the gangs that harass and rob them. Morrison keeps her finger on the jagged edge of black existential pain. Somewhere, she muses, "sometimes good looks like evil; evil sometimes looks like good—you never really know what it is."[96] Sethe's killing of her child upends maternal love, but slavery, with studied cruelty, has accomplished this already. Baby Suggs knows this in her heavy heart and limping body. In love, Sethe has killed her daughter in order to save her from slavery's wanton abuse. Baby Suggs cannot fathom what Sethe has done; it scorches her heart. Yet, in word and deed, *Beloved* mediates this lesson: Even in the face of evil, the deepest and most sacred identity of the human person is realized in *enfleshing love*.

NOTES

1. Toni Morrison, *Beloved* (New York: Alfred Knopf, 1987).

2. Emilie M. Townes, *Womanist Ethics and the Cultural Production of Evil* (New York: Palgrave Macmillan, 2006), 5.

3. Valerie Smith, "Neo-Slave Narratives," in *The Cambridge Companion to the African American Slave Narrative*, ed. Audrey Fisch (Cambridge: Cambridge University Press, 2007); Toni Morrison, "The Site of Memory," in *Inventing the Truth: The Art and Craft of Memoir*, ed. William Zinsser (New York: Houghton Mifflin Company, 1998); and Vincent L. Wimbush, *White Men's Magic: Scripturalization as Slavery* (Oxford: Oxford University Press, 2012), 222.

4. Chela Sandoval, *Methodology of the Oppressed* (Minneapolis: University of Minnesota Press, 2000), 143, 145; and see my *Enfleshing Freedom: Body, Race, and Being* (Minneapolis: Fortress Press, 2009).

5. Sandoval, *Methodology of the Oppressed*, 140.

6. Sandoval, 138.

7. Sandoval, 139.

8. Katherine McKittrick, ed., *Sylvia Wynter: On Being Human as Praxis* (Durham, N.C.: Duke University Press, 2015), 3–4.

9. Several Latin American and Caribbean thinkers deploy an intense and radical critique of the enduring matrix of domination spawned by Western European and North American colonialism. They name this

critique "decolonial/decoloniality" in an effort to understand and effectively respond to the *praxial* (i.e., epistemological *and* practical) aftereffects of colonization and conquest. And, although colonialism has come to a formal end, the "coloniality of power" it produced through "specific social discriminations" now codified as "racial," "ethnic," "anthropological," or "national" linger and are reproduced in the contemporary. These discriminations have been ideologized (i.e., uncritically assumed and appropriated) as "objective" or "scientific" or "natural" phenomena as the history and relations of power responsible for these intersubjective constructions are occluded. See Aníbal Quijano, "Coloniality and Modernity/Rationality," *Cultural Studies* 21, nos. 2–3 (March/May 2007): 168.

The historical emergence of "decolonization" coincides with the 1955 Bandung Conference. Between 1945 and 1990, movements for political liberation or political independence, for decolonization, erupted in European colonies in Asia and Africa. From April 18 through 25, 1955, twenty-nine countries representing more than half the world's population sent delegates to Bandung, Indonesia, for a conference organized by Indonesia, Myanmar (Burma), Ceylon (Sri Lanka), India, and Pakistan. The objective of the Bandung Conference was to organize and unite people of color in opposition to colonialism and to the geopolitical and economic indifference of Western powers in their dealings with Asia.

10. Some key texts by Sylvia Wynter, "Unsettling the Coloniality of Being/Power/Truth/Freedom: Towards the Human, after Man, Its Over-representation—An Argument," *CR: The New Centennial Review* 3, no. 3 (Fall 2003); McKittrick, *Sylvia Wynter*; and David Scott, "The Re-Enchantment of Humanism: An Interview with Sylvia Wynter," *Small Axe* 8 (September 2000).

11. Some key texts by Walter Mignolo: "Epistemic Disobedience, Independent Thought and De-Colonial Freedom," *Theory, Culture, and Society* 26, nos. 7–8 (2009); *The Darker Side of Western Modernity: Global Futures, Decolonial Options* (Durham, N.C.: Duke University Press, 2011); and "Decolonizing Western Epistemology/Building Decolonial Epistemologies," in *Decolonizing Epistemologies: Latina/o Theology and Philosophy*, ed. Ada Maria Isasi-Diaz and Eduardo Mendieta (New York: Fordham University Press, 2012).

12. Jesuit philosopher and theologian Bernard Lonergan would not be considered a decolonial thinker, but his cognitional theory worked out during the 1950s anticipates and addresses similar concerns about the relation between knowing and doing, ethics and action, subjectivity and objectivity, and love as incarnate human authenticity. See his *Insight: A Study of Human Understanding*, 5th ed., vol. 3 of *Collected Works of Bernard Loner-*

gan (1957; Toronto: University of Toronto Press, 1988); and *Method in Theology* (New York: Herder and Herder, 1972).

13. Wynter, "Unsettling the Coloniality of Being Power/Truth/Freedom"; see also Mignolo, *Darker Side of Western Modernity*, esp. 1–21, 35–40.

14. See Johann Baptist Metz, *Faith in History and Society: Toward a Practical Fundamental Theology* (New York: Crossroad Publishing Company, 2007).

15. Walter Mignolo, "Delinking: The Rhetoric of Modernity, the Logic of Coloniality and the Grammar of De-Coloniality," *Culture Studies* 21, no. 2–3 (March/May 2007): 503.

16. Samuel Rayan, "Decolonization of Theology," *JNANADEEPA* 1, no. 2 (July 1998), http://sedosmission.org/old/eng/Rayan.html.

17. Irenaeus of Lyons, *Against the Heresies* (180 CE), vol. 1 of *Ante-Nicene Fathers* (New York: Charles Scribner's Sons, 1925). Irenaeus distinguishes "the image" and "the likeness." He writes: "For in times long past, it was said that *anthropos* was made in the image of God, but it was not shown [to be so]; for the Word was as yet invisible, after whose image *anthropos* was created; and because of this he easily lost the likeness. When, however, the God Word became flesh, he confirmed [the image and the likeness]: for he showed forth the image truly, himself becoming that which was his image, and he reestablished the likeness in a sure manner, by co-assimilating *anthropos* to the invisible Father through the Word become visible." Irenaeus, *Against the Heresies*, 5.6.2.

18. Winthrop D. Jordan, *White over Black: American Attitudes toward the Negro, 1550–1812*, 2nd ed. (Chapel Hill: University of North Carolina Press, 1968), 4.

19. Jordan, *White over Black*, 6.

20. Cited in Jordan, 7.

21. Jordan, 7.

22. Eulalio Baltazar, *The Dark Center: A Process Theology of Blackness* (New York: Paulist Press, 1973), 27; see also Roger Bastide, "Color, Racism, and Christianity," in *Color and Race*, ed. John Hope Franklin (Boston: Beacon Press, 1968); and Robert E. Hood, *Begrimed and Black: Christian Traditions on Blacks and Blackness* (Minneapolis: Augsburg Fortress, 1994). These authors take note of the *positive* meanings and implications of blackness (the opaque) in apophatic theology and the Christian mystical tradition. In these instances, God's splendor is approached as overwhelming all human mental and physical senses. Thus, God is hidden, beyond all images and words; God is as splendid, dazzling darkness.

23. Baltazar, *Dark Center*, 27–28.

24. Baltazar, 29.

25. Baltazar, 29.

26. Wynter, "Unsettling the Coloniality of Being/Power/Truth/ Freedom," 266.

27. Katherine McKittrick, *Demonic Grounds: Black Women and the Cartographies of Struggle* (Minneapolis: University of Minnesota Press, 2006), 124.

28. Baltazar, *Dark Center*, 29.

29. Rinaldo Walcott, "The Problem of the Human: Black Ontologies and 'the Coloniality of Our Being,'" in *Postcoloniality—Decoloniality—Black Critique: Joints and Fissures*, ed. Sabine Broeck and Carsten Junker (New York: Campus Verlag, 2014), 93.

30. Walcott, "Problem of the Human," 93.

31. Matthew Lamb, "The Social and Political Dimensions of Lonergan's Theology," in *The Desires of the Human Heart: An Introduction to the Theology of Bernard Lonergan*, ed. Vernon Gregson (New York: Paulist Press, 1988), 260.

32. Sabine Broeck, "Legacies of Enslavism and White Abjectorship," in *Postcoloniality—Decoloniality—Black Critique: Joints and Fissures*, ed. Sabine Broeck and Carsten Junker (New York: Campus Verlag, 2014), 109.

33. See James Oliver Horton and Lois E. Horton, eds., *Slavery and Public History: The Tough Stuff of American Memory* (Chapel Hill: University of North Carolina Press, 2006).

34. See Enrique Dussel, *The Invention of the Americas: Eclipse of "the Other" and the Myth of Modernity*, trans. Michael D. Barber (New York: Continuum, 1995).

35. Nell Irvin Painter, "Soul Murder and Slavery: Toward a Fully Loaded Cost Accounting," in *U. S. History as Women's History: New Feminist Essays*, ed. Linda Kerber, Alice Kessler-Harris, and Kathryn Kish Sklar (Chapel Hill: University of North Carolina Press, 1995), 127.

36. Consider the plight of those "contracted Chinese and Japanese laborers brought to do much of the hard, dirty work of mining and railroad construction in the nineteenth century; the stoop laborers from Mexico and the Philippines who followed the farm crops—all of them were incorporated into powerful systems of racial thought and practice." Daniel T. Rodgers, *Age of Fracture* (Cambridge, Mass.: Bell Knap Press of Harvard University Press, 2011), 112. Nor should we ever forget the poor and ready-to-work immigrants from Poland, Ireland, Germany, Sweden, Norway, China, the Philippines, and so many other nations.

37. Karla F. C. Holloway, "*Beloved*: A Spiritual," *Callaloo* 13 (1990): 516.

38. Smith, "Neo-Slave Narratives," 175.

39. Morrison, *Beloved*, 3.

40. Morrison coins the neologism *rememory* to express the living quality of recollections of things forgotten and relived when brought to consciousness.

41. Morrison, *Beloved*, 9.

42. Morrison, 149.

43. Morrison, 148–52. Consider the refrain of the Negro Spiritual, "O Freedom": "And before I'd be a slave, I'd be buried in my grave, and go home to my Lord and be free."

44. Morrison, 50.

45. Morrison, 142.

46. Morrison, 65, 163, 249.

47. Morrison, 87.

48. Judylyn S. Ryan, *Spirituality as Ideology in Black Women's Film and Literature* (Charlottesville: University of Virginia Press, 2005), 52.

49. Morrison, *Beloved*, 87.

50. Morrison, 88–89; see 86–89.

51. I borrow the phrase from Charles Taylor, *Modern Social Imaginaries* (Durham, N.C.: Duke University Press, 2004). Certainly, *all* those involved in the operation and management of systemic enslavement or slavocracy (e.g., slave traders, brokers, auctioneers, slaveholders, overseers, etc.) lived *out* and *lived out of* a set of meanings and values that were expressed through particular practices, habits, and customs or mores, and through the appropriation, transmission, and cultivation of particular concepts, judgments, attitudes, and emotions that constructed and maintained slavocracy as "factual and normative" (23). See Walter Johnson, *Soul by Soul: Life inside the Antebellum Slave Market* (Cambridge, Mass: Harvard University Press, 1999).

52. James Pennington, *The Fugitive Blacksmith* (1849; 1850; Kitrinos Publishers, 2015), loc. 25 of 1160, Kindle.

53. Mignolo, "Epistemic Disobedience, Independent Thought and De-Colonial Freedom," 41. To break free fully from the social imaginary of slavocracy (described above in earlier note on Mignolo), the enslaved must "free" their minds, must resist, must assert autonomy in small and large ways—despite continued and increasingly vicious subjugation.

54. See Morrison's epigraph for *Beloved*: "I will call them my people, which were not my people; and her beloved which was not beloved" (Romans 9:25); and Stefano Harney and Fred Moten, *The Undercommons: Fugitive Planning & Black Study* (Brooklyn, N.Y.: Autonomedia, 2013), 97–99.

55. Ryan, *Spirituality as Ideology*, 55.

56. Morrison, *Beloved*, 88.

57. In "Unsettling the Coloniality of Being/Power/Truth/Freedom," Wynter argues that overrepresented "Man" has gobbled up "all" being—i.e.,

devalued all of the "other" ways in which "being" is or has been expressed. "Man" has taken to and made "himself" the repository and font of all power, knowledge, and truth; hence, only "Man" possesses intrinsically and potentially may exercise and live free. To unsettle the totality of this logic requires a new way of knowing, expressing, acting out being/power/truth/ freedom.

58. Mignolo, "Delinking," 503.

59. Janice P. Gump, "Reality Matters: The Shadow of Trauma on African American Subjectivity," *Psychoanalytic Psychology* 27, no. 1 (2010); and Harney and Moten, *Undercommons*, 97–99.

60. Lonergan, *Method in Theology*, 6.

61. Bernard Lonergan, *The Subject: The Aquinas Lecture 1968* (Milwaukee, Wisc.: Marquette University Press, 1968), 19. Again, Lonergan's account is not a decolonial one, but it anticipates the need for the unity and the identification of the interconnectedness *of all life*. He offers a critical cognitional theory whose operations include experiencing, inquiring, imagining, understanding, conceiving, formulating, reflecting, questioning, marshalling and weighing evidence, judging, deliberating, evaluating, and deciding. See his *Method in Theology*, 3–25. On this account, the experiential mode of operation is taken up into the intellectual mode through which the subject becomes a *conscious understanding subject* (intellectual consciousness)—asking and answering questions of what, why, and how. The subject questions whether or not what is presented as true or as knowledge of reality is so. Responses to these questions promote the subject into the mode of *critical* or *rational consciousness*, requiring the subject to pass and verify the truth or falsity of facts or values. Responses to these questions further move the subject to deliberation and evaluation, to decision and action, to responsibility. Here the *conscious rational subject* becomes the *conscious* moral subject who acts.

62. Raúl Fornet-Betancourt, "Para una crítica filosófica de la globalización," in *Resistencia y solidaridad—globalización capitalista y liberación*, ed. Raúl Fornet-Betancourt (Madrid: Editorial Trotta, S.A., 2003), 56, cited in Ada María Isasi-Díaz, "Mujerista Discourse: A Platform for Latinas' Subjugated Knowledge," in *Decolonizing Epistemologies*, ed. Ada María Isasi-Díaz and Eduardo Mendieta (New York: Fordham University Press, 2012), 59.

63. Michael Hardt and Antonio Negri, *Empire* (Cambridge, Mass.: Harvard University Press, 2000), 202.

64. bell hooks, *Killing Rage: Ending Racism* (New York: Henry Holt, 1995), 161.

65. See Ryan, *Spirituality as Ideology*, 54; and Anita Durkin, "Object Written, Written Object: Slavery, Scarring, and Complications of Authorship in *Beloved*," *African American Review* 41, no. 3 (Fall 2007): 550.

66. Morrison, *Beloved*, 89.

67. Alexander G. Weheliye, *Habeas Viscus: Racializing Assemblages, Biopolitics, and Black Feminist Theories of the Human* (Durham, N.C.: Duke University Press, 2014), 131.

68. Julius Yanuck, "The Garner Fugitive Slave Case," *Mississippi Valley Historical Review* 40, no. 1 (June 1953): 47. See Mark Reinhardt, *Who Speaks for Margaret Garner?* (Minneapolis: University of Minnesota Press, 2010). Margaret Garner's 1856 escape and recapture was depicted in an eponymous painting by Thomas Satterwhite Noble in 1867. Albert Boime, in *The Art of Exclusion: Representing Blacks in the Nineteenth Century* (Washington, D.C.: Smithsonian Institution Press, 1990), perceives the painting's aesthetic as depicting Margaret Garner's defiance (144–47). Whereas Delores M. Walters argues that rather than defiance, the painting's aesthetic advances an aesthetic that reinforces the enslaved as "uncontrollable." Delores M. Walters, "Introduction: Re(dis)covering and Recreating the Cultural Milieu of Margaret Garner," in *Gendered Resistance: Women, Slavery, and the Legacy of Margaret Garner*, ed. Mary E. Frederickson and Delores M. Walters (Urbana-Champagne: University of Illinois Press, 2012), 9–11.

69. Northrop Frye, *Anatomy of Criticism: Four Essays* (Princeton, N.J.: Princeton University Press, 1957), 38, 33–34.

70. Frye, *Anatomy of Criticism*, 38.

71. Morrison, *Beloved*, 152.

72. Debra Walker King, *African Americans and the Culture of Pain* (Charlottesville: University of Virginia Press, 2008), 117.

73. Walker King, *African Americans and the Culture of Pain*, 117.

74. Walker King, 117.

75. Wynter, "Unsettling the Coloniality of Being/Power/Truth/ Freedom."

76. Morrison, *Beloved*, 165.

77. Morrison, 191, 193.

78. See Cornel West, *Prophesy Deliverance! An Afro-American Revolutionary Christianity* (Louisville, Ky.: Westminster John Knox Press, 2002), 45–65.

79. Morrison, *Beloved*, 198.

80. See Marlene Nourbese Philip, "Dis Place—The Space Between," in *A Genealogy of Resistance and Other Essays* (Toronto: Mercury Press, 1998), 74–83, 107–10.

81. Achille Mbembe, "Necropolitics," *Political Culture* 15, no. 1 (Winter 2003).

82. Morrison, *Beloved*, 149–50.

83. Walker King, *African Americans and the Culture of Pain*, 116.

84. Walker King, 118, 119.

85. Mary Jane Seuro Elliott, "Postcolonial Experience in a Domestic Context: Commodified Subjectivity in Toni Morrison's *Beloved*," *Meleus* 25, no. 3–4 (Autumn–Winter 2000): 191.

86. Ryan, *Spirituality as Ideology*, 52.

87. Cynthia R. Wallace, *Of Women Borne: A Literary Ethics of Suffering* (New York: Columbia University Press, 2016), 114.

88. Eddie S. Glaude Jr., *In a Shade of Blue: Pragmatism and the Politics of Black America* (Chicago: University of Chicago Press, 2007), 42.

89. Morrison, *Beloved*, 180.

90. Morrison, 3.

91. Morrison, 179.

92. Morrison, 177.

93. Morrison, 179.

94. Morrison, 172.

95. Anna Iatsenko, "Bodies, Music, and Embodied Cognition in Toni Morrison's Fictional Works," in *Living Language, Living Memory: Essays on the Works of Toni Morrison*, ed. Kerstin W. Shands and Giulia Grillo Mikrut (Mölnlycke, Sweden: Elanders, 2014), 63.

96. Robert B. Stepto, "Intimate Things in Place: A Conversation with Toni Morrison," in *Conversations with Toni Morrison*, ed. Danille K. Taylor-Guthrie (Jackson: University Press of Mississippi, 1994), 14.

CHAPTER 5

Nat Turner's Orientation
beyond the Doctrine of Man

Joseph Drexler-Dreis

Sylvia Wynter argues that the "politics of being," or the ways the human person is signified within the modern world-system and the ways this signification is contested, has been the primary struggle within Western modernity.[1] Wynter turns to the "general upheaval of the 1960s" as a set of events that unsettled the delineation of being within European colonialism and the modern world-system that emerged from colonialism. At the same time, the 1960s introduced a conception of the human person that exceeded the imaginative possibilities within European modernity. She specifically locates an alternative vision of the human in liberation movements in the 1960s, rather than in the movements in the 1980s centering on multiculturalism. The former, Wynter argues, contain the possibility of living beyond the assimilationist pull of the destructive crystallization of the human person within Western modernity.[2] It is plausible in Wynter's work that such subversive visions of the human person might exist beyond the 1960s. This essay will consider one of these instances of living beyond a modern/colonial politics of being prior to the general upheaval of the 1960s that stands in continuity with the politics of being that, according to Wynter, unsettles the modern/colonial definitions of the human person.

In the context of a broader resistance to racial slavery in the North Atlantic, Nat Turner presented one option for living beyond the normative definition of the human person produced by European colonialism and European modernity. By 1831, the year that Nat Turner took on a leading role in the Southampton slave rebellion, Southampton County, Virginia, was a relatively isolated area that had a majority black population. Both of these factors, which could suggest a chance of success for a slave rebellion, as well as a half decade of increased protest by slaves in the Western Hemisphere, shaped the context of the revolt.[3]

The most important source of historians' knowledge of the Southampton slave rebellion is "The Confessions of Nat Turner," a document that was physically written by Nat Turner's lawyer, Thomas R. Gray. Gray interviewed Nat Turner during the first three days of November 1831, after Nat Turner had been captured and imprisoned. It is likely Gray knew the vast majority of the over fifty whites killed during the revolt and had a set of motives that differed from Nat Turner's motives in sharing his "confessions." Gray had several interests behind publishing the "Confessions," including a financial motivation and a need to assuage the fear of the white community by showing that Turner's rebellion was impractical and confined to a small area and that Turner was a fanatic and not representative of the general slave population.[4] At the same time, the "Confessions" also conveys Nat Turner's voice. David F. Allmendinger Jr. argues that the "Confessions" was primarily Nat Turner's own narrative, not fabrication. Allmendinger notes that the "Confessions" does not recycle old material Gray had written on the rebellion previously and that it offers a number of previously unknown details. Further, the information collected in the "Confessions" is consistent with what are generally accepted as historical facts related to the rebellion, yet also is not omniscient; the narrative is told from Turner's point of view, without attempting to address events within the rebellion of which Turner would not have been aware.[5]

Herbert Aptheker described the situation after the rebellion as one of "terror and mayhem," including vigilante mobs that gruesomely killed slaves.[6] While impossible to determine how many black people were killed without a trial following the rebellion, it is safe to say it was at least a hundred and possibly several times more.[7] In the weeks and months after the rebellion, there was "frenzied legislative activity of the slave regions" in an attempt to grasp and hold onto the political economy that allowed for the continued hegemony of the white population.[8]

While Nat Turner is distinct as an individual, I understand him to embody a communal politics of being. This claim continues to be contested.[9] In bringing out Nat Turner's specific praxis of being human within the early nineteenth century United States and wrestling with the ways the memories of Nat Turner have been employed, this essay opens up how Nat Turner indicates a politics of being within a religious orientation that exceeds the parameters of understanding within colonial modernity.

Following in a tradition of revolt against designations of the human person that took the conquering European subject as normative, Nat Turner's religious orientation contested the modern Western descriptive statement of the human person. Wynter argues that in the contemporary historical epoch, the conception of the human as bourgeois, white, male, and heterosexual is overrepresented as the human as such, and she calls this overrepresentation "Man." Man as a normative idea of the human legitimizes the logics that undergirded colonialism and racial slavery and that continue to ground hierarchies within colonial modernity. Unsettling Man, therefore, is a central task in combatting the ideological apparatus that maintains the colonial underside of Western modernity.[10] While Wynter generally sees secularism to provide at least the means for a struggle to unsettle the codification of Man, Nat Turner's life unsettles Man through a religious orientation. Nat Turner's life offers one historical instance of unsettling Man within the larger project of contesting the coloniality that constitutes Western modernity.

To support this claim, this essay moves through three areas of reflection. The first section engages the twentieth-century debates regarding how to interpret and carry forward the memory of Nat Turner. The historical unfolding of the task of interpreting who Nat Turner was, which reached a climax after William Styron's 1967 Pulitzer Prize–winning novel, *The Confessions of Nat Turner*, evinces a struggle for a new understanding of the human person. The second section considers Nat Turner's life as a generative site for the struggle beyond Man. In Nat Turner's "Confessions" he cites daily spiritual practices and a religious commitment that shaped his worldview as the ultimate reasons for his participation in the slave rebellion. The final section, again rooted in the "Confessions," moves from Nat Turner's concrete religious orientation and practices to more general claims about the capacity of a religious orientation to provide an opening for living beyond the doctrine of Man.

Interpretations of Nat Turner and the Difficulties of Unsettling Man

Decolonial theorists describe coloniality as a form of domination that emerges from the European discovery and conquest of the Americas, when capitalism became allied with new forms of domination.[11] Furthermore, the sociologist Aníbal Quijano identifies these forms of domination that get tied to capitalism in European colonialism as being codified along the axes of race and forms of labor control. The category of race, Quijano argues, replaces physical domination to legitimize and govern labor relationships.[12] María Lugones subsequently shows that the European conquest of the Americas also imposed a revised gender system.[13] This new gender system "was as constitutive of the coloniality of power as the coloniality of power was constitutive of it. The logic of relation between them is of mutual constitution."[14] In this revised modern/colonial gender system, Lugones argues, nonwhite women were understood to be "without gender" in the sense that "colonized females got the inferior status of gendering as women, without any of the privileges accompanying that status for white bourgeois women."[15] Categories used to define the human person—including but not limited to race and gender—displaced physical domination as the primary means of control and subjugation without, of course, ending the practice of physical exploitation.

The debates in the 1960s surrounding the interpretation of Nat Turner and the Southampton slave rebellion disclose the challenges of holding up Nat Turner as an example of an individual who contested Man. William Styron's 1967 novel, which takes on the name of the original document of Turner's testimony, *The Confessions of Nat Turner*, and speaks in the first person, sparked a debate among US intellectuals. In an "Author's Note," Styron describes his novel as having "rarely departed from the *known* facts about Nat Turner and the revolt of which he was the leader. However, in those areas where there is little knowledge in regard to Nat, his early life, and the motivations for the revolt (and such knowledge is lacking most of the time), I have allowed myself the utmost freedom of imagination in reconstructing events—yet I trust remaining within the bounds of what meager enlightenment history has left us about the institution of slavery."[16] Immediately after the publication of the novel, a group published *William Styron's Nat Turner: Ten Black Writers Respond.* The essays collected in this volume criticize Styron's novel for obscuring the radicalism of Nat Turner. Styron, they charge, neglects the historical evidence of Nat Turner's black wife and instead portrays him as lusting after a white woman. Styron dehumanizes Nat Turner and other black characters, which several of the authors render as "emasculation." Styron often presents slaves as docile and content with slavery.[17] In short, the collection calls attention to how Styron signifies Nat Turner and other black characters in the novel without adequate respect to the historical record and the historical memory alive within black traditions.

To use Wynter's terms, the authors in the *Ten Black Writers* volume identify and criticize how Styron's attachment to Man guides his portrayal of Nat Turner, even as he holds up Nat Turner as a historical example of a rebellious leader. For example, Vincent Harding, one of the contributors to the volume, charges that Styron's novel "becomes an exercise in domestication, assimilation, and finally destruction."[18] Harding supports this claim by focusing on how Styron distorts the reality and memory of Nat Turner by misrepresenting his religious experience. For Harding, the crucial part of Nat Turner's life that Styron misses is that Nat Turner was part of a community deeply shaped by a religious orientation. In reference to Styron's novel, Harding points to a larger pattern within a North Atlantic style of theorizing—namely, concealing origins of knowledge and reference points for knowledge outside the white world.

Harding draws out Styron's treatment of salvation as the most egregious example of how Styron eclipses how the religious center of Nat Turner's life is rooted in black traditions. Styron's Nat Turner experiences separation from God while in jail awaiting execution. This sense of separation is only resolved, in Styron's narration, when Nat Turner repents for killing Margaret Whitehead, a white woman whom Styron constructs as the primary object of Nat Turner's sexual desires.[19] Styron thereby shifts Nat Turner's ultimate reference of salvation from God—and moreover from the traditions black communities have developed about and in reference to God—to the white world. This move, Harding argues, contradicts the vision presented in the original "Confessions." Harding's critique fits within the general critique of the contributors to the *Ten Black Writers* volume: Styron takes Nat Turner out of black traditions and in doing so presents him in a way that minimizes the tradition of black radical thought and protest.[20] The ten black writers argue that Styron's text serves to legitimize colonial modernity through discrediting ways of knowing that reside beyond the purview of Man.

Immediately following the publication of *Ten Black Writers Respond*, the influential US historian Eugene D. Genovese published a long, and generally scathing, review of the collection in the *New York Review of Books*. Genovese took up Styron's defense through an argument regarding what counts as knowledge:

> One might have thought that black and white Americans who are
> committed to racial equality would approve of the fact that William
> Styron, a white Southerner, has rescued the great rebel slave leader,
> Nat Turner, from obscurity. Instead, the claim is made throughout
> these essays that black America has always *known and admired* the
> historical Nat Turner. This is pretense. When Vincent Harding, for
> example, writes of a Nat Turner who exists "in the living traditions of
> black America," he is deceiving himself and, inadvertently, the rest of
> us. . . . *We* have yet to be shown evidence that slaves and postslavery
> blacks kept alive a *politically relevant* legend of Nat Turner or any other
> Southern slave leader.[21]

Genovese, a historian of slavery and of the US American South who operates largely from a Marxist perspective, questions the sources of knowledge that Harding holds to be authoritative. Harding's critique of Styron,
in Genovese's review (and he appreciates Harding's essay much more than
the other essays in the volume), lacks validity because of the epistemic sites
out of which Harding operates, or because of the contested ways black communities have "known and admired the historical Nat Turner."

Several of the "ten black writers" issued a response to Genovese in a following issue of the *New York Review of Books*. In his contribution, Harding
rejects the absolute authority of Genovese's "we" used in the quote above,
which presumably refers to a recognized community of white scholars.
Genovese, it appears, rejects the "living tradition of black America" as a
viable site from which knowledge of Nat Turner can be carried on—or at
least rejects the forms in which it is carried on in these traditions—by questioning whether such knowledge exists in any "politically relevant" way.
Within the context of this debate, Harding sees Genovese participating
in the tragedy represented by Styron's novel:

> In the essay [in the *Ten Black Writers* volume] I referred largely to that
> tragedy created by the non-black authorities on black life who are
> certain that they have eaten and drunk so fully of our experience that
> they are qualified to deliver homilies to us (at the least provocation) on
> how that experience should best be understood, recorded and lived,
> now and in the future. In essence they seek (perhaps unconsciously,
> but nevertheless effectively) to become the official keepers of our
> memories and the shapers of our dreams. I suggested that the society
> which eagerly accepts such assumptions offers to those of us who are
> black a slavery at once more subtle and more damaging than any we
> have known before.[22]

Genovese's reading and defense of Styron fails to perceive how Nat Turner, through the Southampton slave rebellion and the religious life he explains in the "Confessions," draws on a reality underneath or beyond the US politics of being. In other words, Harding questions an interpretation of Nat Turner that does not recognize the existence of his orientations beyond Man. In his response to Styron in *Ten Black Writers Respond*, Harding writes that "the novel has snatched Nat Turner out of the nineteenth century, out of the community of black religious rebels, and placed him totally in our own age of nothingness and fear."[23] Genovese repeats this problem of signifying black communities and praxes and further closes off ways of being human beyond the delimitations of colonial modernity.

Even as Harding recognizes how a politics of being invested in Man shapes knowledge production and the historical memory of Nat Turner, some of the responses of the "ten black writers" unwittingly show the difficulty of unsettling Man within academic contexts.[24] In the responses of the "ten black writers," this difficulty is most apparent in how dynamics of gender play out in the critique of Styron's novel. In a critique that is illustrative of others in the volume, Lerone Bennett Jr. argues that Styron constructs black characters with a pattern of, "most important of all," the "de-balling of black men," as well as "the de-structuring of the black family" and the "deracination" of Nat Turner.[25] Alvin F. Poussaint continues this emphasis on Styron's "emasculation" of Nat Turner. He argues that Styron's insistence that Nat Turner longed for a white woman and his presentation of Nat Turner as having come "closest . . . to a realized sexualized experience . . . through a homosexual one with another black slave . . . implies that Nat Turner was not a man at all" and "suggests that he was unconsciously feminine."[26] This critique of Styron's supposed feminization of Nat Turner and the suggestion that homosexuality compromises something fundamental to "manhood" recalls the gender dimensions of coloniality that Lugones identifies.[27] As such, the "ten black writers" both intentionally reveal the function of race within Man, and, through their debate with Styron, also unintentionally reveal ways that gender functions within Man.

As the debates over the interpretation of Nat Turner taking place in the 1960s indicate, moving beyond Man might be better taken up by contesting dominant epistemes and searching for alternative epistemes, rather than holding up particular individuals as exempla. Thus, I turn to the life of Nat Turner in order to draw out an episteme that indicates a life beyond Man in the next section. The epistemic sources that ground Nat Turner's politics of being, I argue, are generative decolonial sites.

Nat Turner's Life: Contesting Man

The Southampton slave rebellion is a significant manifestation of the possibilities beyond Man that Nat Turner presents. But armed rebellion, while a significant modality of unsettling Man, is not the only opening into Nat Turner's praxis of being human. Moving beyond what Wynter refers to—in a very brief reference to Nat Turner—as the "social construct of the rebellious Nat" that "legitimated the use of force as a necessary mechanism for ensuring regular steady labor" requires considering a wider view of Nat Turner's life than a myopic focus on the Southampton slave rebellion affords.[28] Neglecting Nat Turner's religious practices and epistemology risks forcing Nat Turner to occupy merely the symbolic space of "the rebellious Nat."[29] Wynter sees slave revolts as "punctuations" of the struggle to create "another collective identity whose coding and signification move[s] outside the framework of the dominant ideology."[30] The "constitution of a counterculture" that "provides the basis for the theoretical formulations of the forms of social revolution needed in America today" has histories outside its punctuation in rebellion.[31] Taking seriously the way Wynter focuses on a rigorous politics of being that does more than seek inclusion in the modern world-system requires considering Nat Turner's life as one embedded within a communal politics of being. Situating Nat Turner within a longer history than the "punctuation" of the Southampton slave rebellion opens up the importance of Nat Turner's religious practices and epistemologies cultivated before his armed struggle.

Vincent Harding describes forms of life within black communities in the United States with the metaphor of a river: a continuous movement of black protest in the Americas, "sometimes powerful, tumultuous, and roiling with life; at other times meandering and turgid, covered with the ice and snow of seemingly endless winters, all too often streaked and running with blood."[32] The metaphor of a river uncovers the "soul" or "spirit" of the black radical tradition, which at times found expression in the calls to rebellions and actual rebellions, yet which is by no means limited to these expressions. Albert J. Raboteau brings out this undercurrent of black life in the Americas by looking at the historical expressions of slave religion beyond the paradigm of protest. He draws attention to the complexity of religious life among US slaves, contesting the interpretation of slave religion in two opposing poles of accommodation and rebelliousness. Through prayer, slaves transcended the poles of docility and resistance. Prayer opened an alternative reference point that allowed slaves to be in touch with a reality that transcended the slave system, its moral codes, and its norms.

Prayer allowed slaves to enter into an alternative history—for example, the history of the people of Israel—and actualize a historical identity in reference to this alternative history.[33] While prayer might lead to various forms of submission or protest, the ideas of submission and protest cannot capture the meaning of prayer. Nat Turner demonstrates this recognition within the study of the black radical tradition and slave religion. While the Southampton slave rebellion indicates the intensity or punctuation of a way of living beyond Man, Nat Turner's life in relationship to a divine reality and the religious practices he describes in the "Confessions" reveals a politics of being that exceeds the constraints of Man.

Nat Turner's politics of being beyond Man is apparent in concluding remarks that his lawyer, Thomas R. Gray, makes in the "Confessions" in reference to Nat Turner:

> The calm, deliberate composure with which he spoke of his late deeds and intentions, the expression of his fiend-like face when excited by enthusiasm, still bearing the stains of the blood of helpless innocence about him; clothed with rags and covered with chains; yet daring to raise his manacled hands to heaven, with a spirit soaring above the attributes of man; I looked on him and my blood curdled in my veins.[34]

While certainly related to the revolt, what Gray describes as striking terror in him is Nat Turner's ability to maintain a spirit that resides beyond "the attributes of man." Even when being held in prison before his execution, Nat Turner exudes the capacity to operate beyond the set of expected and accepted dispositions. In his person, Nat Turner reveals the contingency and frailty of Man. He demonstrates a politics of being beyond Man, rooted in an episteme and orientation that exceeds the modern world-system.

A religious orientation cultivated before the specific events of the 1831 rebellion, and which exceeds Nat Turner as an individual protagonist of the rebellion, grounds Nat Turner's mode of life beyond Man, of which Gray catches a glimpse after the rebellion. Through his religious visions and practice, Nat Turner presents in the "Confessions" how he lived out an alternative way of being human prior to 1831 and the specific events of the rebellion. The larger histories of black resistance and slave religion, which Harding and Raboteau describe, shape this alternative vision of the human person that flows through the "Confessions."

A set of practices concretizes Nat Turner's religious orientation. He narrates his early religious life within the scope of the practices of learning, reflection, prayer, and withdrawal:

When I got large enough to go to work, while employed, I was
reflecting on many things that would present themselves to my
imagination, and whenever an opportunity occurred of looking at a
book, when the school children were getting their lessons, I would
find many things that the fertility of my own imagination had depicted to me before; all my time, not devoted to my master's service,
was spent either in prayer, or in making experiments in casting
different things in moulds made of earth.[35]

These practices continue throughout Nat Turner's life. As his community
recognizes him as being endowed with a religious power, Nat Turner says
he "studiously avoided mixing in society, and wrapped myself in mystery,
devoting my time to fasting and prayer."[36] This reflection and prayer, motivated by a recognition by his community, shapes his way of living, as he
attempts "to obtain true holiness" and "to receive the true knowledge of
faith."[37]

Developments in the study of the relationship between an interior faith
life and external ritual practices can shed light on the depth of the alternative to Man that Nat Turner offers. The cultural anthropologists Talal
Asad and Saba Mahmood question the tendency of European anthropologists to detach exterior ritual practices from the interior life of the self.[38]
Asad and Mahmood present a perspective on religious practices that differs
from the dominant view within the anthropology of religion that rituals
have a symbolic function that has to be decoded by the anthropologist.[39] In
her study of the Muslim act of prayer within a contemporary women's piety
movement in Cairo, Egypt, for example, Mahmood argues that becoming
Muslim is a project and is a function of conduct and behavior. This interpretation of ritual practice stands in contrast to the idea that the interiority
of persons is intact and that what they present, for example in religious
practices, is somehow disconnected from this interior essence. Based on
ethnographic research, Mahmood argues that mosque participants "identified the act of prayer as a key site for purposefully molding their intentions,
emotions, and desires" and that prayer is a practice that "should not be understood as a withdrawal from sociopolitical engagement."[40] Using the insights into the relationship between interior life and external practice
Mahmood uncovers within Egyptian women's piety movements as a guide,
it is possible to see the "Confessions" as showing that Nat Turner cultivated
his interior life with external acts and religious practices. His religious
practices of learning, reflection, prayer, withdrawal, and, ultimately, the rebellion are a part of a communal process of an alternative politics of being.

While Nat Turner's project of becoming Christian may have roots in a more general set of religious practices within slave religion, some interpreters have privileged a view of Nat Turner as an exceptional individual, set apart from the "river" Harding identifies. This position is apparent in a review that Styron wrote of Herbert Aptheker's *American Negro Slave Revolts*. This review appeared in the *New York Review of Books* four years before Styron published *The Confessions of Nat Turner*.[41] Styron's basic critique of Aptheker, a historian who would go on to support the "ten black writers" and be used approvingly by them, is that Aptheker's work is merely a reaction against the work of Ulrich B. Phillips, a slavery apologist who presented slaves as docile and content. Styron reads Aptheker to depict slaves as "forever chafing in the bonds of slavery" merely in an attempt to counter Phillips's account.[42] Styron sees both positions as erroneous and ideological and sides with a third view, set forth by Stanley Elkins, that the slave system infantilized slaves and eliminated their desire and ability to resist or form relationships and significant cultural habits and norms.[43] Styron explains his support of Elkins's position:

> The character (not characterization) of "Sambo," shiftless, wallowing happily in the dust, was no cruel figment of the imagination, Southern or Northern, but did in truth exist. But that the plantation slaves *were* often observably docile, *were* childish, *were* irresponsible and incapable of real resistance would seem to be no significant commentary upon the character of the Negro but tribute rather to a capitalist supermachine which swiftly managed to cow and humble an entire people with a ruthless efficiency unparalleled in history.[44]

Significantly, Styron understands Nat Turner to escape this fate (as does Elkins) and to therefore live as an exception to life on the slave compound. This view of Nat Turner as an individual exception does not comport with the historical document of the "Confessions." The complexity of the relationship between the sacred and secular realms and the connection between religion and rebellion presented in the "Confessions" indicate both Nat Turner's connection to his community and his connection to slave religion more generally. He speaks, for example, about "my grandmother, who was very religious, and to whom I was much attached," as well as other "religious persons," including white people.[45] If the "Confessions" is read with an appreciation of this connection—one that Harding shows both Styron and Genovese devalue—then the "Confessions" can indicate a set of religious practices that Nat Turner took up during his life that shaped a politics of being that unsettled the confined space of the Word of Man.

Nat Turner's Theological Epistemology
as a Praxis of Unsettling Man

Because Nat Turner's religious orientation exists within but also beyond a social, political, and economic arrangement supported by a particular descriptive statement of the human within the modern world-system, the episteme out of which he actualizes a politics of being might open up possibilities for the contemporary context. The historian of religions Charles H. Long considers how an "ontological dimension" of the human resists foreclosure in the process of the Western quest to expand and define its own conception of the human in relation to others. Long's work focuses on how communities that have been signified upon by the West have not ceased to offer meaning in sustaining these ontological dimensions.[46] Using Long's framework to understand how Nat Turner—even within the context of racial slavery—resisted foreclosure can open up a paradigm for contesting Man.

To describe this primordial ontological dimension kept open by communities that have been signified within the process of the European conquest of the Americas, Long draws on Rudolf Otto's description of a religious experience as the experience of a *mysterium tremendum*. While what Otto presents as a neutral and objective explanation is no doubt heavily shaped by the Protestant Christian tradition, Long nevertheless finds it illuminating. Otto describes the "tremendum" element of this phenomenon as a feeling of the status of "creaturehood" in the face of the "awefulness" of divinity.[47] He refers to the "urgency" or "energy" of the numinous object and draws attention to this nonrational aspect of religion that is too often "rationalized away."[48] Otto describes the "mysterium" element of the mysterium tremendum as a "wholly other" reality that myths often express but, in the act of expressing the mysterium, depart from it.[49] Humans experience the mysterium tremendum ambiguously. It is negative, oppressive, and overwhelming in the sense that it evokes dependence and humility, and at the same time it provides hope for being human in relation to a reality radically other than an oppressive social-political arrangement. As such, Otto's understanding of religious experience in terms of the mysterium tremendum indicates how a divine reality can be more "oppressive," or obtain a greater hold on the human person, than Man and the modern/colonial matrix.

Long shows how, within black religions in the United States, the phenomenon of the mysterium tremendum plays a crucial role in the subversion of dominant understandings of the human. He argues that the "immediacy" of experience outside the significations of reality imposed by the cultures of conquest is a religious experience—that is, it is an experience of mysterium tremendum.[50] The experience of this reality that cannot be captured and named entails an experience of living beyond Man. This becomes clear in the way Nat Turner narrates the rebellion and his motivations for participating in it.

Nat Turner explains his role in the Southampton slave rebellion in reference to a divine reality and within a communal history of religious experience. In the first line of the "Confessions," he says to Gray, "You have asked me to give a history of the motives which induced me to undertake the late insurrection, as you call it—To do so I must go back to the days of my infancy, and even before I was born."[51] He describes a "belief which has grown with time" that persists even as he is in prison awaiting execution.[52] At least two elements in the "Confessions" shed light on this religious orientation that Turner ventures to explain. First, Turner sees himself to be participating in a divine reality, shaped by but not reduced to his experiences within institutional slavery. Second, he sees this reality to be a common reality, accessible to others in his situation and not limited to his own personal reality. In his explanation of both of these elements of his religious orientation and theological epistemology, Nat Turner conceptualizes his relationship with a divine reality as a relationship shaped by his community and as a relationship that bears on him in a more total way than Man.

Nat Turner's historical experience in slavery shapes his understanding of his participation in a divine reality, yet, in the "Confessions," he consistently refers to a reality that exists beyond the way he has been rendered vis-à-vis the construct of Man. This is already evident in Nat Turner's religious practices to which I referred earlier and is also apparent in aspects of the religious orientation that he shares with the broader phenomenon of slave religion. For example, like Christian slaves more generally, Nat Turner stressed direct revelation from God, alongside revelation in Scripture.[53] And, in continuity with the theologies of slave spirituals, Nat Turner tended to read himself and his community into the Judeo-Christian tradition.[54] As Nat Turner cultivated his religious consciousness through various practices, he told Gray, "I was struck with that particular passage which says: 'Seek ye the kingdom of Heaven and all things shall be added unto you.' I reflected much on this passage, and prayed daily for light on this subject—As I was praying one day at the plough, the spirit spoke to me, saying 'Seek ye the kingdom of Heaven and all things shall be added unto you.'" At this point, Gray asks Turner what he meant by "the spirit," to which he replies, "The Spirit that spoke to the prophets in the former days."[55] Nat Turner, this response suggests, both assumes direct revelation and does not hold to a distinction between the nature of the Israelites' relationship with divinity and his own relationship with divinity. Like in the Israelites' case, and continuing in a long tradition of reading oneself and one's community into biblical narratives, Nat Turner experiences an immediacy to divine revelation. Divine revelation happens in Nat Turner's material reality.

After Nat Turner recounts to Gray signs he encountered within the natural world that indicated that "the time was fast approaching when the first should be last and the last shall be first," Gray asks, "Do you not find yourself mistaken now?" In response, Nat Turner asks rhetorically, "Was not Christ crucified?"[56] Here, Nat Turner again reads himself and his community into biblical narratives. Social and political criteria—in this case, the court's impending decision of his guilt and his death sentence—do not override the religious reality toward which he is oriented. Furthermore, Nat Turner fully commits to this reality. As Gray describes Nat Turner in the prison cell, he relates his fear precisely because of Nat Turner's lack of fear for social arrangements. In Nat Turner's theological epistemology, a religious reality orients actions within mundane reality.[57]

A second element of Nat Turner's theological epistemology revealed in the "Confessions" is his insistence that the divine reality is a larger reality that others can relate to as well. Gray had a political interest in showing that the rebellion was an isolated event when publishing the "Confessions." Doing so could assuage the fear of the white master class in the South and, beyond this, white capitalists in the North and in Europe who benefited from the slave system. Gray discloses this interest in the last part of the "Confessions" when he cross-examines Nat Turner. After Gray asks him if he knew about specific planned rebellions that were happening elsewhere, Nat Turner answers that he did not. Gray then quotes Nat Turner, who says, "I see sir, you doubt my word; but can you not think the same ideas, and strange appearances about this time in the heaven's [sic] might prompt others, as well as myself, to this undertaking."[58] Here Nat Turner indicates a reality and a rationality beyond Man that is shaped by a religious orientation. He discloses a general religious reality, outside the one the slave system has created, to which different people in his situation could connect.

Drawing on the category of the mysterium tremendum and appreciating its ambiguity allows for an understanding of how Nat Turner lived in reference to a reality that makes a claim on his life in a more ultimate way than does the slave system. The concept of the mysterium tremendum can show how Nat Turner moved beyond Man, but understanding this movement also requires recognizing the concept's limitations. Long notes a key limitation in Otto's work: Otto often extrapolates laws of religious experience without adequate attention to "the role of the historical subject undergoing or giving expression to experience in the world."[59] By too quickly moving to laws or abstract principles, delineating a category such as the mysterium tremendum can conceal how the historical experience of oppression operates as a generative site.[60] Furthermore, the mysterium tremendum can suggest a transcendent movement away from the world, rather than a transcendence in history. Nat Turner's religious orientation is not an abandonment of material reality but a way of connecting life on the material level with divinity.

In order to move beyond the abstraction of concepts such as "mysterium tremendum," Long shows how the rationality that the modern world-system takes as valid and the way this rationality operates conceals various ways of being human. In order to engage these concealed modalities of the human, Long moves outside the type of rationality solidified with the Enlightenment and the "ontological givens" it is understood as presenting.[61] He turns to the meaning that comes forth in the process of unmasking as an encounter with a religious reality that moves beyond these ontological givens. The interpretive power of the center is peeled back, revealing "meaning at another level of human existence."[62]

For Long, religious experience is "a primordial experience of that which is considered ultimate in existence," and "implied in this notion of religious experience is that of human orientation—the meaning that human communities give to the particular stances they have assumed in their several worlds."[63] Long describes European voyages to the New World as a religious experience insofar as they created new myths by using the raw material of the peoples of the New World and the peoples they brought there from Africa as an arena of silence on which they could signify. By the seventeenth century, Long argues, these myths become concretized in rhetorics of progress and racialization, which he calls the "linguistic conquest."[64] While Europeans created a discursive reality through their linguistic conquest, Long points to the "oppungent" realities of non-European modes of being human, which remain nontransparent and opaque. The denial of the opacity of these ways of being human allows one to "divorce oneself from the messy, confusing welter of detail that characterizes a particular society at a particular time and to move to the cool realm of abstract principles symbolized by the metaphorical transparency of knowledge."[65] The presumed ability to describe the divine as a prior, abstract reality is but one example of this.

Long's demand to take seriously the visions that were covered over when signified by Europeans excludes an approach that begins with a particular philosophical category or position and applies it to reality. He rather opts for an approach that moves inductively by demanding a study of lived forms of praxis and lived epistemologies. Nat Turner's religious practices that cultivated a self beyond Man, even if these practices can only be somewhat imprecisely grasped at within the historical record, present one such epistemology and praxis.

Conclusion

It is somewhat paradoxical to argue that a way of living out Christian faith contests Man, as Wynter argues that Christianity provides a clear precursor for hierarchical differentiation in the world of Man. Wynter describes an "epochal shift" in subjective understanding that allowed for Christopher Columbus's voyage to the New World in 1492. When the Portuguese rounded the cape of Africa and landed in Senegal, it provided "the first empirical disproof" of earlier Christian geographies marking boundaries between habitable and inhabitable zones.[66] The symbolic representations involved in the Portuguese exploration and exploitation of the peoples of West Africa—namely, the legitimation of exploitation on the grounds of idolatry—provided the "discourse of legitimation" for Columbus's voyage.[67] Columbus had to make the existence of other lands conceptualizable within a world where subjective understanding was based on the habitable/inhabitable divide, as much as he had to "discover" their existence,[68] and he did this by putting forth the humanistic principle that the whole earth needed Christian redemption.[69] For Wynter, Columbus was a part of the revolutionary change in the conception of the relation between God and humans, which posited that "creation had indeed been made by God *on behalf of* and for *the sake of* human kind (*propter nos homines*)."[70] Columbus's "poetics of the *propter nos*," rooted in a theological shift, provided the discursive legitimization for the conquest of the New World and also for Man. By designating the people he encountered in the New World as "idolaters," Columbus was able to interpellate them as exploitable and enslaveable within his objective understanding. He extrapolated the "*nos* of Christendom" and represented it "*as if* it were the *propter nos* of the human species itself."[71] In naming those he encountered in the New

World as idolaters, Columbus began to shift the line that distinguished the inhabitable from the habitable from a physical or territorial referent to a racial one, which Wynter argues "is still encoded in the white/nonwhite and the European/non-European line."[72] As such, Christianity plays a formative role in the creation of the hierarchies that ground Man.[73] Secularization, as represented by Columbus, takes with it (and hypostasizes) the conceptualization of otherness within a Christian theological framework.

Nat Turner draws on Christian faith to subvert Man outside of these categories because he displaces the "poetics of the *propter nos.*" He moves beyond the transcendental Word of Man without moving to a secular discourse, recalibrating the terrain of being and knowing beyond the doctrine of Man within a Christian episteme. The mysterium tremendum element of the divine reality prohibits divinity, even if conceptualized in Christian terms, from being domesticated into a legitimization of Man. The divine reality for Nat Turner remains a reality more oppressive than Man, or a reality that grasps the human person beyond the claims the world of Man is able to make.

Nat Turner's politics of being that cultivates an orientation beyond Man, in his case accessed through a Christian framework, is an option for a constructive movement beyond the way the doctrine of Man has contained being and knowing in a framework grounded in Eurocentered colonialism and its intellectual traditions proceeding from its collective experience as colonizer. As various traditions of theologies of liberation have demonstrated, this move beyond Man is not necessarily tied to a move to secularism; a praxis of taking back the Word can occur, and has occurred, within theological—and even Christian—orientations. Further, a religious orientation, because of its nature of escaping the logic of the world, can move beyond the transcendental Word of Man in ways that orientations bound by rationalities within the modern world-system often cannot.

NOTES

1. Sylvia Wynter, "Unsettling the Coloniality of Being/Power/Truth/ Freedom: Towards the Human, after Man, Its Overrepresentation—An Argument," *CR: The New Centennial Review* 3, no. 3 (Fall 2003): 319.

2. See Sylvia Wynter, "1492: A New World View," in *Race, Discourse, and the Origin of the Americas: A New World View*, ed. Vera Lawrence Hyatt and Rex Nettleford (Washington, D.C.: Smithsonian Institution Press, 1995), 41.

3. See Kenneth S. Greenberg, ed., *The Confessions of Nat Turner and Related Documents* (Boston: Bedford/St. Martins, 1996), 6–7.

4. See Greenberg, *Confessions of Nat Turner*, 7–10. Historians have debated the authenticity of the "Confessions," and it is important to not assume Turner's voice in the "Confessions" uncritically.

5. See David F. Allmendinger Jr., "The Construction of *The Confessions of Nat Turner*," in *Nat Turner: A Slave Rebellion in History and Memory*, ed. Kenneth S. Greenberg (New York: Oxford University Press, 2003). Henry Irving Tragle has compiled source materials that provide context for the "Confessions" in *The Southampton Slave Revolt of 1831: A Compilation of Source Material* (Amherst: University of Massachusetts Press, 1971).

6. Herbert Aptheker, *Nat Turner's Slave Rebellion* (New York: Dover Publications, 2006), 57–71.

7. Thomas C. Parramore, "Covenant in Jerusalem," in *Nat Turner: A Slave Rebellion in History and Memory*, ed. Kenneth S. Greenberg (Oxford: Oxford University Press, 2003), 70; and Aptheker, *Turner's Slave Rebellion*, 62.

8. Aptheker, *Turner's Slave Rebellion*, 74.

9. This was the case even immediately after the revolt. A contemporary newspaper account describes Nat Turner as follows: "A fanatic preacher by the name of Nat Turner (Gen. Nat Turner) who had been taught to read and write, and permitted to go about preaching in the country, was at the bottom of this infernal brigandage. He was artful, impudent, and vindictive, without any cause or provocation, that could be assigned. . . . These wretches are now estimated to have committed *sixty-one murders*! Not a white person escaped at all the houses they visited except *two*." *The Richmond Complier*, August 29, 1831, published in Greenberg, *Confessions of Nat Turner*, 67–68.

10. See Wynter, "Unsettling the Coloniality of Being/Power/Truth/Freedom," 260.

11. See, for example, Nelson Maldonado-Torres, "On the Coloniality of Being: Contributions to the Development of a Concept," *Cultural Studies* 21, no. 2–3 (March/May 2007): 243–44.

12. See Maldonado-Torres, "On the Coloniality of Being," 244; and Aníbal Quijano, "Coloniality and Modernity/Rationality," *Cultural Studies* 21, no. 2–3 (March/May 2007).

13. María Lugones, "Heterosexualism and the Colonial/Modern Gender System," *Hypatia* 22, no. 1 (Winter 2007): 186.

14. Lugones, "Heterosexualism and the Colonial/Modern Gender System," 202.

15. Lugones, 202–3.

16. William Styron, *The Confessions of Nat Turner* (New York: Vintage International, 1992).

17. See John Henrik Clarke, introduction to *William Styron's Nat Turner: Ten Black Writers Respond*, ed. John Henrik Clarke (Boston: Beacon Press, 1968), vii.

18. Vincent Harding, "You've Taken My Nat and Gone," in *William Styron's Nat Turner: Ten Black Writers Respond*, ed. John Henrik Clarke (Boston: Beacon Press, 1968), 25.

19. See Harding, "You've Taken My Nat," 30–31.

20. Lerone Bennett Jr. also strongly renders this critique. He argues, for example, "The man Styron substitutes for Nat Turner is not only the antithesis of Nat Turner; he is the antithesis of blackness." See Lerone Bennett Jr., "Nat's Last White Man," in *William Styron's Nat Turner: Ten Black Writers Respond*, ed. John Henrik Clarke (Boston: Beacon Press, 1968), 5. He goes on to argue that "Styron is writing for his very life, throwing up smokescreen after smokescreen to hide himself from the truth of the American experience" (6).

21. Eugene D. Genovese, "The Nat Turner Case," *New York Review of Books*, September 12, 1968 (emphasis added).

22. Vincent Harding, "An Exchange on 'Nat Turner,'" *New York Review of Books*, November 7, 1968.

23. Harding, "You've Taken My Nat," 30.

24. While he has different emphases than I offer here and makes his argument in different terms, Cedric Johnson has written on the conservative political dynamics within Black Power radicalism that prevented it from addressing the wider matrix of colonial modernity. See Cedric Johnson, *Revolutionaries to Race Leaders: Black Power and the Making of American Politics* (Minneapolis: University of Minnesota Press, 2007).

25. Bennett, "Nat's Last White Man," 8.

26. Alvin F. Poussaint, "*The Confessions of Nat Turner* and the Dilemma of William Styron," in *William Styron's Nat Turner: Ten Black Writers Respond*, ed. John Henrik Clarke (Boston: Beacon Press, 1968), 21.

27. For more on the dynamics of homosexuality and femininity within *Ten Black Writers Respond*, see Vincent Woodard, *The Delectable Negro: Human Consumption and Homoeroticism within U.S. Slave Culture*, ed. Justin A. Joyce and Dwight A. McBride (New York: New York University Press, 2015), 171–208.

28. Sylvia Wynter, "Sambos and Minstrels," *Social Text* 1 (1979): 150–51.

29. See Wynter, "Sambos and Minstrels," 154.

30. Wynter, 156.

31. Wynter, 156.

32. Vincent Harding, *There Is a River: The Black Struggle for Freedom in America* (San Diego: A Harvest Book, 1981), xix.

33. See Albert J. Raboteau, *Slave Religion: The "Invisible Institution" in the Antebellum South* (New York: Oxford University Press, 2004), 306–11.

34. Thomas R. Gray, "The Text of *The Confessions of Nat Turner* . . . as Reported by Thomas R. Gray," in *William Styron's Nat Turner: Ten Black Writers Respond*, ed. John Henrik Clarke (Boston: Beacon Press, 1968), 113.

35. Gray, "Text of *The Confessions of Nat Turner*," 100.

36. Gray, 101.

37. Gray, 103.

38. See, for example, Talal Asad, *Genealogies of Religion: Discipline and Reasons of Power in Christianity and Islam* (Baltimore: Johns Hopkins University Press, 1993), 55–79; and Saba Mahmood, "Rehearsed Spontaneity and the Conventionality of Ritual: Disciplines of *Ṣalāt*," *American Ethnologist* 28, no. 4 (2001).

39. See, for example, Victor Turner, *The Forest of Symbols: Aspects of Ndembu Ritual* (Ithaca, N.Y.: Cornell University Press, 1967).

40. Mahmood, "Rehearsed Spontaneity," 828–29.

41. See William Styron, "Overcome," *New York Review of Books*, September 26, 1963.

42. Styron, "Overcome."

43. See Stanley M. Elkins, *Slavery: A Problem in American Institutional and Intellectual Life* (Chicago: University of Chicago Press, 1974), 81–139.

44. Styron, "Overcome."

45. Gray, "Text of *The Confessions of Nat Turner*," 100.

46. See Charles H. Long, *Significations: Signs, Symbols, and Images in the Interpretation of Religion* (Aurora, Colo.: Davies Group, 1995), 65–67.

47. See Rudolf Otto, *The Idea of the Holy: An Inquiry into the Non-Rational Factor in the Idea of the Divine and Its Relation to the Rational*, trans. John W. Harvey (New York: Oxford University Press, 1958), 20–21.

48. See Otto, *Idea of the Holy*, 23.

49. See Otto, 25–28.

50. See Long, *Significations*, 188.

51. Gray, "Text of *The Confessions of Nat Turner*," 99.

52. Gray, 99.

53. See Raboteau, *Slave Religion*, 242.

54. See Raboteau, 250–51.

55. Raboteau, 101.

56. Raboteau, 104.

57. J. Kameron Carter also argues for how this process of reading oneself into a religious reality contests colonial modernity. Unlike Carter, however, I do not make a claim for the Christian orthodoxy of this process of Nat Turner reading himself into a religious reality, as Carter does with Briton

Hammon, Jarena Lee, and Frederick Douglass, and rather focus on the phenomenon of entering into a religious reality. See J. Kameron Carter, *Race: A Theological Account* (New York: Oxford University Press, 2008).

58. Gray, "Text of *The Confessions of Nat Turner*," 112.

59. Long, *Significations*, 45.

60. In this way, Nat Turner could be understood to be rendered "flesh" in the double sense that Alexander G. Weheliye uses the term. He uses the metaphor of ether, which refers to both (in its ancient usage) one of the elements and (in its modern usage) an anesthetic. As ether, flesh "holds together the world of Man while at the same time forming the conditions of possibility for this world's demise." Weheliye recognizes the way the misnaming of peoples as flesh functions as a constitutive underside of Man, yet also recognizes flesh as a productive site, one that generates alternative versions of the human, beyond Man. Alexander G. Weheliye, *Habeas Viscus: Racializing Assemblages, Biopolitics, and Black Feminist Theories of the Human* (Durham, N.C.: Duke University Press, 2014), 40, 43.

61. Long, *Significations*, 84.

62. Long, 73.

63. Long, 107.

64. See Long, 116.

65. Long, 117.

66. Wynter, "1492," 9.

67. Wynter, 11.

68. See Wynter, 24.

69. See Wynter, 26.

70. Wynter, 27.

71. Wynter, 28.

72. Wynter, 36.

73. J. Kameron Carter articulates a similar formative that Christianity plays within the development of colonial modernity by arguing that whiteness supersedes covenantal identity as a criterion for Christian identity. See Carter, *Race*.

CHAPTER 6

Mystical Bodies of Christ:
Human, Crucified, and Beloved

Andrew Prevot

The bodies crushed at the hands of Christians in the "new world" and globally haunt any contemporary effort to write Christian theology. If one had to choose between affirming the full human dignity of these millions gone and remaining a faithful Christian, one must certainly choose the former and do so as a sheer matter of justice. How could Christian theology warrant any defense if its essential meaning and function were tied to the desecrating violation of the body and the world, which we have witnessed in colonial modernity? The answer is that no such warrant would be possible. Any apologetics would be collusion. Any Christian word would be abuse to the ears of the humane. Yet in the midst of all the horror I have often asked myself whether—and for the moment I still somehow believe that—Christian theology harbors another possible meaning. This is what I aim to explore here in this interpretation of the mystical body of Christ: another meaning of Christian theology that would decolonize it and contribute to the broader decolonial project.

Although I cannot pretend to address all of the problems linking Christianity and coloniality, I do propose three theological shifts that may be part of a better way forward. The first is to rethink the mystical body of

Christ as a doctrine of theological anthropology that, on the basis of the incarnation and certain *nouvelle theological* teachings on grace, affirms a profound unity of Christ with every human body regardless of their beliefs, race, gender, sexuality, and even sinfulness. The second is to develop, on the basis of the experience of Christ's crucifixion among certain Christian mystics and liberation theologians, an understanding of the mystical body of Christ in particular connection with the victims of history. The third is to argue, by drawing on the Christian erotic and spousal imagery of two becoming one flesh and certain contemporary feminist and gender theory critiques, that God loves bodies in Christ in such a way that God both desires and respects their freedom. To show how these three theological shifts have the potential to contribute to a decolonization of Christian theology and to decolonial initiatives more broadly it is necessary for me to treat each one in significantly more detail. I begin by situating these shifts within a general move toward pluralizing the meaning of "the mystical body of Christ," which clarifies, among other things, that it is not merely a name for the church.

Diverse Meanings of the "Mystical Body of Christ"

What does the term "mystical body of Christ" mean? The most common usage today is ecclesiological. The mystical body of Christ is identified with the church seen particularly under the aspect of the unity of diverse members with Christ their head. One finds this meaning throughout Pope Pius XII's 1943 encyclical *Mystici corporis* and in the Second Vatican Council's Dogmatic Constitution on the Church, *Lumen gentium*, sections 7 and 8.[1] I do not wish to contest this ecclesiological usage, which has a venerable history and remains an important way to express the Christic nature and mission of the church today. At the same time, I want to point out that other meanings are possible. Without fear of contradiction, theologians can investigate a variety of different interpretations of the mystical body of Christ, which may all have their own validity and contemporary significance. Let me distinguish just a few. In addition to the ecclesiological, there are sacramental, incarnational, spiritual, eschatological, anthropological, and cruciform meanings that warrant greater attention.

Henri de Lubac's *Corpus Mysticum* retrieves a sacramental meaning, more common in the first millennium of the church's history, according to which "the mystical body of Christ" names Jesus's real, corporeal presence in the Eucharist, hidden under the sensible sign of bread. In the same text, de Lubac argues that both the Eucharist and the church mysteriously signify and make present the historical body of Christ revealed in scripture. Insofar as this historical body is the living human flesh of the divine Word, it can be considered "mystical" in a plenary sense: It is the mystery. Jesus of Nazareth's physical embodiment is thus the foundational referent of "the mystical body of Christ."[2] Furthermore, in recent years, increasing attention has been given to the bodily conditions of Christian spirituality.[3] When mystics and saints (such as Catherine of Siena and Julian of Norwich, whom we shall consider below) speak of a union with Christ taking place in the interior depths of their souls, this by no means excludes physical manifestations of union through sensate experiences of pleasure and pain and through embodied actions of loving service. Such grace-filled bodies, which attest to the unitive heights of Christian spirituality in various ways, can themselves be identified as "mystical bodies of Christ." Finally, Christianity's affirmation of the human body is eschatological. The traditional hope, expressed in 1 Corinthians 15 and in the Apostles' Creed, is that human bodies will be resurrected in a new, glorified state that does not abolish their corporeality. These risen, Christically united "spiritual bodies" (see 1 Cor. 15:44) can be called "mystical" to indicate that they are mysterious to us now and will be forever saturated with divine mystery.

All of these meanings are related to one another and consistent with mainstream commitments of Catholic Christian theology, the tradition in which I write. The sacramental, spiritual, and eschatological interpretations of the term "mystical body of Christ" enrich the ecclesiological interpretation by specifying it further. The church is the place where the eucharistic presence of Christ's body is received, spiritual experiences of union with Christ's body (themselves often sacramentally mediated) are cultivated, and hope in the resurrection of the body is instilled and sustained. The incarnational meaning grounds and justifies the others: Church, sacrament, spirituality, and eschatological hope emerge from the biblically disclosed life, death, and resurrection of Jesus and continually refer back to this originating mystery. None of this should surprise anyone familiar with traditional Catholic doctrines and practices. To be sure, not every Catholic theologian would spontaneously use the term "mystical body of Christ" in all of these ways. Again, the predominant interpretation today remains ecclesiological. But my claim is that it is possible to reflect on these multiple senses without deviating in any substantial respects from this faith tradition.

In the remainder of this essay, I want to develop this already multifaceted understanding of the mystical body (or bodies) of Christ further by reflecting on two other conceivable interpretations that may help with the process of decolonizing Christianity. As decolonial theorists such as Walter Mignolo, Eduardo Mendieta, Sylvia Wynter, and others indicate, decolonization requires major shifts at the levels of theory and practice.[4] It means learning to think and live in ways that seek to undo the unjust power relations that were forged at the origins of modern Europe's colonizing projects, which enslaved Africans, decimated indigenous cultures and peoples, brutalized women, desecrated natural environments, and left generations of human communities in conditions of seemingly interminable poverty and vulnerability. Some may reasonably doubt whether Christian theology has anything positive to contribute to an overcoming of these problems, since these theorists demonstrate that it has been very deeply implicated in their production. Still, my aim in this essay is to seek such a positive contribution if it can be found. Like Pope Pius XII, who turns to a meditation on the mystical body of Christ to address "the sorrows and calamities of these stormy times,"[5] by which he refers to the abysmal circumstances of the Second World War, so too I, in this brief reflection, look to the theme of the mystical body of Christ in search of a more promising Christian response to the recalcitrantly colonial situation of the modern world, which Christians have played a major part in constructing.

The two interpretations of the mystical body of Christ that I shall accent in this discussion, without forgetting those mentioned above, are the *anthropological* and the *cruciform*. Rooted in the incarnational meaning (which is foundational for any legitimate usage of the term "mystical body of Christ"), the anthropological interpretation stresses that the incarnation is God's way of becoming freely and lovingly united with the constitutively corporeal nature of humanity. In Christ, God claims human flesh as such. God assumes it in order to redeem it. Therefore, to live in and as a human body is already to have the sort of nature in which Christ is at least inchoately present. Every human body is in some sense a mystical body of Christ. This anthropological interpretation contributes to the decolonization of Christianity by locating Christ's body in the bodies of all humans, including the many non-Christian victims of colonial modernity who were unjustly abused and murdered for not being members of the church—an even more restrictive category than Wynter's "Man," and indeed its antecedent.[6] In the next section of this essay, I shall connect de Lubac's sacramental and ecclesiological reflections in *Corpus Mysticum* to his theological anthropology in *The Mystery of the Supernatural* in order to establish the possibility of an anthropological meaning of the term "mystical body of Christ" and to clarify its decolonial significance.

The second line of interpretation that I shall explore focuses on Christ's suffering body on the cross and the ways that it signifies God's decision to be united with all those bodies that suffer, especially cruelly and unjustly. This is the cruciform meaning of "the mystical body of Christ," which is clearly displayed in the writings of Catherine, Julian, and other Christian mystics and theologians. It contributes to the decolonization of Christianity by teaching us to perceive the presence of Christ in the bodies of all those who have endured or perished by the violence of the colonial era. Blacks, indigenous peoples, women, the poor—all the victims are in a very particular way united with Christ in his passion. There is a danger here of glorifying suffering and discouraging resistance against it, but recent meditations on Christically united crucified bodies by theologians such as Ignacio Ellacuría, James Cone, and M. Shawn Copeland show how this danger can be overcome.

It is important to note that God decides to become united through Christ with every human body and all suffering bodies out of an intense love for these bodies. The Word becomes flesh not because of any metaphysical necessity to do so but because God creates and recognizes flesh to be beautiful and worthy of immeasurable love. God desires a mutual relationship of intimacy with humans even in their corporeality and their greatest torments and is willing to give everything for them. One way that the Christian tradition has expressed God's amorous motivation in this relationship is by drawing on images of erotic encounter and spousal commitment: the two becoming one flesh. The idea of the mystical body of Christ (composed of head and members) is often distinguished from the theological symbolism of marital union (where spouses join together in love, as in *Lumen gentium*),[7] but these two Christian thought-forms also regularly intermingle and inform each other, with one sometimes making up for what the other lacks. The erotic and spousal imagery of divine-and-human union has received ecclesiological, sacramental, incarnational, spiritual, and eschatological interpretations of its own, perhaps most extensively and controversially in the works of Hans Urs von Balthasar.[8] In the fourth and final section of this essay, I shall argue that, with some critical refinements, this erotic and spousal imagery may also contribute to a decolonial understanding of the anthropological and cruciform ways of participating in Christ's body.

The erotic and spousal imagery of the Christian tradition has been critiqued for the patriarchal and exclusively heterosexual politics that it enshrines, especially in certain Balthasarian formulations,[9] but the goods that a critically revised erotic and spousal imagery has to offer are quite significant and, I would suggest, salvageable from such problematic features. First, this imagery empowers us to make a strong affirmation of the divine loveliness of all human bodies, perhaps especially those bodies branded as ugly or unlovable, as many of those violated within colonial modernity have been. Furthermore, it emphasizes that full union with Christ must be a matter of freedom and consent. This union cannot be coerced. It cannot happen without one's knowledge or against one's will. One danger that comes with treating all human beings, and especially those who suffer, as mystical bodies of Christ simply on the basis of Christ's incarnation and passion is that such a description does not take into account the perspectives and choices of the human participants in this relationship. Using a healthy model of loving mutuality as the basis of Christian theological thinking helps a great deal. The respect for difference and freedom required by current norms of sexual justice guards against the danger of a nonconsensual sexual imagery in Christian theology. Moreover, the refusal to assign any essentialist gender roles to God or humanity (as was often done in the traditional bridegroom-bride framework) potentially frees the idea of an amorous divine-and-human union from oppressive constructs, or at least encourages one to resist them. Although there are limits to such imagery, at its best it reveals God's intense love for the beauty of human flesh and God's unceasing respect for human beings' "enfleshed freedom," as Copeland would call it.

The Mystical Body of Christ as a Doctrine of Theological Anthropology

A major problem with the doctrine of the "mystical body of Christ" is that theologians often reserve this term exclusively for Christians, effectively instructing them to perceive themselves as the sole members of this body. One may lament this restriction out of a general desire to be more inclusive, but the lament will become more pointed the more one recognizes the ways that such a restriction functions to dehumanize those outside the church and to rationalize the brutal treatment of their bodies. History presents us with the bitter hypocrisy of an enormous body of people (Christians) who were better able to appreciate the body of Christ in the sacramentally transfigured sign of bread than in the many human faces of the indigenous and enslaved in their midst and under their abusive control. One thinks of those colonial settlers of Hispaniola who dutifully attended Mass to receive the Blessed Sacrament only to hear with outrage the sermon of Fray Antonio de Montesinos, a sermon that Bartolomé de

Las Casas says "made their flesh tremble." Montesinos forcefully condemns them: "Tell me, by what right or justice do you hold these Indians in such a cruel and horrible servitude?"[10]

From a decolonial perspective, it does not particularly matter whether one seeks to rehabilitate the earlier eucharistic sense of "the mystical body of Christ," which de Lubac unearths in *Corpus Mysticum*, or to hold fast to the modern ecclesiological sense of the "mystical body of Christ," which Pope Pius XII's encyclical *Mystici corporis* most famously represents. In either case, access to the sublime and enduring presence of God in human flesh is reserved for those Christians bound together by faith and sacrament.

Yet one should not assume that such a eucharistically or ecclesially accented treatment of the mystical body of Christ lacks anthropological significance or makes no claims about the meaning of being human simply because it focuses on intra-Christian realities. On the contrary, as de Lubac suggests on the final page of his text, the body of Christ is a mystery in which "God and humankind embrace one another for all eternity."[11] This anthropologically weighty statement follows logically from the incarnational foundation of the doctrine of the mystical body. Both the Eucharist and the church receive their identity as mystical bodies of Christ from the original, historical body of Christ, which is the Word made flesh. According to the creedal tradition, this original Christic body (i.e., Jesus) exists only as the concrete result of the assumption of human nature by the second person of the divine Trinity. It is only on the basis of such a dogmatically affirmed hypostatic union of divine and human natures in the Son that Christians can claim "a real union of our body with that of Jesus Christ"[12] occurring in the church through the Eucharist. The incarnation is foundational, and it is an event of human *nature*, not limited to any one people group, such as Christians. Moreover, although the Word enters the human condition through one singular human body (i.e., as the historical Jesus), with Athanasius Christian theologians must also recognize that the extraordinary effects of this act involve *every* human body.[13]

The fact that de Lubac very traditionally locates the experience of this divine-and-human union in the church, identifying it especially with the celebration of the Eucharist, does not mean that he forgets the anthropological meaning of the Christ-event, which I especially wish to retrieve here. But the mainly ecclesiological and sacramental usage of "the mystical body of Christ" that he and others favor does allow a dangerously restrictive interpretation of this anthropological meaning to gain some traction—that is, an interpretation that humanizes some and dehumanizes others. The positive side of this theological anthropology holds that, in the church, the Eucharist sanctifies one's corporeal humanity and draws it into the divine mysteries of Christ's glorified body. By contrast, the negative side suggests that outside the church one has no reliable access to union with Christ's body. This lack of access implies an absence of any ecclesially mediated divinization. It also jeopardizes the recognizability of the humanity of the non-Christian body for the Christian imagination.[14] According to Chalcedonian orthodoxy, the fullness of divinity *and humanity* coexist and find their truest expression in Christ's body. Hence, to separate non-Christians from Christ's body, even if only terminologically or imaginatively, makes it more difficult for Christians who adhere to this basic Christological teaching to appreciate the full humanity of non-Christian persons. The temptation is to imagine that the non-Christian is, for that very reason, less human or less than human. The question of how to use the term "mystical body of Christ" is thus no trivial matter. Acknowledging an anthropological meaning is important, but one must also make sure not to restrict this anthropological meaning ecclesiologically or sacramentally in such a way that it implicitly dehumanizes those outside the church.

Perhaps if there had never been any idea of the mystical body of Christ, it would be possible now to honor the humanity of non-Christians with less lofty and less mystically charged notions: for instance, Edward Schillebeeckx's "anthropological constants" or more significantly "The Universal Declaration of Human Rights" adopted by the United Nations in 1948.[15] These general testaments to the dignity of the *humanum*, especially the latter document, which has circulated worldwide, remain indispensable in the fight against the lingering injustices of a neocolonial era. Nonetheless, for Christian theology these broad-based affirmations of human nature are insufficient. I would even risk asserting that a doctrine of the *imago Dei* derived from a biblical theology of creation (see Gen. 1:27) is not enough.[16] The idea of humanity has been raised too high by the incarnation for Christian theologians to avoid making an explicit proclamation of the divinely loved and Christically incorporated humanity of all (as in Matt. 25:35–40). A decolonial shift can happen within Christian theology only if Christian theologians reinterpret the mystical body of Christ anthropologically and *without reserve*—that is, as a doctrine that raises up and celebrates human flesh as such, regardless of communal belonging or sacramental status.

De Lubac may be more helpful in this regard than he first appears. In particular, I have in mind his groundbreaking reflections on the relations of the natural and the supernatural within the concrete constitution of the human being. In *The Mystery of the Supernatural,* he argues that Christians must hold in tension two gifts: the gift of a natural (i.e., created, inbuilt, even if only implicit) desire for union with God without which the human would not be human and a supernatural gift of divine union that God freely and lovingly grants human nature without any obligation to do so.[17] The desire that is central to the first gift can only be satisfied by the endlessly full and mysterious experience of the second gift, yet this satisfaction is not "owed" to the human being. De Lubac stresses this point about the unexacted character of grace to guard against problematic misunderstandings, which would curtail divine freedom. Nonetheless, his main concern is to rescue the concrete reality of divinely graced human nature from dissatisfying notions of a "duplex ordo," in which "pure nature" would subsist with its own teleologies on one level and a completely extrinsic framework of grace on another.

De Lubac's search for a more concrete way to discuss the natural and supernatural leads him back to Christology. This Christological re-orientation is reflected in the last lines of the text (a quote from Ephesians 1:3–6): "Blessed be the God and Father of our Lord Jesus Christ, who . . . chose us in him . . . that we should be holy and blameless before him. He destined us in love to be his sons through Jesus Christ, according to the purpose of his will, to the praise of his glorious grace which he freely bestowed on us in the beloved."[18] Here de Lubac indicates that the "supernatural" is not just a philosophical hypothesis but rather a shorthand way to speak about a free choice that God already reveals to humans in history— namely, a choice to love and adopt them in Christ. Without directly endorsing it, de Lubac here opens up the possibility of defining the supernatural precisely *as* the mystical body of Christ. To be incorporated into this body is to be united with God in a way that promises to answer human beings' deepest, innate longings, which are experienced nowhere else if not in their bodies.

On de Lubac's terms, one cannot strictly conclude from the presence of a natural desire alone that God has in fact bestowed a second gift of supernatural grace (a grace that one can now interpret rigorously as oneness with Christ's body). Nonetheless, it is significant that de Lubac does not limit such humanity-defining natural desire to Christians but instead treats it as a universal given. Moreover, it is also significant that he interprets Christ as the revelation of God's free choice to satisfy this desire. This Christological expression of divine freedom—an expression that shows God voluntarily entering into the corporeal condition of *human nature,* not merely the church, and doing so out of supreme love—is what especially supports my argument for a wider, anthropological use of the idea of the "mystical body of Christ."

Within a Christian theological perspective, the decision to consign non-Christians (especially victims of colonial oppression) to a state of "pure nature" simply because they are non-Christian would be another way to dehumanize them and thereby to disregard the good news that is God's indwelling of human flesh. I also submit that a vague sense of the supernatural applied to everyone is not enough. It is important to refine theological language to emphasize that God loves and embraces in Christ the vulnerable bodies that all human beings are. Within this perspective, it is appropriate to speak of "supernatural" grace: Christian theologians need to proclaim a gift of divine love that transcends all natural expectations. But in some sense "supernatural" is the least theology can say about this gift. To speak of a mystical body of Christ that is at least inchoately coextensive with human corporeality is to draw closer to the concrete totality of graced flesh that needs to be named.

As a Catholic theologian, I affirm that membership in the church and participation in its sacraments are true and singular manifestations of the mystical body of Christ; I do not wish to deny this. However, they must not prevent Christians from seeing in human nature itself, and precisely in each of its fleshly appearances, the hidden yet very real presence of Christ. Each body is a mystical body because Christ is there already lovingly in each and every body, seeking desperately to fulfill its profoundest desires for healing and redemption. This intimate divine presence is not necessary or obligatory for God, but it has been revealed as a living mystery of divine freedom and grace. I do not claim that everybody is therefore a Christian, not even "anonymously," as Karl Rahner might want. The Rahnerian theory of anonymous Christianity may be in some sense true or plausible, but it is not the position I want to advance here.[19] My claim, rather, is that Christian theology would do well to understand the incarnation as constituting at the very least an *incipient* divinization and infinite validation of the human body as such, whether or not that body is even anonymously engaged in Christian belief. Hence, Christ would not only be present in the bodies of implicit or explicit Christians or, for that matter, Christian mystics and saints but also be present in the bodies of all those who, merely by virtue of their embodiment, are visibly one with the Word made flesh. This is what it means to take the mystical body of Christ as a doctrine of theological anthropology.

A possible objection, which I cannot fully address here, has to do with the sinfulness of humanity. What sense does it make to affirm the presence of Christ in human bodies that are maliciously governed by vices of various kinds, perhaps even by horrifying evil? In response, I want first merely to insist that this question also troubles the standard ecclesiological interpretation of the term "mystical body of Christ." Membership in the church is no guarantee of sinlessness, as the murderous, rapacious, colonizing behavior of Christians more than attests. To be sure, perfect union with Christ requires a turning away from sin and a graced existence lived in total conformity with God's loving will. But for most of humanity, whether Christian or not, this holiness remains a constant struggle, more nearly a prayer than a possession. Moreover, the fragile condition of sinful humanity has already been anticipated in God's decision to take on and redeem human flesh. God becomes one with human bodies in Christ not because humans are pure and innocent but largely because they are not.[20] The *anthropological* mystical body of Christ is a pure gift, not a reward for righteous conduct.

The Crucified Bodies of Mystics and Victims

De Lubac does not recognize the need for a decolonial shift in Christian theology. But I have argued that the beginnings of such a shift are possible to achieve through a critical and constructive reading of his *Corpus Mysticum* and *The Mystery of the Supernatural*. But only the beginnings. Perceiving every body as a Christic body is one step, rooted in the incarnation. A second step leads to the cross and to a reflection on crucified bodies and crucified peoples, which de Lubac does not develop. First, I shall discuss two medieval Christian women, Catherine of Siena and Julian of Norwich, who establish as traditional doctrine something like the following claim: The suffering body offers a privileged site of intimacy and oneness with Christ. These mystics, or perhaps it would be better to refer to them merely as theologians,[21] teach that experiences of anguish in one's flesh bring one closer to the God who reveals the most intense depths of divine love not merely by becoming flesh but by enduring the visceral and psychological experiences of passion and death.

I want to make explicit, and moreover to investigate, the linkages between this tradition of mystical cruciformity and the more recent series of conversations about crucified bodies and crucified peoples that have appeared in the writings of Ellacuría, Cone, and Copeland, among others. The victims of colonial modernity may not all be Christian mystics, but a theology illuminated by Christian mysticism can perceive in the corporeal suffering of these countless victims the mystical body of Christ hanging battered and bleeding from the cross. Although fraught with perils—for instance, risks of glorifying suffering and weakening the will to resist—I submit that this cruciform interpretation of the mystical body of Christ has liberative potential if it is understood to cherish precisely the bodies that suffer (not the suffering itself) and if it includes a clear awareness that the crucifixion of human flesh is an evil that should not be.

In *The Dialogue* of Catherine of Siena, "eternal Truth" speaks to her in words that suggest that suffering is a privileged context for unity with Christ. For instance, this divine voice says:

> The world makes sport of heaping insults upon me, and you will be saddened in the world when you see them insult me. For when they offend me they offend you, and when they offend you they offend me, since I have become one thing with you. . . . The world has no likeness to me, so it persecuted my only begotten Son even to the shameful death of the cross, and so it persecutes you. Because it has no love for me, the world persecutes you and will persecute you even to the point of death; for if the world had loved me, it would love you as well.[22]

In this passage it becomes clear that the suffering of the Son is one with the suffering of Catherine. Disrespect and violence against either party amount to the same offense. In either instance, we have the same refusal to love, the same act of hatred, and even in some sense the same victim. Catherine may attribute this union with Christ to the fact that she belongs to "the Mystic Body of Holy Church,"[23] but we also find God explaining to her that "I united my nature with you, hiding it in your humanity,"[24] suggesting the possibility of an anthropological interpretation of the mystical body of Christ even in her work.

But more apposite at this point in the present argument is a consideration of cruciform suffering as the site, and perhaps evidence, of such union. On the one hand, we may welcome the idea that any violation of a human body, such as Catherine's, would be, according to her understanding of Christian faith, a direct violation of the God who is humanly embodied in Christ. Every body may be recognized as a mystical body of Christ, but according to this divine discourse the body in pain deserves a special kind of attention insofar as it is united with Christ in his passion. From this claim, one might develop an ethically powerful understanding of God's "preferential option" for victims. God chooses in a particular way to be one with them.

Consider the difference between this message of compassion, spoken directly by God, and the sorts of messages given by Christian missionaries to the victimized natives of colonial Hispaniola—such as the noble Hatuey who was instead told by a friar, before being burned at the stake, that he must believe in Christ or go to hell.[25] The doctrine that Christ takes into himself and radically identifies with each and every wounded body (a doctrine central to Catherine's theology) enables Christian theologians today to rediscover the true meaning of the gospel and rescue it from such violent distortion. Christ is present in the victims of history, and if he condemns anyone it would most assuredly be those who falsely use the memory of his name as a pretext to harm or destroy the bodies of others.

On the other hand, there are aspects of *The Dialogue*'s treatment of suffering from which Christian theologians may now want to distance themselves. For instance, the divine utterance received by Catherine that states that "the more you bear, the more you show your love for me"[26] could easily be used to encourage an active pursuit of suffering as a way to draw closer to Christ and, similarly, discourage any effort to resist or overcome unjust suffering that is imposed upon one. Catherine's divine interlocutor does mitigate this danger to some extent by clarifying that "I want works of penance and other bodily practices to be undertaken as means, not as your chief goal."[27] That is, an ascetical welcoming of suffering should happen, not for its own sake, but only insofar as it helps to open one to the infinite love of God and thereby prepares one to share this love better with one's neighbors through compassionate actions and intercessory prayers. This clarification ameliorates, but perhaps does not wholly remove, the risks.

Similar points can be made about Julian's theology. At the beginning of the "Long Text" of her *Showings*, she expresses a desire for both a "bodily sight, in which I might have more knowledge of our savior's bodily pains" and a "bodily sickness . . . so severe that it might seem mortal."[28] Both wishes are granted. So ill as to be on the verge of death, she is simultaneously immersed in a multistaged visionary experience of Christ's suffering body. She sees the blood from the crown of thorns, the discoloration of skin, the lacerations, the dryness and fragmentation of the flesh. She writes: "Here I saw a great unity between Christ and us, as I understand it; for when he was in pain we were in pain, and all creatures able to suffer pain suffered with him."[29] Notably, she does not limit the potential to be united with God in the suffering of Christ only to members of the church; she does not even limit this potential to humans. She recognizes divine anguish in "all creatures able to suffer pain."[30] Like *The Dialogue*, *Showings* empowers Christians to turn with special attention to every suffering body and perceive therein the God who loves human flesh so much as to enter into its most terrifying and agonizing experiences. Yet once again, also like *The Dialogue*, *Showings* may (if not carefully interpreted to avoid this possibility) seem to put suffering on a spiritual pedestal that valorizes it as a desirable and ennobling instrument of divine union. The traditional doctrine of mystical cruciformity, whether in Catherine or Julian, therefore does not unambiguously support contemporary efforts to combat suffering's many unjust historical appearances.

Nevertheless, recent theological works by Ellacuría, Cone, and Copeland contribute significantly to the disambiguation of mystical cruciformity. The key text by Ellacuría in this regard is "The Crucified People." Here he argues that "salvation . . . cannot be made exclusively a matter of the mystical fruits of Jesus' death, separating it from his real and verifiable behavior."[31] Informed by modern biblical criticism and Ignatian spirituality, Ellacuría traces both the historical reasons and the theological meaning of Jesus's crucifixion back to the way that he lived—namely, his proclamation and embodiment of the reign of God. The cross is a direct consequence of his uncompromising way of confronting evil in service of God's reign. Unlike Catherine and Julian, Ellacuría does not isolate the crucifixion as a moment of profound mystical oneness with Christ but rather historicizes the event, stressing its inseparability from Jesus's, the church's, and humanity's socially prophetic action. There are indications of this social action in Julian and especially Catherine, but in Ellacuría it is much more pronounced.

Yet Ellacuría's historicizing critique of a mystical fixation on the cross does not make him de-emphasize the cross or the Christian call to participate in it. On the contrary, he is very critical of any theology that would direct its attention almost exclusively toward creation and resurrection in order to avoid dealing with the negativity of the crucifixion. He considers such cross-marginalizing interpretations of Christianity to be "even more dangerous."[32]

For Ellacuría, the cross is mainly significant as an outcome of Jesus's particular way of life, which Christians are called to follow now. But the cross is also for this very reason highly significant. To be united with Christ in his way of life one must be willing to remain with him and to follow him (if circumstances demand) even to the sort of scandalously violent death that his confrontational sort of life is likely to provoke. Archbishop Oscar Romero and the other martyrs of El Salvador, including eventually Ellacuría himself, testify to this cruciform character of true Christian discipleship with their blood.

Ellacuría insists that the question for Christians now must be "who continues to carry out in history what his [Jesus's] life and death was about."[33] Significantly, Ellacuría does not answer this question here by mentioning martyrs or other saintly witnesses to Christ. His answer, instead, is the "crucified people" as a whole, by which he means "that collective body that, being the majority of humanity, owes its situation of crucifixion to a social order organized and maintained by a minority that exercises its dominion through a series of factors, which, taken together and given their concrete impact within history, must be regarded as sin."[34] This victimized "majority of humanity" (many of whom are certainly not Christian in any explicit sense), this wounded population in which one might include the conquered, the enslaved, and their numerous descendants, this immeasurable "collective body" is for Ellacuría the most important continuation of Christ's life and death in the present age. Without using the expression, Ellacuría gestures here toward the idea that these victims should be perceived as a decisive manifestation of the mystical body of Christ. This title is appropriate not only because they are victims but also because "the Lord" praised by the Suffering Servant songs of Second Isaiah is embodied in this modern crucified people as a loving and liberating presence. Ellacuría claims: "It is the Lord himself who adopts this condition. God takes our crimes on himself."[35]

Reading this text in continuity with Christian mystical theologians such as Catherine and Julian is helpful because such a reading draws out the theocentric nature of the doctrine of the crucified people. Ellacuría's focus on structural similarities between characteristics of the Suffering Servant and the crucified people may not sufficiently stress the theologically essential point (which he does acknowledge in passing) that the Christological status of this people is established not merely by formal comparison (i.e., as an abstract analogy) but by a free decision on God's part to enter compassionately into human corporeality and suffering. To honor victims with the title of "crucified people" is to recognize the living presence of the crucified Christ in their midst. At the same time, Ellacuría develops the core insight of traditional mystical cruciformity—namely, that Christ is one with the afflicted—in critically important ways by tethering it, on the one hand, to the practice of actively following Jesus's prophetic, reign-centered life and, on the other hand, to the collective and physical bodies of victims worldwide, whether or not they be in the church. Christian theology needs no longer be hampered by the threats of idealized suffering and political passivity. Instead, Ellacuría enables one to reconceive Christian theology through the decolonially efficacious affirmations of martyrial discipleship and the divinely united bodies of those who unjustly suffer. Christ is present in both.

Cone makes a comparable contribution in *The Cross and the Lynching Tree*.[36] At the opening of the fourth chapter (a chapter that on its own must be considered a stunning breakthrough in black theological aesthetics), he observes that "many black poets, novelists, painters, dramatists, and other artists saw clearly what white theologians and clergy ignored and what black religious scholars and ministers merely alluded to: that in the United States, the clearest image of the crucified Christ was the figure of an innocent black victim, dangling from a lynching tree." He quotes several poems worth remembering. Countee Cullen's "Christ Recrucified" offers the haunting lines: "The South is crucifying Christ again" and "Christ's awful wrong is that he's dark of hue." Lorraine Hansberry's "Lynchsong" sings the pain-fractured verses "Laurel:/Name sweet like the breath of peace/Blood and blood/Hatred there/White robes and/Black robes/And a burning/burning cross." And Langston Hughes's "Christ in Alabama" cries: "Christ is a nigger,/Beaten and black—/*Oh, bare your back*" and "Most holy bastard/Of the bleeding mouth,/*Nigger Christ/On the cross of the South*."[37]

These poems clarify what it means to call God black and, moreover, why Cone was compelled to do so. God is none other than the ever-faithful one who enters history in the incarnate and crucified Christ. In continuity with such perceptive black artists, Cone stresses that this event of divine entrance into the corporeal condition of human suffering is not merely a happening in the past, confined to some other context that does not concern people today, but rather a thoroughly self-implicating doctrine about who God is in every era and situation, including the present. In the midst of the US society's ongoing brutalization of black bodies precisely as black, God is assuredly black. This means: God is there in darkly hued crucified bodies. Billie Holiday's "strange fruit hanging from the poplar trees" is paschal Christology hidden in the at once bodily and "soulful" practice of the blues.[38]

Like Ellacuría, Cone acknowledges dangers in some Christian ways of embracing the cross as a privileged site of unity with Christ, dangers that we have seen in Catherine and Julian. In agreement with Delores Williams and other womanist critics of redemptive suffering, he states clearly: "I find nothing redemptive about suffering in itself." He sees suffering, especially born of the history of racism, as an evil, indeed as a sign of idolatry. "But," he continues, "in the end I am in closer agreement with other womanist theologians like Shawn Copeland, . . . JoAnne Terrell, . . . and Jacquelyn

Grant, . . . who view the cross as central to Christian faith, especially in African American communities."[39] The cross is central for Cone's theology because it enables him to identify the real presence of Christ in the victims of white oppression and because, as Ellacuría argues and embodies in his own way, it inspires courageous martyrial action for the sake of liberation. Cone writes beautifully about this latter point in his chapter on Martin Luther King Jr.[40] Ultimately, there are good reasons to read Cone's black theology as a decolonial development and refinement of the Christian tradition of mystical cruciformity—*decolonial* because slave labor and its enduring aftermath, which Cone resists theologically, are constitutive features of colonial and neocolonial America; *mystical cruciformity* because he sees the broken body of Christ on the lynching tree.

Finally, I would like to turn to Copeland, who, in *Enfleshing Freedom* and other works, contributes to the sort of decolonial re-visioning of the mystical body of Christ crucified that I have already attempted to elucidate in Ellacuría and Cone. After lamenting Christians' all-too-common forgetfulness of the victims of history, she writes: "But there is one who does not forget—Jesus of Nazareth, who is the Christ of God. He does not forget poor, dark, and despised bodies. For these, for all, for us, he gave his body in fidelity to the *basileia tou theou*, the reign of God, which opposes the reign of sin. Jesus of Nazareth is the paradigm of enfleshing freedom: he is freedom enfleshed."[41] Jesus's memory of suffering bodies and his giving of his body for them culminates in an act of welcoming into his body. Copeland argues that "the only body capable of taking us *all* in as we are with all our different body marks—certainly including the mark of homosexuality—is the body of Christ." The "marks" that distinguish "our red, brown, yellow, white, and black bodies—our homosexual and heterosexual bodies, our HIV/AIDS infected bodies, our starving bodies, our prostituted bodies, our yearning bodies, our ill and infirm bodies, our young and old and joyous bodies" become through the saving praxis of the reign *Christ's own body marks*.[42]

In passages such as these, we see Copeland articulating a theological anthropology and mystical cruciformity centered in the enfleshing and enfleshed freedom of Jesus. Like Ellacuría's, Copeland's Christology highlights Jesus's reign-oriented life and also the crucifixion that results from such a life. Moreover, with Cone and the black poetic tradition he cites, Copeland sees the cross *in* the lynching tree.[43] Like him, too, she does not thereby glorify suffering. On the contrary, she argues that "the cross of Jesus of Nazareth demonstrates, at once, the redemptive potential of love and the power of evil and hatred."[44] It is love, not suffering, that redeems, and the crucifixion itself is a clear evil. The love of God for the bodies of those who suffer is simply so great that Christ forever enters solidaristically into their suffering.

Like de Lubac, Copeland associates the mystical body of Christ with his real presence in the Eucharist and the church.[45] At the same time, she enacts a decolonially relevant expansion of the concept of the mystical body of Christ by associating it with the endlessly pluriform corporeality of human existence and in a very special way with the bodies of those bearing the weight of the world's suffering. This more expansive vantage point enables her to reappraise the significance of the Eucharist and the church. In effect, these two interdependent and vital Christian institutions must manifest and verify their God-given identities as mystical bodies of Christ by cultivating in themselves—more precisely, as their very Christological essence—an explicit and active solidarity with all human bodies, and especially the most despised bodies, which Christ freely and lovingly claims as his very own flesh.[46] The mystical corporeality of the Eucharist and the church is thus, in a very real sense, *contingent* on the solidaristic attention they give to all bodily forms, including extra-ecclesial and not explicitly sacramental forms, of human and crucified existence.

Beloved Flesh

Thus far, I have proposed theological anthropology and mystical cruciformity as two decolonially significant and doctrinally sound ways to interpret the mystical body of Christ. At this point, it would be possible to develop the argument in various directions to continue decolonizing the theme of the mystical body of Christ and Christian theology more broadly. For instance, one might reflect on the practical stakes of Christian hope in the resurrection of the body, as Ellacuría begins to do at the end of his essay on the crucified people.[47] One might rethink the central contention of this paper from a pneumatological perspective: What decolonial significance might there be in the perception of the human body as a temple of the Holy Spirit?[48] One might bring in numerous sources from scripture, tradition, and various contemporary contexts to refine or adjust the argument in this way or that. All of this would be possible and worthwhile.

In the small space that remains, however, I want to take up a different task. In short, I want to consider what might be added to the preceding anthropological and cruciform interpretations of the mystical body of Christ by an alternative way of imagining the same divine-and-human corporeal relationship through an emphasis on its amorous quality. Is there any decolonial significance in the depiction of God and humanity as lovers becoming one flesh? I contend that this imagery makes at least two very important contributions. First, it proclaims the loveliness of the human body as seen and held by God, in opposition to the hurtful aesthetic regimes of colonial modernity. Second, it insists that union is ultimately a composition of two freedoms and, therefore, impossible without genuine consent.

Copeland quotes a scene from Toni Morrison's *Beloved*. The character Baby Suggs is preaching in the clearing to a community of the formerly enslaved, declaring with bold and insistent words: "Yonder they do not love your flesh. They despise it. They don't love [it]. *You* got to love it, *you*! This is flesh I'm talking about here. Flesh that needs to be loved."[49] The good news that Christian theology is supposed to clarify, if possible, is that flesh is already loved, and with an infinite love. That is the mystery of the triune God in history. Christian theology interprets corporeal life—including not only the body of the Christian but also, as we have seen, all other human bodies and especially the bodies of the crucified—as Christic in a rather strong sense. The open question that I want to reflect on here is how to understand this Christic union of God and human flesh as an act of love.

One possibility is to stress compassion. Christ suffers with those who suffer. That is certainly an act of compassionate love. But Christian theology also speaks of a divine eros, which unifies through an intimacy born of mutual desire, attraction, and fulfillment. God's love, perhaps especially as experienced by the mystics, is not only compassionate, that is, solidaristic in pain. It is also passionate: pressing longingly toward union with the beautiful. In other words, the love that leads God to indwell human bodies is not defined merely by a crushing, self-sacrificial commitment to endure whatever may befall them; it also involves a spontaneous and lasting affection for these bodies, which celebrates them and seeks to glorify them in their highly diverse, richly colored, delicately textured, and unrepeatably featured phenomenality. Having created them, God sees and loves them, desperate for every fine detail that composes them. And what is the beautiful if not that which appears lovely in God's eyes? We humans are the only ones who would dare to consider any bodies (including, perhaps, our own) hideous. God, by contrast, is madly enamored with them. This is the amorous answer to Anselm's classic theological question, *cur Deus homo*? My claim is that it has untapped decolonial potential.

To accent this aspect of divine love, Christian theology makes metaphorical and allegorical use of sexual and nuptial imagery, speaking often of Christ as bridegroom and the soul as bride. Its sources have been courtly love literature and the biblical love poetry of *The Song of Songs*. To be sure, Christian theologians cannot afford to interpret the mystical eroticism of the Christian tradition any longer without reflecting critically on the patriarchal and heteronormative constructions of gender that it expresses, the ways that particular bodies and kinds of bodies have been devalued, the ways that certain notions of masculinity have been taken as most representative of the divine, the ways that gender binaries have been broken down and new possibilities of language and practice opened up, the ways that sex and certain regulated abstentions from it have become vehicles of power (for better or worse), and countless other complicating factors. To account for all of this, an entire history of sexuality would need to be developed in close relation to the history of theology, a task lying far beyond the scope of the present argument.[50] Nevertheless, presupposing the need for such critical awareness, I want to focus on what can be positively retrieved from this highly ambiguous history.

I have already hinted at the first point: The love poetry of the Christian tradition ought to encourage Christian theologians to appreciate the divinely beloved beauty of every body, regardless of religion, race, sex, gender, sexuality, size, age, ability, and so on. In this regard, it supplements the all-inclusive anthropological reading of the mystical body of Christ given above. The idea that God sees and loves the beauty of all flesh disrupts certain harmful mass-marketed regimes of contemporary aesthetics, such as those prizing whiteness, thinness, and "normalcy" of various kinds, which many people unthinkingly assume as a basis for critical judgment against supposed bodily deviations.[51] Coloniality functions aesthetically. It distributes power by determining which sorts of bodies are valued in what ways, how they are used and represented, how they are seen and touched and experienced. As Alejandro Vallega argues, there is a need for a liberative decolonial aesthetics to counteract such colonial or neocolonial forms.[52] In theological terms, such a decolonial aesthetics begins with the conviction that God loves human flesh without exception and without any of the typical consumer-driven hierarchizations that distort modern conceptions of beauty.

The second point is that God makes human bodies to be free. Any union of love presupposes such freedom. By contrast, this enfleshed freedom is precisely what colonial regimes of power have refused to acknowledge and often sought to destroy. As Copeland and Andrea Smith demonstrate, violence against the victims of colonial modernity, particularly indigenous and enslaved women, was often of an explicitly sexual nature. It was rape and worse: brutal beatings, murder, and genocide connected to sexual exploitation.[53] Margaret Farley persuasively shows that a just sexual relationship requires mutuality, consent, and above all a fundamental respect for the concrete reality and freedom of the other.[54] Reimagining God through the lens of this sort of just eroticism could allow the Christian imagination to contribute to the healing of deep personal and cultural wounds related to profound sexual violations at the roots of this colonial epoch. While deadly idols of power and wealth have been venerated through the sexually violent sacrifice of female, black, and indigenous bodies, the God of love desires only that these bodies become and remain free—free to love whomever they will and free to be loved and respected in their irreplaceable singularity.

Within a decolonized Christian theology, the doctrine of the mystical body of Christ, which left to itself may seem too theocentric—that is, too passive and quietist—is helpfully supplemented by the idea of *two* bodies *voluntarily* agreeing to become one flesh. God's desire for this union is passionate and relentless, to be sure. The cross shows the shocking extents to which God is willing to go in an effort to win human affection. Nevertheless, the potential human partner may, if she or he chooses, refuse the incessant divine call to spousal levels of intimacy and commitment. One who is united to Christ mystically by virtue of the incarnation, even by virtue of Jesus's willing entrance into human anguish, may very readily withhold an affirmative response to these most zealous of divine pleas, and any God who is really just and loving will respect that decision. This is one of the reasons why I wish to avoid an ersatz universalization of Christian faith as "anonymously" occurring everywhere even when any particular person denies it. Choices to return or not to return Christ's overtures of love (however extravagant these gestures become, however ontologically significant they may be) must be accepted as real choices. This seems, in fact, to be the key insight in Las Casas's approach to missiology, which compared to other alternatives at the time was much more humane and respectful of the freedom of the other.[55]

Yet because God is divine and not merely a human love partner, matters do become more complicated. To be sure, when talking about God, all images falter. God's love may also be represented as that of a parent, whether father or mother,[56] or as that of a friend. These traditional theological symbols give rise to different theoretical possibilities and challenges. Moreover, unlike ideal human relationships, the relationship between Creator and creature cannot be entirely equal or symmetrical. The *kenosis* of the Word into human flesh makes some genuine mutuality possible, but there remains, within the Christian tradition, an infinite asymmetry at the level of divine and human natures. Patriarchal theological uses of erotic and spousal imagery have harmfully presupposed that a male-female gender differentiation helps to express not only the loving but also the asymmetrical character of the divine-and-human relationship. I argue, on the contrary, that Christian theologians ought to treat any inevitable asymmetry in the divine-and-human relationship as a *radical departure* from the egalitarian logic implied by the image of a just and loving sexual relationship, as analyzed by Farley. In accord with Elizabeth Johnson, I contend that the divine essence is beyond gender, not definitionally masculine; moreover, God is always greater than any human partner because God is infinite, not because of any gender specification on either side of the relationship.[57]

Whatever limitations and perils remain in this sort of amorous symbolism, it does offer an opportunity to contemplate the idea that God intensely loves my body and its freedom, not out of some abstract duty but because of its inestimable loveliness. This idea may be a powerful and life-restoring thought for anyone whose body has been abused and discarded as trash, declared ugly and therefore unlovable, or made to feel worthless in any way, including through an impersonal exotification of the flesh that replaces intimacy with objectification or through the grisly realities of sex slavery and sex trafficking.[58] The idea that the eyes, the ears, the teeth, the nose, the lips, the neck, the cheeks, the hair, the chest, the stomach, the navel, the fingers, the legs, and the feet that are mine—that phenomenalize me uniquely in this world of shared flesh—are so dear and precious that God would long to be one with them is a liberating message, if Christian theologians only carefully receive it as such.

Jean-Louis Chrétien's *Symbolique du corps: La tradition chrétienne du "Cantique des Cantiques"* unveils God's tender love for each of these body parts.[59] Jacques Derrida has, in a way, suggested a preference for Jean-Luc Nancy's phenomenology of the body over Chrétien's.[60] I, however, see the deeply mystical and theological character of Chrétien's phenomenology of the body to be a major advantage. Baby Suggs is right that the oppressed must love their bodies in defiance against those "yonder" who do not love them, but it would help, I suspect, to have at least at some point heard the thought that the Creator loves them in such a radical way as to want to be near and with them, to glorify them in their endless unnoticed minutiae (the numbered hairs on the head of Luke 12:7), and to keep and hold and cherish them for all eternity. Christian faith is the new life of relational freedom that results from continual consent to this possibility.

Conclusion

In this essay, I have sought to pluralize the meaning of the mystical body of Christ. Without dismissing the prevalent ecclesiological sense of the term or breaking with the central tenets of the Catholic tradition, I have emphasized the Christian theological possibility and decolonial significance of anthropological and cruciform interpretations, which invite Christians to contemplate the presence of Christ in every human body and particularly in the bodies of victims. Through Christ, God enters into and unites with human beings (and, indeed, all creatures) in their physical vulnerability, even in their suffering and death. This is a supreme act of divine love, which responds to the beauty and respects the freedom that make each of us uniquely who we are. Though often despised and exploited in this neocolonial world, flesh is beloved by God. This is the true gospel message. To underscore this point, I found it helpful to supplement the discussion of anthropological and cruciform interpretations of the mystical body of Christ with a critical retrieval of the amorous imagery in the Christian tradition of two becoming one flesh. We are faced here with an astounding mystery that demands multiple images and vantage points and that ultimately surpasses them all. The body is no lamentable prison of the soul (as crude philosophical dualism would have it); nor is it a mere product of ambiguous force relations (as in the more reductive versions of poststructuralist theory). The captains of colonial modernity who would like to give it some value on the market or dispose of it as though it were valueless gravely misunderstand it. The body is the gift, the dwelling place, and the desire of God.

NOTES

1. Pius XII, *Mystici corporis Christi*, encyclical letter, Vatican website, June 29, 1943, http://w2.vatican.va/content/pius-xii/en/encyclicals /documents/hf_p-xii_enc_29061943_mystici-corporis-christi.html; and Pope Paul VI, *Lumen gentium*, encyclical letter, Vatican website, November 21, 1964, http://www.vatican.va/archive/hist_councils/ii_vatican_council /documents/vat-ii_const_19641121_lumen-gentium_en.html.

2. See Henri de Lubac, *Corpus Mysticum: The Eucharist and the Church in the Middle Ages*, trans. Gemma Simmonds, C.J., with Richard Price and Christopher Stephens (Notre Dame, Ind.: University of Notre Dame Press, 2006).

3. See Beverly Lanzetta, *Radical Wisdom: A Feminist Mystical Theology* (Minneapolis: Fortress, 2005), 155–73.

4. See Walter D. Mignolo and Arturo Escobar, eds., *Globalization and the Decolonial Option* (New York: Routledge, 2013); Ada María Isasi-Díaz and Eduardo Mendieta, eds., *Decolonizing Epistemologies: Latino/a Philosophy and Theology* (New York: Fordham University Press, 2012); and Sylvia Wynter, "Unsettling the Coloniality of Being/Power/Truth/Freedom: Towards the Human, after Man, Its Overrepresentation—An Argument," *CR: The New Centennial Review* 3, no. 3 (Fall 2003).

5. Pius XII, *Mystici corporis Christi*, section 3.

6. See Wynter, "Unsettling the Coloniality of Being/Power/Truth/Freedom," 262–63.

7. Pope Paul VI, *Lumen gentium*, 6.

8. See, among many texts, Hans Urs von Balthasar, *Theo-Drama: Theological Dramatic Theory*, vol. 5, *The Last Act*, trans. Graham Harrison (San Francisco: Ignatius, 1998).

9. See Linn Marie Tonstad, "Sexual Difference and Trinitarian Death: Cross, Kenosis, and Hierarchy in the *Theo-Drama*," *Modern Theology* 26, no. 4 (October 2010); and Elizabeth T. Vasko, "The Difference Gender Makes: Nuptiality, Analogy, and the Limits of Appropriating Hans Urs von Balthasar's Theology in the Context of Sexual Violence," *Journal of Religion* 94, no. 4 (October 2014).

10. Bartolomé de Las Casas, "Are Not the Indians Men?," in *Witness: The Writings of Bartolomé de Las Casas*, ed. and trans. George Sanderlin (Maryknoll, N.Y.: Orbis, 1992), 67.

11. De Lubac, *Corpus Mysticum*, 261, quoting Rupert of Deutz, *Liber de divinis officiis*, ed. Rabanus Haacke, Corpus christianorum continuation medievalis 7 (Turnhout, Belgium: Brepols, 1967).

12. De Lubac, *Corpus Mysticum*, 252.

13. See the classic treatment of this issue by Athanasius in *On the Incarnation*, trans. John Behr (Yonkers, N.Y.: St. Vladimir's Press, 1996), ch. 2.

14. Willie James Jennings shows that dehumanizing distortions of Christian imagination lie at the origins of colonial modernity in his *The Christian Imagination: Theology and the Origins of Race* (New Haven, Conn.: Yale University Press, 2010).

15. See Edward Schillebeeckx, *Christ: The Experience of Jesus as Lord*, trans. John Bowden (New York: Crossroad, 1981), 733–43; and Johannes Morsink, *The Universal Declaration of Human Rights: Origins, Drafting, and Intent* (Philadelphia: University of Pennsylvania Press, 1999).

16. But see the notable proposal by Mary Catherine Hilkert in "The Threatened Humanum as *Imago Dei*: Anthropology and Christian Ethics," in *Edward Schillebeeckx and Contemporary Theology*, ed. Lieven Boeve, Frederick Depoortere, and Stephan van Erp (New York: T&T Clark, 2010).

17. Henri De Lubac, *The Mystery of the Supernatural*, trans. Rosemary Sheed (New York: Crossroad, 1998), 76, 179.

18. De Lubac, *Mystery of the Supernatural*, 238.

19. See Karl Rahner, "Anonymous Christianity and the Missionary Task of the Church," in *Theological Investigations*, vol. 12, trans. David Bourke (New York: Seabury, 1974).

20. See Athanasius, *On the Incarnation*, ch. 2; and Thomas Aquinas, *The Summa Theologia*, trans. Fathers of the English Dominican Province (New York: Benzinger Bros., 1948), tertia pars, q. 1, a. 3.

21. As in Denys Turner, *Julian of Norwich: Theologian* (New Haven, Conn.: Yale University Press, 2011); and Elizabeth A. Dreyer, *Accidental Theologians: Four Women Who Shaped Christianity* (Cincinnati: Franciscan Media, 2014).

22. Catherine of Siena, *The Dialogue*, trans. Suzanne Noffke, O.P. (Mahwah, N.J.: Paulist, 1980), sec. 12, p. 46.

23. Catherine of Siena, *Dialogue*, sec. 110, p. 205.

24. Catherine of Siena, sec. 12, p. 46.

25. Bartolomé de Las Casas, "A 'Very Brief Account' of Spanish Cruelty," in *Witness: The Writings of Bartolomé de Las Casas*, ed. and trans. George Sanderlin (Maryknoll, N.Y.: Orbis, 1992), 147.

26. Catherine of Siena, *Dialogue*, sec. 5, p. 33.

27. Catherine of Siena, sec. 11, p. 43.

28. Julian of Norwich, *Showings*, trans. Edmund Colledge, O.S.A., and James Walsh, S.J. (Mahwah, N.J.: Paulist, 1978), "Long Text," ch. 2, p. 178.

29. Julian of Norwich, *Showings*, "Long Text," ch. 18, p. 210.

30. One might find an affinity here between Julian's thought and ecoliberationist theology, such as Leonardo Boff, *The Cry of the Earth, the Cry of the Poor*, trans. Philip Berryman (Maryknoll, N.Y.: Orbis, 1997).

31. Ignacio Ellacuría, "The Crucified People: An Essay in Historical Soteriology," in *Ignacio Ellacuría: Essays on History, Liberation, and Salvation*, trans. and ed. Michael E. Lee (Maryknoll, N.Y.: Orbis, 2013), 207.

32. Ellacuría, "Crucified People," 201.

33. Ellacuría, 208.

34. Ellacuría, 208.

35. Ellacuría, 217.

36. James Cone cites Ellacuría's discussion of the "crucified people" in *The Cross and the Lynching Tree* (Maryknoll, N.Y.: Orbis, 2011), xiv. See also my "Hearing the Cries of Crucified Peoples: Ignacio Ellacuría and James Cone," in *Witnessing: Prophecy, Politics, and Wisdom*, ed. Maria Clara Bingemer and Peter Casarella (Maryknoll, N.Y.: Orbis, 2014).

37. Cone, *Cross and the Lynching Tree*, 93, 111, 114.

38. Cone, 134. Would not the use of "soul" within Christian theology function more meaningfully if textured by the soulfulness of black life? I take this soulfulness to be nothing other than a deepening of connection with the communally experienced rhythms of the body, in its sorrows and its joys, often (not always) in explicit recognition of bodily intimacy with God.

39. Cone, 150.

40. Cone, 65.

41. M. Shawn Copeland, *Enfleshing Freedom: Body, Race, and Being* (Minneapolis: Fortress Press, 2009), 53.

42. Copeland, *Enfleshing Freedom*, 83.

43. Copeland, 121.

44. Copeland, 124.

45. Copeland, 81, 109.

46. On this point, see also M. Shawn Copeland, "The New Anthropological Subject at the Heart of the Mystical Body of Christ," *CTSA Proceedings* 53 (1998). If the new *anthropological* subject is poor, despised women of color, the *theological* subject is arguably the same God who became flesh out of love. The mystical body of Christ is the hidden, historical unity of these two.

47. Ellacuría, "Crucified People," 224.

48. Flannery O'Connor's eucharistic meditation on intersex embodiment in "A Temple of the Holy Ghost" could be an interesting source for such reflection. See O'Connor, *The Complete Stories* (New York: Farrar, Straus, and Giroux, 1971), 236–48.

49. Copeland, *Enfleshing Freedom*, 52.

50. See, among many sources, Sarah Coakley, *The New Asceticism: Sexuality, Gender, and the Quest for God* (New York: Bloomsbury, 2015); Grace M. Jantzen, *Power, Gender, and Christian Mysticism* (New York: Cambridge University Press, 1995); Amy Hollywood, *The Soul as Virgin Wife: Mechthild of Magdeburg, Marguerite Porete, and Meister Eckhart* (Notre Dame, Ind.: University of Notre Dame Press, 1995); and Mark D. Jordan, *Convulsing Bodies: Religion and Resistance in Foucault* (Stanford, Calif.: Stanford University Press, 2015).

51. See Lisa Isherwood, *The Fat Jesus: Christianity and Body Image* (New York: Seabury, 2008); Monique Roelofs, "Racialization as an Aesthetic Production: What Does the Aesthetic Do for Whiteness and Blackness and Vice Versa," in *White on White, Black on Black*, ed. George Yancy (Lanham, Md.: Rowman & Littlefield, 2005); and Lennard J. Davis, *Enforcing Normalcy: Disability, Deafness, and the Body* (New York: Verso, 1995).

52. Alejandro A. Vallega, *Latin American Philosophy from Identity to Radical Exteriority* (Bloomington: Indiana University Press, 2014), 196–218.

53. See M. Shawn Copeland, "Wading through Many Sorrows," in *A Troubling in My Soul: Womanist Perspectives on Evil and Suffering*, ed. Emilie M. Townes (Maryknoll, N.Y.: Orbis, 1993); and Andrea Smith, *Conquest: Sexual Violence and American Indian Genocide* (Durham, N.C.: Duke University Press, 2015).

54. See Margaret A. Farley, *Just Love: A Framework for Christian Sexual Ethics* (New York: Continuum, 2006).

55. See de Las Casas, "The 'Only Method' of Converting the Indians," in *Witness: The Writings of Bartolomé de Las Casas*, ed. and trans. George Sanderlin (Maryknoll, N.Y.: Orbis, 1992).

56. As in Julian, *Showings*, "Long Text," chs. 58–60, pp. 293–99.

57. See Elizabeth A. Johnson, *She Who Is: The Mystery of God in Feminist Theological Discourse* (New York: Crossroad, 2007).

58. See Anne Dondapati Allen, "No Garlic, Please: We Are Indian: Reconstructing the De-eroticized Indian Woman," in *Off the Menu: Asian and Asian North American Women's Religion and Theology*, ed. Rita Nakashima Brock et al. (Louisville, Ky.: Westminster John Knox, 2007), 183–95; and Siddharth Kara, *Sex Trafficking: Inside the Business of Modern Slavery* (New York: Columbia University Press, 2009).

59. Jean-Louis Chrétien, *Symbolique du corps: La tradition chrétienne du "Cantique des Cantiques"* (Paris: Presses Universitaires de France, 2005).

60. Jacques Derrida, *On Touching—Jean-Luc Nancy*, trans. Christine Irizarray (Stanford, Calif.: Stanford University Press, 2005), 262.

CHAPTER 7

African Humanism: Between the Cosmic and the Terrestrial

Patrice Haynes

African religion is a kind of humanism.

—DOMINIQUE ZAHAN, *The Religion, Spirituality and Thought of Traditional Africa*

Man is the ideology of dehumanization.

—THEODOR ADORNO, *Jargon of Authenticity*

Preamble: African Humanism and Liberation

Modern African humanism emerged in response to the comprehensive dehumanization of black (i.e., sub-Saharan) Africans by Europeans who, since at least the fifteenth century, would fatefully bind the lives and experiences of Africans—including here the African diaspora—to the impact of that unholy trinity of racism, slavery, and colonialism. At the height of the trans-Atlantic slave trade, Europeans considered Africans devoid of reason, living solely in accordance with their bodily appetites and lacking moral sense. However, by the nineteenth century another perception of Africans gained prominence: benighted, heathen souls to be saved by the light of Christ. The modern missionary movement in Africa seemed to effect a reversal of the dehumanization of Africans insofar as those Africans who had converted to Christianity could be viewed as fellow brothers and sisters in Christ. Yet this reversal demanded a high price. The humanity of Africans could only be achieved by way of "a systematic program of de-Africanization"[1] delivered by European missionaries and the colonialist project more generally. The humanitarian impulse driving the expansion of missionary activity in Africa proclaimed an emancipatory universalism, yet behind such proclamations laid the idea of the human as European Man, rational, civilized, cosmopolitan, and white. Unsurprisingly, anticolonialist theorist Frantz Fanon claims that while Europeans endlessly broadcast their concern for human welfare, whether through missionary or commercial enterprises, "today we know with what sufferings humanity has paid for every one of their triumphs."[2] It was only by violently negating their "Africanness"—their languages, cultures, and religions—that Eurocentric humanism could admit the humanity of Africans.

The nationalist movements sweeping across the African continent in the late 1950s and 1960s were in no small part motivated by the desire to wrest back the humanity of Africans by way of a humanism that affirmed *African* ways of being. Indeed, a key driver toward winning independence from European colonialists would be the notion of a shared African identity. The Negritude movement, led by Léopold Sédar Senghor (Senegal), Aimé Césaire (Martinique), and Léon Damas (French Guiana) in the 1930s, sought to articulate this idea of a collective African identity (founded, rather controversially, on race as a biological concept), the recovery of which would be concomitant with the recovery of freedom from Western colonial powers. The quest for both a reclaimed African identity and the liberation of Africa would crystallize around the idea of an African humanism. Furthermore, for postwar African leaders enthused by Marxist politics—Kwame Nkrumah (Ghana), Julius K. Nyerere (Tanzania), Kenneth Kaunda (Zambia) and Negritude advocate Senghor—African humanism would become synonymous with African socialism.[3]

Importantly, for these figures humanism was not considered to be an alien doctrine illegitimately imported from Europe to Africa. Rather, it was understood as a principle implicitly underpinning precolonial African societies and cultures. As Senghor puts it, "We had achieved socialism [i.e., humanism] before the coming of the European."[4] Richard H. Bell explains that African humanism is fundamentally communal in character. Whereas Western humanism derived from the liberal tradition emphasizes individual freedom and rights, African humanism, Bell points out, "is rooted in traditional values of mutual respect for one's fellow kinsman and a sense of position and place in the larger order of things: one's *social* order, *natural* order, and the *cosmic* order. African humanism is rooted in *lived dependencies*."[5] The primacy of the communal in traditional African societies is famously expressed by Kenyan philosopher John S. Mbiti in his seminal work *African Religions and Philosophy*:

Only in terms of other people does the individual become conscious of his own being, his own duties, his privileges and responsibilities towards himself and towards other people. . . . The individual can only say: "I am, because we are; and since we are, therefore I am." This is a cardinal point in the understanding of the African view of man.[6]

Similarly, the South African term *Ubuntu* employed in the country's post-apartheid truth and reconciliation process is a word of Bantu origin that broadly means "respect for human dignity." Here the human is once again envisaged as fundamentally communal, a position captured by the proverb "A person is a person through other people" (in Zulu, "umuntu ngumuntu ngabanye").

For some African writers, African humanism promised a vision of the human that could inspire the world beyond Africa. According to Kaunda,

To a certain extent, we in Africa have always had a gift for enjoying Man for himself. It is at the heart of our traditional culture. . . . Let the West have its Technology and Asia its Mysticism! Africa's gift to world culture must be in the realm of Human Relationships. . . . The way things are going, Africa may be the last place where Man can still be Man.[7]

From the standpoint of the twenty-first century, such effusive praise for African humanism strikes a discordant note. Postcolonial Africa has seen black Africans assailed by deadly, often genocidal, civil wars in Nigeria, Liberia, Sierra Leone, the Democratic Republic of Congo, Sudan, and Rwanda, as well as the baleful consequences of global capitalism, corruption, ethnocentrism, the AIDS and Ebola epidemics, food insecurity, and climate change. The perturbing disconnect between the values espoused by African humanism and the reality of contemporary life for many black Africans requires careful scrutiny, not least because of the suspicion that African humanism, generally premised on an idealized precolonial African past, is no more than an ideology serving to bolster ethnocultural and political power struggles.[8] Constraints of space mean that I am unable to respond to this problem here. Instead, the focus of this essay is the legacy of African indigenous religions in shaping a contemporary African humanism. Whereas post-Enlightenment, Western humanism is predominantly framed in secular terms, African humanism and its vision of the human is, for the most part, thoroughly entwined with religion.[9]

Without wishing to homogenize the vast array of African indigenous religions, it is generally agreed by scholars that they are deeply humanistic in orientation. As Mbiti puts it, African religiosity concentrates "on earthly matters, with man at the centre of this religiosity."[10] Even more plainly, Dominique Zahan writes, "African religion is a kind of humanism."[11] In this essay I examine the anthropocentrism characteristic of African indigenous religions, highlighting how these seek to affirm the fleshly, embodied lives of humans in both their communal and individual aspects. Moreover, such an exploration of African anthropocentrism allows the emergence of a conception of the human foreclosed by what Sylvia Wynter calls "the doctrine of Man," whereby Euro-American man—the white, bourgeois, heterosexual, and purely rational man at the heart of Western modernity—is upheld as the paradigm human.[12] Concentrating on the indigenous religion of the Yorùbá (a people who now mainly inhabit the southwestern region of present-day Nigeria), I first outline the Yorùbá cosmic order as this provides the ontological coordinates for human life. I then go on to consider how best to understand the anthropocentrism evident in African indigenous religions. One way might be along Feuerbachian lines, whereby African indigenous religions are held to be a projection of African societal life and experiences. I am sympathetic to such a reading, particularly given Feuerbach's emphasis on human, fleshy sensuousness in response to Hegel's Absolute Idealism. Nevertheless, I will delineate the Eurocentric assumptions in Feuerbach's anthropological analysis of religion that are at odds with attempts to outwit the doctrine of Man. Following this critique of Feuerbach, I offer some preliminary reflections on what I call "animist humanism," an idea informed by both ritual studies and recent efforts to retrieve the term *animism* in ways that contest its unsavory association with early anthropologists who use it to denote "primitive" religions. I will contend that animist humanism suggests a religious anthropocentrism that eschews the divinization of Man and instead envisions the human as part of a cosmic matrix comprising ambiguous relations and forces by virtue of which human life may be enhanced (or impaired).[13]

Yorùbá Cosmology: An Outline

In outlining Yorùbá cosmology and religion, I am aware of making generalized claims about African indigenous religions based on a single religious tradition—in this case the Yorùbá, who are also a heterogeneous group. Nevertheless, I take my cue from those scholars who point out that there are certain recurring themes in indigenous African religions that make it reasonable to suppose that they share, to a greater or lesser extent, some key features.[14] The ensuing discussion on Yorùbá cosmology sketches a particular religious tradition that nevertheless illuminates features that grant a degree of coherence and determinateness to the diversity of indigenous West African religions.

The Yorùbá cosmos comprises two planes of existence: the visible plane (*ayé*) of material, tangible things and the invisible plane (*ọ̀run*) of heavenly or spiritual entities. Importantly, while these two planes are distinct from each other, their boundaries are permeable, enabling continuous interaction between the two. Thus, the Yorùbá cosmos is a holistic one—the visible and invisible planes constitute an integrated yet dynamic whole with mutual interplay between the forces and elements of both. The visible plane is the earthly world of humans, animals, plants, rivers, hills, etc. It also includes a subterranean level (*ilé*) wherein the dead dwell. Furthermore, this chthonic space is the realm of the earth deity who is revered as the source of life and regeneration. The invisible plane is the world of manifold spiritual powers and deities. This plane is typically described in terms of a hierarchical ordering of diverse spirit-beings. At the highest level is the Supreme Deity, Olódùmaré, a disembodied (therefore sexless) spirit who is "the source of being [*orise*], the owner and giver of life breath [*ẹlẹ̀mí*], and the most perfect and just."[15]

In addition to Olódùmaré there are at least 401[16] deities (*òrìṣà*) of varying status in the Yorùbá pantheon. These include three primordial deities who have always existed alongside Olódùmaré: Ọrunmila/Ifá, the god of wisdom and knowledge; Ọbàtálá/Òrìṣàńlà, the god of moral purity; and Eṣu, the trickster god who maintains cosmic order and balance. There are also deified ancestors and personified natural phenomena such as the earth, rivers, and mountains. Each divinity governs a particular area of earthly life, but the ultimate source of their power is held to be Olódùmaré.[17]

The question of the relationship between the multitude of deities (òrìṣà) and the Supreme Deity Olódùmaré has provoked debates on whether the Yorùbá religion (and other African indigenous religions more widely) is best understood as polytheistic or as some sort of qualified monotheism.[18] So as to avoid shoehorning African indigenous religious thought into Western, philosophical, and theological categories such as "polytheism" and "monotheism," some recent authors have found A. Okechukwu Ogbonnaya's notion of "communotheism" instructive. This term emphasizes the significance of relationship and community in the heavenly realm such that notions of "supremacy" and "hierarchy" are inapt.[19]

A further class of spirit-beings in the invisible plane are the ancestors (*ará-ọ̀run*). These are human beings who have died a "nonsorrowful

death" (i.e., died an elder, left progeny, and received a proper burial) that
ensures their transformation from a physical being living in the world
(*ayé*) to a spiritual being living in the realm of the dead (*ilé*). Notably, the
ancestors are not to be regarded simply as disincarnate humans. For the
transition to ancestorhood involves not only a change in ontological status from natural to supernatural being but also an elevated moral status
that lends ancestors a near divine-like status. For the Yorùbá, the ancestors are deemed spiritual moral guardians to their lineage, protecting
their descendants from various misfortunes and guiding them in the development of good character (*ìwà pẹ̀lẹ̀*). However, should the living neglect
their moral and ritual obligations, then the ancestors will cease protecting their lineage against the harms and tribulations of various evil states
and forces.

There are three salient and related points to highlight from the preceding comments. First, as Jacob Olupọna notes, for the Yorùbá "the living
and the ancestors depend upon one another for survival."[20] The living seek
assistance from the ancestors in order to elude, or at least withstand, ad-
versity. Vice versa, the ancestors rely on their earthly family to sustain their
vitality with offerings (in the form of libations) and sacrifices (the latter
being required if the cosmic order has been disrupted by a transgressive
act). Second, given the reciprocal relationship said to obtain between embodied human beings and spiritual ancestors, communication between the
two must be possible. The Yorùbá believe this occurs in a variety of ways,
most of which are forms of rituals. Finally, the ancestors may be considered ontologically liminal since they move fluidly between the spiritual and
the material, the human and the divine. E. Bolaji Idowu captures something of this when he writes,

> The deceased are truly members of the family on earth; but they are
> no longer of the same fleshly order as those who are still actually
> living in the flesh on earth. They are closely related to this world; but
> they are no longer ordinary mortals. . . . To some extent they are
> intermediaries between Deity or the divinities and their own children:
> this is a continuation of their earthly function.[21]

In this passage, Idowu places the accent on the extrahuman quality of the
ancestors. Yet Olupọna reminds us that, for the Yorùbá, ancestors are not
entirely divorced from corporeal life since they are believed to "drink, eat
and excrete" as humans do.[22]

The final group of entities populating the invisible plane is spirits. These
are indistinct forces and may be directed toward good or evil ends. A num-

ber of spirits are associated with natural phenomena like the earth, rivers, mountains, trees, and wind. Early anthropologists such as Edward Tylor would call religions that upheld beliefs in a spirit-infused nature "animism," which would stand in direct contrast with theism, the latter hailed as representing the highest form of religion. J. Ọmọṣade Awolalu argues that while there are some elements of animism in Yorùbá beliefs, "it would be wrong to call the whole religion animism."[23] However, as we will see later, I think that recent attempts to rehabilitate the concept of "animism," in ways that distance it from a Eurocentric anthropology, illuminate fresh perspectives on African cosmologies and its implications for thinking the human. In anticipation of the discussion in the final section of this essay, Graham Harvey explains that given sufficient revision, "animism labels those efforts to live well in a world that is a community of persons, most of whom are 'other-than-human' [e.g., natural objects, mythic characters, and things seen in dreams]."[24] Such an understanding of animism coheres with the holistic, relational ontology expressed by African cosmologies such as can be found in Yorùbá thought.

From the above overview of the Yorùbá cosmic order we can identify at least four of its key features. First, the underlying ontology is a holistic one. Although Yorùbá cosmology posits two planes—the invisible and the visible—these do not constitute a dualistic system but an integrated whole, with the invisible and the visible interpenetrating each other. Second, the Yorùbá cosmos is thoroughly relational; its plurality of spirits composes a web of relations that confound theological descriptions such as "theistic" or "polytheistic" (and even "pantheistic"). Third, given that spiritual power can be oriented toward life and flourishing or death and disintegration, the Yorùbá cosmos is a dynamic one. While the invisible and the visible planes can mutually enhance each other in ways conducive to life, there can be no evading death. The human hope is that death can be the right sort of death at the right time. Finally, the Yorùbá cosmos is shot through with the various personalities of deities, ancestors, spirits, and humans, giving it color and vibrancy, as well as enabling and impeding communication between the visible and the invisible planes.

On Making Gods

Traditional Yorùbá religiosity does not demand the disavowal of the body in the attempt to attain contemplative union with God. Rather, the focus is on the flourishing of communal (and, consequently, individual) life. As Olupọna puts it,

> African traditional religions typically strive for a *this-worldly salvation*—measured in terms of health, wealth, and offspring—while at the same time maintaining a close contact with the otherworldly realm of the ancestors, spirits, and gods who are seen as having a strong influence on the events and people in the here and now.[25]

The life that is of concern here is a *mortal* life, a vulnerable, carnal life: the "life of flesh."[26] Careful attention is paid to the invisible, spirit realm not for the glorification of God (or deities or the ancestors) as an end in itself, but to cultivate good relations with those invisible beings populating the cosmos so that embodied, human life may thrive. Yorùbá religiosity is, therefore, of a pragmatic, utilitarian nature. It is anthropocentric rather than theocentric. Okot p'Bitek cogently expresses this point when he writes of African indigenous religions, "Even the deities are there to serve the interests of men. The African deities are for man, and not man for them."[27]

Ghanaian philosopher Kwasi Wiredu explains that in African religious traditions deities are praised for the benefits they are expected to deliver. If these are not forthcoming then the deities in question will be held in contempt—indeed, devotees can withdraw their attention from a deity altogether, leaving it to languish "in fatal solitude."[28] Wiredu recounts how the Nigerian playwright Wole Soyinka once "startled an audience of African scholars at the University of Ghana when, in remarks enthusiastic of the Yorùbá 'gods,' he pointed out quite serenely that the Yorùbás create their own 'gods' (such as the god of electricity) and can on occasion kill them."[29]

Indeed, a popular Yorùbá proverb asserts: "Without humanity, the deities perish" ("Ibití enià kò sí, kò sí imalé").[30] In a paper titled, "How Man Makes God in West Africa: Yorùbá Attitudes towards the *Òrìṣà*," Karin Barber argues that "relations between humans and *òrìṣà* [deities] are in some sense a projection of relations between people in society. . . . If the Yorùbá see the *òrìṣà's* power as being maintained and augmented by human attention, this is because they live in a kind of society where it is very clear that the human individual's power depends in the long run on the attention and acknowledgement of his fellow-men."[31] Barber explains that although hierarchical, traditional Yorùbá society is also dynamic such that there is room for the rise of the self-made "Big Man." Key to becoming a "Big Man" is the securing of followers, gaining their attention and fidelity precisely by displaying and distributing wealth and political influence. Given this social structure, Barber presses for a sociological interpretation

of Yorùbá òrìṣà devotion, which she maintains reflects Yorùbá sociopolitical relations. Unless an òrìṣà maintains the attention of human devotees
by improving their lives, it loses its significance and potency and is "reduced to nothing."[32] Barber suggests that it was this pragmatic attitude to
religion that paved the way for Christianity and Islam in Yorùbáland—
there was a willingness to "test," as it were, the extent to which divine
power in these religions could serve human life.[33]

One point on which there is unanimity in scholarship on African indigenous religions is their concrete and pragmatic character. This can invite a Feuerbachian interpretation of these religions. For Ludwig Feuerbach,
"theology is anthropology"[34]—that is, religion is an expression of human
aspirations and ideals that have been unconsciously projected onto a transcendent ideality: God. The problem is, Feuerbach argues, that God then
confronts human beings as an independent, objective reality leaving humanity alienated from itself (as "species-being" [*Gattungwesen*]), unable to
realize, through collective effort, human ideals such as love, charity, and
wisdom.

Although Feuerbach considers the Christian God of faith to be an illusion, it is an idea that nevertheless has *instrumental value* insofar as the cardinal Christian tenet, "God is love," can excite a humanitarian love that
affirms all humans in their embodied existence, reconciling the individual
"I" with the "thou" that is collective humanity. Commenting on the Christian doctrine of the Incarnation, Feuerbach claims that its import stems
from how it makes evident "the divine significance of my [and all human]
nature."[35] He later cites Luther as follows: "'He who can truly conceive
such a thing (namely, the incarnation of God) in his heart, should, for the
sake of the flesh and blood which sits at the right hand of God, bear love
to all flesh and blood here upon the earth and never more to be able to be
angry with any man.'"[36] For Feuerbach, religion becomes problematic when
its true essence is shrouded by a theological edifice that hinders human
freedom and loving solidarity with one another.

In the next section I argue that there is a Eurocentric core running
through Feuerbach's anthropotheism that would overly compromise efforts
to think the human beyond the figure of Euro-American Man. While I
find Barber's account of indigenous Yorùbá religion insightful, I want to
explore ways in which traditional Yorùbá religion can be understood outside the parameters of Feuerbach's projection model and, in doing so, make
visible a mode of human living that does not orbit around Man.

Feuerbach's Sensuous Materialism

In criticizing Hegel's Absolute Idealism for advancing no more than a series of lifeless abstractions, Feuerbach's work, in particular *The Essence of
Christianity* (1841), would play a pivotal role in the materialist turn occurring in the wake of post-Hegelian German philosophy. In his *Science of
Logic*, Hegel begins with the concept of "pure being," which slips into its
opposite concept "nothing" in a dialectical movement that produces the
concept of "becoming," and with this the reconciliation of "being" and
"nothing" that raises speculative thought to a higher, more comprehensive level. By contrast, Feuerbach argues that "the antithesis of being . . .
is not nothingness, but sensuous and concrete being."[37] For Feuerbach,
the universalizing trajectory of spirit must—if it is to be truly reconciled
with real rather than ideal being—ceaselessly tarry with sensuous particularities rather than process through determinations of thought alone.
As Feuerbach puts it, "Dialectics is not a monologue that speculation carries on with itself, but a dialogue between speculation and empirical
reality."[38]

Feuerbach is keen to elaborate a philosophy that valorizes the sensible
finitude of human life. As noted earlier, he targets religion as that which is
most denigrating of this-worldly human life. The transcendent, supernatural God of monotheism is particularly charged with thwarting awareness of the infinite powers that (collectively) belong to humanity alone.
Feuerbach is unconvinced by Hegel's account of the doctrine of the Incarnation as the reconciliation of the human and the divine because he thinks
Hegel only achieves this at the level of an absolute spirit that progresses
to self-consciousness by purging itself of all sensuous particularity. In
Feuerbach's words:

> Reason, however, knows nothing . . . of a real and absolute incarnation
> of the species in a particular individuality. It is true that the spirit or
> consciousness is "species existing as species," but, no matter how
> universal, the individual and his head—the organ of spirit—are always
> designated by a definite kind of nose, whether pointed or snub, fine or
> gross, long or short, straight or bent. . . . The god of limitation stands
> guard at the entrance to the world.[39]

Even when nature mystics such as F. W. J. Schelling and Jakob Böhme
admit physical nature, in all its darkness and irrationality, into God's eternal being, Feuerbach demurs, "Instead of the rude, but hence all the more
striking expression, *flesh*, it [nature mysticism] substitutes the equivocal,

abstract words, *nature* and *ground*."[40] Feuerbach's materialism envisions the human as a fleshy, sensuous particularity.

The numerous references in Feuerbach's writings to human beings in their flesh and blood concreteness serve primarily as a way of underscoring the everyday carnal existence of human life. Guarding against turning the body into yet another abstraction, he reminds us that "a body does not exist without flesh and blood."[41] Moreover, flesh and blood bodies are "nothing without the oxygen of sexual distinction."[42] It is precisely the self's sensuous awareness of the *distinctiveness* of the other—which, for Feuerbach, is nowhere more manifest than in sexual difference—that marks a clear break from Hegelian idealism, whereby, on Feuerbach's understanding, the ego sucks the very marrow out of the other's sensuous particularity,[43] reducing otherness to a moment in the journey toward self-consciousness. Feuerbach's promotion of love as a feeling directed toward human beings in general may well have its basis in the sexual love he celebrates between a particular woman and a particular man.[44] Feuerbach's sensualism is also evident in his longstanding interest in the human need to consume food. As he once wrote, "Eating and drinking is the everyday and therefore unadmired and even disdained incarnation, nature become human."[45] The life of flesh—the everyday life of eating, drinking, sex, joys, pains, and ultimately death—is a life Feuerbach counterposes to the abstractions of Hegel's dialectic that, for Feuerbach, is unable to deliver the concrete universal it promises. "The deepest secrets," Feuerbach tells us, "are to be found in the simplest natural things."[46]

Insofar as Feuerbach develops an anthropocentric materialism, I do not think he can be easily categorized as a reductive materialist for whom the human is understood to be solely a biophysiological entity. In his pragmatic deconstruction of religion, Feuerbach denies the "unhuman" aspects of religion and speculative philosophy, particularly the transcendent God of monotheism, precisely so that there can be the revelation of the human—the revelation that is the essence of all religions. For Feuerbach, the absolute objective reality that the human can both feel and contemplate is not God but humanity in its universal species-being. It is by virtue of the particular human's mediation (both sensuously and cognitively) by the concrete universal that is human species-being that the human rises above the animal ("who has no religion"[47]) and is thereby divinized. Thus, Feuerbach writes:

> The mystery of the inexhaustible fullness of the divine predicates is
> therefore nothing else than the mystery of human nature considered
> as an infinitely varied, infinitely modifiable, but consequently,

phenomenal being. Only in the realm of the senses, only in space and time, does there exist a being of really infinite qualities or predicates.[48]

In rethinking the human, Feuerbach rejects both theistic and purely materialist frames of reference. Instead, he describes the human, understood collectively, as a mystery, irreducible to any final conceptualization for human beings have infinite ways of thinking, willing, and loving.[49]

Of course, in his pithy "Theses on Feuerbach" Marx, while deeply inspired by Feuerbach, famously criticizes his materialism for being merely contemplative. The problem, for Marx, is that Feuerbach's materialism remains too rationalistic insofar as it fails to "comprehend sensuousness as practical activity,"[50] contenting itself with simply *thinking* sensuous particularity. Most damningly, Marx argues that Feuerbach's notion of human species-being is no more than an ahistorical "dumb generality,"[51] no more, that is, than an abstraction. I do not think Marx's appraisal of Feuerbach as a contemplative materialist is entirely fair. Certainly, it is true that Feuerbach does not understand human practice in the political-economic terms of Marx's materialism. However, as we have seen, his "flesh and blood" humanism repeatedly focuses on the ordinary, quotidian activities of human life. Furthermore, as Mark Wartofsky points out, Feuerbach does not overlook history in his understanding of human nature, for in *The Essence of Christianity* he traces the historical emergence of human self-consciousness as this passes through progressive stages of (alienating) objectification in religious concepts until it is finally grasped as human species-being.[52]

Nevertheless, while I find Feuerbach's attention to the sensuous particularities of everyday, embodied life an important intervention in the context of the baroque systems of post-Kantian German idealism, I think that his flesh and blood humanism cannot disregard those ways in which fleshly materiality is constituted by shifting sociocultural, economic, and historical forces and thereby imbricated in relations of power. As ever, Marx has a point. In what follows, I outline how Feuerbach's appeal to the redemptive power (and therefore revolutionary potential) of humanitarian love rests on a pernicious Eurocentric teleology that demands the (often murderous) negation of those fleshy, sensuous particularities that are thought to frustrate the accomplishment of human self-knowledge as species-being.

The Problem of Humanitarian Love

For Feuerbach it is monotheistic Judaism that gives to human consciousness the first glimmers of human universality. But it would be a distorted universality. For, according to Feuerbach, Judaism is an egoistic and utilitarian religion with a tyrannical God "who is nothing but the personified selfishness of the Israelitish people, to the exclusion of all other nations."[53] Furthermore, while Feuerbach affirms sensuousness elsewhere, when he discusses Jewish sensuousness it is to emphasize their devouring carnality. Thus he writes, "The Israelite did not rise above the alimentary view of theology."[54] Here, and throughout *The Essence of Christianity*, Feuerbach reinforces the seething anti-Semitism of nineteenth-century German Protestants that within a few generations would manifest itself in reducing to ashes the flesh and blood particularity of millions of European Jews.

Whereas Judaism offers only a partial image of human universality (since only the Jews are valued by God), Feuerbach would consider Christianity the most exalted form of religious consciousness. The love embodied by and through Christ, the incarnate God, represents for Feuerbach the penultimate stage in the development of human self-knowledge.

However, the truly concrete universal, according to Feuerbach, is human species-being, which is precisely not an abstraction because "it exists in feeling . . . in the energy of love."[55] This humanitarian love realizes the ideality of Christ's love (which was only ever an image) for it wishes to "bless and unite" all human beings "without distinction of sex, age, rank or nationality."[56] But the seemingly benevolent embrace of this universal love is far from tender. It presupposes the hateful abjection of Jews, and non-Christians more generally, who serve as flesh and blood testimonies of all that base sensuousness (Jews) and irrationality (heathens) that must be surpassed in the realization of (divine) humanity.

When Marx complains that Feuerbach's notion of "species-being" is no more than a "dumb generality" he is not without warrant (though whether Marx's own use of the concept fares any better is debatable). The emergence of "species-being" through progressive transformations of religious thought is the emergence of "Man-God" at the expense of flesh and blood humans. However, as Peter Caldwell notes, there are elements in Feuerbach's work that seem to defy the dangerous teleological history of humanity's redemption by "Man-God" presented in *The Essence of Christianity*.[57] For example, while he contends that polytheism is to be superseded by monotheism he nevertheless has a particular appreciation for the polytheism of ancient Greece. He tells us that "polytheism is the frank, open, unenvying sense of all that is beautiful and good without distinction, the sense of the world, of the universe."[58] Polytheism expresses an appreciation of difference. Feuerbach's admiration of polytheism would deepen in his later works where, troubled by the criticisms of those such as Marx, he sought to exorcise once and for all the specter of "abstract Rational Being . . . as distinct from the actual sensuous being of nature and humanity"[59] that haunted *The Essence of Christianity*. The concept of "species-being" would be significantly deflated. It would refer not to an idealized universal essence of humanity but to the sensuous encounter with a flesh and blood "thou" that discloses the human to be fundamentally relational. Commenting on Feuerbach's later interest in myth—in which truths about human nature could be revealed in the stories of human beings responding to concrete situations rather than the abstract speculations of philosophy— Caldwell suggests that Feuerbach abandons his teleological account of species-being, along with its concomitant anti-Semitism, in favor of envisioning "humanity as involving a plurality of forms."[60] On this picture, the human world could be viewed as "individuals in a set of overlapping groups, with many different concrete wishes and self-representations."[61]

Feuerbach sought to resist what he believed to be the effacement of actual flesh and blood human beings in Hegel's account of the world in terms of the historical unfolding of *Geist*. By considering religious ideas in terms of their local material contexts, Feuerbach's philosophy would galvanize materialist responses to Hegelian idealism, most notably that of Marx. However, the appeal to a universal, teleological history culminating in the liberating recognition that "Man's God is Man" ("Homo homini Deus Est"[62]) would reinstate, in the notion of species-being, precisely the sort of fleshless abstraction Feuerbach wished to avoid.

While it might be tempting to offer a Feuerbachian analysis of the anthropocentric pragmatism characteristic of indigenous African religions, such as that of the Yorùbá people, I strongly caution against this. This is for two main reasons. First, the contention that religious thought is simply the projection of human wishes and ideals is implicated in an Enlightenment story[63] that promises freedom yet only by virtue of a grim and powerful subplot: the invention of racialized others abstracted from flesh and blood human beings, serving to index an enigmatic materiality that both imperils freedom and provides the dehumanized backdrop against which Man's freedom can be asserted.

Even if anthropological or sociological interpretations of religion jettison Feuerbach's (early) commitment to a universal, redemptive history— and here is my second reason—such interpretations generally remain caught up with a Eurocentric rationalism insofar as they conceive religion primarily in terms of *beliefs*. When religion is understood in terms of belief systems upheld by "believers" what is overlooked is religion as it is *lived* in dynamic and mutable ways by embodied, sensuous subjects in particular material contexts. This point is especially pertinent with respect to African indigenous religions. For these, as Emmanuel Lartey explains, are not so much a matter of "beliefs, dogmas and creeds" but rather center on "the performance of powerful rituals and the expression of communal solidarity through participation in such rituals."[64]

In the next and final section, I briefly consider the role of ritual in indigenous Yorùbá religion. I will suggest that many Yorùbá rituals can be viewed as dramatizing in the flesh the cosmic forces of the invisible realm, not so much for the apotheosis of the human but for the enrichment of earthly, human life both individually and communally. I also offer some preliminary remarks on the idea of an animist humanism, which, I maintain, indicates a way to understand the anthropocentric character of African indigenous religions, without referring to Feuerbachian projection theory of religion and its attendant Eurocentrism, and promises to open up and tread a new pathway beyond Man toward the human. We will see that an important feature of the animist humanism I begin to outline is a conception of the human as profoundly relational, bound up with other human beings and the cosmos more widely. Now Feuerbach's appreciation of dialectics means that he too conceives the human as inherently relational: The self-identical "I" is but an abstraction and must be understood in its constitutive (sensuous) relation to a "Thou." However, when Feuerbach, in his later work, seeks to abandon the concept of species-being as that idealized human essence by virtue of which humanity is united, he struggles to articulate a relational anthropology, often rooting this rather insecurely in heterosexual love. The animist humanism proposed below affirms the relationality of both humanity and the cosmos, particularly through communal ritual practices that also, I maintain, yield an open-ended anthropology that moves beyond the racist dictates of Man.

Toward an Animist Humanism

Like *religion, ritual* is a fuzzy term that eludes easy definition. For the purpose of this essay, I will assume a loose, working definition of *ritual* as that which refers to specific ways of acting that both disclose and constitute religious meaning. Until the turn of the twenty-first century, scholars (mostly anthropologists) have tended to view ritual as unthinking, mechanical action. In doing so, a dualism between belief and practice is presupposed, grounded by that most basic dualism between mind and body that historically steers so much Western discourse. Given the pre-eminence of mind in Western theorizing, the lack of sacred books typical of African indigenous religions is, from a Eurocentric perspective, yet one more justification for deeming such religions "primitive," dependent on noncognitive, rote practices (orthopraxy) rather than systematic and coherent beliefs (orthodoxy).[65]

However, in recent years the study of rituals has seen attempts to cut through oversimplifying dualisms in order to show that ritual is neither thoughtless action nor purely "symbolic," the "mere physical expression of logically prior ideas,"[66] but constitutes what Laura S. Grillo calls "bodily ways of knowing."[67] Ritual generates profound bodily experiences that do not simply mediate predetermined meaning but are meaningful in and of themselves—their meaningfulness is *felt*, is made sense of, in the flesh. This is not to emphasize ritual meaning over ritual performance, thus capitulating to the mind-body dualism once again, but is intended to show their reciprocal determination. Commenting on the emphasis given to the body in its fleshy materiality in African rituals, Grillo writes, "Ritual enables participants *literally* to make *sense* of themselves and the world. Through its appeal to the *senses* and the *sensational* nature of the experience that it elicits, ritual reveals alternate realities and new modes of being."[68] By exciting and orchestrating the senses—through, for example, dance, song, consuming certain foods and drink, performing specific gestures, etc.— African rituals can reconfigure bodily sensibilities in ways that heighten awareness of diverse liminal powers and actualities promissory of concrete, material transformations.

The reappraisal of ritual as bodily ways of knowing is significant in efforts to think the human beyond Man. Ritual is integral to African indigenous religions and foregrounds the body in an emphatic way. Here the body is neither reduced to inarticulate, inanimate flesh (the fate of enslaved, racialized African bodies) nor is it idealized to the point that its fleshy materiality evaporates in a cloud of metaphors and discourses. Rather, in African religiosity the body is a vibrant, sensuous particularity, at once subject, insofar as it is generative of meaning, and object, insofar as action is directed toward it in ritual practices. We might think of this in terms of what Vivian Sobchack refers to as "embodiment."[69] For Sobchack, embodiment is such that "we [human beings] matter and we mean through processes and logics of sense-making that owe as much to our carnal existence as they do to our conscious thought."[70]

The embrace of embodied human life evident in African rituals recalls Feuerbach's sensuous materialism. As we saw earlier, Feuerbach goes against the grain of post-Hegelian idealism, and the prevailing view of Western philosophy more broadly, by arguing that it is not rational thought that is definitive of human being but rather the unique sensibility of human bodies. I have wanted to resist a Feuerbachian reading of African indigenous religions insofar as this appeals to the contentious idea of human species-being emerging from the grand sweep of a universal history. However, where Feuerbach's work suggests that the everyday activities of sensuous human life carry religious import we find points of convergence with his sensuous materialism and the world-sense[71] generally upheld by African indigenous religions.

Seeking to show how religion permeates all aspects of life in traditional African cultures, such that there is no notion of distinct secular and sacred spheres, Mbiti writes, "Wherever the African is, there is his religion: he carries it to the fields where he is sowing seeds or harvesting a new crop; he takes it with him to the beer party or to attend a funeral ceremony."[72] What is important here is the earthbound orientation of African religiosity. It is unsurprising, then, that African indigenous religions are widely held to be instrumental in essence, with human interests as the primary concern. I do not disagree with this depiction. However, given that most African indigenous religions assert a cosmological milieu within which human life takes place, an example of which is the Yorùbá cosmology sketched earlier, it is clear that for all the adoration of the terrestrial, African indigenous religions do not consider tangible earthliness in wholly materialist terms.

One way we might try to marry the geocentric anthropocentrism and the cosmological narratives simultaneously advanced by African indigenous religions is to maintain that these cosmologies are the unconscious projections of a people's consciousness. However, I hope to have shown that the trouble with such Feuerbachian accounts is that they are difficult (perhaps impossible) to disconnect from a linear, progressive conception of history, one that would see humanity arrive at a point of transparent self-understanding, and with this freedom, but only at the expense of the dehumanization of those humans deemed less than Man. In contrast to Feuerbachian readings of African indigenous religions, I want to suggest that the unmitigated anthropocentrism often attributed to African indigenous religions is overstated and should be qualified in light of the animist ontology implied by the cosmologies and rituals upheld by these religions. To do this, I will highlight spirit possession as a ritual that powerfully intimates a vision of the human as a "relational being [or better 'becoming'] in a relational cosmos"[73] that includes invisible extrahuman forces that can be enfleshed and dramatized in ways transformative of human life.

Baldly put, spirit possession in a ritual context describes the temporary overcoming of a person's embodiment by a deity such that their conscious agency is wholly displaced. It most often occurs during ritual dance and is a phenomenon primarily associated with women. When referring to possession trance the Yorùbá use the word *gún*, a polysemic term usually translated as "to mount" that can be used to convey the idea of a deity (òrìṣà) mounting and then riding the possessed devotee like a horse, indeed, the possessed individual is called the "horse of the god."[74] Spirit possession establishes a particularly dramatic expression of the visible and invisible planes intersecting each other. In their possessed state, devotees "incarnate and embody the unseen" mainly in ways that are "for the good of the human community."[75] According to Margaret Drewal in her important study on Yorùbá ritual, once possessed by a deity the devotee is thought to *become* that deity. Drewal describes how the presence of the deity is made evident in concrete, bodily ways. She recounts a festival in which a medium of Ògún, the god of war and iron, fully transforms into the deity: Once mounted by Ògún, the medium's movement becomes agitated, her body trembles, her head falls back until Ògún signals his presence when the medium emits a deep, guttural yell; thereafter, Ògún takes giant steps toward the crowd, hands on his hips and moving in a stylized manner, he goes on to dance, sing, and pray until he leaves the medium.[76] Grillo explains that devotees (who are not mediums) witnessing possession trance "recognize archetypal gestures and behaviours as indications of the presence of particular spirits and divinities among them."[77] Deities choreograph bodies according to their unique signatory style, announcing their presence in vividly sensory ways and, in doing so, commending enfleshed bodiliness.

From these brief remarks on possession trance, I wish to draw attention to an issue that at first blush seems to undermine my claim that traditional African thought rejects Cartesian dualistic accounts of mind and body, spirit and matter. The idea of spirit possession easily invites the impression that there are disembodied deities and forces capable of "spiritualizing" material objects ranging from human bodies to lakes to artifacts, objects that would simply be inert stuff if not for the animating, form-giving work of spirit. There are certainly grounds for defending a dualistic reading of spirit possession.[78] However, I want to show how contemporary reformulations of animism circumvent modern mind-body dualism and offer insights that can develop an animist humanism.

In a fascinating and resonant article in which he explores African and African diaspora literature, society, and culture through the lens of what he calls "animist materialism," Harry Garuba writes:

> Perhaps the single most important characteristic of animist thought—in contrast to the major monotheistic religions—is its almost total refusal to countenance unlocalized, unembodied, unphysicalized gods and spirits. . . . Instead of erecting graven images to symbolize the spiritual being, animist thought spiritualizes the object world giving the spirit a local habitation.[79]

The above comments raise two interrelated points that I wish to examine further: 1) the nonrepresentational expression of spiritual forces, and 2) the spiritualization of objects.

The first point cautions against viewing the manifestation of gods and spirits in animist thought in representational terms, such that a statue of Esu or a lake is regarded as symbolizing something immaterial and so other than the signifying material object. In possession trance, for example, the medium does not just signify a deity but *becomes* that deity. Thus, I would argue, it is not so much that the human is divinized in such rituals but rather held in a kind of liminal suspense.

This takes us to the second point concerning the spiritualization of objects—and, conversely, the materialization of spiritual forces—central to animist thought. In trying to make sense of these without conceding substance dualism, I have found it helpful to turn to Soyinka's notion of "fourth space" in his discussion of African (especially Yorùbá) ritual and drama.[80] In addition to the three realms of the ancestors, the living, and the unborn, Soyinka identifies a fourth space, "the dark continuum of transition where occurs the inter-transmutation of essence-ideal and materiality."[81] By "essence-ideal" Soyinka means the idealization of archetypal aspects of the human self; essence-ideals are "a product of the conscious creativity of man,"[82] human images "fashioned in the shape of gods."[83] Such an explanation of essence-ideals seems to return us to a Feuerbachian account of African cosmologies. Indeed, Caribbean social theorist Paget Henry holds that the creative matrix that is Soyinka's fourth space ultimately has its locus in human consciousness, so much so that he suggests that the primacy given to (human) spirit in Soyinka's vision of the African cosmos "links traditional African thought to global traditions of idealism."[84] While Henry pushes Soyinka's account of African cosmology in an idealist direction, I want to suggest that Soyinka's fourth space need not be rendered in terms of what Henry calls "the vertical dramas of ego consciousness"[85] but, given an animist twist, a space of *creative transition*, that point of traffic between the invisible and the visible, the cosmic and the terrestrial.

An animist perspective invites us to think the fourth space as a dynamic, opaque matrix where dualistic oppositions—mind and body, subject and object, spirit and matter, etc.—have no place and where the fundamental relatedness of all things is particularly acute. On this picture, the spiritualization of matter, and materialization of spirit, are best understood in terms of a relational, processual ontology rather than a substance one. Spiritualization and materialization thus name a reconfiguration of cosmic relations and, consequently, powers. As Tim Ingold emphasizes, animacy (that is, life or spirit) is not a property or quality of things but is the creative, relational dynamic generative of all persons and things. "The animacy of the lifeworld," Ingold tells us, "is not the result of infusion of spirit into substance, or of agency into materiality, but is rather ontologically prior to their differentiation."[86]

It is also worth appreciating that animism complicates ideas about time. It defies the secular notion of time unfolding in a progressive, linear manner and instead recognizes, as Garuba writes, "the complex embeddedness of different temporalities . . . within the same historical moment."[87] In a similar vein, Soyinka emphasizes the protean vitality of time within human daily life for the Yorùbá, for whom the present is a conceptual notion and also "contains within it manifestations of the ancestral, the living and the unborn."[88] With animism there is no superseding of cyclical, mythic time by linear, historical time, no overcoming of the premodern by the modern. Instead, a liminal temporality persists between linear time and cyclical time enabling the creative renewal of the present by way of (still potent) past powers such that the future can be imagined in new ways. In Garuba's elegant words, "animist culture . . . opens up a whole new world of poaching possibilities, *prepossessing the future*, as it were, by laying claim to what in the present is yet to be invented."[89] The renowned *egúngún* masquerade in which the ancestors are ritually honored can be considered an example of Yorùbá efforts to prepossess the future. The masked performers do more than symbolize ancestral spirits; they incarnate those spirits and in doing so reanimate lines of connection between the invisible and visible worlds. Through ritual performance, as Drewal explains, the maskers reshape and transform the everyday, sensible world, the "*as if* becomes *is* as illusion becomes its own reality, or, . . . reveals otherwise undisclosed reality."[90] African ritual has always sought to consolidate and revitalize relations between the invisible and the visible world precisely so that the latter can be transformed in life-promoting ways.

In contemporary Africa, ancestral masking rituals, such as the *egúngún* masquerade, continue to be performed. However, it would be a mistake to think that such rituals merely re-enact fixed traditional practices in order to protest a unitary modernity. Rather, African masking rituals (and religious practices more generally) have *always* responded to changing social conditions, for just as they are informed by tradition they are also experimental[91] since this enables them to respond to the material realities of the community in their current and particular situation. Garuba is critical of a double-aspected process he calls, following Africanist Patrick Chabal, "re-traditionalization," which sees "modern" African elites recuperate pre-colonial practices into forms of Western modernity and "traditional" African elites assimilate modern European elements into traditional customs.[92] The problem is that such retraditionalization generally serves to buttress the interests of local leaders, particularly the modern elites who control economic and political power in Africa's nation-states. Nevertheless, Garuba is keen to point out that "an animistic understanding of the world applied to the practice of everyday life has often provided avenues of agency for the dispossessed in colonial and postcolonial Africa."[93] Animism offers an alternative conception of both space and time that can subvert the teleological image of human history perpetuated by colonial modernity and, in doing so, open up possibilities for the sort of creative agency—often centered on bodily rituals—needed to transform the embodied, daily lives of Africans, and similarly situated peoples, in the wake of the bleak encounter with Europe.

While Garuba highlights the prospects of animism for empowering postcolonial Africans with creative agency, in developing an animist humanism I would like to draw attention to another form of agency that emerges from reflection on African indigenous religions. In her work on women and spirit possession in various religious traditions, Mary Keller challenges the model of religious subjectivity inflected by Enlightenment ideals, particularly as this enshrines a certain conception of agency. According to Keller, the modern, European conception of religious subjectivity centers on: an individual's experience, beliefs that exist in consciousness, a matter of choice and/or invention, and the promotion of one's autonomy.[94] Such a conception of religious subjectivity, Keller argues, can only interpret the phenomenon of possessed women as a primitive form of religious subjectivity.

Resisting the Eurocentrism informing such an evaluation, Keller proposes the concept of "instrumental agency" to describe the agency of
women's possessed bodies. She explains that here instrumentality "refers
to the *power of receptivity*, comparable metaphorically to a hammer, flute or
horse that is wielded, played or mounted."[95] Even as Feuerbach's sensuous
materialism foregrounds the (sexed) body in its flesh and blood materiality, he does not depart from a model of subjectivity based on self-conscious,
autonomous agency and so is unable to recognize the "power of receptivity" of the possessed female body, and thus the power of the flesh as "a seat
of passivity and affectivity."[96] What interests me in Keller's notion of instrumental agency is how it alludes (even if unintentionally) to an animist
world-sense insofar as this posits the human existing in a relational cosmos replete with extrahuman as well as sociocultural (i.e., human) forces.
I think Keller is onto something important when she writes:

> If we shift from the Western habit of thought and consider religious-
> ness to be practices that have been developed to negotiate with power,
> then the question about whether or not religiousness is "real" dis-
> appears. The religious body engages with ritualising practices that
> make it stronger in order to deal with external forces that have greater
> power than does the individual. The ancestors . . . are not [abstract]
> beliefs that float about; they are [concrete, felt] forces which people
> must contend and negotiate.[97]

This pragmatic approach to religion significantly differs from Feuerbach's
because there is no apotheosis of Man who has managed to reclaim for
himself the creative power once attributed to God (or, in what Feuerbach
considers to be less advanced religions, various deities and/or spiritual
forces). Instead, human beings are envisaged as situated in overlapping
force fields of power that can—particularly in ritual contexts—both over-
whelm and empower them in ways affirmative of communal human life
but also in ways that can be injurious of that life, inattentive to the pro-
nouncements of the ancestors who keep watch for justice.

Conclusion

According to Garuba, "animist understandings of the natural and social
world functioned within discourses of colonial modernity as the aberra-
tion, the past-in-the-present, to be disciplined to create civilized worlds
and subjects."[98] In the attempt to think beyond the doctrine of Man so that
we (Westernized theorists) can begin to imagine the human, I have sug-

gested that animism harbors various conceptual resources that can exert pressure on the tensions and interstices of a totalizing but not wholly totalized colonial modernity.

The appeal to animism is bound to make some decolonial and postcolonial thinkers restive, and I admit that I use the term with a degree of uneasiness. This is because animism is a European construct, one invoked, as Garuba says, to signify the denigrated Other against which colonial modernity defines itself. Particularly troubling for me, in light of my critique of Feuerbach, is how animism, in the modern European imaginary, is only meaningful insofar as it names a primeval moment in the evolutionary history of Man. Nevertheless, I hope to have shown how animism can actually dislocate the appearance of time as a progressive linearity. The endurance of what can be called animist practices in twenty-first century, everyday African life (as well as in some of the lives of the African diaspora and other formerly colonized peoples) can be, and often is, considered to be the endurance of a primitive outlook that impedes African development (i.e., modernization). However, theorists such as Garuba urge us to refrain from conceding too quickly to such simplistic appraisals. Instead, a deeper scrutiny of the endurance of traditional culture in places like Africa can disclose the coexistence of multiple temporalities at a single historical juncture.

"Without humanity," a famous Yorùbá saying tells us, "the deities perish." It is very tempting to read this, as have some scholars (both European and African), according to Feuerbach's anthropological account of religion. In this essay I have wanted to make explicit the ways in which the Feuerbachian legacy in the study of religion is deeply invested in the logic of colonial modernity. Feuerbach performs an important materialist inversion of Hegelian idealism that seeks to do justice to flesh and blood human beings in their sensuous particularity. However, his idea of "species-being" coupled with a teleological conception of history betrays his vision of universal human freedom and humanitarian love since it is predicated on a racist superseding of those who are deemed not yet Man-God.

The humanity referred to in the Yorùbá saying is one that could be explored in terms of what I am calling an "animist humanism." There is no doubt that African indigenous religions, like that of the Yorùbá, are anthropocentric: Religious practices are meant to bear fruits in this life, not some otherworldly hereafter. That being said, most African indigenous religions uphold a cosmology comprising invisible spiritual forces and deities (including a Supreme Deity) as well as the visible terrestrial plane. Animism, I maintain, offers a way to take seriously the cosmologies of

African indigenous religions. While an animist humanism can preserve the anthropocentric focus typical of African indigenous religions, this must be with the proviso that the human is to be conceived as fundamentally relational, a node of relatedness entangled in a relational cosmos where a multiplicity of creative/destructive forces can effect innumerable transformations. Ritual is central to animist humanism for ritual practices encourage a receptive attentiveness to extrahuman realities, due in no small part to the import of the body, its fleshy materiality, in ritual performance. Keller's concept of "instrumental agency" is one I find particularly helpful in developing an animist humanism. This is because it establishes distance between a Eurocentric model of the human as an autonomous body and mind and a postcolonial model that acknowledges a radical, nonautonomous agency that, by way of embodied practices, fosters connections between the invisible and visible, spirit and body, the dead, the living, and the unborn so that living human communities may flourish. While the deities are said to perish without humanity, given an animist humanism, it would seem that humanity would perish with them.

Before drawing this essay to a close, a final point I wish to note is Garuba's reference to Soyinka's description of animist spirituality as "a non-doctrinaire mould of constant awareness."[99] This is a significant observation because it underscores the inclusive elasticity of animism. The famous syncretism of African and African diaspora religions is testimony to animism's accommodative logic. Such a logic could potentially encompass what at one level are conflicting religious, political, and ideological commitments. Rather than seeking to drive out (often violently) ostensible impurities from what are held to be hermetically sealed doctrines and identities, animism encourages constant awareness of humanity's "cosmic entanglement"[100] with various powers and relations. Through "observances, rituals and mytho-historical recitals,"[101] communities try to apply such awareness (inevitably mediated by local contexts) to the often-tricky task of securing mundane goods that promote the well-being of earthbound, living communities. Recalling an animist world-sense could help recover and realize the life-affirming values espoused by twentieth-century African humanism—values that all too often have been tragically betrayed by a postcolonial Africa continuing to grapple with the legacy of Man.[102]

NOTES

1. Kwasi Wiredu, "Introduction: African Philosophy in Our Time," in *Blackwell Companion to African Philosophy*, ed. Kwasi Wiredu (Malden, Mass.: Blackwell, 2006), 1.

2. Frantz Fanon, *The Wretched of the Earth*, trans. Constance Farrington (London: Penguin Classics, 2001), 251.

3. Richard H. Bell, *Understanding African Philosophy: A Cross-Cultural Approach to Classical and Contemporary Issues* (London: Routledge, 2002), 37.

4. Senghor cited by Bell, *Understanding African Philosophy*, 37.

5. Bell, *Understanding African Philosophy*, 40.

6. John S. Mbiti, *African Religions and Philosophy* (London: Heinemann, 1969), 108–9.

7. Kenneth Kaunda, *A Humanist in Africa* (London: Longmans, 1966), 22.

8. See Rob Gaylard, "Welcome to the World of Our Humanity," *Journal of Literary Studies* 20, no. 3/4 (2004); and Michael Onyebuchi Eze, "Ubuntu/Botho: Ideology or Promise?," in *Exploring Humanity: Intercultural Perspectives on Humanism*, ed. Mihai I. Spariosu and Jörn Rüsen (Göttingen, Germany: V&R unipress, 2012).

9. These are, of course, generalizations: Christian humanism is upheld by certain strands of European thought, and secular/atheistic humanism is defended by African thinkers such as Frantz Fanon and Okot p'Bitek.

10. Mbiti, *African Religions and Philosophy*, 5.

11. Dominique Zahan, *The Religion, Spirituality and Thought of Traditional Africa* (Chicago: University of Chicago Press, 1970), 5.

12. See, for example, Sylvia Wynter, "Unsettling the Coloniality of Being/Power/Truth/Freedom: Towards the Human, after Man, Its Over-representation—An Argument," *CR: The New Centennial Review* 3, no. 3 (Fall 2003). For Wynter, the Western bourgeois conception of "Man" "overrepresents itself as if it were the human itself" (260).

13. I do not wish to imply that all claims regarding the divinization of the human, particularly in the context of Christian theology, are necessarily problematic. Nevertheless, in Feuerbach's work at least it can be shown that such divinization amounts to the dangerous self-aggrandizement of Man who eclipses other modes of being human.

14. See, for example, Zahan, *Religion, Spirituality and Thought of Traditional Africa*, 4.

15. Segun Gbadegesin, *African Philosophy: Traditional Yoruba Philosophy and Contemporary African Realities* (New York: Peter Lang, 1991), 88.

16. "The 'plus 1' . . . does not refer to any particular divinity. Rather it is a principle of elasticity by which the Yorùbá account for any newly deified Òrìṣà." Kola Abimbola, *Yorùbá Culture: A Philosophical Account* (Birmingham, England: Iroko Academic Publishers, 2005), 50.

17. Segun Gbadegesin, "African Religions," in *The Routledge Companion to Theism*, ed. Charles Taliaferro, Victoria S. Harrison, and Stuart S. Goetz (New York: Routledge, 2013), 108.

18. E. Bọ́lájí Ìdòwú labels the Yorùbá religion a "diffuse monotheism." See *African Traditional Religion: A Definition* (London: SCM Press, 1973), 136.

19. See, for example, Monica A. Coleman, "Invoking *Oya*: Practicing a Polydox Soteriology through a Postmodern Womanist Reading of Tananarives Due's *The Living Blood*," in *Polydoxy: Theology of Multiplicity and Relation*, ed. Catherine Keller (New York: Routledge, 2011), 191; Dianne Stewart, *Three Eyes for the Journey* (Oxford: Oxford University Press, 2005), 24; and Emmanuel Y. Lartey, *Postcolonializing God: An African Practical Theology* (London: SCM Press, 2013), 27.

20. Jacob K. Olupọna, *African Religions: A Very Short Introduction* (Oxford: Oxford University Press, 2014), 29.

21. Idowu, *African Traditional Religion*, 184.

22. Jacob K. Olupọna, "To Praise and Reprimand: Ancestors and Spirituality in African Societies and Cultures," in *Ancestors and Post-Contact Religion: Roots, Ruptures and Modernity's Memories*, ed. Steven J. Friesen (Cambridge, Mass.: Harvard University Press, 2001), 50.

23. J. Ọmọṣade Awolalu, *Yoruba Beliefs and Sacrificial Rites* (London: Longman, 1979), 49.

24. Graham Harvey, *Food, Sex and Strangers: Understanding Religion as Everyday Life* (Abingdon, England: Routledge, 2014), 126.

25. Olupọna, *African Religions*, 3 (emphasis added).

26. John Caputo, "Bodies Without Flesh: Overcoming the Soft Gnosticism of Incarnational Theology," in *Intensities: Philosophy, Religion and the Affirmation of Life*, Katharine Sarah Moody and Steven Shakespeare (London: Routledge, 2016), 80.

27. Okot p'Bitek, *Decolonizing African Religions: A Short History of African Religions in Western Scholarship* (New York: Diasporic African Press, 2011), 51.

28. Kwasi Wiredu, "African Religions from a Philosophical Point of View," in *Blackwell Companion to Philosophy of Religion*, Philip L. Quinn and Charles Taliaferro (Malden, Mass.: Blackwell, 2000), 39.

29. Wiredu, "African Religions from a Philosophical Point of View," 39.

30. E. Bọ́lájí Ìdòwú, *Olódùmarè: God in Yorùbá Belief* (Long Island, N.Y.: African Tree Press, 2011), 63 (translation modified).

31. Karin Barber, "How Man Makes God in West Africa: Yoruba Attitudes towards the 'Orisa,'" *Africa* 51, no. 3 (1981): 724.

32. Barber, "How Man Makes God," 724.

33. Barber, 741.

34. Ludwig Feuerbach, *Essence of Christianity*, trans. George Eliot (Amherst, N.Y.: Prometheus Books, 1989), xvii.

35. Feuerbach, *Essence of Christianity*, 57.

36. Feuerbach, 58.

37. Ludwig Feuerbach, "Towards a Critique of Hegel's Philosophy," in *The Fiery Brook: Selected Writings of Ludwig Feuerbach*, ed. and trans. Zawar Hanfi (New York: Doubleday, 1972), 72. Also available online at: https://www.marxists.org/reference/archive/feuerbach/works/critique/.

38. Feuerbach, "Towards a Critique of Hegel's Philosophy," 72.

39. Feuerbach, 56–57.

40. Feuerbach, *Essence of Christianity*, 89.

41. Feuerbach, 93.

42. Feuerbach, 93.

43. Feuerbach, "Towards a Critique of Hegel's Philosophy," 54.

44. Note here the heteronormativity of Feuerbach's account. Moreover, he fails to note how flesh is marked by determinations such as race, class, and abilities.

45. Feuerbach cited in Peter C. Caldwell, *Love, Death and Revolution in Central Europe: Ludwig Feuerbach, Moses Hess, Louise Dittmar, Richard Wagner* (New York: Palgrave Macmillan, 2009), 138. See also "Eating and drinking is the mystery of the Lord's supper—eating and drinking is, in fact, in itself a religious act; at least, ought to be so." Feuerbach, *Essence of Christianity*, 277.

46. Feuerbach, "Towards a Critique of Hegel's Philosophy," 94.

47. Feuerbach, *Essence of Christianity*, 1.

48. Feuerbach, 23.

49. According to Feuerbach, reason, will, and feeling are the distinctive characteristics of human nature. Feuerbach, *Essence of Christianity*, 3.

50. Karl Marx, "Theses on Feuerbach," in *Karl Marx: Selected Writings*, ed. David McLellan, 2nd ed. (Oxford: Oxford University Press, 2000), 173.

51. Marx, "Theses on Feuerbach," 172.

52. Mark W. Wartofsky, *Feuerbach* (Cambridge: Cambridge University Press, 1977), 225.

53. Wartofsky, *Feuerbach*, 113–14.

54. Wartofsky, 115.

55. Wartofsky, 268.

56. Wartofsky, 268.

57. Caldwell, *Love, Death and Revolution in Central Europe*, 25–26.

58. Feuerbach, *Essence of Christianity*, 114.

59. Feuerbach, cited by Van A. Harvey, "Ludwig Andreas Feuerbach," *The Stanford Encyclopedia of Philosophy* (Winter 2013 Edition), http://plato.stanford.edu/entries/ludwig-feuerbach/.

60. Caldwell, *Love, Death and Revolution in Central Europe*, 131.

61. Caldwell, 131.

62. Feuerbach, *Essence of Christianity*, 159.

63. It must be recognized that the Enlightenment story is not mono-lithic; nevertheless, what is identified here are its predominate aspects.

64. Lartey, *Postcolonializing God*, 28.

65. Laura S. Grillo, "African Rituals," in *The Wiley-Blackwell Companion to African Religion*, ed. Elias Kifon Bongmba (Oxford: Blackwell, 2012).

66. Catherine Bell, *Ritual Theory, Ritual Practice* (New York: Oxford University Press, 1992), 19.

67. Grillo, "African Rituals," 114.

68. Grillo, 114.

69. Vivian Sobchack, *Carnal Thoughts: Embodiment and Moving Image Culture* (Berkeley: University of California Press, 2004), 4.

70. Sobchack, *Carnal Thoughts*, 4.

71. This is a term coined by Oyèrónké Oyěwùmí, who uses it to avoid the Western privileging of sight over other senses. Oyèrónké Oyěwùmí, "Visualizing the Body," in *The African Philosophy Reader*, ed. P. H. Coetzee (London: Routledge, 2003), 458.

72. Mbiti, *African Religions and Philosophy*, 2.

73. Harvey, *Food, Sex and Strangers*, 203.

74. Margaret Thompson Drewal, *Yoruba Ritual: Performers, Play, Agency* (Bloomington: Indiana University Press, 1992), 183. The term *gun* also has a sexual connotation insofar as it describes a male mounting a female during sex.

75. Lartey, *Postcolonializing God*, 28.

76. Drewal, *Yoruba Ritual*, 183–84.

77. Grillo, "African Rituals," 119.

78. See, for example, Emma Cohen, "What Is Spirit Possession? Defin-ing, Comparing, and Explaining Two Possession Forms," *Ethnos* 73, no. 1 (March 2008).

79. Harry Garuba, "Explorations in Animist Materialism: Notes on Reading/Writing African Literature, Culture and Society," *Public Culture* 15, no. 2 (Spring 2003): 267.

80. See Wole Soyinka, *Myth, Literature and the African World* (Cam-bridge: Cambridge University Press, 1976), esp. "The Fourth Stage."

81. Soyinka, *Myth, Literature and the African World*, 26.

82. Soyinka, 2.

83. Soyinka, 12.

84. Paget Henry, *Caliban's Reason: Introducing Afro-Caribbean Philosophy* (New York: Routledge, 2000), 59.

85. Harvey, *Caliban's Reason*, 121, 123.

86. Tim Ingold, "Rethinking the Animate, Re-animating Thought," *Ethnos* 71, no. 1 (March 2006): 10.

87. Harry Garuba, "On Animism, Modernity/Colonialism, and the African Order of Knowledge: Provisional Reflections," *e-flux* 36 (July 2012): 7, http://www.e-flux.com/journal/on-animism-modernitycolonialism-and -the-african-order-of-knowledge-provisional-reflections/.

88. Soyinka, *Myth, Literature and the African World*, 144.

89. Garuba, "Explorations in Animist Materialism," 271.

90. Drewal, *Yoruba Ritual*, 90.

91. Drewal, 104.

92. Garuba, "Explorations in Animist Materialism," 265.

93. Garuba, 285.

94. Mary L. Keller, "Divine Women and the Nehanda *Mhondoro*: Strengths and Limitations of the Sensible Transcendental in a Post-Colonial World of Religious Women," in *Religion in French Feminist Thought: Critical Perspectives*, ed. Morny Joy, Kathleen O'Grady, and Judith L. Poxon (London: Routledge, 2003), 68.

95. Mary L. Keller, *The Hammer and the Flute: Women, Power and Spirit Possession* (Baltimore: Johns Hopkins University Press, 2002), 9 (emphasis added).

96. Caputo, "Bodies without Flesh," 81.

97. Keller, "Divine Women and the Nehanda *Mhondoro*," 77.

98. Garuba, "On Animism, Modernity/Colonialism, and the African Order of Knowledge," 4.

99. Garuba, "Explorations in Animist Materialism," 276. Garuba is quoting Soyinka, *Myth, Literature and the African World*, 54.

100. Soyinka, *Myth, Literature and the African World*, 54.

101. Soyinka, 54.

102. I am aware that for some readers the animist humanism I am exploring sails too closely to the sentiments of the Negritude movement and its attendant problems, especially the romanticization of precolonial African society and religion. For sure, the appeal to animism in attempting to reimagine the human beyond Man is a risky maneuver. However, mindful of the pitfalls bedeviling Negritude writings I hope to make the dangers of these visible while bypassing them in developing animist humanism further.

PART III

Biopolitics and the Project
of Unsettling Man

CHAPTER 8

Bodies That Speak

Linn Marie Tonstad

> There is something in the pursuit of liberation that
> feels exactly like—that is—prayer.
>
> —THOMAS GLAVE, "Toward a Queer Prayer"

Can the queer prophet stop the deadly forward march of contemporary global capitalism, that vast empire of dispossession variously characterized as financialized, neoliberal, or late? In this essay, I proffer a qualified "yes" to that question. The queer prophet is a figure of shifting embodiment and mysterious forms of agency. An amalgam formed out of biblical stories about bodies moving in enigmatic ways and queer performance theory, the queer prophet promises to lead the way toward transformations previously unimagined, yet materializable. Approaching prophetic performances as bodied practices that rematerialize the relations that configure the world makes the elements of social transformation apparent: the way imagination opens up past, present, and future to occluded perspectives while dislodging dominant stories; the necessary labor to sustain the spaces—and the bodies—in and through which alternative visions of the future can materialize with enough depth to form (even evanescent) communities; the detailed analyses of geographies of domination that reshape space itself, situating performers and audiences in relation to histories and futures refused by the dispossessive logic of capital; the utopian forms of identification that generate transitory collective subjects.

In recent writing, I have explored two synecdoches for some of the most important ways in which features of contemporary global capitalism rob us of capacities for effective collective action toward an otherwise: debt time and the entrepreneur.[1] In both cases, these figures encapsulate pressures that deny or remove possibilities for willed social transformation. A brief rehearsal of the features of these synecdoches sets up the problem that I believe needs to be solved.[2] Debt time—a time in which large swaths of people are subjected to unsustainable, crushing debt burdens—doubly determines the present by the need to order present and future to fulfill promises that were made in the past. These promises of debt repayment create money out of nothing. That "nothing"—the future income and choices of debtors—eats up any slack we might have for making radically different choices, especially in the case of increasingly large debt loads. Without a significant social safety net, there is no possibility of redirecting the economic order, because the indebted one has to concentrate on staying in a precarious balance between risk and destruction. She cannot step out of an economy in which her choices are always constrained, nor does she have the resources left over to work toward a radical transformation of that economic order. In the case of the entrepreneurial subject—a subject that increasingly extends through every economic level as well as transnationally—the figure of the entrepreneur fatally occludes the difference between the pieceworker in the "gig economy" and the beneficiary of Silicon Valley venture capital. Nevertheless, the entrepreneur becomes a figure for what all independently responsible social subjects ought to be. The entrepreneur exhibits features—often praised or read as axiomatically positive in theoretical and theological literature—like "risk-taking, vulnerability, orientation to the other, irreversible commitment to an unpredictable future, self-transcendence, fluidity (and responsivity), and self-creation through ascetic practices."[3] Such practices, valuable though they are, may not then counter the features of globalized Euro-American capitalism that the dissolution of the subject promised to transform.

Since debt and entrepreneurialism are ideologically and materially coded into the constitution of capitalism, it may seem odd to suggest that such figures encapsulate tendencies particularly germane to the present. At the same time, albeit for vastly different reasons, many economists, cultural analysts, entrepreneurs, and workers share a sense that capitalism's current form is irreducible to its normal patterns (to the extent that they may be said to exist) due to radically transformative strategies of intensification, expansion, and innovation that incorporate and expand on existing cultural and social formations. Thus, I worry that "we cannot rest content with the hope that the dissolution of the subject—the end of m/Man—will also be the end of capitalism. The dissolution of the subject may be one of the means by which capitalism preserves itself."[4] How, then, do we move beyond the doctrine of Man? To counter capital's reformation of time and space, subjugation of the many to the outsized profit of the few, and insusceptibility to the application of brakes to its acquisitive instincts, I contend that (at least) the following features are necessary: the creation of spatial and temporal contiguities that allow the formation of a social subject (a "we") that can identify the structuring features of the contemporary order, make demands of it in order to redirect it, and believe (despite the current order's "monopoly on actuality"[5]) in an impossible and unimaginable future that might nonetheless offer a "better," especially for the most vulnerable among us.

I align myself with those who see the global financial order as having been transformed in unprecedented ways during the last thirty-five years—less because of neoliberalism's well-known "financialization of everyday life" (Randy Martin) than because of the effects financialization has in global economic terms, particularly with regard to the concentration of wealth and evasion of even transnational attempts at regulation and redistribution. The intensification practiced by contemporary capitalism changes its strategies, making ineffective many previously developed strategies for resistance. For instance, capitalism does not so much flatten differences as make use of them. Lisa Lowe explains Cedric Robinson's "racial capitalism" as the way "actually existing capitalism exploits through culturally and socially constructed differences such as race, gender, region, and nationality, and is lived through those uneven formations."[6] She continues: "Capitalism expands not through rendering all labor, resources, and markets across the world identical, but by precisely seizing upon colonial divisions, identifying particular regions for production and others for neglect, certain populations for exploitation and still others for disposal." Lowe worries that many discussions of contemporary neoliberalism forget not only colonialism's capacity for turning human beings into literal capital but also the decolonial struggles that form an alternative horizon for "the political."[7] Respect for difference or recognition of the full humanity of differently racialized people may then assist "actually existing capitalism's" ability to make use of such constructed differences. As a result, the task of developing strategies for transformation becomes yet more difficult.

The Queer Prophet

With these caveats in mind, and the brief list of diagnostic criteria enumerated above, let me turn to a description of the tasks I have assigned to the queer prophet: creation of temporal and spatial contiguity among people who live in different times and differently spatialized places, the formation of a "we" as a result of such proximity, the identification of the salient processes (or quilting points) of global capital (processes that are in a nonintentional sense well designed to obscure themselves from view), the utterance of demands[8] indexed to the transformation of such salient processes by the "we," and, in the processes, the development of "our" ability to believe in an impossible and unimaginable future.[9]

Two biblical scenes stand at the heart of my vision of prophecy: Joel's description of the last days ("Your sons and daughters will prophesy, your old men will dream dreams, your young men will see visions. Even on my servants, both men and women, I will pour out my spirit in those days"[10]) and Ezekiel's tormented body on the ground with its face set against Jerusalem.[11] Joel's description suggests the transsocial, transgenerational, and transgender aspects of the prophetic—the indiscriminate distribution of visions of an *otherwise* that grounds a transformed community. These lines from Joel focus on dreams and visions, as well as on the relation to an other ("my spirit") that opens up ordinary time to another time (those days) in which such dreams and visions are realized. Prophecy is not, then, about foretelling the future. Rather, prophecy is a practice of reshaping the present to become other than what it is. Prophetic speech performances sometimes denounce injustice and inequality and promise transformation. However, my interest in this context is less in the *content* of prophetic speech than in prophetic material actions, located in the body and its (in)capacities, that reorder the world.

When Ezekiel lies down with one arm tied to his side and sets his face against Jerusalem, he joins or even inaugurates a genealogy of prophets whose performing bodies are the material of their prophecy. Ezekiel's inexplicable vignettes are, Rhiannon Graybill suggests, "sign acts" that offer "a series of peculiar and generally ineffective embodied performances that mark the beginning of his prophecy."[12] Ezekiel's prophetic acts are "instigated in crisis and located in the body."[13] Without speaking, Ezekiel's "prophecy begins as a series of performances . . . that leave no indication of their success."[14] For Graybill, "dumbness and other difficulties with speech characterize prophecy in disaster."[15] These scenes suggest the partial indeterminacy of prophecy: It confounds intention as well as clear determinations of agency and resistance.[16]

I propose understanding prophecy as bodied acts, often baffling even to the prophet, that have transformative potential in relation to the current order but that require reception and mediation (and thus relation) in order to actualize that potential—reception and mediation that may not at the time, or ever, appear.[17] The effects of prophetic practice are thus finitely deferred, potentially (although not necessarily) nonevidentiary at the moment of encounter, yet not outside any testing by effects. Prophetic acts often have a diagnostic character in relation to the present and its practices of concealment, but prophecy also entails a relation to the "otherwise than actual," where the "actual" refers to the monopoly on actuality claimed by the current order.[18] But prophecy is less about incorporation (Word-takes-flesh) of a radically different social order somehow uncontaminated by present distortions than it is about incarnation (Word-made-flesh) that reveals the true nature of our socioeconomic order and draws us toward new ways of being. Prophecy also traverses the visible and invisible. In body-form, prophecy is also always visible and potentially communicative, yet its visibility is irreducible to a brute empiricism; instead, prophecy makes visible the demonically hidden (where "demonic" signifies what in capitalism is larger-than-life yet contingent—more below) and changes the vantage point from which the world, and its necessities, is regarded.

Prophecy may also involve speech (always also a bodied act), whether understood or not. For example, the performance artist Ron Athey transforms his body into a specular site of subjection and resistance, incorporating blood, sex, and prophetic speech (glossolalia) in ritual re-enactments of sainthood. Athey's work often reflects the AIDS crisis (he himself is HIV-positive). Athey's performances, which most of the time involve extreme and bloody forms of body-art, form new, only partly evanescent communities, constituted by the experiences of empathy and specularization. Audiences feel empathy for Athey but also enjoy the voyeuristic thrill of seeing someone "in the flesh" push his flesh as far as Athey does; this dual reaction is extended even further in performances like *Incorruptible Flesh: Messianic Remains*, where at one point members of the audience salve Athey's naked, tortured body as he lies with eyelids pinned back with fishhooks. As the title *Incorruptible Flesh* suggests, Athey simultaneously lays claim to the reality of flesh, its carnal truth and the impress such carnal truth has on those present (one of the reasons he prefers that his performances not be recorded), *and*, in the flesh, constitutes himself as a secular saint whose (in)voluntarily ravaged, beautiful, HIV-positive body is both his truth and his medium—that is, a body that neither refuses nor is overcome by the reality of death, risk, and suffering in human lives. Athey was brought up to be a prophet, a chosen one, who "was to sacrifice the playthings of the world, in order to fulfil the plans of God."[19] He even sought the stigmata as a child.[20] In *Sebastiane*, Athey at one point breaks into glossolalia while crucified and pierced with arrows made of syringes. At that point, agency and self-possession are no longer adequate to describe what is happening. By speaking in tongues, Athey embodies and enacts relations to that which is otherwise: ways of being human in which a nonagential agency emerges, identification is rendered open to nonhuman powers, and clear-cut distinctions between the religious and the secular are undone.

Much has been written about the ways in which queer performance art—indeed, queer art of many kinds—develops in the context of experiences of abjection, disidentification, and condemnation to death (in connection with AIDS, which continues to hit people of color, especially women, particularly hard). But there are also other genealogies of queer and racialized performance.[21] Performance is often considered the most widely accessible art form, since it requires nothing other than the body. Uri McMillan argues that some acts under conditions of slavery may be read through the interpretive lens of what he terms "self-objectification" as a strategy for (not guarantee of) "an emancipated subjectivity."[22] The implication is that self-possession of the body (to be "body" rather than "flesh") is not an absolute condition for such performances. In McMillan's reading, "forms of subjectivity and agency are always present, however miniscule they may be." He seeks to "rescrambl[e] the dichotomy between objectified bodies or embodied subjects by reimagining objecthood as a performance-based method that disrupts presumptive knowledges of black subjectivity."[23] In a series of astonishing studies, McMillan uses the notion of an "embodied avatar" to think about the possibilities of black women's performances in the United States over a period of nearly two hundred years: "Avatars . . . act as mediums—between the spiritual and earthly as well as the abstract and the real—and . . . their attendant meanings . . . continue to multiply."[24] Black women's performances of "avatar production" are "a means of highlighting (and stretching) the subordinate roles available to black women."[25] Black women's performances have not historically had illusions of escapism or dematerialized utopian idealism available to them.[26]

McMillan's understanding of the avatar can be juxtaposed (but not equated) with the ways in which notions of possession, prophetic, or ecstatic speech have been used as gendered strategies for resistance, claiming authority, and transformation. Aihwa Ong's classic study *Spirits of Resistance and Capitalist Discipline* shows how spirit possession offered female Malay factory workers ways to resist the disciplines imposed on them, even as the forms of resistance reflected the contestations over bodies, sexuality, and production that constricted these women: "Their struggles to pose new questions and redefine the meaning of morality represented a quest for self-determination against agencies of power and capital which treat human beings like raw resources, disposable instruments, and fractured sensibilities."[27] Mary Keller picks up Ong's descriptions in her study of gender, agency, and possession when she argues for "instrumental agency as a corrective framework for interpreting the agency of possessed bodies, which are not conscious agents but instead are functioning as instrumental agencies for the ancestors, deities, or spirits that possess them."[28] Instrumental agency avoids Western, colonial overwriting of possession into more "palatable" terms.[29] Instead, instrumental agency leaves a space for the "otherwise" that manifests itself in the possessed. Keller argues that the instrumental agency of the possessed changes the relation to the past, "thereby producing an altered knowledge of the present. With the woman's body as the instrumental agency for a reterritorialization of time, the ancestors, deities, or spirits re-create perpetual beginnings . . . such that the past reinstantiates itself as constitutive of the present."[30] Struggles over possession, agency, and prophetic authority also take place as the prophetic and ecstatic are distinguished from the rational and discursive, as Laura Nasrallah cautions. Such distinctions can reproduce the "periodization" on which Western ideas of progress depend.[31] Nasrallah makes evident that the contestations encoded in prophecy involve debates over what counts as knowledge, as well as over whose knowledge counts.[32]

Developing the figure of the queer prophet through a collision between biblical stories and contemporary performance art has the capacity to confound historical periodization as well as colonial assignations of reason to some and unreason to others. Because the queer prophet practices within and in relation to global capitalism, the prophetic cannot be dismissed as a romantic search for an "outside" that will avoid the pressures and contradictions of "Western modernity." Nor is the prophet archaic, a vestige of an outmoded religiosity soon to be surpassed. Instead, the prophet often emerges from the lively, in-between, invisibilized spaces that geographer Katherine McKittrick describes and to which we now turn.

If the prophet's body is the material of diagnostic and transformative becoming in relation to an otherwise, the questions that follow reflect both the situation of the prophet's body and its sign-character. Prophets, as not-quite-agential agents of transformation, cannot magically accomplish the reshaping of the world that is hinted at or momentarily incarnated in them. The many stories of prophets whose acts are not understood or whose warnings are not believed (Cassandra, most famously) remind us that prophecy without reception becomes a trace of what could have been rather than of what might still be.[33] In what follows, then, I want to tarry for a while with the space and time of change. Into what sedimented cultural formations, and against which larger-than-life powers, must prophets intervene? If a prophetic performance is received, what happens? How is the world reordered?

The Space of Change

Describing the poetry of Dionne Brand, McKittrick says that "geography, the material world, is infused with sensations and distinct ways of knowing: rooms full of weeping, exhausted countries, a house that is only as safe as flesh. Brand's decision . . . to disclose that geography is always human and that humanness is always geographic . . . suggests that her surroundings are speakable."[34] McKittrick reads geography through "space, place, and location in their physical materiality and imaginative configurations,"[35] in particular through the histories of black women that disclose the constructed nature of seemingly given geographies. These histories open up "an interpretive alterable world, rather than a transparent and knowable world."[36] Seeing from the vantage point of the historical geographies of black women discloses "domination as a visible spatial project that organizes, names, and sees social differences (such as black femininity) and determines *where* social order happens."[37] The "cartographies of struggle," then, are "respatializations."[38]

Following Édouard Glissant and Sylvia Wynter, McKittrick argues that such respatializations issue neither in a unitary framework nor in repossession of stolen landscapes but instead in "a grammar of liberation, through which ethical *human*-geographies can be recognized and expressed."[39] Examining the construction of space leads to "'a *public* genealogy of resistance': histories, names, and places of black pain, language, and opposition, which are 'spoken with the whole body' and present to the world, to our geography, other rhythms, other times, other spaces."[40] The histories of black women's geographies generate "a workable terrain through which respatialization can be and is imagined and achieved."[41] Rather than transparent, naturalized, and hierarchically arranged landscapes, these geographies are contested; they are where struggle takes place.[42] McKittrick insists, however, that black women's geographies are neither marginal to the production of space nor only histories of dispossession.[43] Instead, they offer critical terrain within and across geographies of domination that naturalize hierarchical difference.

It is from Sylvia Wynter that McKittrick develops her understanding of the demonic as a participative, possessive (in the "supernatural" sense), opaque concealment that discloses.[44] "The demonic . . . is a nondeterministic schema; it is a process that is hinged on uncertainty and non-linearity because the organizing principle cannot predict the future."[45] "Demonic grounds" are both the geographies through which difference is hierarchically organized—through prisons, borders, the reordering of global cities, economic domination, and more—and geographies already "life-filled and poetic."[46] While this is not McKittrick's language, I think she imagines a geography of contiguities and relations that avoids the atomization and isolation of single-issue struggles that continually bedevil left efforts at social transformation, while mobilizing extant geographic knowledges toward transformation. Demonic grounds indicate what already is, the territory from which the otherwise must be made, but the demonic is also a way to indicate the future's potential difference from the present as well as the present's own contingency.

Seeing geography from the vantage point of black women's histories of struggle discloses the "intimacies" discussed by Lisa Lowe: "the range of laboring contacts that are necessary for the production of bourgeois domesticity, as well as the intimacy of captured workers surviving together, the proximity and affinity that gives rise to political, sexual, intellectual collaborations, subaltern revolts and uprisings."[47] Lowe draws attention to the revolutionary potential of spatial proximity when it becomes spatial contiguity (relational inhabitation of contiguous nonidentical space). The wild hypergentrification currently transforming cities like New York and London ensures that the economically powerful are spared contiguity with the less powerful, experiencing only proximity mediated by economic disparity. Respatialization requires works like Yinka Shonibare's *Nelson's Ship in a Bottle*, an artwork exhibited in Trafalgar Square that, Lowe says, makes visible "a new 'grammar' for referring to the concealed histories of empire, slavery, and migration that linked the trades in goods and peoples between Europe, Asia, Africa, and the Americas."[48] By materializing the intimacies rendered ideologically invisible or forgotten, Shonibare's ship remaps the geography of Trafalgar Square in relation to empires past and present. In my terms, Shonibare's creation is a past-oriented prophetic disclosure that tells a story of how things came to be the way they are. Learning to see the occluded past is one aspect of learning to see the present more truthfully.[49] Respatialization in service of the creation-discovery of contiguity (also always bodily) between the relationally nonidentical thus offers the potential to counter the naturalized geographic order of the world.[50] Respatialization accompanies struggle and is effected by it, just as spatiality is itself a history of struggle.

That respatialization is necessary is shown by work like Ruth Wilson Gilmore's brilliant *Golden Gulag*, in which she examines the spatial landscape of prisons in California. As she points out, the expanse and scale of California prisons "belies the common view that prisons sit on the edge—at the margins of social spaces, economic regions, political territories, and fights for rights. This apparent marginality is a trick of perspective, because . . . edges are also interfaces. . . . They also connect places into relationships with each other and with non-contiguous places." The more hopeful implication is that there are more possibilities for collective, connected action toward change, even between struggles that seem distant from each other.[51] Through an analysis of four different kinds of surplus— "finance capital, land, labor, and state capacity"[52]—she demonstrates how the vast expansion of prison capacity became a possible, but not inevitable, partial solution to the crises involved in those surpluses. Gilmore shows how shifts in state financial structure, land and water use, unemployment and defense spending, voting patterns, concern about violent crime, and the relationships between state, municipal, and corporate interests combined to generate the hugely expanded prison population in California, despite the drop in the crime rate that began well before the prison boom.[53] That carceral state depends on and intensifies antiblackness even as it ensnares many Latinx, API, and other minoritized people.[54] Throughout, she reminds us that "prison siting, like all industrial siting, is a question of land use . . . [and so] a question about horizontal and vertical social and economic planning,"[55] the planning that California abandoned while "the corporate and banking forces' determining the movement of capital across the land feature central planning as a fundamental activity."[56] There is much more to be said about Gilmore's analysis, which I return to briefly below. For our purposes here, she makes clear that, as McKittrick also points out, social, economic, political, and racial struggles are also always geographic, spatial, situated struggles. The reorder of economic relations cannot take place without, and indeed depends on, respatialization: "We make places, things, and selves, but not under conditions of our own choosing. . . . [Yet] persistent small changes, and altogether unexpected consolidations, [have] added up to enough weight, over time and space, to cause a break with the old order."[57] In order to act toward such a break, we must learn to read, and then reorganize, the spatial configurations that organize our lives, separate us from one another, and produce the lively and the "forgotten places"[58] in which many of us live.

In his study of Black ballroom culture in Detroit, Marlon Bailey describes the "performance labor" that creates both alternative kinship networks for "multiply marginalized communities" and the spaces within which such worlds come into being.[59] "Black LGBT people have a vexed relationship with space (built environments)," he points out.[60] Space for communal transformation has to be created; it is not simply given. Building spaces—renting them, paying for them, rearranging them into the "proper" arrangements that allow for balls to take place—requires labor in the most concrete of senses,[61] but the work also expands the very meaning of labor itself.[62] Bailey's investigation of the material and social labor that stages the ritual performances of the multiply marginalized ends on a note of reflection about the challenges and limitations of dominant HIV/AIDS prevention strategies. He argues that "ballroom culture offers . . . just the beginning of a cultural practice of survival that is desperately needed."[63] The need for practices of survival, along with memorializing those lost to HIV/AIDS, turns our attention to times past, present, and future.

Times and Other Times

Respatialization also involves queer forms of temporality: learning to see the past in the present, as in Lowe's discussion of Shonibare; remembering the dead in the body of the prophet-performer; crossing between capital's many presents. As in McKittrick's work, retemporalization may take place on the demonic grounds of historical memory. It also involves the "future anterior,"[64] which is a more promising version of what theologians call the already-not yet. Harry Harootunian discusses capital's encounters with the temporal differences that it also produces: "The time of capital is . . . complex; it presents a smooth, unbroken surface that resembles national time, yet it also works to unify immense temporal irregularities—uneven time—in the sphere of production, circulation, and distribution—thus totalizing the various temporal processes resulting from the division of labor. . . . Capitalist time situates the global at the level of the everyday and local, unsettling and segregating it into heterogeneous units."[65] Capital's ability to smooth temporal irregularities while also producing and using them striates time, allowing those who live in consonance with different times to pass each other by without lasting entanglement even when they encounter each other directly. In Johannes Fabian's classic *Time and the Other*, he demonstrates how anthropology denies contemporaneity (what he terms "coevalness") between itself and its objects in ways that actively produce and reproduce the imperial, colonial, and capitalist relations through which exploitation and domination continue.[66] We have already noted the way historical periodization also contributes to the production of the colonial other who remains stuck, mired in the past and unable to come up to or be contemporaneous with a flattened modernity. The challenges of the time of capital thus emerge both from its striating or segregating capacities, and from its integrating capacities.

Queer theories of temporality, following Carolyn Dinshaw, have looked into the possibility of "touching across time."[67] Queer theory, especially in its most influential forms, is tightly bound up with memories of a lost and partly idyllic past, pre-HIV/AIDS, as well as with the losses and mourning that still attach to all the missing. In addition, queer is bound up with—and skeptical of—the articulation of regimes of sexuality that do not have historical names. Thus, queering, both in performance and text, involves the reading and rereading of texts in which one cannot find oneself, or if one finds oneself, it is only obliquely, in unexpected ways.[68] One of the most famous performances of the group Split Britches was their reenactment of *A Streetcar Named Desire*, *Belle Reprieve*, in which butch lesbian Peggy Shaw plays Stanley. *Belle Reprieve* offers resignification on resignification, in relation to the play as well as the iconic status the movie—especially Marlon Brando and Vivien Leigh's performances—has taken on in relation to a certain kind of heteromasculinity, as Sue-Ellen Case points out. Displacement and doubling are unavoidable.[69] In Joshua Lubin-Levy and Carlos Motta's *Petite Mort: Recollections of a Queer Public*,[70] they gather maps drawn by primarily gay male participants in the public sex cultures of New York City. Overlaying others' memories of public sex onto familiar locations in the city doubles with one's own memories. Such maps trace the movements of others' bodies, without proffering reciprocal recognition. The traces are both historical and potentially hostile for some. Such queer, not always affirmative, forms of temporality provide possible models of seeing oneself in relation to what one did not know one was intimate with, to adapt Lowe's language. Capital's intensification of temporal irregularities, while smoothing the always almost instantaneous present for its own transactions, allows the coexistence of striated times that have to become connected, become intimate, with each other. Queer performances are one way of learning to do that interpretive work.

Temporal and spatial reorganizations are distinguishable but never separable. Temporal contestation emerges repeatedly around the relationship between woman, feminist, lesbian, and queer. The Split Britches, or perhaps more accurately Lois Weaver and Peggy Shaw, cofounders of the WOW Café Theatre in New York, are at the heart of many such stories told by performance scholars. If the antisex, staid, lesbian-feminist is to be left behind by the parodically playful queer, one way to rescue lesbian attachment might be to demonstrate that lesbian-feminist performance anticipates in its practice the theory that will only emerge a decade later, as Kate Davy argues.[71] Unfortunately, the way in which Davy makes the case reproduces, rather than undoes, some of the most distortive stereotypes of lesbian and feminist life in the 1970s and 1980s. Further, in order to ensure that the WOW Café lands on the "right" side of history (i.e., shows itself in line with typical histories of the overcoming of monolithic white feminism by new attention to intersectionality and diversity), Davy works hard to make the case that performances at WOW were attentive to race even though the vast majority of central performers[72] and participants were white: "If the racialization that produces whiteness is deployed through the construct of white womanhood, then the aggressively oppositional stance WOW women take . . . flies in the face of that process. . . . There is something 'not quite white' about WOW."[73] Even though Davy wants to critique simplistic feminist histories, and even as she worries about racial politics, she ends up reproducing what she critiques in its overcoming.[74]

Davy's stories, and my critiques, bring us to another necessary form of retemporalization that concerns the politics of storytelling itself. In *Why Stories Matter*, Clare Hemmings marks out three dominant narrative forms of feminist self-narration: stories of progress, of loss, and of return.[75] As Hemmings points out, these narratives depend on generationalism and a temporalization that assigns different feminist theorists to different decades based on whatever "turn" they are symbolically thought to inaugurate or represent, while investing those different decades with positive or negative affect depending on which narrative form is being invoked.[76] Generationalism overwrites political disagreement within any given period[77] while producing subjects who are "now" always at the crest of the right wave.[78] Feminist temporal stories do not only recode contestation, disagreement, and diversity as generational stories.[79] They also allow us to deflect our own self-implication in "the complicity others necessarily remain mired within."[80] Generational stories are a strategy for maintaining positive affect around our status as subjects of feminism, Hemmings argues.[81]

The generationalism Hemmings describes also has other worrisome aspects. The ever-renewed Western production of the non-Western as its temporal and spatial Other takes place through narratives of feminist and queer progress. And many of the stories Hemmings describe hinge, like Davy's above, on where race—particularly black lesbian feminism—is placed in the narrative. In progress narratives, feminists of color, many but not all lesbian, are firmly placed in the 1980s in order to set up the grand discovery of difference that marks the 1990s.[82] Return narratives keep "black, postcolonial, and/or lesbian critiques" in the 1980s, but as part of a story of descent and loss.[83] Return narratives, which call for a return to materiality, find the conditions requiring material amelioration outside the West. They thus produce "a temporal as well as spatial dynamic between 'the West' and 'the rest.'"[84] They also erase the critiques of this dynamic that have emerged over several decades both from within and, more importantly, from without white Western feminist spaces,[85] leading the white Western feminist to confront the disturbing realization "that she may not be the subject of history at all."[86]

Retemporalizing (and to some extent "detemporalizing") might in part require a strategy of evasion: evasion of the obsessive need many Western feminist and queer theorists have to rehearse the shared just-so stories of "our" disciplines and disciplining[87] in order to secure both a shared past and "our" own right positioning at the theoretical and political cutting edge of a different future. The politics of storytelling are, well, *political*. In Wynter's terms, these stories constitute only a minor variation in the story of Man's overrepresentation. And each generational narrative involves varying claims for when and whether feminism became attentive to race and when and whether feminism became aware of its Anglo-American, Eurocentric, and colonial biases.[88]

That last sentence reproduces in its form the way, as Janet Jakobsen points out, a "we" of feminism that intends to overcome feminism's oft-cited and oft-repudiated association with white, heterosexual, middle-class, Western women might instead stabilize that association.[89] Rather than asking how to make allies out of the different, Jakobsen argues that allies emerge *from* alliance among the different: "Alliance is . . . the necessary pre-requisite to movement."[90] Thus "solidarity shifts the site of agency away from identity and to alliance. . . . The 'I' who is an ally becomes so only in and through the process of working together ('with others')."[91] If

Jakobsen is right, activated solidarity precedes rather than results from acting together with others toward ends that may only take on form in the process of struggle.

Gilmore's *Golden Gulag* stunningly illustrates the latter dynamic. Her analysis of the antiprison activism of Mothers Reclaiming Our Children shows how the individuation and fragmentation resulting from arrest mobilized mothers (biological and fictive) to work against what is often called the prison-industrial complex in California.[92] The members of the group "arrived at their art through critical action."[93] While each person came to Mothers ROC primarily because a specific loved one was ensnared by California's vicious "anti-crime" laws,[94] they brought different, more or less formal, experiences of organizing with them.[95] "In the context of shared opposition, the activists 'discovered' . . . —which is to say, created—shared values; in turn, that collective work produced community solidarity . . . enabling further action."[96] Gilmore's complex case study sets up the way in which collective subjects acting together for change can both form alliances across difference and be vulnerable to fragmentation.

"We" Demand a Future

Having considered some of the challenges and opportunities for respatialization and retemporalization, let us briefly tarry with the "we" that can demand a future different from the present. Jill Dolan's *Utopia in Performance* begins with the claim that "live performance provides a place where people come together, embodied and passionate, to share experiences of meaning making and imagination that can describe or capture fleeting intimations of a better world."[97] What's especially important to her is the way theater has the capacity to expand the audience's notion of the "humankind" for which one hopes and seeks a better future. Along related but nonidentical lines, Weheliye envisions humanity as "a relational ontological totality, however fractured this totality may be."[98] Dolan joins the many scholars in recent years who have turned toward affect as a way to explore human sensibilities. For my purposes, Dolan's emphasis on the didactic (my word, not hers) qualities of certain performances and shared experiences— that they teach "us" what it might look like to *become* an "us" that "we" are not yet—is especially useful. The affective form of expansive humanism that she seeks broadens one's sense of community and identification, but not at the cost of particularity. Rather, particularity becomes a medium *for* identification—with a performer, in some cases, with the rest of the audience, and with those unknown others who might also want to be part of the transformed world possibilities held out in those moments. Dolan reads "performance as a public practice, as a rehearsal for an example that yearns toward something better and more just than the social arrangements that divide us now, [so that] theater becomes a sort of temple of communion with a future we need to practice envisioning."[99] Dolan explicitly seeks an ethical rather than religious temple, but rigid distinctions between sacred and secular belong to the politics of time that create the colonial other; McKittrick's and Wynter's demonic otherwise avoids any fixed distinctions of that kind. And many biblical stories about prophetic acts reflect contestation among different gods rather than between god and not-god.

Moving beyond sacred-secular divides is only one of the many forms of alliance required to redirect capital's complex network of powers to separate, striate, and interconnect. Judith Butler argues for a politics of alliance (which is how she understands queer[100]) that follows from interdependency and "our shared exposure to precarity."[101] The creation of a "we" should not be a matter of indistinguishability or identity, but in performance one might imagine oneself as part of a different "we," or one might see a differently organized sociality represented. Redrawing naturalized, sedimented, separating social relations becomes easier if and when one is made aware of the limits of one's identifications, but perhaps especially when different socialities are represented and one finds oneself irresistibly drawn to them. Such "we"s may not be permanent, or even long-term "we"s, but they may allow for the creation and recognition of contiguity rather than proximity among those who have not known themselves in relation to one another.

Many of our diagnostic and theoretical tools lag capital's developments. Critical theorists worry about naturalization and essentialism, while capital promotes fluidity and transformation.[102] Some of our hopefully resistant practices might then miss their target and might turn out to be only too consonant with capitalism's new capacities to orient us from within.[103] The prophet, however, stands in relation to an *otherwise* (possessed by a god, perhaps) that reveals hidden mysteries (albeit in mysterious ways). A queer prophetic practice is one, then, in which we learn to see, to know, the present differently. Such practice might eventuate in, as Alexander Weheliye puts it, the recognition that "the functioning of blackness as both inside and outside modernity sets the stage for a general theory of the human, and not its particular exception."[104] The "hidden places" (McKittrick) are the places from which we might learn to see differently and, more accurately, across and aslant sedimented spatiotemporal formations of Man.

A "we" formed by alliances between the different genres of the human that already exist has the capacity to make demands. Kathi Weeks argues that a crucial component of the utopian demand is its ability to "alter our connection to the present [and] . . . shift our relationship to the future; one is productive of estrangement, the other of hope."[105] For Weeks, estrangement from the conditions of apparent necessity (there is no alternative) that our current social arrangements seek to imbue in us is an essential condition for the demand that can shift and reorder one's sense of the possible. The demand also works against the insistence on individual responsibility that does so much work in contemporary politics and economics—the way each of us is made to be responsible for ourselves. The prophetic performative whose outlines I am trying to delineate can be seen, for instance, in the bodily performances of Black Lives Matter activists, whose demands[106] follow from their worldmaking practices. Any possible enactment of those demands depends on alliances among the different. Butler emphasizes the infrastructural nature of demands that are implied by taking to the streets—streets that are, after all, a public good.[107] While the performances (and performatives) I describe do not depend on a particular kind of infrastructure, their inhabitability over time may depend on *some* kind of infrastructure, like the experimental theaters near my home in New York that bought their buildings cheaply from the city and are now partially, but not totally, immune to the immense real estate pressures brought by hypergentrification.

The future in which prophetic performance teaches us to believe is also no future, at least from the perspective of continuity. Kathi Weeks asks whether we "could . . . bear to will our own transformation. . . . Can we want, and are we willing to create, a new world that would no longer be 'our' world, a social form that would not produce subjects like us?"[108] Yet this world was never "our" world to begin with, for some of "us" "were never meant to survive."[109] The future that is better, the one to which we are led by the queer prophet, may look like the end of the world. Yet human beings always act toward unknown and unknowable futures; the question is whether we can find ways to become contiguous with each other in alliances that will shout transformative demands together.

NOTES

1. Linn Marie Tonstad, "Debt Time Is Straight Time," *Political Theology* 17 no. 5 (September 2016); and Linn Marie Tonstad, "The Entrepreneur and the Big Drag: Risky Affirmation in Capital's Time," in *Sexual Disorientations: Queer Temporalities, Affects, Theologies*, ed. Kent Brintnall, Joseph

Marchal, Stephen Moore, and Catherine Keller (New York: Fordham University Press, 2018).

2. As I write elsewhere, any brief discussion that pretends to deal with the dynamics of global capitalism risks overgeneralization, excessive historicization, and dematerialization.

3. Tonstad, "Entrepreneur and the Big Drag," 223.

4. Tonstad, "Entrepreneur and the Big Drag," 226–27.

5. Richard Dienst, *The Bonds of Debt: Borrowing against the Common Good* (London: Verso, 2011), 2; and Karen Ho, *Liquidated: An Ethnography of Wall Street* (Durham, N.C.: Duke University Press, 2009), 34–38.

6. Lisa Lowe, *The Intimacies of Four Continents* (Durham, N.C.: Duke University Press, 2015), 149–50.

7. Lowe, *Intimacies of Four Continents*, 196–98n54.

8. I am thinking here with Kathi Weeks, although I, to some extent, prefer the manifesto to the utopian demand for which she argues. See Kathi Weeks, *The Problem with Work: Feminism, Marxism, Antiwork Politics, and Postwork Imaginaries* (Durham, N.C.: Duke University Press, 2011).

9. These elements derive from three primary sources. The first is experiences of the visionary and imaginative capacities of performance art. The second is analyses distilled from a variety of accounts of contemporary (and especially financialized) capitalism. The third reflects my attempt to think through the relationships between institutions and the imagination that are required to generate—to *materialize*—transformation.

10. Joel 2:28–29.

11. See Ezekiel 4:1–5:4 for a description of the tasks set him during this period. There are many other relevant body-acts in biblical prophecy that also inform this account. They include stories like the odd (and oddly doubled) body-acts in 1 Samuel when Saul comes among the prophets, falls into a frenzy, and strips himself naked (19:18–24; see also 10:9–16); Jeremiah sunk in mud in a cistern (Jeremiah 38:6), punished for demoralizing soldiers in an unrighteous war; Daniel's interpretive skills, employed to denounce Belshazzar, who rewards him for his sagacity (Daniel 5); Hosea's horrifically sexist body-acts (expressed through denigration of sex workers, procreation, slave-trading, and adultery; Hosea 1–3); Jonah's adventures in sailing, whaling, and worming, combined with his incomprehension of why God would care about 120,000 people in Nineveh "and also many animals" (Jonah 4:11); the body-acts of John the Baptist, who ate locusts and honey in the wilderness before being beheaded by an unjust ruler and whose pointing hand identifies the Lamb of God (Matthew 3:4; John 1:29); Jesus's inaugural act (the transformation of water into wine), inexplicable cursing of the fig tree (Mark 11:12–14), his crucifixion and resurrection; and the scroll eaten

by the first-person narrator of Revelation (10:8–10) as well as his measuring practices (11:1). In many of these stories, prophets contest with each other for symbolic authority, setting prophet against prophet.

12. Rhiannon Graybill, "Voluptuous, Tortured, and Unmanned: Ezekiel and Daniel Paul Schreber," in *The Bible and Posthumanism*, ed. Jennifer L. Koosed (Atlanta: Society of Biblical Literature, 2014), 137.

13. Graybill, "Voluptuous, Tortured, and Unmanned," 138.

14. Graybill, 139. Graybill suggests that most attempts to read Ezekiel as a form of performance art neglect the fact that Ezekiel, unlike the performance artist, does not have a choice about what he does (140). Yet choice, in each case, is not a transparent site of self-identical autonomy; the relational character of performance also troubles any straightforward search for the volition of the prophet-performer.

15. Graybill, 144.

16. While I disagree with Alexander G. Weheliye that agency and resistance require "full, self-present, and coherent subjects working against something or someone," I strongly agree that these concepts may not be the most illuminating ways to consider the "genres" of human being that offer alternatives to the totalizing desires of contemporary capitalism. See Weheliye, *Habeas Viscus: Racializing Assemblages, Biopolitics, and Black Feminist Theories of the Human* (Durham, N.C.: Duke University Press, 2014), 2.

17. I thus align myself with those thinkers who have recently done much to draw attention to the *contingencies* of history, the it-might-have-been that haunts many accounts of how-it-was.

18. This is related to, but not identical with, Sylvia Wynter's description of the dominance of *homo oeconomicus*: "The genre-specific preprescribed 'truth' of economics must itself analogically elaborate an ethno-class *descriptive statement* mode of *material provisioning* that can, law-likely, be *only that* of *homo oeconomicus's* single absolute model of free-market capitalism. . . . This model can, at the same time, be enacted only on the homogenized basis of the systemic repression of all other alternative modes of material provisioning. . . . There can ostensibly be no alternative to its . . . free-market capitalist economic system, in its now extreme neoliberal transnational technocratic configuration." Sylvia Wynter and Katherine McKittrick, "Unparalleled Catastrophe for Our Species? Or, To Give Humanness a Different Future: Conversations," in *Sylvia Wynter: On Being Human as Praxis*, ed. Katherine McKittrick (Durham, N.C.: Duke University Press, 2015), 22.

19. Ron Athey, "Gifts of the Spirit," in *Pleading in the Blood: The Art and Performances of Ron Athey*, ed. Dominic Johnson (Chicago: Intellect/University of Chicago Press, 2013), 42.

20. Athey, "Gifts of the Spirit," 42.

21. José Esteban Muñoz's hugely influential *Cruising Utopia: The Then and There of Queer Futurity* (New York: New York University Press, 2009) reads queer performance as holding open the possibility of a queer utopia that we have not yet become and that cannot be specified in advance. I share with Muñoz the sense that performance art constitutes, even now, a vital resource for social transformation. Because my concern is especially with the need to shift currents in contemporary capitalism, my argument focuses on what queer performance art does when it helps to generate new imaginative possibilities in relation to specific features of the current order. As a result, my criteria are material and concrete in ways that Muñoz's are not; they are also flatter and less possibility-filled. Peggy Phelan made the now-implausible argument that performance intrinsically resists capitalism because it is not subject to reproduction in *Unmarked: The Politics of Performance* (New York: Routledge, 1993).

22. Uri McMillan, *Embodied Avatars: Genealogies of Black Feminist Art and Performance* (New York: New York University Press, 2015), 8.

23. McMillan, *Embodied Avatars*, 9.

24. McMillan, 11.

25. McMillan, 12.

26. Here we might think of Hortense J. Spillers on "garretting" and Katherine McKittrick's respatialization, discussed below, developed from Spillers. See Spillers, "Mama's Baby, Papa's Maybe: An American Grammar Book," in *Black, White, and in Color: Essays on American Literature and Culture* (Chicago: University of Chicago Press, 2003), 223; and Katherine McKittrick, *Demonic Grounds: Black Women and the Cartographies of Struggle* (Minneapolis: University of Minnesota Press, 2006), 59–63.

27. Aihwa Ong, *Spirits of Resistance and Capitalist Discipline: Factory Women in Malaysia*, 2nd ed. (Albany: SUNY Press, 2010), 221. The women were not always able to target the forces working on them directly, however (210–13).

28. Mary Keller, *The Hammer and the Flute: Women, Power and Spirit Possession* (Baltimore: Johns Hopkins University Press, 2002), 22.

29. Keller, *Hammer and the Flute*, 74.

30. Keller, 79.

31. Laura Nasrallah, *An Ecstasy of Folly: Prophecy and Authority in Early Christianity* (Cambridge, Mass.: Harvard Theological Studies, 2003), 202.

32. Nasrallah, *Ecstasy of Folly*, 202–3.

33. Whether what could have been can be transformed into what might still be is another question, one that depends heavily on valid analogies between what was and what is.

34. McKittrick, *Demonic Grounds*, ix.

35. McKittrick, x.

36. McKittrick, xiii.

37. McKittrick, xiv.

38. McKittrick, xix.

39. McKittrick, xxiii.

40. McKittrick, xxvii, quoting Marlene Nourbese Philip, *A Genealogy of Resistance and Other Essays* (Toronto: Mercury Press, 1997), 25 (McKittrick's emphasis). From a different vantage point, Lowe suggests that "colonial difference" now "is not a fixed binary distinction; it operates precisely through various modes of spatial differentiation and temporal development, . . . flexibly designating . . . contemporaneity or extinction, and so forth." *Intimacies of Four Continents*, 189n24.

41. McKittrick, *Demonic Grounds*, xxxi.

42. McKittrick, 6, 31, 122.

43. McKittrick, 62.

44. McKittrick, xxiv, 123.

45. McKittrick, xxiv.

46. McKittrick, 133.

47. Lowe, *Intimacies of Four Continents*, 35.

48. Lowe, 135.

49. As Lowe suggests, somewhat differently, in *Intimacies of Four Continents*, 137.

50. See also Judith Butler, who argues that "assembly and speech reconfigure the materiality of public space" even as assemblies of bodies (an emergent "we" that can ally on the basis of shared precarity [58]) cross and trouble distinctions between public and private. Butler, *Notes toward a Performative Theory of Assembly* (Cambridge, Mass.: Harvard University Press, 2015), 71.

51. Ruth Wilson Gilmore, *Golden Gulag: Prisons, Surplus, Crisis, and Opposition in Globalizing California* (Berkeley: University of California Press, 2007), 10–11.

52. Gilmore, *Golden Gulag*, 57.

53. Gilmore, 8–9, *passim*.

54. Gilmore reports that members of Mothers Reclaiming Our Children concluded that "you have to be white to be prosecuted under white law, but you do not have to be Black to be prosecuted under Black law." *Golden Gulag*, 227.

55. Gilmore, 175.

56. Gilmore, 179.

57. Gilmore, 242.

58. Gilmore, 247.

59. Marlon M. Bailey, *Butch Queens Up in Pumps: Gender, Performance, and Ballroom Culture in Detroit* (Ann Arbor: University of Michigan Press, 2013), 127.

60. Bailey, *Butch Queens*, 145.

61. Bailey, 146–47.

62. Bailey, 208–9.

63. Bailey, 220.

64. Lowe, *Intimacies of Four Continents*, 164, quoting Kenneth Surin on C. L. R. James.

65. Harry Harootunian, "Remembering the Historical Present," *Critical Inquiry* 33, no. 3 (Spring 2007): 473n3. See also Lowe, *Intimacies of Four Continents*, 60–61, on the irredeemable past.

66. Johannes Fabian, *Time and the Other: How Anthropology Makes Its Object* (New York: Columbia University Press, 1983), 149.

67. Carolyn Dinshaw, *Getting Medieval: Sexualities and Communities, Pre- and Postmodern* (Durham, N.C.: Duke University Press, 1999), 36.

68. See Sandra K. Soto, *Reading Chican@ Like a Queer: The De-Mastery of Desire* (Austin: University of Texas Press, 2015), 87–120, for one example of what such a reading might look like. See also David Halperin, *How to Be Gay* (Cambridge, Mass.: Belknap/Harvard University Press, 2012), 452–55.

69. Sue-Ellen Case, introduction to *Split Britches: Lesbian Practice/ Feminist Performance*, ed. Sue-Ellen Case (New York: Routledge, 1996), 28.

70. Joshua Lubin-Levy and Carlos Motta, *Petite Mort: Recollections of a Queer Public* (New York: Forever & Today, 2011).

71. Kate Davy, *Lady Dicks and Lesbian Brothers: Staging the Unimaginable at the WOW Café Theatre* (Ann Arbor: University of Michigan Press, 2010), 86–89.

72. With the significant exception of Carmelita Tropicana, who is central to Muñoz's earlier work in *Disidentifications: Queers of Color and the Performance of Politics* (Minneapolis: University of Minnesota Press, 1999), ch. 5.

73. Davy, *Lady Dicks*, 178.

74. For somewhat different reasons, Muñoz worries about Davy's earlier discussion, in "Fe/Male Impersonation," of camp's function in lesbian and gay male performance in Muñoz, *Disidentifications*, 128–35. Muñoz's concern is that Davy "limit[s] or foreclose[s] the possibility of lesbian camp" (131) by assigning camp primarily to gay men, but Davy appears to depoliticize camp as such. Kate Davy, "Fe/Male Impersonation: The Discourse of Camp," in *The Politics and Poetics of Camp*, ed. Moe Meyer (New York: Routledge, 1993).

75. Clare Hemmings, *Why Stories Matter: The Political Grammar of Feminist Theory* (Durham, N.C.: Duke University Press, 2011), 3–5.

76. Hemmings, *Why Stories Matter*, 5.

77. Hemmings, 5–7.

78. See Robyn Wiegman, *Object Lessons* (Durham, N.C.: Duke University Press, 2012), for a careful analysis of the desires encoded in that affective position.

79. Hemmings, *Why Stories Matter*, 156.

80. Hemmings, 83.

81. Hemmings, 25–26, 131–59.

82. Hemmings, 52–54.

83. Hemmings, 67.

84. Hemmings, 125.

85. Hemmings, 126–27.

86. Hemmings, 214.

87. Wiegman, *Object Lessons*, 8.

88. Hemmings, *Why Stories Matter*, 6, 8–10.

89. Janet R. Jakobsen, *Working Alliances and the Politics of Difference: Diversity and Feminist Ethics* (Bloomington: Indiana University Press, 1998), 118.

90. Jakobsen, *Working Alliances*, 120.

91. Jakobsen, *Working Alliances*, 166.

92. Gilmore, *Golden Gulag*, 235–36.

93. Gilmore, 236.

94. Gilmore points out that they sometimes encountered one another because "people who drive long distances to see loved ones [in prison] will make small talk in parking lots and discover an identity in their immediate purpose." *Golden Gulag*, 234.

95. Gilmore, 186–96, 206–8.

96. Gilmore, 238.

97. Jill Dolan, *Utopia in Performance: Finding Hope at the Theater* (Ann Arbor: University of Michigan Press, 2005), 2. See also Teresa Brennan, *The Transmission of Affect* (Ithaca, N.Y.: Cornell University Press, 2004).

98. Weheliye, *Habeas Viscus*, 32.

99. Dolan, *Utopia in Performance*, 135. At 136–37, she discusses what she sees as the religious or spiritual elements of this view.

100. Butler, *Notes toward a Performative Theory*, 70.

101. Butler, 218.

102. See Rosemary Hennessy, *Profit and Pleasure: Sexual Identities in Late Capitalism* (New York: Routledge, 2002).

103. Frédéric Lordon, *Willing Slaves of Capital: Spinoza & Marx on Desire*, trans. Gabriel Ash (London: Verso, 2014).

104. Weheliye, *Habeas Viscus*, 19.

105. Weeks, *Problem with Work*, 204–5.

106. "We Can End Police Violence in America," Campaign Zero, http://www.joincampaignzero.org/#vision.

107. Butler, *Notes toward a Performative Theory*, 125–29.

108. Weeks, *Problem with Work*, 202.

109. Audre Lorde, "A Litany for Survival," in *The Black Unicorn* (New York: Norton, 1995), 32.

CHAPTER 9

Life beyond the Doctrine of Man: Out of This World with Michel Henry and Radical Queer Theory

Kristien Justaert

On different levels, Sylvia Wynter's critique of the historical-social reality that she calls "Man" has led to a negative attitude toward "the world." The world, in this case, is to be distinguished from "life." The world is the realm of representation, the symbolic order, the "center" (as opposed to the periphery), where meaning resides and identity is possible. This essay starts from the assumption that negativity is the form under which Wynter's critique of "Man" has reached the Western world in which I reside. I would like to study this existential attitude of negativity toward the world (or *Grundstimmung*, in a Heideggerian term), which has nothing to do with psychological states of mind such as pessimism or depression, on both a philosophical and an ethical-cultural level, but rather with a deep, fundamental questioning of what Lacan calls the "symbolic order," the world as it is revealed to us and often gives meaning to our lives. In this essay, I investigate the critique of "Man" philosophically as well as culturally. I examine the reasons why the world is rejected, as well as the positive account of life that undergirds that critique and that allows for drawing the sketches of an alternative. This alternative, as I will demonstrate, is situated in matter or, more specifically, in living flesh.

In its rejection of the "world," and of a logic of inclusion (everybody should be able/enabled to belong to and participate in the world), this essay differs somewhat from other essays in this book. Indeed, the dystopian perspective partially laid out here contrasts with the more utopian contributions in this volume from, for example, Mayra Rivera and M. Shawn Copeland that exhibit more trust in the world and its capacity for transformation and in an all-inclusive future. At the same time, the topic of this essay aligns with the intuitions of Linn Tonstad when she points to the indeterminability and the impossibility of the future, while at the same time suggesting an alternative formation of a "we" that expresses belief in the prophetic and transformative power of art and communities.[1]

Philosophically, this "turn to negativity" seems to be following (and questioning) the usually world-affirming linguistic/hermeneutical turn. In this sense, I interpret this turn to negativity as part of the material turn.[2] The latter is a logical outcome of the growing insights into the nature of matter and its entanglement with meaning, or into the involvement of "the knower" in knowledge production. The increasing attention to the agency of matter ("vibrant matter"[3]) questions the gap between meaning (signifier) and matter (signified), which forms the basis of modern European philosophy, as well as the postmodern linguistic and hermeneutical paradigms. It is these dualistic paradigms that create a hierarchy (meaning and, by extension, the human being as (co-)creator of meaning, has power over matter) from which the existential attitude of negativity is turning away. Moreover, the past emphasis on hermeneutics and dialogue did not "listen" to matter: Several "voices," such as that of the environment, were simply ignored, whereas the dialogue itself turned out to have a devastating effect on that very environment. Naturally, the attention for "matter" has always been a central concern of feminist theory[4] and in that sense is not new.[5] What is new is, among other things, that a "new materialist" approach to reality is detaching itself from modern philosophical paradigms and is gaining credibility in "malestream" philosophy as well.[6]

Culturally and ethically, the turn to negativity has manifested itself in several movements within the margins of society. In the context of this essay, I will refer to a mainly Western movement, because I situate myself within that context and these experiences belong to a certain extent to my own lived experience as a European white woman. Nevertheless, it goes without saying that the borders between Europe and the (still) colonized world are nowadays blurred, that it is not so easy (anymore) to draw the line of the "colonial difference."[7] Indeed, the negative queer theory to which I will turn in this chapter is an activist and intellectual movement that emerged from the "underside" of modernity, albeit geographically mainly in the Western world. The problems its theorists address, however—namely, the possibility and the desirability of inclusion of queer people—are widespread over the earth.[8]

After a short presentation of the queer antipolitics, in order to enter the problematic from a concrete perspective, I turn to the French philosopher Michel Henry's (1922–2002) understanding of flesh (mainly in his work *Incarnation: A Philosophy of Flesh* [2000]), which will form the bulk of this essay. Henry's critique of modernity and of the subject-object dualism that has governed our world since modernity does not result in a dissolution of the subject itself in his thought, as it did for Deleuze and Guattari and other postmodern thinkers.[9] To the contrary, Henry deepens the notion of the subject by detaching it from the world and from objectivity. Whereas this rigorous phenomenological perspective precludes him from describing life in nonhuman beings,[10] his phenomenological approach allows Henry to conceptualize subjective life as a nonrepresentational givenness situated in the flesh, not in the world of representation. The ethics that comes forth from this philosophy of the flesh, I will demonstrate, aligns with queer antisocial politics, which I introduce in the first section. In the third part of this essay, I will revisit the antisocial queer theory in order to concretize Henry's antipolitical, but not unethical or apolitical, "ethics of life." I conclude by evaluating this seemingly gnostic position toward the word of Man as a creative locus of alternative ways of life.

Out of This World: Radical Queer Politics

Recent queer theory has rejected the world through rejecting the future. The future, even if it is not human-centered anymore, is what usually remains unquestioned in any critique: Alternatives to our current way of life in the neoliberal order demonstrate a stubborn belief in the (existence of the) future. Or do they? Recent developments in queer theory have done just that, questioning the future itself, in what Jack Halberstam calls the "negative" or "antisocial" turn in queer studies. This turn away from the future and from the belief in social change is based on an antisocial understanding of sexuality: Rather than connected to relation, intimacy, or romance, sexuality is understood, in this context and in line with psychoanalytical theory, as closely linked to the death drive. The negative turn, Halberstam contends, "produces a counter-intuitive but crucial shift in thinking away from projects of redemption, reconstruction, restoration and reclamation and towards what can only be called an anti-social, negative and anti-relational theory of sexuality."[11] The antisocial turn can be said to divide queer theorists into two camps: those fighting for inclusion into the social (heteronormative) order, equal rights, gay marriage, equal participation, etc., and those who refuse doing this. The "narrative of inclusion," indeed, is highly criticized by this new line of thought in queer theory as, in Halberstam's words, "another self-congratulatory, feel-good narrative of liberal humanism that celebrates homo-heroism and ignores the often overlapping agendas of the state and homosexuals, or the family and homosexuals, or decency and homosexuals."[12] The category of "queer" is, necessarily, also defined negatively, as "antinormative" and anti-identitarian. I will later qualify this definition of "queer." While theorists such as Lee Edelman and Leo Bersani like to dwell on the negative in their work, focusing on the necessity of a queer standpoint of negation,[13] Halberstam points to the possibility of creating something in that space of negativity. He refers, for example, to the "tiny queer archives" of the gay male literature to which Edelman and Bersani refer, or the antisocial archive of feelings such as anger, despair, rage, or the political negativity that promises to fail, to mess up, to make people "less happy."[14] Bersani too does not give up on art as a whole but stresses that the function of art is not to redeem us from traumatic experiences, or, more generally, from our *Weltschmertz*, but to show us the eternal existence of the space of negativity in which meaning falls apart.[15] In the last part of this essay, I will elaborate more on queer theory's relation to the future.

However negative this movement is toward the world, one could state that, in general, it does not give up on life (even if life is located in a position of negativity, as is the case for Bersani, for example). Being, as I will argue in the following, is equated with life, but this life and its meaning is simply not situated in the world. Below, I elaborate on Michel Henry's understanding of life, because for him (human) flesh is the seat of life.

Michel Henry: Life, Auto-Affection, and Flesh

Trained as a philosopher in the tradition of phenomenology, Michel Henry, who had been a professor of philosophy at the University of Montpellier, France, for most of his working life, eventually moves beyond Husserl when asking questions on the *origins* of intentionality, which makes him an exception within the domain of phenomenology. This question allows Henry to make a "move inward." He distinguishes between two modes of phenomenality, the "classical," exterior mode that is oriented toward the world and its appearances, and the interior mode of phenomenality, which will be Henry's life project as a philosopher. For Henry, life can only be experienced when one turns away from one's intentionality or being-oriented toward the world. Life, then, reveals itself as auto-affection through the flesh. In this section, I will elaborate on both these life-defining concepts—auto-affection and flesh. Toward the end of his life, Henry will express this insight in Christian terms, not in the sense that his Christian faith provokes his phenomenology of life, but inversely: His phenomenology leads him to find, in the Gospels (especially in the one ascribed to John), an intuition of life akin to his own.[16]

It is not my intention to give a complete account of Henry's philosophy here, but I want to briefly touch on his core intuitions and insights in order to demonstrate the meaning and the connection of life, auto-affection, and flesh in his work and then connect these with antisocial queer theory to indicate how Henry's perspective on enfleshment can allow us to think beyond "Man." While, at first sight, one could be tempted to think that Henry works with a modern, abstract, and universalist account of subjectivity, I hope it will become clear in what follows that Henry's understanding of subjectivity and flesh is all but universalizing and that in his description of what he calls a "clandestine subjectivity" (a term that emerged from his lived experiences as part of the resistance movement in France and Spain during the Second World War) he demonstrates an affinity with a perspective on life outside of this world. Apart from these critical elements in Henry's philosophy itself, the connection of Henry's thought to the political movement of antisocial queer theory is meant to evoke, stress, and even enhance the concreteness of his thinking. However, the discourse of this essay differs from most other essays in that my reflection on the dynamics and meaning of flesh will primarily *not* be held in terms of power and power differences/inequalities but in terms of life as a force that escapes the worldly power dynamics. Henry appeals to a dimension of life that is able to bracket the "colonial difference." The presupposition of his philosophy is thus that such "bracketing" is at all possible. It expresses a belief in something other than the world. In this respect, it is probably not a coincidence that Henry turned to Christian faith to highlight this possibility—although again, Henry will highlight a very specific and rather marginal interpretation of Christianity. I come back to this seemingly gnostic Christian philosophy in the conclusion.

LIFE: THE INDIVIDUAL'S EXPERIENCE OF AUTO-AFFECTION

For Henry, the subjective experience of life is phenomenologically accessible. It is the territory laid bare when phenomenology starts thinking about its condition: What enables me to experience objects? What makes intentionality possible? This question urges the move inward. The answer to it, for Henry, is the givenness or revelation of life as auto-affection, of life feeling its own activity,[17] the fact that we first experience our selves, our own life, before anything else is apprehended.[18] There is no mediation (of language, for example) involved in the experience of life: "Life is nothing other than that which experiences itself without differing from itself, such that this experience is an experience of self and not of something else, a self-revelation in a radical sense."[19] The immediate character of the experience of life as auto-affection also entails that (the experience of) life comes *before* the relation with the other.[20] Henry's is a nonrelational understanding of the subject. This does not mean, however, that collectivity or community is impossible. Referring to the German fourteenth-century mystic Meister Eckhart, Henry explains that there is an absolute unity between "all living Selves": We are all One in Christ, because we share in His Life. Human beings are connected to each other in their experience of life. Henry conceives of the other not from the perspective of the ego but from the concrete experience of life, an experience that is first of all affective.

> Is the experience of the other not what an ego has of another ego? For each of them, is it a question of anything other than having access, not only to the other's thought, but also to his or her very life, of living from it in a certain way? Is this not the reason why, always and everywhere, such an experience is first affective, so that in each one it is affectivity that opens her to this experience, or closes her to it?[21]

All living beings thus have a relation to absolute life ("absolute" here meaning that it is not affected by worldly dynamics, only by itself). This is how Henry understands relationality, not as the interconnectedness of all beings or the responsibility for the other as other but as something that Gilles Deleuze called a "disjunctive synthesis": We all have an equal relation to absolute life and that is what connects us. In *Incarnation*, Henry describes this while referring to Heidegger's tonality:

> We should examine again and directly the possibility for being-in-the-world to be a "being-with" qua "being-with-the-other"—where the other is no longer any "other" in general, and still less alterity as such, but the other: an other who is what I am myself, an other self [*moi*].[22]

Henry's is thus a radically egalitarian philosophy, in which differences eventually do not matter. To him, it is the perversion of our culture of barbarism that creates differences; they are not essential to life itself. Although Henry seems to speak about "all human beings" here, in a general, universalizing sense, the experience of life for him is never an abstract event. It is always subjective and concrete. With his account of subjectivity, Henry is in opposition to Kant's anonymous and impersonal understanding of the subject.[23] From a more political stance, Henry's account of the subject is developed as an antidote to the praise of "objectivity" in the world in which positive sciences co-constitute the dominant worldview. This kind of objectivity has distanced human beings from the experience of their own life as auto-affection: There is no life in the visible world.[24] In *The Essence of Manifestation*, Henry writes:

> By tearing existence away from the absolute milieu of exteriority, these present investigations wish to draw attention to the "subjective" character of this existence; we are invited to ask ourselves if it would not be better today to give a new meaning to the concept of "interior life."[25]

Henry thus understands the self apart from the world in which subjects are separated from objects through a logic of representation, installing both identity and difference. Like "the other," "difference" for Henry is not a primary category. Difference is a category related to the world. It is an effect of the "culture of barbarism," installed by the dominance and logic of calculation of positive science and technology. Unity and immanence are thus more fundamental, in that they express the truth of life, whereas difference and transcendence, for Henry, belong to the world of representation. Of course, this entails neither a suspension nor an ignorance of all differences. As indicated above, Henry understands intersubjectivity, akin to Deleuze, in a "univocal" sense: All beings are different, but they express life (being) in the same manner. Referring to Christianity and interpreting the Word that became flesh as life, Henry describes this unity as follows:

> This absolute unity between all living Selves, far from signifying or implying the dissolution or destruction of the individuation of each one, is on the contrary constitutive of it, in as much as each of them is joined to himself or herself in the phenomenological effectuation of Life in its Word, and generated in themselves as this irreducibly singular Self, irreducible to any other.[26]

Against more popular philosophies of alterity and difference, Henry constructs a philosophy of self-awareness, of emotions, of affects. Self-awareness, for Henry, has nothing to do with (self-)consciousness. Self-awareness is self-experience that comes before consciousness and representations. In this sense, a baby has self-awareness too. Self-awareness is the self-affection of the self by itself, or auto-affection. Henry also names this the "pulses of life" (*pulsions*).[27] Moreover, these affections are not psychological "feelings," they are material. The locus of auto-affection is, in other words, the flesh.

Flesh: The Site of Auto-Affection

For Henry, flesh is both a material and a transcendental concept. While the materiality of flesh speaks for itself, its transcendental character indicates that for Henry, flesh is the condition for life, before everything else. Flesh is, moreover, a concrete and at the same time universal concept in the sense that it is something that all living beings share (a statement, obviously, that does not render all living beings similar). Henry's central problem is the observation that life and flesh are usually defined in terms of "world" or "power dynamics." This is the reason why he eventually distinguishes between "body" and "flesh." With regard to the body, Henry distinguishes two bodies: the *subjective body*, which is "enfleshed" (the body as flesh), and the *body of the world*, which is inorganic and is not moveable (i.e., it does not know affectivity). The body as flesh "is likely to feel the body that is exterior to it, to touch it as well as to be touched by it. This is what the exterior body, the inert body of the material universe, is in principle incapable of."[28] That the distinction between body and flesh, and the choice for the concept of "flesh" to say something about life, is not merely a theoretical problem is shown, for example, in the work of Mayra Rivera and even more clearly in that of disability theologian Sharon Betcher. In her book *Poetics of the Flesh*, Rivera depicts the body as "an entity complete in itself and visible to those around it. In contrast, flesh is conceived as formless and impermanent, crossing the boundaries between the individual body and the world."[29] While the body has "reifying tendencies,"[30] flesh exposes us to our materiality and vulnerability. Betcher, for her part, questions the "delusion of wholeness"[31] that is exhaled by the body. Initially revalued by feminist thinkers to counter men's focus on the (masculine) mind, the body, under the sway of capitalism, has become a space of control and discipline.[32] From a disability perspective, Betcher questions the body and its norm of "ability" and proposes flesh as a concept able to reveal life's vulnerability (as I will show later, this idea is close to Butler's account of "precariousness"). Flesh indicates a dynamic embodiment—it is the locus where life is exposed in all its complexity, like a "teacup crackled with ten thousand veins."[33] Flesh is necessary to experience life.

The margins of this world, the places of negativity, where there is no meaningful identity, are where life is. In the context of his critical analysis of the Western capitalist society in *From Communism to Capitalism: Theory of a Catastrophe*, Henry gives an interesting example of this, referring to the topical issue of refugees in order to make clear that, even though refugees come to the West because they want to live, they do not find life here:

> Those who seek to escape from death by going to the West do not yet know that death awaits them at a rendezvous. Regardless of being devalued, oppressed, exhausted, and overtaken, the force that lifts up individuals is the force of life. The lures in cardboard—the fries at McDonald's—will only deceive them once. The truth that shines in their eyes is neither the truth of democracy nor of capitalism—nor is it the truth of technology or science fiction. The truth is a cry: it is the cry of life, which says that it is life and that it wants to live.[34]

Paradoxically, and painfully, there seems to be more life in the cry of the refugees than in the safe haven they are seeking in the West. The capitalism that reigns in the West is, for Henry, a negation of life. While at first sight, this position might come across as very elitist out of the mouth of a European philosopher, I believe it sides with a fundamental intuition of Christian liberation theology. Situating life, or God, in the poor and the oppressed does not mean that it is somehow "better" to be poor or oppressed. It acknowledges that poverty and oppression are the result of worldly dynamics. It expresses the belief that God sides with the poor, that God is present in their cry, and that liberation, or the "Reign of God," will come from the poor or from within the margins.

Flesh is a transcendental category, in the sense that being in the flesh through auto-affection is the condition of (comes before) being with the other/other beings. In the case of Henry, the qualification "transcendental" has nothing to do with an ideal construct of the mind, meant to reconstruct the origins of events and things. To the contrary, the transcendental is a material, unconscious reality. A very concrete example of this, one that Henry himself also hints at, is the experience of the runner. On a transcendental level, the runner who runs is "in touch with her body," experiences life in an immediate fashion. This is an unconscious experience, not thematized but felt by the runner. It cannot be perceived, unless in the interior. Henry uses the term "auto-affectivity" for this transcendental experience of life. The transcendental experience, writes Henry, opens up "a field of presence interior to which this life and its contents might be able to rise up before us as 'phenomena.'"[35] On another level, this experience of running can also be represented in statistics. It can be described in terms of speed, averages, health, etc.—all these parameters could be included in the total experience of running. But these "stats" only come *after* the direct experience of life in the act of running: First, there is auto-affectivity, then there is being "in the world" of representation, of the other or other beings, or parameters.

That flesh is more than a material and transcendental locus for Henry, as a space from which one can start living, thinking, and acting alternatives, is demonstrated by its status as "living." Flesh, for Henry, is a living force, it has the power to feel itself.[36] Henry's ethics of life can thus be phrased as the enhancement, or the intensification, of this power.[37] This entails the refusal to be objectified and, at the same time, a return to life as a source. This source is not an intellectual one; it is the experience of auto-affection in the flesh.

Queer Antipolitics: We Die So We May Live!

Henry's understanding of life and flesh might be called unpolitical, in the sense that the question of truth always comes before pragmatic considerations, but, as indicated above, definitely not unconcerned with ethics. The other dimension of life he invokes "opens up the possibilities of living differently in this world,"[38] as Inna Viriasova formulates it. Life itself escapes the domain of the political, because it is nonobjectifiable, but precisely in this way, it can be transforming.

In an attempt to translate Henry's philosophical account of flesh into a more sociopolitical discourse, I connect it to Judith Butler's notion of "precariousness" as an existential and political condition and its socioeconomic meaning as developed by Isabell Lorey. Butler's understanding of life as precarious indicates that for her, as for Henry, there is "something" beyond representation and beyond particular identities and, secondly, that it is not because precariousness is not defined in sociopolitical terms (beyond all differences, it is something we all share) that a reflection on it does not have ethical consequences.

"When is life grievable?" is the guiding question and subtitle of Judith Butler's *Frames of War.* In this book, Butler wonders why some people's lives seem to matter more than others. But rather than focusing on the plurality and multiplicity of today's forms of lives, and rather than asking attention for all these different forms, she draws our attention to the notion of precariousness. Precisely the recognition that every life is precarious makes the value of life appear: Life becomes grievable. Butler also stresses that precariousness comes with birth—it is not something that is added up, or developed, afterward, in the course of life. Moreover, she affirms that precariousness will never be fully understood (and, therefore, it will never be in our full control):

> Precariousness itself cannot be properly recognized. It can be apprehended, taken in, encountered, and it can be presupposed by certain norms of recognition just as it can be refused by such norms. Indeed, there ought to be recognition of precariousness as a shared condition of human life (indeed, as a condition that links human and non-human animals), but we ought not to think that the recognition of precariousness masters or captures or even fully recognizes what it recognizes.[39]

From this quote, it is clear that precariousness is itself a precarious, fragile category: It is not representable, it is invisible, but at the same time, it is a condition we all share.

Isabell Lorey too, in her book *State of Insecurity: Government of the Precarious*, uses precariousness as a concept to describe the existential condition of human beings today. Precariousness, as living with the unforeseeable, with contingency, is indeed a general *condition humaine*. What is typical for our day, however, is that the dynamic of precarization is used as a power tool from governments (pushed by economics) to control human beings' behaviors and that precarization nowadays has become *normalized* as a strategy of governing.[40] Whereas the welfare state was able to protect citizens from their own vulnerability, "what we are currently experiencing is the 'return of mass vulnerability.'"[41] Indeed, the question is not, Lorey writes, "how to prevent and end the threat of precarity that is driving the disintegration of order. It is rather a matter of understanding how we are governed and keep ourselves governable specifically through precarization."[42] "Precarity" is, for both Lorey and Butler, the sociopolitical dimension of precariousness—it is considered a threat and a hierarchizing tool of power. This is what ultimately causes certain lives to be more valuable than others in the "world."[43]

Butler's notion of precariousness is akin to Michel Henry's concept of "passivity" as transcendental life. Life as auto-affectivity is *pathos*—passion and suffering as grounding tonalities of the subject's experience of life. Recognizing this, Butler argues to no longer consider precariousness as a threat.⁴⁴ Instead, she proposes to recognize our common vulnerability as an *affirmative* basis for politics.⁴⁵ The difference between Butler and Henry, however, is that for Henry, the relation to the self, or the experience of the self (the auto-affectivity), always comes *before* the relation with the other—it is the condition for it. While for Butler, ethics is always "an ethical relation . . . because I am from the start implicated in the lives of the other,"⁴⁶ the "I" for Henry is first and foremost not social but self-affecting. So, whereas Butler discovers the precariousness of life *through* the life of others, it is crucial for Henry to experience one's own precariousness directly and unmediated and to recognize that we share this with every living being.

Reconnecting Henry's materialist phenomenology to the antipolitics within queer theory again, as developed by Jack Halberstam, Lee Edelman, and Leo Bersani, I contend that both Henry and queer theory sense the "culture of death" we live in today, unmasking our "culture of redemption" (Bersani) as a culture of capitalist deception and eventually of death and revealing the creative potential of failure, of the incapability to live in our world of success and competition (Halberstam). It is important that, thinking about what comes after this "failure," it is not simply a reconstruction of the same logic.⁴⁷ Bersani has therefore given up the idea of an alternative: There is no beyond, according to him. Thus, the moment of "undoing" our culture must be endlessly repeated.⁴⁸ Although Henry equally rejects the modern world, he would never say that there is no "outside" or "beyond" of our culture. To the contrary, for him the world *is* the exteriority: "[The world] withdraws Being from all that is shown And this is because *giving in Exteriority and thus placing each thing in its own exteriority, it empties them of their own reality*." ⁴⁹ These "negative politics" of queer theorists radically reject Western modernity, connecting the latter with the figure of the "child" in order to critique its orientation toward the ever positive future. In *No Future: Queer Theory and the Death Drive*, Edelman focuses on the figure of the "Child" as the "excuse" for everything,⁵⁰ as the Child is connected to our future and is the symbol of it. A reference to the Child accounts for all kinds of political decisions, right and left wing. Edelman terms this phenomenon "reproductive futurism": "[a set of] terms that impose an ideological limit on political discourse as such, preserving in the process the absolute privilege of heteronormativity by rendering unthinkable, by casting outside the political domain, the possibility of a queer resistance to this organizing principle of communal relations."⁵¹ Children, and by extension that which they represent, our future, are unquestionable. Reproductive futurism is the dominant ideology of our time. But constructing an alternative is equally impossible: A queer utopia, for

Edelman, does not exist, for it would be a world where there is no dissent and no difference—it would be a world without politics.[52] Edelman points at the unavoidable negativity that is a part of life, a part pre-eminently incarnated by the nonheterosexual person who often does not fulfill her or his reproductive "duty" and thus does not affirm this reproductive futurism. "To be queer, in fact, is not to be, except insofar as queerness serves as the name for the thing that is not, for the limit point of ontology, for the constitutive exclusion that registers the no, the not, the negation in being."[53] Queer theory, Edelman holds, cannot agree with a vision of a harmonized future. Queer formulates a "constant no against the symbolic."[54] He refers to psychoanalytical insights[55] to stress the necessity of not ignoring the negative in view of not denying difference altogether. As Halberstam writes with regard to Edelman: "The queer subject, [Edelman] argues, has been bound epistemologically, to negativity, to nonsense, to anti-production, to unintelligibility and, instead of fighting this characterization by dragging queerness into recognition, he proposes that we embrace the negativity that we anyway structurally represent."[56] The position of the queer is the position of negativity, a position, Halberstam rightly remarks, that might be antipolitical but is certainly not apolitical.[57] As such, queers, with their ambiguous stand toward reproduction (and their sexual lives that are usually not bringing forth any children), are, according to Edelman, in a unique position to disrupt the reproduction of the social order. Linking the queer with the negative, according to Halberstam, reveals at the same time an "oppositional politics which has both anti-racist and anti-capitalist dimensions."[58]

Eventually, Henry and the negative queer theorists have in common a radical rejection of modernity, but Michel Henry's thought might also help to find life outside of the modern world through his account of the flesh. Indeed, as queer theorist Jasbir Puar points out in her book *Terrorist Assemblages*, what remains after all this negativity is the flesh. Defining flesh negatively, as having no meaning or power within the modern world, Puar interprets the body of the suicide bomber as a queer form of resistance (a "queer assemblage"). It is the only resistance that is left for people that are not listened to, thus relocating queerness from the Western world into the "subaltern." Puar refers to Gayatri Spivak's notorious text "Can the Subaltern Speak?" and cites:

> Suicidal resistance is a message inscribed on the body when no other means will get through. It is both execution and mourning, for both self and other. For you die with me for the same cause, no matter which side

you are on. Because no matter who you are, there are no designated killees in suicide bombing. No matter what side you are on, because I cannot talk to you, you won't respond to me, with the implication that there is no dishonor in such shared and innocent death.[59]

In this act of dying, all differences are suspended. But negative politics does not necessarily have to end here. Halberstam refers to the DreamWorks film *Over the Hedge*, in which a possum plays dead and explains to his daughter: "We die so we may live!"[60] Henry, indeed, turns away from the world of politics and representation so that real life may manifest itself. Viriasova remarks that Aristotle already warned for the totalizing nature of the political discourse: "The totalizing ambition of politics should be contradicted by an affirmation of life itself, notwithstanding the political order that attempts to contain it."[61]

Queer Gnosis of the Flesh

Browsing through the work of Michel Henry and its reception, it is striking that Henry has not been brought much into dialogue with other thinkers or other disciplines. Of course, his turn away from all things worldly might have isolated him in these times of connection and networking. At first sight, it might thus seem strange to combine Henry with queer thought—the latter being a movement pre-eminently emerging from unbalanced worldly power dynamics and disciplining normativities. In the confrontation, however, Henry just might have shifted the meaning of queer a bit: Instead of situating its antinormative discourse *within* the world, we might consider antinormativity as *more* than an oppositional stance, more anormative than antinormative, more non-identity-oriented than another expression of identity politics, more apolitical than antipolitical. Negative queer theory, with its rejection of the world, with its giving up of any kind of participation in it, exactly points at such a position.

This "gnostic" position, reflecting the tension between representation and life, however, is not without problems. One could say that a gnostic worldview threatens to simply repeat the world "elsewhere," as Adam Kotsko notes in response to Giorgio Agamben's analysis of fourteenth-century monastery life and its ideal of poverty.[62] Also referring to Agamben, Alexander Weheliye points at the problem of a universalization of the position of exception. Thinking life out of this world "in general," he writes, falls in the universalizing trap of modernity that Agamben wants to avoid: "The universalization of exception disables thinking humanity creatively."[63]

Agamben's mistake is that he continues to talk about "bare life" "from the horizon of jurisprudence and hegemony,"[64] instead of trying to understand life in its own terms. Here, the difference with Henry's project becomes clear. While life is a transcendental experience, it is not a transcendent (in the sense of beyond immanent materiality) category. Salvation, or the experience and enhancement of life, still happens within history—though for Henry, this is not the history of the world; it is the materiality of an immediately experienced life in the flesh that is the condition for every other experience. Reflecting on the force of this gnosis of the flesh, he writes:

> When in its innocence each modality of our flesh undergoes experiencing itself, being nothing other than itself, when suffering says suffering and joy joy, it is actually flesh that speaks, and nothing has power against its word.[65]

The flesh contains the power of life, but it needs the unworldly subjective experience of auto-affectivity in order to live.

Beyond the Gnosticism and negativity, there is an affirmative ground, which lies in the meaning of life as auto-affection in the flesh. Turning away from the world is not a simple oppositional move. The negative turn, when grounded in flesh, has an affirmative undercurrent, a strong belief in life itself, in life beyond Man, as well as in an alternative politics. Not wanting to go along with a logic of inclusion in the world does not mean embracing exclusion—it might mean trying, or providing a strategy, to live on other, material terms.

NOTES

1. See Linn Marie Tonstad's contribution to this collection and also Linn Marie Tonstad, "The Limits of Inclusion: Queer Theology and Its Others," *Theology and Sexuality* 21, no. 1 (2015).

2. I fully recognize that this categorizing of a specific paradigm in a specific era is an artificial, and political, act and that this negative existential attitude toward the world is not necessarily connected to a materialist worldview. Moreover, it is not a recent phenomenon at all. Nevertheless, for the sake of my argument—the connection to flesh and the affirmative undercurrent—I understand the "turn to negativity" within the context of materiality. On the politics of theoretical genealogies, see Clare Hemmings, *Why Stories Matter: The Political Grammar of Feminist Theory* (Durham, N.C.: Duke University Press, 2011).

3. See Jane Bennett, *Vibrant Matter: A Political Ecology of Agency and Politics* (Durham, N.C.: Duke University Press, 2010).

4. See, for example, Paul Reid-Bowen, "Vital New Matters: The Speculative Turn in the Study of Religion and Gender," *Religion and Gender* 1, no. 1 (2011); Karen Barad, *Meeting the Universe Halfway: Quantum Physics and the Entanglement of Matter and Meaning* (Durham, N.C.: Duke University Press, 2007); Rosi Braidotti, *The Posthuman* (Cambridge: Polity Press, 2013); Diana Coole and Samantha Frost, eds., *New Materialisms: Ontology, Agency, and Politics* (Durham, N.C.: Duke University Press, 2011); Bennett, *Vibrant Matter*; Vicki Kirby, *Quantum Anthropologies: Life at Large* (Durham, N.C.: Duke University Press, 2011); and Stacy Alaimo and Susan Hekman, eds., *Material Feminisms* (Bloomington: Indiana University Press, 2008).

5. On the genealogy of new materialism as a new paradigm, see Iris van der Tuin, "Deflationary Logic: Response to Sara Ahmed's 'Imaginary Prohibitions: Some Preliminary Remarks on the Founding Gestures of the "New Materialism,"'" *European Journal of Women's Studies* 15, no. 4 (2008).

6. See, for example, the so-called speculative materialist thinkers, such as Ray Brassier, Bruno Latour, Quentin Meillassoux, and others.

7. See Nelson Maldonado-Torres, "On the Coloniality of Being: Contributions to the Development of a Concept," *Cultural Studies* 21, no. 2–3 (March/May 2007): 257.

8. Another movement that can be situated within a negative materialist paradigm is the environmental Dark Mountain Project. The Dark Mountain Project is an artistic collective or network that started in the United Kingdom with Paul Kingsnorth and Dougald Hine but quickly found soulmates globally in the English-speaking world. Disillusioned after twenty-five years of utopian environmental activism, the Dark Mountain group has decided to retire from society and to testify of what can be called an "apocalyptic nature mysticism." Dark Mountain's rejection of this world is grounded in its harsh critique of the Western myth of progress and of the inscription of the environmental movement in this myth. Dark Mountain wants us to step out of the human bubble in order to encounter the nonhuman world. What is crucial is to save the planet. The survival of our civilization, let alone of the individual, is of secondary importance. Dark Mountain wishes to create a space of its own, outside of the dominant framework of society. The collective fills this space with art as a means to create other, "uncivilized," and ecocentric imaginaries that could be the result of our encounter with nature. See the Dark Mountain Project website at https:// dark-mountain.net.

9. See, for example, Gilles Deleuze and Félix Guattari, *A Thousand Plateaus: Capitalism and Schizophrenia*, trans. Brian Massumi (New York: Continuum, 2004).

10. See Michel Henry, *Incarnation: A Philosophy of Flesh* (Evanston, Ill.: Northwestern University Press, 2015), 3: "We will leave living beings other than human beings outside the field of our investigation. A decision like this is not arbitrary. It is justified by a methodological choice to speak of what we know rather than of what we do not."

11. Jack (Judith) Halberstam, "The Anti-Social Turn in Queer Studies," *Graduate Journal of Social Science* 5, no. 2 (2008): 140.

12. Halberstam, "Anti-Social Turn in Queer Studies," 143.

13. See Lee Edelman, *No Future: Queer Theory and the Death Drive* (Durham, N.C.: Duke University Press, 2005); and Leo Bersani, *The Culture of Redemption* (Cambridge, Mass.: Harvard University Press, 2000).

14. See Halberstam, "Anti-Social Turn in Queer Studies," 151–54.

15. See Bersani, *Culture of Redemption*.

16. See Frédéric Seyler, *"Barbarie ou culture": L'ethique de l'affectivité dans la phénoménologie de Michel Henry* (Paris: Editions Kimé, 2010), 65. Kevin Hart formulates Henry's relation to Christianity more critically: "There is no doubt that Henry wishes to assimilate Christianity to his philosophical position and that he trims the faith as Fichte had done earlier before he does so." See Kevin Hart, "Inward Life," in *Michel Henry: The Affects of Thought*, ed. J. Hanson and M. R. Kelly (New York: Continuum, 2012), 103. Henry's is a particular interpretation of Christianity, mainly based on his reading of the Gospel of John, but not entirely exceptional within the Christian tradition, especially in the more Gnostic early Christian readings.

17. Hart, "Inward Life," 98–99.

18. This experience, however, has nothing to do with self-consciousness. One could indeed ask: "What about the baby who does not have any self-awareness yet?" But then, we have misunderstood Henry's account of the "self"; he understands the self apart from the world in which subjects are separated from objects through a logic of representation, installing both identity and difference. Self-awareness, moreover, has nothing to do with (self-)consciousness. What Henry does is not affirming the subject-object divide but protesting against the observation that the subject in the world is being objectified.

19. Michel Henry, *Incarnation: Une philosophie de la chair* (Paris: Seuil, 2000), 89 (author's translation).

20. This is a conception of life strange to philosophers such as Emmanuel Lévinas or Maurice Merleau-Ponty, who have influenced the domain of philosophical ethics far more than Henry. Gilles Deleuze's understanding of "the other" is more similar to Henry's: Both consider the other as belonging to the world, providing in its predictability. See, for example, Gilles Deleuze, *Logique du sens* (Paris: Les éditions de minuit, 1969), 354. Henry refers to

Meister Eckhart to explain the all-encompassing and unifying character of life: "Life is without a why. And this is because it does not tolerate in itself any outside itself to which it would need to manifest itself" (*Incarnation*, 224). Moreover, life does not "care about itself" (225), because that would entail a distance from itself, something that is impossible.

21. Henry, *Incarnation*, 242.

22. Henry, 241. Henry's understanding of flesh and incarnation stands in sharp contrast to Merleau-Ponty's conception of flesh. For Merleau-Ponty, flesh is related to exteriority, to our relation with the world. See Mayra Rivera, *Poetics of the Flesh* (Durham, N.C.: Duke University Press, 2015).

23. See Michel Henry, *Auto-donation: entretiens et conférences* (Paris: Beauchesne, 2004), 77: "Il est vrai que chez les phénoménologues, qui retrouvent d'ailleurs la situation kantienne, on a affaire à une subjectivité à la fois anonyme et impersonnelle. Ma position est totalement différente: je pense qu'il s'agit d'une subjectivité qui est ni universelle, ni impersonnelle, ni générale, et que sa structure est telle qu'elle est nécessairement individuelle."

24. Hart, "Inward Life," 98–99: "When life's mode of appearing is suborned to visible phenomena, when subjectivity and individuality are denied by the world (i.e., by abstractions such as 'the economy' and 'the state' . . .) or are drained by its forces (the will to busyness, the preoccupation with objectivity, and especially today, the enervating fascination with television, Facebook, the web, etc.) does it succumb to diminishment: a situation arising in early modernity that Henry calls 'barbarism.'"

25. Michel Henry, *The Essence of Manifestation* (The Hague, Netherlands: Nijhoff, 1973), 45.

26. Henry, *Incarnation*, 248.

27. See for example Henry, *Auto-donation*, 107–8: "Ce monde de la représentation et de ses déterminations n'est intelligible qu'à partir d'une instance à lui irréductible, celle des pulsions, des désirs, du besoin, de l'action, du travail, qui lui donnent sa forme, une forme plus ancienne que celle de la pensée et que celle-ci ne peut que retrouver après-coup."

28. Henry, *Incarnation: Une philosophie de la chair*, 9 (author's translation).

29. Rivera, *Poetics of the Flesh*, 2.

30. Rivera, 7.

31. Susan Betcher, "Becoming Flesh of My Flesh: Feminist and Disability Theologies on the Edge of Posthumanist Discourse," *Journal of Feminist Studies in Religion* 26, no. 2 (Fall 2010): 108.

32. See also the important work done by Angela McRobbie, *The Aftermath of Feminism: Gender, Culture, and Social Change* (London: Sage, 2009); and *Be Creative: Making a Living in the New Culture Industries* (Cambridge: Polity, 2016).

33. Betcher, "Becoming Flesh of My Flesh," 108.

34. Michel Henry, *From Communism to Capitalism: Theory of a Catastrophe* (London: Bloomsbury, 2014), 118.

35. Henry, *Essence of Manifestation*, 29.

36. Henry, *Incarnation*, xi.

37. Henry was well aware of the fact that life is not to be found in philosophy either. He himself was a fervent hiker and skier, among other sports.

38. Inna Viriasova, "Unpolitical Life: Michel Henry and the Real Limits of Biopolitics," *Diacritics* 42, no. 3 (2014): 85.

39. Judith Butler, *Frames of War: When Is Life Grievable?* (New York: Verso, 2009), 13.

40. Isabell Lorey, *State of Insecurity: Government of the Precarious* (London: Verso, 2015), 60ff.

41. Lorey, *State of Insecurity*, 52. Lorey quotes Robert Castel, *From Manuel Workers to Wage Laborers: Transformation of the Social Question* (New Brunswick, N.J.: Transaction Publishers, 2003), 445.

42. Lorey, *State of Insecurity*, 2.

43. Lorey, *State of Insecurity*, 22: "Precarity can therefore be understood as a functional effect arising from the political and legal regulations that are specifically supposed to protect against general, existential precariousness."

44. Henry would affirm that life, in the world, is "weakened." Henry also develops this thought in his interpretation of Marx, where he describes that, in capitalism, life is being pushed out of the labor process, and labor becomes an alienating activity that is no longer connected to the living individual. See Michel Henry, *Le socialisme selon Marx* (Paris: Sulliver, 2008).

45. Butler, *Frames of War*, 32.

46. Judith Butler and Athena Athanasiou, *Dispossession: The Performative in the Political* (Malden, Mass.: Polity, 2013), 107.

47. See Tim Dean et al., "A Conversation with Leo Bersani," *October* 82 (1997).

48. Dean et al., "Conversation with Leo Bersani," 4.

49. Michel Henry, "Speech and Religion: The Word of God," *Phenomenology and the Theological Turn*, ed. D. Janicaud (New York: Fordham University Press, 2000), 221.

50. Edelman, *No Future*, 3: Edelman figures the Child as the "fantasmatic beneficiary of every political intervention."

51. Edelman, *No Future*, 2.

52. See IPAK Centar, "Interview with Prof Lee Edelman," September 21, 2015, YouTube video, 7:03, https://www.youtube.com/watch?v=NjTDLyKP2po.

53. Lee Edelman, "Against Survival: Queerness in a Time That's out of Joint," *Shakespeare Quarterly* 62, no. 2 (2011): 149.

54. Edelman, *No Future*, 5.

55. See also Edelman, "Against Survival," 169: "'What is someone who has been psychoanalyzed?' asks psychoanalyst Jean Allouch, in the course of his own compelling reading of Derrida's *Mal d'archive*. And he answers without hesitation, 'He is . . . someone who no longer has a future.' We might say that he is someone who faces the empty page of 'freedom' in a world with no promise of meaning in advance, a world with no master whose teaching protects against the death drive such teaching enacts."

56. Halberstam, "Anti-Social Turn in Queer Studies," 141.

57. Halberstam, 148.

58. Halberstam, 141.

59. Jasbir Puar, *Terrorist Assemblages: Homonationalism in Queer Times* (Durham, N.C.: Duke University Press, 2007), 218.

60. Halberstam, "Anti-Social Turn in Queer Studies," 153.

61. Viriasova, "Unpolitical Life," 85. Viriasova refers to Laurent Dubreuil, "Leaving Politics: Bios, Zōē, Life," trans. Clarissa C. Eagle, *Diacritics* 36, no. 2 (2006): 97.

62. See Colby Dickinson and Adam Kotsko, *Agamben's Coming Philosophy: Finding a New Use for Theology* (London: Rowman & Littlefield, 2015), 183–201.

63. Alexander G. Weheliye, *Habeas Viscus: Racializing Assemblages, Biopolitics, and Black Feminist Theories of the Human* (Durham, N.C.: Duke University Press, 2014), 11.

64. Weheliye, *Habeas Viscus*, 133.

65. Henry, *Incarnation*, 262.

CHAPTER 10

Black Life/Schwarz-Sein: Inhabitations of the Flesh

Alexander G. Weheliye

> To have one's belonging lodged in a metaphor is voluptuous intrigue;
> to inhabit a trope; to be a kind of fiction. To live in the Black
> Diaspora is I think to live as a fiction—a creation
> of empires, and also self-creation.
>
> —DIONNE BRAND, *A Map to the Door of No Return: Notes to Belonging*

> Indeed some of us did not die . . .
>
> And what shall we do, we who did not die? . . .
>
> I don't know the answer to that.
>
> —JUNE JORDAN, "Some of Us Did Not Die"

> Look for the life
>
> Look for the reflections of the living
>
> —JUNE JORDAN, "Nowadays the Heroes"

> Only by becoming inhuman can the human being
> pretend that they are.
>
> —JAMES BALDWIN, *The Price of the Ticket*

Black Life is that which must be constitutively abjected—and as such has represented the negative ontological ground for the Western order of things for the last five hundred years—but cannot be included in the Western world of Man as such. As an ontological formation, Black Life not only forms a part of the modern West but must be understood as constitutive of this domain. The Middle Passage, transatlantic racial slavery, the plantation system, and the gendered racial terror erected on Black people were not one-time events; they spanned almost five hundred years, from the early fifteenth century to well into the nineteenth century, and their consequences can still be felt around us in many other places around the globe, including continental Africa. Although the "proper" colonization of continental Africa did not extend over the same period, it must be seen as part of this continuum if we consider that the "scramble for Africa" took place almost contemporaneously with the abolition of slavery in Brazil, thus extending this form of racial terror to the 1970s, when Portugal "ceded" its African colonies. The subjugation, expropriation, enslavement, rape, and killing of Black Life continues today under different guises in, among other places, the prison industrial complex in the United States and the economic neocolonization of many African nations by the West.

Given this historical sedimentation, Blackness and Black Life have become a negative fleshly foil for the being of white Western Man.[1] Nevertheless, Black Life is continually made to appear as mere ontic scaffolding vis-à-vis the-world-Man—that is, as historical happenstance rather than as a force that fundamentally structures every part of being in the world Man. Black Life, which is intimately tied to anti-Black racism but never reducible to it, provides the ontological conditions of possibility for the historical or ontic existence of Black people, Black diasporas, Black culture and whiteness, modernity writ large. As a result, focusing only on the ontic leaves intact the structural basis for racial slavery, Jim Crow, neocolonial exploitation, and the prison industrial complex.[2]

Continuing the exploration of Hortense Spillers's notion of the flesh in my book *Habeas Viscus*, my essay focuses on Black Life/Schwarz-Sein as a constitutive ontological limit for the workings of modern life and being.[3] For Spillers the flesh—both opposed to the body and in a parasitic relationship to it—represents the pivotal domain through which Man marks the hierarchical species-level difference between himself and his various others, for instance, Latino, poor, incarcerated, indigenous, disabled, gender-nonconforming subjects, but especially African-descended populations. To say it more succinctly and in the inimitable words of Hortense Spillers, this means fundamentally misrecognizing how Black is vestibular not simply to culture but also to life and being in this here prison house of modernity.[4] If, indeed, the flesh supplies the constitutive relation to the world and, thus, to the earth, then we would do well to version Amiri Baraka, who, in the heady days of 1960s, said that Black was neither a nation nor chained to particular territories but a country. That is, we ought to insist on the flesh being our country, the enfolded mattering of the ungendered belonging to unbelonging.[5] As a result, it becomes paramount to understand and amplify alternate modes of being that do not rest on abjuring Black Life—and not sell our "birthright for a mess of pottage," as James Weldon Johnson's unnamed protagonist did—but embrace its possibilities, albeit without erasing the traces of violence that give rise to them.[6]

One of the main ways in which this putatively natural difference between Man and his Black others becomes legible is through what Spillers refers to as the "ungendering and defacing project of African persons."[7] Accordingly, the genders and sexualities of Black Life are deemed incompatible with the world of Man, because Black subjects are projected to be in possession of either a surplus (hyperfemininity/hypermasculinity and hypersexualization) of gender and sexuality or a complete lack thereof (desexualization). As Spillers phrases this constellation: "The unsexed black female and the supersexed black female embody the very same vice, cast the very same shadow, since both are an exaggeration of the uses to which sex might be put."[8] In other words, the histories of racial slavery, colonialism, Jim Crow, the prison regime, etc., have congealed to debilitate Black subjects' ability to conform to normative genders and sexualities. The iconography of the restroom signs during the era of legal segregation in the US South underscores this disavowal of gender difference in no uncertain terms seeing that the white side is split into two doors, one for "ladies" and one for "gentlemen," whereas there is only one entryway on the "colored" side: The vestibule to the ungendering of the door of no return.[9]

This means that often if Black people sought recognition as properly human, they have needed not only to accept and perform an idea of humanity steeped in white supremacy and colonialism but also to don the drag of normative genders and sexualities. My point is, though, that this represents an opportunity for imaging gender/sexuality otherwise, for embracing and inhabiting the ungendered flesh, for fully and differently inhabiting the gift of Black Life. The post–civil rights era so clearly shows that pursuing a respectability politics based on disparaging different facets of Black Life such as wearing sagging pants, speaking AAVE (African American Vernacular English), patois, or even standard English with a newly immigrated accent from the non-Anglophone Black world, creating nontraditional social formations, and living nonnormative genders and sexualities, in favor of proper masculinity and femininity, nuclear families, speaking standard English without bringing your non-Anglo linguistic communities with you, etc., has not led to Black folks reaping the political, economic, and cultural benefits of full humanity. Far from it, given that the modern state bestows and rescinds humanity as an individualized legal status in the vein of property. Allocating personhood in this way maintains the world of Man and its attendant racializing assemblages. Accordingly, the entry fee required of Black folks for legal recognition is the conformity to and acceptance of categories thoroughly marinated in the sanguine fluids of white supremacy and colonialism and stewed in the bitter sauce of normative genders and sexualities. In order for individual Black lives to be recognized as suitably human by the law their Blackness must be killed.

Denise Ferreira da Silva describes the affectability of the Black subject in Western modernity, which she sets off against the transparency of the white, masculine master subject, thus:

> In this ontological context, globality, the horizon of death, scientific signification has deployed the racial to produce modern subjects that emerge in exteriority/affectability and exist between two moments of violence: (a) engulfment, that is, "partial negation," the productive violent act of naming, the symbolic appropriation that produces them, inaugurating a relationship precisely because, in the regimen of representation interiority governs, it institutes unsublatable and irreducible subjects, and (b) murder, total annihilation, that which obliterates the necessary but haunting relationship between an I instituted by the desire for transparency (self-determination) and the affectable, always already vanishing others of Europe that the scientific cataloguing of minds institutes.[10]

Ungendering represents one pivotal mode of engulfment in the force field of Black Life/Schwarz-Sein as an ontology of affectability, which provides violent abjection and opens up possibilities for being otherwise. For instance, Toni Cade Bambara asks us "to let go of all notions of manhood and femininity and concentrate on Blackhood. . . . It perhaps takes less heart to pick up the gun than to face the task of creating a new identity, a self, perhaps an androgynous self, via commitment to the struggle. . . . I'm not arguing the denial of manhood or womanhood, but rather a shifting of priorities, a call for Selfhood, Blackhood."[11] My point is that the shifting of priorities Bambara demands with regard to the affectability of Black ungendering already exists in a variety of guises, and we ought to consult the histories, myths, speculations, and conjurings in order to embrace more fully the gift of Schwarz-Sein's nonnormative genders.

Using the racialized performances of gender of Joss Moody, the main character in Jackie Kay's 1998 novel *Trumpet*, and the musician Sun Ra as launchpads, my argument pays particular attention to the complex ways gender and sexuality function in the barring of Black flesh from the category of the human-as-Man. In addition, both Sun Ra and Joss Moody embody nonnormative figurations of Black masculinity that deploy the violent ungendering of Black subjects as a condition of possibility for alternate ways of inhabiting the world. As Spillers remarks, "black men can't afford to appropriate the gender prerogatives of white men because they have a different kind of history; so you can't just simply be patriarchal. You have to really think about something else as you come to that option. . . . Men of the black diaspora are the only men who had the opportunity to understand something about the female that no other community had the opportunity to understand, and also vice versa."[12] Joss Moody and Sun Ra represent inhabitations of the flesh that bring to light the relational being-in-the-world of Black Life/Schwarz-Sein, in the process making the constitutive ungendered displacement of Black Life from origin and belonging habitable in the present and in the future by staging the affectability of Black ontological mattering as second sight, as one of the most luminous gifts Black Life/Schwarz-Sein has bestowed upon our world.[13] In focusing on the affectability of ungendered mattering in Joss Moody's and Sun Ra's conjurings, my aim is to highlight the different ways the histories of Schwarz-Sein/Black Life offer an archive of alternatives to being-in-the-World-of-Man in the vein suggested by Bambara. Both Moody and Ra confront us with "the terrifying and overwhelming possibility that there are no models, that we shall have to create from scratch," and as a result affectably stand in the flesh as both the fiction of empires and as self-creations.[14] In order to think more deeply about Black Life's relationship to the nonhuman, I will also briefly consider an underdiscussed aspect of Henrietta Lacks's cellular afterlife. The larger project will focus on other texts that welcome the ungendering of Black Life as speculative inhabitations of the flesh, such as Audre Lorde's *Zami*, Samuel R. Delany's *Stars in My Pocket Like Grains of Sand*, Nuruddin Farah's *Maps*, Octavia Butler's two Parable novels, Ama Ata Aidoo's *Our Sister Killjoy*, and Luke Sutherland's *Venus as a Boy*, as well as the ungendered Schwarz-Sein of Black public figures such as Michael Jackson, Prince, Whitney Houston, Mariah Carey, and Janet Jackson.

Partially based on the life of white US-American jazz musician Billy Tipton, Jackie Kay's brilliant and beautiful 1998 novel, *Trumpet*, tells the story of Joss Moody, an Afro-Scottish jazz musician, who dies before the present tense of the novel is set in motion and is "revealed" to have been assigned female at birth and given the name Josephine Moore to everyone except his white Scottish wife, Millie. The novel is told almost exclusively through the retrospective narrations of Millie, who now has to come to grips with everybody knowing Joss's "secret," and their adopted son, Colman Moody. Joss's life is narrated by those who did not die, only some of whom are looking for life. The readers also encounter how government officials, medical professionals, and a journalist enforce dimorphic gender norms and sensationalize Joss's gender expression. Take, for instance, the doctor, who certifies Joss's death:

> Doctor Krishnamurty got her red pen out from her doctor's bag. What she thought of as her emergency red pen. She crossed "male" out and wrote "female" in her rather bad doctor's handwriting. She looked at the word "female" and thought it wasn't quite clear enough. She crossed that out, tutting to herself, and printed "female" in large childish letters.[15]

Dr. Krishnamurty is only one of the many characters in Kay's novel who believe that they have the right to inspect Joss's genitalia and use this privilege to measure, tabulate, and sensationalize his personhood.

Over the course of the novel, readers encounter Joss as a trans man, father, husband, musician, friend, daughter, young queer woman, and a corpse. In the wake of his death Joss becomes a diffractive reflection of the other characters' own struggles with identification and belonging. What is striking, however, is that barely anyone except his wife and son mentions that Joss is a Black man, which seems peculiar in the spatiotemporal context of Scotland and England from the 1950s to the 1990s, a time period during which policy and discourse made abundantly clear that there was to be no Black in the Union Jack and the United Kingdom did not care for or about Black people. Hence, my question: What role does Blackness play in the will to know and therefore violently determine a supposedly mimetic correlation between Joss's anatomy and gender expression?[16] In order to better understand this, we should note that what Spillers calls the ungendering of Black Life appears in the arenas of sexuality and gender expression, among other places, in the mainstream deficitary imaginary concerning Black Life's constitutive not-queerness or transness, which is reinscribed through the incessant recurrence on the "innate" homophobia and transphobia of Black communities, whether they are located in the United States, the Caribbean, or different parts of the African continent—and, of course, in the constant stream of studies and articles that claim to show that Black people are not exceptionally homophobic or transphobic. Just to be transparent: I am in no way saying that homophobia and transphobia do not exist in African-descended populations but describing the putative excessiveness and surplus projected onto Blackness.

In a related fashion, yet also deviating from the norm, often Black public figures such as Caster Semenya, Michael Sam, Brittney Griner, Jason

Collins, Janet Mock, Frank Ocean, and Laverne Cox have been summoned as spokespersons for nonnormative genders and sexualities—whether they agree to take up these positions or not—which highlights the excessive queerness and transness of Black Life (surplus). In addition, we have to consider the long intertwined histories of genital policing and sexual violence Black folks have been subject to during the Middle Passage and plantation slavery and since, for example, the inspection of Black folks' genitalia on the auction block, the systematic use of rape and other forms of sexual violence during slavery and Jim Crow, as well as the long history of medicalized genital surveillance and experimentation, of which the Tuskegee experiment is only the most prominent example, and the very public court cases for the criminal transmission of HIV of Michael Johnson, a.k.a. Tiger Mandingo, and Nushawn Williams, a.k.a. Shyteek Johnson, in the United States and Nadja Benaissa in Germany.[17]

Of course, there is the case of Khoisan woman Sarah Baartman, who was "exhibited" throughout Europe during the early nineteenth century, while after her date Baartman's preserved genitals, her skeleton, and a plaster cast of her nude body were displayed at the Museum of Man in Paris until 1974, when these were removed from public view. Nevertheless, Baartman's remains were not repatriated to South Africa until 2002. We also see this inclination in the often now retrospectively submerged genitality of lynching, which I will underscore only through one example: the 1934 lynching of Claude Neal in Marianna, Florida. Neal was imprisoned because he was accused of killing a white woman, with little to no evidence, and abducted by a lynch mob. The local and national press printed announcements for the lynching, which drew over seven thousand white onlookers from eleven states, some of whom staged a riot after they arrived too late to witness the spectacle. Among many forms of torture, Neal was subjected to castration and the mob forced him to orally consume his severed penis and testicles. This tendency also appears in less "spectacular" arenas such as the Moynihan Report and in the recent billboards about the most dangerous place in the world for a child being the womb of a Black woman.

Overall, we see a clear relationship between visibility and knowability and their intimate ties to the inherent killability of Black Life. Black people's presumed excessive and pathological deviance becomes the ground for the disposability of Black Life. The frequently literal and at times only intimated genital policing and violation of Black folks I have cursorily outlined here forms a crucial part of both the persistent practices of "racializing surveillance" in slavery and its afterlives Simone Browne charts in her recent book *Dark Matters* and C. Riley Snorton's argument about the different ways Black sexuality in the Western world is firmly encased in a glass closet, which according to Snorton is defined by "hypervisibility and confinement, spectacle, and speculation."[18] The history of the different ways Black Flesh is subject to violent genital surveillance brings together all four factors Snorton associates with the glass closet while at the same time gesturing toward the entombment W. E. B. Du Bois associates with the "thick sheet of invisible but horribly tangible plate glass [that] is between [Black people] and the world," as the partition of racial difference during de jure segregation in his 1940 autobiography, *Dusk of Dawn*.[19] While Du Bois is less concerned with the surveillance aspect of this haptically and sonically impermeable but visually traversable pane of glass, his metaphor of Black people being seen but not heard in this enclosure emphasizes just how fundamental to Black Life this enclosure is. As a consequence, to be Black is always already tantamount to inhabiting the glass confinement of "racializing surveillance."

This is all a circuitous way of getting at how Joss's Blackness is at once projected onto, displaced by, and a fundamental component of the uncovered "secret" of his gender expression after his death. The crisis Joss's death causes in the other characters and the presumed right of some to know and determine the ultimate truth imagined to inhere in Joss's genitalia results from both Joss's race and gender. The fundamental point to be made here is that Joss Moody, suspended in a perpetual state of vestibularity, is not supposed to exist in this context, not as a Black person, not as queer Black woman, and most definitely not as a Black trans man, which is why he is forced to invent himself, give birth to himself. Here, I am less interested in the jazz structure of the novel than I am in what Joss's irreducibly specific story, grounded as it is in a particular time and place, can tell us about Black Life and "the transgender potential for remaking Black manhood in the diaspora," to use Matt Richardson's words and Black un/genders in general.[20]

Jackie Kay writes about this perpetual state of vestibular unbelonging in a poem from her 1999 collection, *Off Colour*, entitled "Somebody Else":

If I was not myself, I would be somebody else.
But actually I am somebody else.
I have been somebody else all my life.
It's no laughing matter going about the place
all the time being somebody else:
people mistake you; you mistake yourself.[21]

Because Joss must invent and reinvent himself, he listens for signs of Black Life elsewhere, he looks to the suave Black masculinity of jazz performers. When Colman, Joss and Millie's adopted son, remembers his father, he thinks that Joss "looked real enough playing that horn in those smoky clubs; he looked real and unreal like a fantasy of himself. All jazz men are fantasies of themselves, reinventing the Counts and Dukes and Armstrongs, imitating them . . . Black people and music. Black people and music; what would the world be without black people and music" (*Trumpet*, 104). The perpetual self-reincarnation of the Counts and Dukes and Armstrongs serve as Joss's templates for living in Blackness and in masculinity in a spatiotemporal zone that resolutely denies his existence by demanding him to be somebody-else, anybody-else. This raises the questions: How does Black Life come to exist in spaces where there is no Black culture to speak of? How do you *be* Black without recourse to models for Schwarz-Sein, like Joss Moody in Scotland?

Jackie Kay also records how in the absence of other Black people in 1960s Scotland, Bessie Smith becomes her portable cypher for Black Life in very similar terms to how Spillers construes community as a "moveable feast":

> I was adopted in 1961 and brought up in a suburban house in a
> suburban street in the north of Glasgow. . . . I never saw another black
> person. There was my brother and me. That was it. . . . So the first
> time I saw Bessie it was like finding a friend. I saw her before I heard
> her. . . . I realized that I could choose always to have Bessie Smith in
> my life. . . . Nobody could take her away from me. And when I grew
> up and went away, I could take her with me. And I did.[22]

Being-somebody-else entails the demise of the not-somebody-else, it demands coming to grips with the death of languages, cultures, archives, genders, origins, homes, and belonging. Yet, being-somebody-else also engenders, in the words of Katherine McKittrick, "possibilities that are iterations of black life that cannot be contained by black death."[23] For "it is only when you are stranded in a hostile country that you need a romance of origins; it is only when you lose your mother that she becomes a myth," as Saidiya Hartman remarks.[24] In Kay's novel, Colman is far less captivated by his maternal ancestry than he is by his patrilineal descent, which leads Matt Richardson to write the following about the status of maternity in *Trumpet*:

> She (Josephine) is the absent presence of Black female experience in
> the diaspora, the denied past that sustains the present and the future.

> Without her, there can be no Joss. He is his own mother, so to speak.
> However, in order to be a (Black) "man," he has to deny his own
> reproduction. That is, his biological mother and his figurative
> "mother" in Josephine constitute the feminine that must be displaced
> from desire in order to fulfill the oedipal contract. To be a proper
> oedipalized male requires the phobic denial of identification with the
> (castrated) mother in favor of becoming the father.[25]

Though I agree largely with Richardson's analysis of the vicissitudes of maternity in the construction of Joss's and Colman Moody's Black mascu-
linities, I would add that in both cases it becomes necessary to disavow
maternity to a certain extent, because in the schema of racializing assemblages the white mother is not able to bestow symbolic significance of the
benefits of whiteness on the Black child, nor can she serve as a guide for
how to be in Blackness or explain the somebody-elseness of the Black child,
especially when the assumption in this context is always already that the
Black child cannot "belong" to the white mother and thus the British
nation.[26]

In a video recording, Jackie Kay offers an emblematic anecdote before
she reads of a few of her poems, including "Somebody Else," of a white
woman asking her mother "Is that your daughter?" and demanding to know
from Kay: "Where do you come from?"[27] Kay responds with her poem "In
My Country":

> a woman passed round me
> in a slow watchful circle,
> as if I were a superstition;
> or the worst dregs of her imagination,
> so when she finally spoke
> her words spliced into bars
> of an old wheel. A segment of air.
> *Where do you come from?*
> "Here," I said, "Here. These parts."[28]

It seems as though in this particular constellation the loss of the white
mother is a forgone conclusion, giving the existential question "Where
do you come from?" a double signification since it presupposes not only
that Kay as a Black person cannot form a part of Scotland's imaginary
bloodlines but also that she cannot be of her mother. In "'Mama's Baby,
Papa's Maybe': An American Grammar Book," Spillers takes the Moynihan Report, which argued that the "tangle of pathology" found in the

African American family was defined by a matriarchal structure because of the laws of racial slavery that yoked enslaved children to the status of the mother rather than the father, as her point of departure. Fusing this historical configuration with the law of the father in Lacanian psycho-analysis, Spillers refutes the Black matriarchy thesis in order to show how, instead, for Black people in the West "motherhood as female blood-rite is outraged, is denied, at the very same time that it becomes the founding term of a human and social enactment; 2) a dual fatherhood is set in motion, comprised of the African father's banished name and body and the captor father's mocking presence. In this play of paradox, only the female stands in the flesh, both mother and mother-dispossessed."[29] As Heather Russell reasons in her assessment of Spillers's overhaul of the Oedipus complex through the prism of the Middle Passage and planta-tion slavery, "the 'law of the Mother' . . . is fraught with intrinsic tension for black men, within both the symbolic and public/institutional orders. Rejecting the 'law of the Mother' and unable to name the Father, the 'law of Race' thus becomes guarantor of racial and masculine identity. Hence, the 'law of Race' becomes a metonym for the Father's name, the Father's law."[30] The whiteness of the mother compounds the rejection of the maternal in this context, because the social environment continually re-minds both Kay and Colman that their mothers must be somebody else, and because the Black father remains outside this schema, the visual taxon-omy of race becomes the proxy for both paternity and the father's law. Accordingly, while the law of race erases maternity altogether, it inti-mates that the father's Blackness can bequeath subjectivity to children like Colman.

This is one reason why Colman recollects continually pestering his father to relay to him a narrative of their familial origin, especially how his grandfather John Moore came to Scotland. Joss does reveal his father's story to Colman in a posthumous letter, but only in relatively broad brush-strokes, partially because he himself knows so little about this history: A Black man who arrived in Scotland in the early part of the twentieth century to be educated but wound up working as a servant, whose name, John Moore, was given to him by his employers, never saw his family again. John Moore's "story could be the story of any black man who came from Africa to Scotland. His story, I told you, was the diaspora. Every story runs into the same river and the same river runs into the sea" (*Trumpet*, 271). At an earlier point in the narrative Colman also recollects a different type of genealogical wisdom Joss imparted to him while he was still alive: "He said they didn't belong anywhere but to each other. . . . He said you make up your own bloodline, Colman. Make it up and trace it back. Design your own family tree—what's the matter with you? Haven't you got an imagination?" (*Trumpet*, 59). It is this knowledge that Colman must come to understand and internalize, which necessitates becoming a permanent resident alien of the flesh as a country.

Similarly, in a dreamlike chapter of the novel entitled "Music," readers become privy to a glimpse of Joss's inhabitation of his music:

> The music is his blood. His cells. But the odd bit is that down at the bottom, the blood doesn't matter after all. . . . So when he takes off he is the whole century galloping to its close. The wide moors. The big mouth. Scotland. Africa. Slavery. Freedom. He is a girl. A man. Everything, nothing. He is sickness, health. The sun. The moon. Black, white. Nothing weighs him down. Not the past or the future. He hangs on to the high C and then he lets go. Screams. Lets it go. Bends his notes and bends his body. . . . He is blowing his story. His story is blowing in the wind. He lets it rip. He tears himself apart. He explodes. Then he brings himself back. Slowly, slowly, piecing himself together. (*Trumpet*, 136)

Although ultimately the blood might be irrelevant, it would be difficult to get under it without the mattering of its existence, and, not to put a too fine point on it, the bottom is also where the music plays "loud and long," which like Nel's Urschrei at the end of Morrison's *Sula* "had no bottom and it had no top," but surely enfolds much more than "just circles and circles of sorrow."[31]

Like Joss Moody, another jazz musician, Sun Ra, also knew all too well what it meant to live "all the time being somebody else" and, thus, create yourself from the rivers of blood that course through the veins of Black Life. According to gossip circulating and the official documents fabricated by the Feds after his death, Ra was born in Birmingham, Alabama, in 1914 and assigned the name Herman Sonny Blount. However, Sun Ra, throughout his lifetime, vehemently denied these rumors, choosing instead to flip the "mistake" of being-somebody-else on its head, for instance, when he states: "People say I'm Herman Blount, but I don't know him. That's an imaginary person, he never existed. . . . If I tried to do anything with the name Sonny Blount, I couldn't. . . . I'm not terrestrial, I'm a celestial being."[32] Besides presaging Mariah Carey's infamous "I don't know her" by a few decades, though no less resplendent with glitter than Mimi, it must be said, Ra's insistence in word, sound, image, and deed that his roots are incontrovertibly otherworldly hints at another form of realness, which pivots on both his personal somebody-elseness and the common conditions of Black Life.[33]

Sun Ra's 1972 film, *Space Is the Place*, depicts Ra and his Arkestra traveling to another planet via the medium of sound waves. Yet, in order to populate this new planet with Black people, Ra and his Arkestra must voyage back to Earth and, using their otherworldly music, save Black people from the daunting pimp figure named Overseer. Eventually, planet Earth combusts after the saviors (Sun Ra and his Arkestra) have returned to their new home planet. In one of the central scenes from the film, set in an Oakland community center during the Black Power era, Ra, who has just returned from his intergalactic travels, is confronted by young Black people about his racial and political realness; one woman asking Ra, "How do we know *you ain't somebody else?*" This is the response he offers: "How do you know I am real? I am not real, I am just like you. You don't exist in this society. If you did, your people wouldn't be seeking equal rights. You're not real. . . . So we're both, myths. I do not come to you as a reality. I come to you as the myth. Because that's what black people are. Myths."[34] Nevertheless, this did not preclude Sun Ra from exercising patriarchal power in his Arkestra, for instance, by relegating female members of his family of invented bloodlines, such as Vertamae Grosvenor and Rhoda Blount, to "ornamental" roles such as choreography, costuming, and vocalizing. Even one of his most consistent collaborators, June Tyson, was initially confined to this status and was sometimes asked to leave the recording studio if things were not going well: "I can't create with women in my environment," said Ra. Rumored to be gay and/or asexual during his time on this planet, Sun Ra resolutely refused any semblance of recognizable human sexuality,[35] more often refusing any hint of what might be considered sexuality and ungendering himself through his clothing, voice, and stage presence. He also articulated this ungendering as it applies to Black folks in toto in one of his broadsides from the 1950s:

> Negroes are not men.
> Negroes do not belong to
> the race called man. . . .
> The truth is that negroes
> are human beings, and
> in trying to be a man
> they are all out of course[36]

Ra lays bare here not only that Black folks dwell beyond the imaginary bloodlines of the world-of-Man but also, and, more importantly, that these currents of imagined co/sanguinity transport racializing qua ungendering. In other words, in unbelonging to the "race called man," Black men cannot be "men" and Black women are not able to conform to the category of "woman" in the world-of-Man. Even though Ra, as opposed to Joss, is said to have been born into a Black community in early twentieth-century Birmingham, he still felt it necessary to invent his own bloodline, or rather do away with earthly sanguine waters altogether. Feeling out of place, Sun Ra recognized and lived according to the maxim that he *wasn't-never-nobody-else*. Whether he was feeling like a woman and looking like a man, or vice versa, he made sure that planet Earth had some inkling of what it feels like to sound like a no-no.[37]

The recent embrace of all that is nonhuman and inhuman in the broader field of cultural studies, appearing under the guise of posthumanism, animal studies, new materialism, object-oriented realism, has once again failed to systematically address the question of Blackness and the mattering of Black Life, even though, as Zakiyyah Iman Jackson states, the very "terrestrial movement toward the nonhuman is simultaneously movement toward blackness, whether blackness is embraced or not, as blackness constitutes the very matter at hand."[38] Which is to say, there is no sphere of the nonhuman untouched by the forces of racialized gendering, and *vice versa*. This means that seeking to better understand the nonhuman, we would do well to route this journey through and root it in the relational mattering of Black Life, in the fleshy ether of concocted bloodlines. If negro blood, indeed, has a message for the world as W. E. B. Du Bois prophesied in 1903, how is it transmitted when "making generations" is not an option and you have always already lost your mother, father, aunties, and uncles, which is another way of asking how the message radiates when the blood is not pumping through the veins of individuals designated as Black?[39] Let me give you a more concrete example. While most of you are now familiar with the story of Henrietta Lacks and the eternal afterlife of the HeLa cells, and their productive vestibularity for so many fields of science and industry, what has garnered far less attention is how the cervical cancer cells—the first human cell culture to exist independently of their humanoid form in the laboratory—of a poor Black woman from Virginia shaped the purported first complete genetic map of the human genome.[40]

Twenty years before the sequencing through the Human Genome Project in 2000, another sequence was completed in 1981 in the United Kingdom, albeit not using nuclear DNA (the forty-six chromosomes found in the nucleus) but mitochondrial DNA (mtDNA).[41] The primary difference between these two forms of biological mattering lies in the fact that mtDNA is transmitted to succeeding generations *only* through the maternal line. What later came to be known as the Anderson sequence served as the reference for both the Human Genome Project and the Human Genome Diversity Project, which, as opposed to the Human Genome Project's avowed goal of charting the overall sequence of human DNA, was studying and preserving current human genetic diversity for the future, especially as it pertained to non-European indigenous populations—i.e., those parts of the human genome most likely to face "extinction."[42] Of course, why the "rare specimens" of specific genetic mattering associated with different indigenous populations around the globe might cease to exist or why they constitute distinct populations (racial groups) did not really figure into this project. In any case, at some point in the process it was revealed that against the grain of previous suppositions the Anderson line, now the standard against which all other genome cartographic renderings were measured, contained HeLa cells and did not consist of purely melanin deficient genetic material—i.e., British or European mtDNA. Once this knowledge became public, Anderson was resequenced in 1999 with the scientists "correcting" the map to conform to the Euro norm, thus excising not only any trace of Africanity but also any remnant of the HeLa cell line. I guess this is what happens when the "family of Man" meets the door of no return. What is the message for the world encoded in the somebody-elseness of Henrietta Lacks's genetic material? As an altogether different form of creating bloodlines ex nihilo, the retroactive transformation of the Anderson sequence had to be forcibly and retroactively made white and British, which is to say, we are not dealing with mere absence but with the violent killing and erasure of Black Life by any means necessary. As a result, Black Life must be excised from even the purportedly most fundamental parts of human life in order for it to even begin resembling human life, whether this occurs on the street, in the boardroom, in the university, or in the laboratory: *the Un-Blackening of human life*. While we can certainly debate whether the "Negro identifies being with life; more precisely with the vital force [because] his metaphysics are an existentialist ontology," as Léopold Sédar Senghor would have it, we would be remiss to not acquiesce to the fact that this represents, for all intents and purposes, an "ontology written in blood."[43]

Though the HeLa cell line was and continues to be so fundamental to scientific practice, it has also accrued much more narrative baggage than other cell lines. Much of the discourse around the HeLa line in the scientific community, particularly after Henrietta Lacks became known as the mother of these cells, has been about how these cells multiply so prolifically and how they have a tendency to aggressively displace other cells with which they come into contact. If you, too, out here, suddenly realize the only music they are playing in the adjoining room is Hortense Spillers's voice telling us, "Let's face it. I am a marked woman, but not everybody knows my name," get comfortable, grab some popcorn, and cue up that Michael Jackson, because you are most definitely not alone.[44] But make sure to take your time listening, otherwise you might miss not-quite-yet observable and the barely audible frequencies of the murmurs beneath the blood. Even though Michael might have proclaimed that "it don't matter if you're black or white" in the chorus of the song that inaugurated the late imperial period in his oeuvre, we do well to remember the concluding ad libs in this song: "It's black, it's white/It's tough for you to get by/It's black, it's white, woo," which are of course accompanied by his singular woohoohoos. Apparently, it do matter whether you are Black or white even at the cellular level, even after death.[45] You really could not make this shit up, even if you tried.

Michael too had to invent himself, because he was not supposed exist, because he was a fiction. Black boys with Afros from Gary, Indiana, were not supposed to become the world's biggest pop stars and most recognized public figures, and, if we are being honest, eleven-year-old children were not envisaged to sound the way Michael sings on "I'll Be There." How else can we explain the layers of somebody-elseness in the following descriptions of Jackson's first recordings for Motown: First, Greg Tate, "Yet part of the tyke's appeal was being able to simulate being lost in the hot sauce way before he was supposed to know what the hot sauce even smelt like. No denying he sounded like he knew the real deal."[46] And, second, Nelson George: "Whereas the folks at Steeltown [the Local Gary, Indiana, record company the group recorded for before Motown], Joe, and Bobby Taylor had all seen Michael's voice as a vehicle for a kid to sing as an adult, Gordy saw that the real money was in having a kid with adult skills sing as a kid."[47] As a child, Jackson's vocal apparatus mimicked being a grown Black man, only to relinquish both the twin "birthright" of his Blackness and masculinity once he had transmorphed into an adult Black man.

Was there ever a period when Michael was not engaged in the labor of being-somebody-else, where he did not hum to himself: *Wo Er war, soll Ich niemals werden?* Was Jackson being-somebody-else during the very public discourse about the shape, color, and size of his genitalia and buttocks as part of the first round of allegations of child sexual abuse against Jackson in 1993? Has there been a day in recent memory in which Oprah Winfrey was *not* asked to *be anybody but* a Black woman born in rural Mississippi and raised in Milwaukee and Memphis? What modalities of somebody-elseness did eighteen-year-old Mariah Carey exhibit in her "relationship" with and subsequent marriage to her employer, Tommy Mottola, who was not only over twice her age but also the president of the record company that styled her in ways that would facilitate Carey's crossover success through racial passing? What form of somebody-elseness was Prince performing when he scrawled "slave" on his cheek and changed his public name to an icon, which typographically fuses the signs for male (♂) and female (♀) but cannot itself be phonated: ♀, bringing to (Black) Life his lyrics from the previous decade: "I'm not a woman/I'm not a man/I am something that you'll never understand"?[48] Was there one moment in time when Whitney Houston was not vocalizing this self-same melody, killing us and herself with her songs? My queries are less concerned with authenticity, either personal or cultural, or with the fact that there are hardly any white celebrities with the same level of fame as Oprah, Prince, Mariah, Whitney, and Michael than with the still very much operative structural principle, or primal scene, if you prefer that lexicon, of Black Life that demands the annihilation and mortality of Blackness for Black people to exist in the mainstream of the Western world.

In his philosophy of Being, Martin Heidegger deploys the term *Dasein*, which in German signifies a mode of being rather than subjectivity or individuality, and he does so with the purpose of not collapsing being and the human. *Dasein* denotes the sphere of being that establishes beings and things as entities. Still, Heidegger differentiates between man's capacity for world-forming, the animal's poverty in world (*Weltarm*), and the absolute worldlessness of the stone.[49] For Heidegger, the tiered distinction between humans, animals, and minerals comes into existence primarily through the different ways these entities relate to death: "Death is the *ownmost* possibility of Dasein. Being toward it discloses to Dasein its *ownmost* potentiality-of-being in which it is concerned about the being of Dasein absolutely. . . . The ownmost possibility is *nonrelational* (unbezügliche)."[50] The nonrelational finality of death, or finitude in Heideggerian phrasing, creates self-reflexivity for the individual, revealing to them that they are a particular being and form a part of the ontological sphere of Dasein. The knowledge of one's own possible death leads to an authentic recognition of Dasein, which also constitutes the basis of Man's world-formingness. However, still lingering in the clearing of being-toward-death Heidegger argues, "We do not experience the dying of others in a genuine sense; we are at best always just 'there' too."[51] Even as Man's genuine encounter with the potentiality of his/her own mortality grants him/her the coveted entry into to the exclusive Dasein club, the death of others, according to Heidegger, must remain stranded outside the establishment on a cold and rainy Friday night. Somebody must have forgotten to put them on the guest list.

I am left pondering, what if in all the hard work of always having to be somebody-else, we cannot but experience relationally the death of others, because it is also our ownmost mortality? Put differently, what might all of this mean for Black Life's relationship to death or, in Saidiya Hartman's formulation, "the intimacy of our experience with the lives of the dead," be they in the form of humans, cultures, languages, genders, origins, belonging, and so on.[52] In what sense does this familiarity with, not the dead per se but the "lives of the dead"—and this is a very important distinction— supply an ontology of Schwarz-Sein? I use this term both to inoculate the Heideggerian corpus with some much-needed melanin, and because it is the translation for the English language term *Blackness* as it circulates in German activist and academic circles. In addition, in strict opposition to the majority of words in the German language, particularly those associated with the worldliness of humans and animals, *Dasein* is not clothed in a dimorphically gendered definite article (*die/der*), Being is qualified by the gender neutral *das*.[53] I want the passage from Dasein to Schwarz-Sein to play an important role in theorizing the ontological silhouette of ungendering in Black Life as the enfolded mattering of the belonging to unbelonging, being-somebody-else as a way of life, the way of Black Life/ Schwarz-Sein. In an analogous fashion Sylvia Wynter asks, "How can we come to know/think/feel/behave and subjectively experience ourselves— doing so for the first time in our human history consciously now—in quite different terms? How do we be, in Fanonian terms, hybridly human?"[54] In this formulation Wynter deploys the "habitual Be," also referred to as Be_2, nonfinite Be, Invariant be, which is one of the grammatical hallmarks of Black American English.

Russell and John Rickford describe this use of the verb *to be* as "distinctive because it occurs rarely or not at all in white vernaculars," adding that "outsiders . . . believe that black folk replace Standard English is and are with invariant be all the time . . ., but AAVE is actually more discriminating. For one thing, invariant habitual be describes only an event that is performed regularly or habitually. . . . Furthermore, unlike ashy, invariant habitual be is more than an isolated AAVE word; it is part of the grammatical system, an integral tile in the mosaic of the dialect."[55] Though in some cases ashiness might also be performed repeatedly, Be_2 emphasizes the active and continual Being of Schwarz-Sein, the praxis of Black Life.

This praxis is, according to June Jordan, a result of Black Life's "intimacy with the lives of the dead" given that it "has been constantly threatened by annihilation or, at least, the swallowed blurring of assimilation," and consequently AAVE "is a system constructed by people constantly needing to insist that we exist, that we are present." Jordan continues her rumination on the ontological dimensions of Black English in the following fashion: "There is no passive voice construction possible in Black English. For example, you cannot say, 'Black English is being eliminated.' You must say, instead, 'White people eliminating Black English.' The assumption of the presence of life governs all of Black English."[56] Thus, the Be$_2$ and the overall necessary ontological vivacity of AAVE provide linguistic instantiations of Black Life just as Schwarz-Sein modifies and envelops the Heideggerian notion of Dasein; they represent the somebody-elseness of Dasein.

It gets very tiring having to be-somebody-else and still knowing full well what it feels like to be a problem. And, though Michael might have endeavored to make himself and the rest of the planet relinquish the memory about the little Black boy with that big Afro and those Jackson 5 nostrils, the unmistakable welling up of the ungendering of Black Life in his voice, or rather his singing styles, always transmitted different stories drenched as they were in the bygone vocal sweat beneath the blood of Jackie Wilson, Diana Ross, Sylvester, Levi Stubbs, and Frankie Lymon.[57] Do we have the language to get at the virtually infinite layers of somebody-elseness of Jackson's "Rock with You" music video that marked his transition to adulthood? The video intermittently doubles the central image of Jackson dancing while strobe lights and backlighting refract from the sheen of his Jheri curl and the asymmetrically arranged sequins and sparkles that adorn Michael's long-sleeved shirt, pants, and boots completely cover his body from the neck down.[58] We see a diffractive cornucopia of Jackson's future and past somebody-elses. Perhaps the glittery Black fantastic in this video represents Michael Jackson's response to "Where are you from?" Maybe the optic dissemblance achieved by the soft ricocheting of the shimmering lights and gleam suggest his and our version of "Here. These parts." As does the burst of affectable mattering of Black Life that welled up in the quasi-resurrection of Jackson by professional MJ impersonator, Dimitri Reeves, during the 2015 Baltimore uprisings. More important, Jackson's voice and its afterlives can offer a glimpse of dwelling below the viscous mattering of Joss Moody's, Henrietta Lacks's, Michael Jackson's, and Sun Ra's imaginary bloodlines, as they mellifluously susurrate their ungendered messages of unbelonging for the world.

I should think that it would take a good long time for us to learn to hear the messages well.

NOTES

1. See, for instance, Sylvia Wynter and Katherine McKittrick, "Unparalleled Catastrophe for Our Species? Or, To Give Humanness a Different Future: Conversations," in *Sylvia Wynter: On Being Human as Praxis*, ed. Katherine McKittrick (Durham, N.C.: Duke University Press, 2015); and M. Shawn Copeland, *Enfleshing Freedom: Body, Race, and Being* (Minneapolis, Minn.: Fortress Press, 2009).

2. On the ways historical sedimentation becomes ontology, see Ian Hacking, *Historical Ontology* (Cambridge, Mass.: Harvard University Press, 2004).

3. See Alexander G. Weheliye, *Habeas Viscus: Racializing Assemblages, Biopolitics, and Black Feminist Theories of the Human* (Durham, N.C.: Duke University Press, 2014).

4. "At this level of radical discontinuity in the 'great chain of being,' black is vestibular to culture." Hortense J. Spillers, "Interstices: A Small Drama of Words," in *Black, White, and in Color: Essays on American Literature and Culture* (Chicago: University of Chicago Press, 2003), 155. See also Hortense J. Spillers, "The Idea of Black Culture," *CR: The New Centennial Review* 6, no. 3 (2006); and Sylvia Wynter, "On How We Mistook the Map for the Territory and Re-Imprisoned Ourselves in Our Unbearable Wrongness of Being, of Désêrte: Black Studies toward the Human Project," in *Not Only the Master's Tools: African-American Studies in Theory and Practice*, ed. Lewis Ricardo Gordon and Jane Anna Gordon (Boulder, Colo.: Paradigm, 2006).

5. See Amiri Baraka, "'Black' Is a Country," in *Home: Social Essays* (New York: Morrow, 1966).

6. James Weldon Johnson, *Autobiography of an Ex-Colored Man* (Boston: Sherman, French, & Company, 1912), 207.

7. Hortense J. Spillers, "'Mama's Baby, Papa's Maybe': An American Grammar Book," in *Black, White, and in Color: Essays on American Literature and Culture* (Chicago: University of Chicago Press, 2003), 214.

8. Spillers, "Interstices," 164.

9. Margo Crawford, *Dilution Anxiety and the Black Phallus* (Columbus: Ohio State University Press, 2008), 8.

10. Denise Ferreira da Silva, *Toward a Global Idea of Race* (Minneapolis: University of Minnesota Press, 2007), 29. Much gratitude goes to Brittnay Proctor for drawing my attention to the pertinence of Ferreira da Silva's concept of affectability for the study of Black ungendering. See Proctor's

"'They Say I'm Different': Theories of Black Gender and the Grammatologies of Funk" (PhD diss., Northwestern University, 2018).

11. Toni Cade Bambara, "On the Issue of Roles," in *The Black Woman: An Anthology*, ed. Toni Cade Bambara (New York: Penguin, 1970), 103. I am indebted to Cheryl Clarke for reminding me about Bambara's essay and its theorization of Black gender.

12. Hortense J. Spillers et al., "'Whatcha Gonna Do?': Revisiting 'Mama's Baby, Papa's Maybe: An American Grammar Book': A Conversation with Hortense Spillers, Saidiya Hartman, Farah Jasmine Griffin, Shelly Eversley, & Jennifer L. Morgan," *Women's Studies Quarterly* 35, no. 1/2 (2007): 304.

13. On the constitutive displacement of Blackness from both origin and habitus, see Nahum Dimitri Chandler, "Originary Displacement," *boundary 2* 27, no. 3 (2000).

14. Bambara, "On the Issue of Roles," 104.

15. Jackie Kay, *Trumpet* (New York: Pantheon Books, 1998), 34. Hereafter parenthetically cited in the text.

16. Though I will not dwell too much on this point here, recent "scientific" evidence has shown that the biological basis of the dimorphic system of sexual difference is far from uncomplicated. See, for instance, Anne Fausto-Sterling, *Myths of Gender: Biological Theories about Women and Men*, 2nd ed. (New York: Basic Books, 1992); and Claire Ainsworth, "Sex Redefined," *Nature* 518 (2015): 288.

17. On the Benaissa case, see Tinka Dippel, *Nadja Benaissa - Alles wird gut* (Hamburg, Germany: Edel Books, 2010); on Nushawn Williams and transgender rumors about Black celebrities, see C. Riley Snorton, *Nobody Is Supposed to Know: Black Sexuality on the Down Low* (Minneapolis: University of Minnesota Press, 2014); and on Tiger Mandingo, see Steven Thrasher, "A Black Body on Trial: The Conviction of HIV-Positive 'Tiger Mandingo,'" *BuzzFeed*, November 20, 2015, http://www.buzzfeed.com/steventhrasher/a-black-body-on-trial-the-conviction-of-hiv-positive-tiger-m. On HIV decriminalization as an important cornerstone of the Black radical tradition, see Jordan Mulkey, "Black Radical Tradition and HIV-Decriminalization," *Queer Black Millennial*, December 1, 2017, https://queerblackmillennial.com/black-radical-tradition-hiv-decriminalization/.

18. See Simone Browne, *Dark Matters: On the Surveillance of Blackness* (Durham, N.C.: Duke University Press, 2015), 16 and Snorton, *Nobody Is Supposed to Know*, 4. We should also note how the histories of racial passing figure into this equation, since, on the one hand, they heightened the dangers of surveillance and, on the other, they were always already about gender passing. In other words, there is no racial passing without the

embodiment of racialized gender roles. As Cheryl Wall notes, "'Passing' does not refer only to the sociological phenomenon of blacks crossing the color line. It represents instead both the loss of racial identity and the denial of self required of women who conform to restrictive gender roles." See Cheryl A. Wall, "Passing for What? Aspects of Identity in Nella Larsen's Novels," *Black American Literature Forum* 20, no. 1/2 (1986): 105.

19. W. E. B. Du Bois, "Dusk of Dawn: An Essay toward an Autobiography of a Race Concept," in *Writings*, ed. Nathan Huggins (New York: Library of America, 1986), 650.

20. Matt Richardson, *The Queer Limit of Black Memory: Black Lesbian Literature and Irresolution* (Columbus: Ohio State University Press, 2013), 109.

21. Jackie Kay, *Off Colour* (Newcastle, England: Bloodaxe Books, 1999), 27.

22. Jackie Kay, *Bessie Smith* (New York: Absolute Press, 1997), 9–11. Spillers states: "Community so that it could now stand for a 'moveable feast'. The idea that community is not strictly defined by four stakes in the ground, and you stand on that spot in the center. The idea is that community is a place that I never leave because I always take it with me, because it's now something inside me." Tim Haslett, "Hortense Spillers Interviewed by Tim Haslett for the Black Cultural Studies Website Collective in Ithaca, NY February 4, 1998," blackculturalstudies.org, http://www.blackculturalstudies .org/spillers/spillers_intvw.html.

23. Katherine McKittrick, "Mathematics Black Life," *Black Scholar* 44, no. 2 (2014): 20.

24. Saidiya V. Hartman, *Lose Your Mother: A Journey along the Atlantic Slave Route* (New York: Farrar, Straus and Giroux, 2007), 98.

25. Richardson, *Queer Limit of Black Memory*, 125–26.

26. For an ethnographic consideration of how white women navigate being mothers of Black children in the United Kingdom that empirically gives credence to my remarks, see France Winddance Twine, *A White Side of Black Britain: Interracial Intimacy and Racial Literacy* (Durham, N.C.: Duke University Press, 2010).

27. Pamela Robertson-Pearce, "Jackie Kay," *In Person: 30 Poets* (London: Bloodaxe Books, 2008), DVD.

28. Jackie Kay, *Other Lovers* (Newcastle, England: Bloodaxe Books, 1993), 24.

29. Spillers, "Mama's Baby, Papa's Maybe," 228. Though referred to as the Moynihan Report after its principal author, Daniel Patrick Moynihan, the document is officially titled *The Negro Family: The Case for National Action*, see United States Department of Labor, *The Negro Family: The Case for National Action* (Washington, DC: U.S. Government Printing Office, 1965). In Lacan's reformulation of the Freudian Oedipus complex,

"the law of the father" denotes the symbolic principle of differentiation and separation in language, which enacts the originary splitting of the subject.

30. Heather Russell, *Legba's Crossing: Narratology in the African Atlantic* (Athens: University of Georgia Press, 2009), 39.

31. Toni Morrison, *Sula* (New York: Plume, 1987), 174.

32. Sun Ra, liner notes to *Sound Sun Pleasure!!*, El Saturn Records, 1970, audio recording. I thank Evie Shockley for first suggesting that I incorporate Sun Ra into my argument.

33. When Mariah Carey, whose nickname is Mimi, was interviewed on German television in 2001 and asked about Jennifer Lopez she stated, "I don't know her," while knowingly smiling. In recent years, clips from the interview as well as still images and GIFs from it have widely circulated on social networks, especially Tumblr and Twitter, because it represents a classic instance of insulting someone without expressly doing so. In other words, Mariah Carey indirectly says that Jennifer Lopez, despite her immense fame, is so beneath her stature that Carey need not even know who she is.

34. John Coney, dir., *Sun Ra & His Intergalactic Arkestra: Space Is the Place* (Plexifilm, 1974).

35. As with the discussion of Michael Jackson later, I am not interested in categorically determining and delimiting Sun Ra's sexual identity. First, gender or ungendering is the far more operative category in this scenario than any simple notion of sexuality, and, second, we should take seriously Ra's refusal to enact and define himself through the legibility of homo/hetero/bisexuality. If we do venture out into the spaceways of Ra's sexuality, we should be prepared for the possibility of no models and, thus, that his sexuality might have been glittery Blackhood or saturnine sparkle.

36. Sun Ra, "Negroes Are Not Men," in Sun Ra, *The Wisdom of Sun-Ra: Sun Ra's Polemical Broadsheets and Streetcorner Leaflets*, ed. John Corbett (Chicago: White Walls Press, 2006), 76.

37. Grace Jones, *Walking in the Rain*, Island Records, 1981, audio recording.

38. Zakiyyah Iman Jackson, "Outer Worlds: The Persistence of Race in Movement 'Beyond the Human,'" *Dossier: Theorizing Queer Humanisms* 21, no. 2–3 (2015): 217. For a critique of posthumanism's failure to address racial difference and Blackness, see Alexander G. Weheliye, "'Feenin': Posthuman Voices in Contemporary Black Popular Music," *Social Text* 20, no. 2 (2002).

39. W. E. B. Du Bois, *The Souls of Black Folk*, ed. Donald B. Gibson (New York: Penguin Classics, 1996), 5. The phrase "making generations" is taken from Gayl Jones, *Corregidora* (Boston: Beacon Press, 1986).

40. On Henrietta Lacks, see Karla F. C. Holloway, *Private Bodies, Public Texts: Race, Gender, and a Cultural Bioethics* (Durham, N.C.: Duke University Press, 2011), 2–6; Paul Gilroy, *Against Race: Imagining Political Culture beyond the Color Line* (Cambridge, Mass.: Da Capo Press, 2010), 19–24; Ferreira da Silva, *Toward a Global Idea of Race*, 8–10; Weheliye, *Habeas Viscus*, 79–81; and Jayna Brown, "Being Cellular: Race, the Inhuman, and the Plasticity of Life," *GLQ: A Journal of Lesbian and Gay Studies* 21, no. 2 (2015).

41. On the significance of the Anderson sequence and HeLa for the Human Genome Diversity Project, see Amade M'charek, "Race, Time and Folded Objects: The HeLa Error," *Theory, Culture, & Society* 31, no. 6 (2014); and *The Human Genome Diversity Project: An Ethnography of Scientific Practice* (Cambridge: Cambridge University Press, 2005).

42. On the problems of and the resistance to the Human Genome Diversity Project vis-à-vis indigenous populations, see Joanne Barker, "The Human Genome Diversity Project: 'Peoples,' 'Populations' and the Cultural Politics of Identification," *Cultural Studies* 18, no. 4 (2004); and Kimberly TallBear, *Native American DNA: Tribal Belonging and the False Promise of Genetic Science* (Minneapolis: University of Minnesota Press, 2013).

43. Léopold Sédar Senghor, "The Spirit of Civilization, or the Laws of African Negro Culture," *Presence Africaine* 8–10 (1956): 53.

44. Spillers, "Mama's Baby, Papa's Maybe," 203.

45. Moreover, the full version of the 1991 "Black and White" music video was banned in the United States, because Jackson grabs his crotch too frequently and vociferously and breaks some windows while dancing. We should also note the pertinence of Janet Jackson being banned from US radio and television after one of her breasts was forcibly exposed by a white man (Justin Timberlake) during the 2004 Super Bowl half-time show. In addition, the incident led to the FCC "crackdown" on televised "indecency" and the institution of a four-second delay in televised live broadcasts.

46. Greg Tate, "I'm White! On Michael Jackson," *Village Voice*, September 22, 1987, 15.

47. Nelson George, *Thriller: The Musical Life of Michael Jackson* (Cambridge, Mass.: Da Capo Press, 2010), 33.

48. Prince and the Revolution, *I Would Die 4 U*, Warner Bothers Records, 1984, audio recording. Prince adopted the ⚤ symbol from 1993 to 2000 during a labor dispute with his record company, Warner Brothers, about the ownership of his recording masters.

49. See Martin Heidegger, *The Fundamental Concepts of Metaphysics: World, Finitude, Solitude*, trans. William McNeill and Nicholas Walker (Bloomington: Indiana University Press, 1995).

50. Martin Heidegger, *Being and Time*, trans. Joan Stambaugh (Albany: State University of New York Press, 1995), 263–64. Martin Heidegger, *Sein und Zeit* (Tübingen, Germany: Niemeyer, 1979), 263: "Der Tod ist eigenste Möglichkeit des Daseins. Das Sein zu ihr erschließt dem Dasein sein eigenstes Seinkönnen, darin es um das Sein des Daseins schlechthin geht . . . Die eigenste Möglichkeit ist unbezügliche." All the original German quotations are taken from Heidegger, *Sein und Zeit*.

51. Heidegger, *Being and Time*, 239. Heidegger, *Sein und Zeit*, 239: "Der Tod enthüllt sich zwar als Verlust, aber mehr als solcher, den die Verbleibenden erfahren. Im Erleiden des Verlustes wird jedoch nicht der Seinsverlust als solcher zugänglich, den der Sterbende 'erleidet.' Wir erfahren nicht im genuinen Sinne das Sterben der Anderen, sondern sind höchstens immer nur 'dabei.'"

52. Saidiya Hartman, "Venus in Two Acts," *Small Axe: A Caribbean Journal of Criticism* 26 (2008): 4.

53. The pronomic gendering of the German language also makes it difficult to create/use pronouns that move beyond this dimorphism, as is the case with the third person singular in English (they), which is feminine in German (*Sie*).

54. Wynter, "Unparalleled Catastrophe for Our Species," 45.

55. Russell Rickford and John Rickford, *Spoken Soul: The Story of Black English* (New York: John Wiley & Sons, 2000), 113–14.

56. June Jordan, *Some of Us Did Not Die: New and Selected Essays of June Jordan* (New York: Basic/Civitas Books, 2002), 171.

57. Though we can be fairly certain that he was moving away from traditional masculinity and Blackness visually, I am not convinced that, as some claim, Jackson was in the process of remaking himself surgically in the image of a white woman. As Francesca Royster remarks: "I don't think there has been enough theorization of Jackson's becoming gender as experienced through less material modes like voice, however. Through his cries, whispers, groans, whines, and grunts, Jackson occupies a third space of gender, one that often undercuts his audience's expectations of erotic identification." Francesca Royster, *Sounding Like a No-No: Queer Sounds and Eccentric Acts in the Post-Soul Era* (Ann Arbor: University of Michigan Press, 2013), 119.

58. Krista A. Thompson writes the following of the many uses of blinding, shimmering, and glittery lights in US and Caribbean Black popular culture: "We might understand the use of material goods and the production of blinding light as a shield or apotropaic, simultaneously reflecting and deflecting the deidealizing gaze on black subjects. Moreover, the photographic effect of light, bling, visually suspends that which is not of the subject, the cultural screen. The popular expressions analyzed here, with

their attention to the reflection of light off of surfaces, highlight a space just beyond the surface, lingering on the gap between the viewer and the subject." Krista A. Thompson, *Shine: The Visual Economy of Light in African Diasporic Aesthetic Practice* (Durham, N.C.: Duke University Press, 2015), 33. On the Black fantastic, see Richard Iton, *In Search of the Black Fantastic: Politics and Popular Culture in the Post–Civil Rights Era* (New York: Oxford University Press, 2010).

ACKNOWLEDGMENTS

This volume began with a colloquium, titled "Beyond the Doctrine of Man: Perspectives on Enfleshment," hosted by the Centre for Liberation Theologies (CLT) at KU Leuven in Leuven, Belgium, on December 18 and 19, 2015. The existence of the CLT, and its commitment to theological reflection and research in the service of promoting, advancing, and disseminating theologies of liberation, provided the possibility of this colloquium. Georges De Schrijver, with a group of international KU Leuven students, provided the vision of the CLT that sustained it for twenty-five years up to the "Beyond the Doctrine of Man" colloquium. Jacques Haers, as well as numerous KU Leuven students who assisted in the ongoing intellectual and practical work of the centre, continued the CLT's legacy by continuing to prioritize research in theologies of liberation.

The colloquium itself was a success because of the quality of the papers, presentations, and discussions. The strength of the presentations, from Steven Battin, M. Shawn Copeland, Joseph Drexler-Dreis, Patrice Haynes, Kristien Justaert, Andrew Prevot, Mayra Rivera, Linn Tonstad, and Alexander G. Weheliye, gave us the impetus to work to publicize these ideas. In addition to the presenters, Sarah Bracke, Stephan van Erp, Phillip J. Linden Jr., Jacques Haers, and Yves De Maeseneer responded to the papers in ways that significantly improved the quality of discussion and debate at the colloquium and, consequently, the quality of the work that appears in this volume. The colloquium, and this subsequent volume, would not have been possible without the support of the aforementioned people. We wish to thank all participants in the colloquium for their insightful and inspiring contributions.

Finally, we want to thank Richard Morrison at Fordham University Press for his continued support of this project. His encouragement and suggestions, along with suggestions from the anonymous reviewers, have significantly improved the quality of this work.

Abimbola, Kola. *Yoruba Culture: A Philosophical Account*. Birmingham, England: Iroko Academic Publishers, 2005.

Adorno, Theodor. *Jargon of Authenticity*. Translated by Knut Tarnowski and Frederic Will. New York: Routledge, 2003.

Ainsworth, Claire. "Sex Redefined." *Nature* 518 (2015): 288–91.

Alaimo, Stacy, and Susan Hekman, eds. *Material Feminisms*. Bloomington: Indiana University Press, 2008.

Alexander, M. Jacqui. *Pedagogies of Crossing: Meditations on Feminism, Sexual Politics, Memory, and the Sacred*. Durham, N.C.: Duke University Press, 2006.

Allen, Paula Gunn. *The Sacred Hoop: Recovering the Feminine in American Indian Traditions*. Boston: Beacon Press, 1986.

Allmendinger Jr., David F. "The Construction of *The Confessions of Nat Turner*." In *Nat Turner: A Slave Rebellion in History and Memory*, edited by Kenneth S. Greenberg, 24–42. New York: Oxford University Press, 2003.

Anzaldúa, Gloria. *Borderlands: la frontera*. 3rd ed. San Francisco: Aunt Lute, 1987.

Aptheker, Herbert. *Nat Turner's Slave Rebellion*. New York: Dover Publications, 2006.

Aquinas, Thomas. *The Summa Theologica*. Translated by the Fathers of the English Dominican Province. New York: Benzinger Bros., 1948.

Asad, Talal. *Genealogies of Religion: Discipline and Reasons of Power in Christianity and Islam*. Baltimore: Johns Hopkins University Press, 1993.

Athanasius. *On the Incarnation*, translated by John Behr. Yonkers, N.Y.: St. Vladimir's Press, 1996.

Athey, Ron. "Gifts of the Spirit." In *Pleading in the Blood: The Art and Performances of Ron Athey*, edited by Dominic Johnson, 42–53. Chicago: Intellect/University of Chicago Press, 2013.

Awolalu, J. Ọmọṣade. *Yoruba Beliefs and Sacrificial Rites*. London: Longman, 1979.

Bailey, Marlon M. *Butch Queens Up in Pumps: Gender, Performance, and Ballroom Culture in Detroit.* Ann Arbor: University of Michigan Press, 2013.

Baldwin, James. *The Price of the Ticket: Collected Nonfiction, 1948–1985.* New York: St. Martin's Press, 1985.

———. "Uses of the Blues." In *The Cross of Redemption: Uncollected Writings.* New York: Knopf Doubleday Publishing Group, 2010.

Baltazar, Eulalio. *The Dark Center: A Process Theology of Blackness.* New York: Paulist Press, 1973.

Bambara, Toni Cade. "On the Issue of Roles." In *The Black Woman: An Anthology,* edited by Toni Cade Bambara, 101–10. New York: Penguin, 1970.

Barad, Karen. *Meeting the Universe Halfway: Quantum Physics and the Entanglement of Matter and Meaning.* Durham, N.C.: Duke University Press, 2007.

Baraka, Amiri. "'Black' Is a Country." In *Home: Social Essays,* 82–86. New York: Morrow, 1966.

Barber, Karin. "How Man Makes God in West Africa: Yoruba Attitudes towards the 'Orisa.'" *Africa* 51, no. 3 (1981): 724–44.

Barker, Joanne, ed. *Critically Sovereign: Indigenous Gender, Sexuality, and Feminist Studies.* Durham, N.C.: Duke University Press, 2017.

Barker, Joanne. "The Human Genome Diversity Project: 'Peoples,' 'Populations' and the Cultural Politics of Identification." *Cultural Studies* 18, no. 4 (2004): 571–606.

Barnes, Natasha. "Reluctant Matriarch: Sylvia Wynter and the Problematics of Caribbean Feminism." *Small Axe* 5 (March 1999): 34–47.

Bastide, Roger. "Color, Racism, and Christianity." In *Color and Race,* edited by John Hope Franklin, 34–49. Boston: Beacon Press, 1968.

Bell, Catherine. *Ritual Theory, Ritual Practice.* New York: Oxford University Press, 1992.

Bell, Richard H. *Understanding African Philosophy: A Cross-Cultural Approach to Classical and Contemporary Issues.* London: Routledge, 2002.

Bennett, Jane. *Vibrant Matter: A Political Ecology of Agency and Politics.* Durham, N.C.: Duke University Press, 2010.

Bennett Jr., Lerone. "Nat's Last White Man." In *William Styron's Nat Turner: Ten Black Writers Respond,* edited by John Henrik Clarke, 3–16. Boston: Beacon Press, 1968.

Bersani, Leo. *The Culture of Redemption.* Cambridge, Mass.: Harvard University Press, 2000.

Betcher, Susan. "Becoming Flesh of My Flesh: Feminist and Disability Theologies on the Edge of Posthumanist Discourse." *Journal of Feminist Studies in Religion* 26, no. 2 (Fall 2010): 107–18.

Big K.R.I.T. *Cadillactica*. Def Jam Recordings, B0021368-02, 2014, compact disc.

Boff, Leonardo. *The Cry of the Earth, the Cry of the Poor*. Translated by Philip Berryman. Maryknoll, N.Y.: Orbis, 1997.

Boime, Albert. *The Art of Exclusion: Representing Blacks in the Nineteenth Century*. Washington, D.C.: Smithsonian Institution Press, 1990.

Braidotti, Rosi. *The Posthuman*. Cambridge: Polity, 2013.

Brand, Dionne. *A Map to the Door of No Return: Notes to Belonging*. Toronto: Doubleday Canada, 2001.

Brennan, Teresa. *The Transmission of Affect*. Ithaca, N.Y.: Cornell University Press, 2004.

Broeck, Sabine. "Legacies of Enslavism and White Abjectorship." In *Postcoloniality—Decoloniality—Black Critique*, edited by Sabine Broeck and Carsten Junker, 1–21. Chicago: University of Chicago Press, 2014.

Brown, Jayna. "Being Cellular: Race, the Inhuman, and the Plasticity of Life." *GLQ: A Journal of Lesbian and Gay Studies* 21, no. 2 (2015): 321–41.

Browne, Simone. *Dark Matters: On the Surveillance of Blackness*. Durham, N.C.: Duke University Press, 2015.

Busia, Abena. "Silencing Sycorax: On African Colonial Discourse and the Unvoiced Female." *Cultural Critique* 14 (Winter 1989–1990): 81–104.

Butler, Judith. *Frames of War: When Is Life Grievable?* New York: Verso, 2009.

———. *Notes toward a Performative Theory of Assembly*. Cambridge, Mass.: Harvard University Press, 2015.

Butler, Judith, and Athena Athanasiou. *Dispossession: The Performative in the Political*. Malden, Mass.: Polity, 2013.

Caldwell, Peter C. *Love, Death and Revolution in Central Europe: Ludwig Feuerbach, Moses Hess, Louise Dittmar, Richard Wagner*. New York: Palgrave Macmillan, 2009.

Caputo, John. "Bodies without Flesh: Overcoming the Soft Gnosticism of Incarnational Theology." In *Intensities: Philosophy, Religion and the Affirmation of Life*, edited by Katharine Sarah Moody and Steven Shakespeare, 79–94. London: Routledge, 2016.

Carew, Jan. *Black Midas*. London: Secker & Warburg, 1958.

———. "The Fusion of African and Amerindian Folk Tales." *Caribbean Quarterly* 23, no. 1 (1977): 7–21.

Carter, J. Kameron. *Race: A Theological Account*. New York: Oxford University Press, 2008.

Case, Sue-Ellen. Introduction to *Split Britches: Lesbian Practice/Feminist Performance*, edited by Sue-Ellen Case, 1–34. New York: Routledge, 1996.

Castel, Robert. *From Manual Workers to Wage Laborers: Transformation of the Social Question*. New Brunswick, N.J.: Transaction Publishers, 2003.

Catherine of Siena. *The Dialogue*. Translated by Suzanne Noffke, O.P. Mahwah, N.J.: Paulist, 1980.

Césaire, Aimé. "Notebook on a Return to the Native Land." Translated by Clayton Eshleman and Annette Smith. *Montemora* 6 (1979): 9–37.

———. "Poetry and Knowledge." Translated by Krzystof Fijlkowski and Michael Richardson. In *Refusal of the Shadow: Surrealism and the Caribbean*, edited by Michael Richardson, 134–46. London: Verso, 1996.

Chandler, Nahum Dimitri. "Originary Displacement." *boundary 2* 27, no. 3 (2000): 249–86.

Chrétien, Jean-Louis. *Symbolique du corps: La tradition chrétienne du "Cantique des Cantiques."* Paris: Presses Universitaires de France, 2005.

Clarke, John Henrik. Introduction to *William Styron's Nat Turner: Ten Black Writers Respond*, edited by John Henrik Clarke, vii–x. Boston: Beacon Press, 1968.

Coakley, Sarah. *The New Asceticism: Sexuality, Gender, and the Quest for God*. New York: Bloomsbury, 2015.

Cohen, Emma. "What Is Spirit Possession? Defining, Comparing, and Explaining Two Possession Forms." *Ethnos* 73, no. 1 (March 2008): 1–25.

Coleman, Monica A. "Invoking *Oya*: Practicing a Polydox Soteriology through a Postmodern Womanist Reading of Tananarives Due's *The Living Blood*." In *Polydoxy: Theology of Multiplicity and Relation*, edited by Catherine Keller, 186–202. New York: Routledge, 2011.

Combahee River Collective. *The Combahee River Collective Statement: Black Feminist Organizing in the Seventies and Eighties*. New York: Kitchen Table: Women of Color Press, 1977.

Cone, James. *The Cross and the Lynching Tree*. Maryknoll, N.Y.: Orbis, 2011.

———. *The Spirituals and the Blues: An Interpretation*. Maryknoll, N.Y.: Orbis, 1992.

Coney, John, dir. *Sun Ra & His Intergalactic Arkestra: Space Is the Place*. Plexifilm, 1974.

Coole, Diana, and Samantha Frost, eds. *New Materialisms: Ontology, Agency, and Politics*. Durham, N.C.: Duke University Press, 2011.

Copeland, M. Shawn. *Enfleshing Freedom: Body, Race, and Being*. Minneapolis: Fortress Press, 2009.

———. "The New Anthropological Subject at the Heart of the Mystical Body of Christ." *CTSA Proceedings* 53 (1998): 25–47.

———. "Wading through Many Sorrows." In *A Troubling in My Soul: Womanist Perspectives on Evil and Suffering*, edited by Emilie M. Townes, 109–29. Maryknoll, N.Y.: Orbis, 1993.

Crawford, Margo. *Dilution Anxiety and the Black Phallus*. Columbus: Ohio State University Press, 2008.

Dance, Daryl C. *Folklore from Contemporary Jamaicans*. Knoxville: University of Tennessee Press, 1985.

Davis, Angela Y. *Blues Legacies and Black Feminism: Gertrude Ma Rainey, Bessie Smith, and Billie Holiday*. New York: Knopf Doubleday Publishing Group, 2011.

Davis, Lennard J. *Enforcing Normalcy: Disability, Deafness, and the Body*. New York: Verso, 1995.

Davy, Kate. "Fe/Male Impersonation: The Discourse of Camp." In *The Politics and Poetics of Camp*, edited by Moe Meyer, 130–49. New York: Routledge, 1993.

———. *Lady Dicks and Lesbian Brothers: Staging the Unimaginable at the WOW Café Theatre*. Ann Arbor: University of Michigan Press, 2010.

Dean, Tim, Hal Foster, Kaja Silverman, and Leo Bersani. "A Conversation with Leo Bersani." *October* 82 (1997): 3–16.

de Las Casas, Bartolomé. "Are Not the Indians Men?" In *Witness: The Writings of Bartolomé de Las Casas*, edited and translated by George Sanderlin, 66–71. Maryknoll, N.Y.: Orbis, 1992.

———. "The 'Only Method' of Converting the Indians." In *Witness: The Writings of Bartolomé de Las Casas*, edited and translated by George Sanderlin, 137–42. Maryknoll, N.Y.: Orbis, 1992.

———. "A 'Very Brief Account' of Spanish Cruelty." In *Witness: The Writings of Bartolomé de Las Casas*, edited and translated by George Sanderlin. Maryknoll, N.Y.: Orbis, 1992.

Deleuze, Gilles. *Logique du sens*. Paris: Les éditions de minuit, 1969.

Deleuze, Gilles, and Félix Guattari. *A Thousand Plateaus: Capitalism and Schizophrenia*. Translated by Brian Massumi. New York: Continuum, 2004.

de Lubac, Henri. *Corpus Mysticum: The Eucharist and the Church in the Middle Ages*. Translated by Gemma Simmonds, C.J., with Richard Price and Christopher Stephens. Notre Dame, Ind.: University of Notre Dame Press, 2006.

———. *The Mystery of the Supernatural*. Translated by Rosemary Sheed. New York: Crossroad, 1998.

Derrida, Jacques. *On Touching—Jean-Luc Nancy*. Translated by Christine Irizarray. Stanford, Calif.: Stanford University Press, 2005.

Dickinson, Colby, and Adam Kotsko. *Agamben's Coming Philosophy: Finding a New Use for Theology*. London: Rowman & Littlefield, 2015.

Dienst, Richard. *The Bonds of Debt: Borrowing against the Common Good*. London: Verso, 2011.

Dinshaw, Carolyn. *Getting Medieval: Sexualities and Communities, Pre- and Postmodern.* Durham, N.C.: Duke University Press, 1999.

Dippel, Tinka. *Nadja Benaissa - Alles wird gut.* Hamburg, Germany: Edel Books, 2010.

Dolan, Jill. *Utopia in Performance: Finding Hope at the Theater.* Ann Arbor: University of Michigan Press, 2005.

Dondapati Allen, Anne. "No Garlic, Please: We Are Indian: Reconstructing the De-eroticized Indian Woman." In *Off the Menu: Asian and Asian North American Women's Religion and Theology,* edited by Rita Nakashima Brock, Jung Ha Kim, Kwok Pui-Lan, and Seung Ai Yang, 183–95. Louisville, Ky.: Westminster John Knox Press, 2007.

Dotson, Kristie. "Between Rocks and Hard Places." *Black Scholar* 46, no. 2 (2016): 46–56.

Douglas, Kelly Brown. *Black Bodies and the Black Church: A Blues Slant.* New York: Palgrave Macmillan, 2012.

Drewal, Margaret Thompson. *Yoruba Ritual: Performers, Play, Agency.* Bloomington: Indiana University Press, 1992.

Dreyer, Elizabeth A. *Accidental Theologians: Four Women Who Shaped Christianity.* Cincinnati: Franciscan Media, 2014.

Du Bois, W. E. B. "Dusk of Dawn: An Essay toward an Autobiography of a Race Concept." In *Writings,* edited by Nathan Huggins, 549–802. New York: Library of America, 1986.

———. *The Souls of Black Folk.* Edited by Donald B. Gibson. New York: Penguin Classics, 1996.

Dubreuil, Laurent. "Leaving Politics: Bios, Zōē, Life." Translated by Clarissa C. Eagle. *Diacritics* 36, no. 2 (2006): 83–98.

Durkin, Anita. "Object Written, Written Object: Slavery, Scarring, and Complications of Authorship in *Beloved.*" *African American Review* 41, no. 3 (Fall 2007): 541–56.

Dussel, Enrique. *The Invention of the Americas: Eclipse of "the Other" and the Myth of Modernity.* Translated by Michael D. Barber. New York: Continuum, 1995.

Edelman, Lee. "Against Survival: Queerness in a Time That's out of Joint." *Shakespeare Quarterly* 62, no. 2 (2011): 148–69.

———. *No Future: Queer Theory and the Death Drive.* Durham, N.C.: Duke University Press, 2005.

Elkins, Stanley M. *Slavery: A Problem in American Institutional and Intellectual Life.* Chicago: University of Chicago Press, 1974.

Ellacuría, Ignacio. "The Crucified People: An Essay in Historical Soteriology." In *Ignacio Ellacuría: Essays on History, Liberation, and Salvation,* edited and translated by Michael E. Lee, 195–226. Maryknoll, N.Y.: Orbis, 2013.

Eze, Michael Onyebuchi. "Ubuntu/Botho: Ideology or Promise?" In *Exploring Humanity: Intercultural Perspectives on Humanism*, edited by Mihai I. Spariosu and Jörn Rüsen, 247–60. Göttingen, Germany: V&R unipress, 2012.

Fabian, Johannes. *Time and the Other: How Anthropology Makes Its Object.* New York: Columbia University Press, 1983.

Fanon, Frantz. *Black Skin, White Masks.* New York: Grove Press, 1967.

———. *Black Skin, White Masks.* Translated by Richard Philcox. New York: Grove Press, 2008.

———. *The Wretched of the Earth.* Translated by Constance Farrington. London: Penguin Classics, 2001.

Farley, Margaret A. *Just Love: A Framework for Christian Sexual Ethics.* New York: Continuum, 2006.

Fausto-Sterling, Anne. *Myths of Gender: Biological Theories about Women and Men.* 2nd ed. New York: Basic Books, 1992.

Ferguson, Roderick A. *Aberrations in Black: Toward a Queer of Color Critique.* Minneapolis: University of Minnesota Press, 2003.

Ferreira da Silva, Denise. *Toward a Global Idea of Race.* Minneapolis: University of Minnesota Press, 2007.

Feuerbach, Ludwig. *Essence of Christianity.* Translated by George Eliot. Amherst, N.Y.: Prometheus Books, 1989.

———. "Towards a Critique of Hegel's Philosophy." In *The Fiery Brook: Selected Writings of Ludwig Feuerbach*, edited and translated by Zawar Hanfi, 53–96. New York: Doubleday, 1972. Available online at https://www.marxists.org/reference/archive/feuerbach/works/critique/.

Figueroa, Yomaira. *Decolonizing Diasporas: Radical Mappings of Afro-Atlantic Literature.* Evanston, Ill.: Northwestern University Press, forthcoming.

———. "Reparation as Transformation: Radical Literary (Re)Imaginings of Futurities through Decolonial Love." *Decolonization: Indigeneity, Education & Society* 4, no. 1 (2015): 41–58.

Fornet-Betancourt, Raúl. "Para una crítica filosófica de la globalización." In *Resistencia y solidaridad—globalización capitalista y liberación*, edited by Raúl Fornet-Betancourt, 55–80. Madrid: Editorial Trotta, S.A., 2003.

Frye, Northrop. *Anatomy of Criticism: Four Essays.* Princeton, N.J.: Princeton University Press, 1957.

Garuba, Harry. "Explorations in Animist Materialism: Notes on Reading/Writing African Literature, Culture and Society." *Public Culture* 15, no. 2 (Spring 2003): 261–86.

————. "On Animism, Modernity/Colonialism, and the African Order of Knowledge: Provisional Reflections." *e-flux* 36 (July 2012): http://www.e-flux.com/journal/on-animism-modernitycolonialism-and-the-african-order-of-knowledge-provisional-reflections/.

Gaylard, Rob. "Welcome to the World of Our Humanity." *Journal of Literary Studies* 20, no. 3/4 (2004): 26–82.

Gbadegesin, Segun. *African Philosophy: Traditional Yoruba Philosophy and Contemporary African Realities.* New York: Peter Lang, 1991.

————. "African Religions." In *The Routledge Companion to Theism*, edited by Charles Taliaferro, Victoria S. Harrison, and Stuart S. Goetz, 102–13. New York: Routledge, 2013.

Genovese, Eugene D. "The Nat Turner Case." *New York Review of Books*, September 12, 1968.

George, Nelson. *Thriller: The Musical Life of Michael Jackson.* Cambridge, Mass.: Da Capo Press, 2010.

Giggie, John M. *After Redemption: Jim Crow and the Transformation of African American Religion in the Delta, 1875–1915.* New York: Oxford University Press, 2007.

Gilroy, Paul. *Against Race: Imagining Political Culture beyond the Color Line.* Cambridge, Mass.: Da Capo Press, 2010.

Glaude Jr., Eddie S. *In a Shade of Blue: Pragmatism and the Politics of Black America.* Chicago: University of Chicago Press, 2007.

Glave, Thomas. "Toward a Queer Prayer." In *Among the Bloodpeople: Politics and Flesh*, 51–56. New York: Akashic Books, 2013.

Gonzalez, Michelle A. "Who We Are: A Latino/a Constructive Anthropology." In *In Our Own Voices: Latino/a Renditions of Theology*, edited by Benjamín Valentín, 64–84. Maryknoll, N.Y.: Orbis, 2010.

Gray, Thomas R. "The Text of *The Confessions of Nat Turner* . . . as Reported by Thomas R. Gray." In *William Styron's Nat Turner: Ten Black Writers Respond*, edited by John Henrik Clarke, 92–117. Boston: Beacon Press, 1968.

Graybill, Rhiannon. "Voluptuous, Tortured, and Unmanned: Ezekiel and Daniel Paul Schreber." In *The Bible and Posthumanism*, edited by Jennifer L. Koosed, 137–47. Atlanta: Society of Biblical Literature, 2014.

Greenberg, Kenneth S., ed. *The Confessions of Nat Turner and Related Documents.* Boston: Bedford/St. Martins, 1996.

Grillo, Laura S. "African Rituals." In *The Wiley-Blackwell Companion to African Religion*, edited by Elias Kifon Bongmba, 113–26. Oxford: Blackwell, 2012.

Gump, Janice P. "Reality Matters: The Shadow of Trauma on African American Subjectivity." *Psychoanalytic Psychology* 27, no. 1 (2010): 42–54.

Hacking, Ian. *Historical Ontology*. Cambridge, Mass.: Harvard University Press, 2004.

Halberstam, Jack (Judith). "The Anti-Social Turn in Queer Studies." *Graduate Journal of Social Studies* 5, no. 2 (2008): 140–56.

Halperin, David. *How to Be Gay*. Cambridge, Mass.: Belknap/Harvard University Press, 2012.

Harding, Vincent. "An Exchange on 'Nat Turner.'" *New York Review of Books*, November 7, 1968.

———. *There Is a River: The Black Struggle for Freedom in America*. San Diego: A Harvest Book, 1981.

———. "You've Taken My Nat and Gone." In *William Styron's Nat Turner: Ten Black Writers Respond*, edited by John Henrik Clarke, 23–33. Boston: Beacon Press, 1968.

Hardt, Michael, and Antonio Negri. *Empire*. Cambridge, Mass.: Harvard University Press, 2000.

Harney, Stefano, and Fred Moten. *The Undercommons: Fugitive Planning & Black Study*. Brooklyn, N.Y.: Autonomedia, 2013.

Harootunian, Harry. "Remembering the Historical Present." *Critical Inquiry* 33, no. 3 (Spring 2007): 471–94.

Harrison, Daphne Duval. *Black Pearls: Blues Queens of the 1920s*. New Brunswick, N.J.: Rutgers University Press, 1988.

Hart, Kevin. "Inward Life." In *Michel Henry: The Affects of Thought*, edited by J. Hanson and M. R. Kelly, 87–110. New York: Continuum, 2012.

Hart, William David. *Afro-Eccentricity: Beyond the Standard Narrative of Black Religion*. New York: Palgrave MacMillan, 2011.

Hartman, Saidiya V. *Lose Your Mother: A Journey along the Atlantic Slave Route*. New York: Farrar, Straus and Giroux, 2007.

———. "Venus in Two Acts." *Small Axe: A Caribbean Journal of Criticism* 26 (2008): 1–14.

Harvey, Graham. *Food, Sex and Strangers: Understanding Religion as Everyday Life*. Abingdon, England: Routledge, 2014.

Haynes, Tonya. "Sylvia Wynter's Theory of the Human and the Crisis School of Caribbean Heteromasculinity Studies." *Small Axe* 20, no. 1 (49) (2016): 92–112.

Heidegger, Martin. *Being and Time*. Translated by Joan Stambaugh. Albany: State University of New York Press, 1995.

———. *The Fundamental Concepts of Metaphysics: World, Finitude, Solitude*. Translated by William McNeill and Nicholas Walker. Bloomington: Indiana University Press, 1995.

———. *Sein und Zeit*. Tübingen, Germany: Niemeyer, 1979.

Hemmings, Clare. *Why Stories Matter: The Political Grammar of Feminist Theory*. Durham, N.C.: Duke University Press, 2011.

Hennessy, Rosemary. *Profit and Pleasure: Sexual Identities in Late Capitalism*. New York: Routledge, 2002.

Henry, Michel. *Auto-donation: entretiens et conférences*. Paris: Beauchesne, 2004.

———. *The Essence of Manifestation*. The Hague, Netherlands: Nijhoff, 1973.

———. *From Communism to Capitalism: Theory of a Catastrophe*. London: Bloomsbury, 2014.

———. *Incarnation: A Philosophy of Flesh*. Evanston, Ill.: Northwestern University Press, 2015.

———. *Incarnation: Une philosophie de la chair*. Paris: Seuil, 2000.

———. *Le socialisme selon Marx*. Paris: Sulliver, 2008.

———. "Speech and Religion: The Word of God." In *Phenomenology and the Theological Turn*, edited by D. Janicaud, 217–42. New York: Fordham University Press, 2000.

Henry, Paget. *Caliban's Reason: Introducing Afro-Caribbean Philosophy*. New York: Routledge, 2000.

Hilkert, Mary Catherine. "The Threatened Humanum as *Imago Dei*: Anthropology and Christian Ethics." In *Edward Schillebeeckx and Contemporary Theology*, edited by Lieven Boeve, Frederick Depoortere, and Stephan van Erp, 127–41. New York: T & T Clark, 2010.

Ho, Karen. *Liquidated: An Ethnography of Wall Street*. Durham, N.C.: Duke University Press, 2009.

Holloway, Karla F.C. "*Beloved*: A Spiritual." *Callaloo* 13 (1990): 516–25.

———. *Private Bodies, Public Texts: Race, Gender, and a Cultural Bioethics*. Durham, N.C.: Duke University Press, 2011.

Hollywood, Amy. *The Soul as Virgin Wife: Mechthild of Magdeburg, Marguerite Porete, and Meister Eckhart*. Notre Dame, Ind.: University of Notre Dame Press, 1995.

Hong Kingston, Maxine. *China Men*. New York: Vintage, 1980.

Hood, Robert E. *Begrimed and Black: Christian Traditions on Blacks and Blackness*. Minneapolis: Augsburg Fortress, 1994.

hooks, bell. *Killing Rage: Ending Racism*. New York: Henry Holt, 1995.

Horton, James Oliver, and Lois E. Horton, eds. *Slavery and Public History: The Tough Stuff of American Memory*. Chapel Hill: University of North Carolina Press, 2006.

Hucks, Tracey E. *Yoruba Traditions and African American Religious Nationalism*. Albuquerque: University of New Mexico Press, 2012.

Iatsenko, Anna. "Bodies, Music, and Embodied Cognition in Toni Morrison's Fictional Works." In *Living Language, Living Memory: Essays on the*

Works of Toni Morrison, edited by Kerstin W. Shands and Giulia Grillo Mikrut, 55–66. Mölnlycke, Sweden: Elanders, 2014.

Ìdòwú, E. Bólájí. *African Traditional Religion: A Definition.* London: SCM Press, 1973.

———. *Olódùmarè: God in Yorùbá Belief.* Long Island, N.Y.: African Tree Press, 2011.

Ingold, Tim. "Rethinking the Animate, Re-animating Thought." *Ethnos* 71, no. 1 (March 2006): 9–20.

IPAK Centar. "Interview with Prof Lee Edelman." September 21, 2015, YouTube video, 7:03, https://www.youtube.com/watch?v =NjTDLyKP2po.

Irenaeus of Lyon. *Against the Heresies.* Volume 1. *Ante-Nicene Fathers.* New York: Charles Scribner's Sons, 1925.

Isasi-Díaz, Ada María. "Mujerista Discourse: A Platform for Latinas' Subjugated Knowledge." In *Decolonizing Epistemologies: Latino/a Philosophy and Theology,* edited by Ada María Isasi-Díaz and Eduardo Mendieta, 44–67. New York: Fordham University Press 2012.

Isasi-Díaz, Ada María, and Eduardo Mendieta, eds. *Decolonizing Epistemologies: Latino/a Philosophy and Theology.* New York: Fordham University Press, 2012.

Isherwood, Lisa. *The Fat Jesus: Christianity and Body Image.* New York: Seabury, 2008.

Iton, Richard. *In Search of the Black Fantastic: Politics and Popular Culture in the Post-Civil Rights Era.* New York: Oxford University Press, 2010.

Jackson, Zakiyyah Iman. "Outer Worlds: The Persistence of Race in Movement 'Beyond the Human.'" *Dossier: Theorizing Queer Humanisms* 21, no. 2–3 (2015): 215–18.

Jakobsen, Janet R. *Working Alliances and the Politics of Difference: Diversity and Feminist Ethics.* Bloomington: Indiana University Press, 1998.

Jantzen, Grace M. *Power, Gender, and Christian Mysticism.* New York: Cambridge University Press, 1995.

Jennings, Willie James. *The Christian Imagination: Theology and the Origins of Race.* New Haven, Conn.: Yale University Press, 2010.

Johnson, Cedric. *Revolutionaries to Race Leaders: Black Power and the Making of American Politics.* Minneapolis: University of Minnesota Press, 2007.

Johnson, Elizabeth A. *She Who Is: The Mystery of God in Feminist Theological Discourse.* New York: Crossroad, 2007.

Johnson, Walter. *Soul by Soul: Life inside the Antebellum Slave Market.* Cambridge, Mass.: Harvard University Press, 1999.

Jones, Gayl. *Corregidora.* Boston: Beacon Press, 1986.

Jones, Grace. *Walking in the Rain.* Island Records, 1981. Audio Recording.

Jones, Leroi. *Blues People: Negro Music in White America*. New York: Harper Collins, 1999.

Jordan, June. "Nowadays the Heroes." In *Directed by Desire: The Collected Poems of June Jordan*, edited by Jan Heller Miles Levi and Sara Miles, 24. Port Townsend, Wash.: Cooper Canyon Press, 2005.

———. *Some of Us Did Not Die: New and Selected Essays of June Jordan*. New York: Basic/Civitas Books, 2002.

Jordan, Mark D. *Convulsing Bodies: Religion and Resistance in Foucault*. Stanford, Calif.: Stanford University Press, 2015.

Jordan, Winthrop D. *White over Black: American Attitudes toward the Negro, 1550–1812*. 2nd ed. Chapel Hill: University of North Carolina Press, 1968.

Josephs, Kelly Baker. "The Necessity for Madness: Negotiating Nation in Sylvia Wynter's *The Hills of Hebron*." In *Disturbers of the Peace: Representations of Madness in Anglophone Caribbean Literature*, edited by Kelly Baker Josephs, 45–68. Charlottesville: University of Virginia Press, 2013.

Julian of Norwich. *Showings*. Translated by Edmund Colledge, O.S.A., and James Walsh, S.J. Mahwah, N.J.: Paulist, 1978.

Kara, Siddharth. *Sex Trafficking: Inside the Business of Modern Slavery*. New York: Columbia University Press, 2009.

Kaunda, Kenneth. *A Humanist in Africa*. London: Longmans, 1966.

Kay, Jackie. *Bessie Smith*. New York: Absolute Press, 1997.

———. *Off Colour*. Newcastle, England: Bloodaxe Books, 1999.

———. *Other Lovers*. Newcastle, England: Bloodaxe Books, 1993.

———. *Trumpet*. New York: Pantheon Books, 1998.

Keller, Mary L. "Divine Women and the Nehanda *Mhondoro*: Strengths and Limitations of the Sensible Transcendental in a Post-Colonial World of Religious Women." In *Religion in French Feminist Thought: Critical Perspectives*, edited by Morny Joy, Kathleen O'Grady, and Judith L. Poxon, 68–82. London: Routledge, 2003.

———. *The Hammer and the Flute: Women, Power and Spirit Possession*. Baltimore: Johns Hopkins University Press, 2002.

Kirby, Vicki. *Quantum Anthropologies: Life at Large*. Durham, N.C.: Duke University Press, 2011.

Kvam, Kristien E. "Anthropology, Theological." In *Dictionary of Feminist Theologies*, edited by Letty M. Russel and J. Shannon Clarkson, 10–12. Louisville, Ky.: Westminster John Knox Press, 1996.

Lamb, Matthew. "The Social and Political Dimensions of Lonergan's Theology." In *The Desires of the Human Heart: An Introduction to the Theology of Bernard Lonergan*, edited by Vernon Gregson, 255–84. New York: Paulist Press, 1988.

Lanzetta, Beverly. *Radical Wisdom: A Feminist Mystical Theology.* Minneapolis: Fortress, 2005.

Lara, Irene. "Beyond Caliban's Curses: The Decolonial Feminist Literacy of Sycorax." *Journal of International Women's Studies* 9, no. 1 (2007): 80–98.

Lartey, Emmanuel Y. *Postcolonializing God: An African Practical Theology.* London: SCM Press, 2013.

Levins Morales, Aurora. *Medicine Stories: History, Culture and the Politics of Integrity.* New York: South End Press, 1998.

Linden, Phillip J. "Letting Go of Race: Reflections from a Historical Theological View." *Voices* 36, no. 1 (January–March 2013): 75–88.

Lonergan, Bernard. *Insight: A Study of Human Understanding.* 5th ed. Vol. 3 of *Collected Works of Bernard Lonergan.* Toronto: University of Toronto Press, 1988.

———. *Method in Theology.* New York: Herder and Herder, 1972.

———. *The Subject: The Aquinas Lecture 1968.* Milwaukee, Wisc.: Marquette University Press, 1968.

Long, Charles H. *Significations: Signs, Symbols, and Images in the Interpretation of Religion.* Aurora, Colo.: Davies Group, 1995.

Lorde, Audre. "A Litany for Survival." In *The Black Unicorn,* 31–32. New York: Norton, 1995.

———. *Sister Outsider: Essays and Speeches.* New York: Crossing Press, 2002.

Lordon, Frédéric. *Willing Slaves of Capital: Spinoza & Marx on Desire.* Translated by Gabriel Ash. London: Verso, 2014.

Lorey, Isabell. *State of Insecurity: Government of the Precarious.* London: Verso, 2015.

Lowe, Lisa. *The Intimacies of Four Continents.* Durham, N.C.: Duke University Press, 2015.

Lubin-Levy, Joshua, and Carlos Motta. *Petite Mort: Recollections of a Queer Public.* New York: Forever & Today, 2011.

Lugones, María. "Heterosexualism and the Colonial/Modern Gender System." *Hypatia* 22, no. 1 (Winter 2007): 186–209.

———. *Peregrinajes/Pilgrimages: Theorizing Coalitions against Multiple Oppressions.* Lanham, Md.: Rowman and Littlefield, 2003.

Mahmood, Saba. "Rehearsed Spontaneity and the Conventionality of Ritual: Disciplines of Ṣalāt." *American Ethnologist* 28, no. 4 (2001): 827–53.

Maldonado-Torres, Nelson. "On the Coloniality of Being: Contributions to the Development of a Concept." *Cultural Studies* 21, no. 2–3 (March/May 2007): 240–70.

Marcos, Sylvia. *Taken from the Lips: Gender and Eros in Mesoamerican Religions.* Vol. 5. Leiden, Netherlands: Brill Academic Publishers, 2006.

Marx, Karl. "Theses on Feuerbach." In *Karl Marx: Selected Writings*, edited by David McLellan, 171–73. Oxford: Oxford University Press, 2000.

Mbembe, Achille. "Necropolitics." *Political Culture* 15, no. 1 (Winter 2003): 11–40.

Mbiti, John S. *African Religions and Philosophy*. London: Heinemann, 1969.

M'charek, Amande. *The Human Genome Diversity Project: An Ethnography of Scientific Practice*. Cambridge: Cambridge University Press, 2005.

———. "Race, Time and Folded Objects: The HeLa Error." *Theory, Culture, & Society* 31, no. 6 (2014): 29–56.

McKittrick, Katherine. *Demonic Grounds: Black Women and the Cartographies of Struggle*. Minneapolis: University of Minnesota Press, 2006.

———. "Mathematics Black Life." *Black Scholar* 44, no. 2 (2014): 16–28.

McKittrick, Katherine, ed. *Sylvia Wynter: On Being Human as Praxis*. Durham, N.C.: Duke University Press, 2015.

McMillan, Uri. *Embodied Avatars: Genealogies of Black Feminist Art and Performance*. New York: New York University Press, 2015.

McRobbie, Angela. *The Aftermath of Feminism: Gender, Culture, and Social Change*. London: Sage, 2009.

———. *Be Creative: Making a Living in the New Culture Industries*. Cambridge: Polity, 2016.

Méndez, Xhercis. "Decolonizing Feminist Methodologies from the Dark Side." Manuscript in progress.

———. "Decolonial Feminist *Movidas*: A *Caribeña* (Re)thinks 'Privilege,' the Wages of Gender, and Building Complex Coalitions." In *Theories of the Flesh: Latinx and Latin American Feminisms, Transformation, and Resistance*, edited by José Medina, Mariana Ortega, and Andrea Pitts. New York: Oxford University Press, Forthcoming.

———. "Notes toward a Decolonial Feminist Methodology: Revisiting the Race/Gender Matrix." *Trans-Scripts* 5 (2015): 41–59.

———. "Transcending Dimorphism: Afro-Cuban Ritual Praxis and the Rematerialization of the Body." *Power* 3, no. 3 (2003): 47–69.

Metz, Johann Baptist. *Faith in History and Society: Toward a Practical Fundamental Theology*. New York: Crossroad Publishing Company, 2007.

Mignolo, Walter. *The Darker Side of Western Modernity: Global Futures, Decolonial Options*. Durham, N.C.: Duke University Press, 2011.

———. "Decolonizing Western Epistemology/Building Decolonial Epistemologies." In *Decolonizing Epistemologies: Latina/o Theology and Philosophy*, edited by Ada Maria Isasi-Diaz and Eduardo Mendieta, 19–43. New York: Fordham University Press, 2012.

———. "Delinking: The Rhetoric of Modernity, the Logic of Coloniality and the Grammar of De-Coloniality." *Culture Studies* 21, no. 2–3 (March/May 2007): 449–514.

———. "Epistemic Disobedience, Independent Thought and De-Colonial Freedom." *Theory, Culture, and Society* 26, no. 7–8 (2009): 1–23.

———. *Local Histories/Global Designs: Coloniality, Subaltern Knowledges, and Border Thinking.* Princeton, N.J.: Princeton University Press, 2000.

Mignolo, Walter D., and Arturo Escobar, eds. *Globalization and the Decolonial Option.* New York: Routledge, 2013.

Morrison, Toni. *Beloved.* New York: Alfred Knopf, 1987.

———. "The Site of Memory." In *Inventing the Truth: The Art and Craft of Memoir,* edited by William Zinsser, 183–200. New York: Houghton Mifflin Company, 1998.

———. *Sula.* New York: Plume, 1987.

Morsink, Johannes. *The Universal Declaration of Human Rights: Origins, Drafting, and Intent.* Philadelphia: University of Pennsylvania Press, 1999.

Mulkey, Jordan. "Black Radical Tradition and HIV-Decriminalization." *Queer Black Millennial,* December 1, 2017, https://queerblackmillennial.com/black-radical-tradition-hiv-decriminalization/.

Muñoz, José Esteban. *Cruising Utopia: The Then and There of Queer Futurity.* New York: New York University Press, 2009.

———. *Disidentifications: Queers of Color and the Performance of Politics.* Minneapolis: University of Minnesota Press, 1999.

Murray, Albert. *Stomping the Blues.* Cambridge, Mass.: Da Capo Press, 1976.

Nasrallah, Laura. *An Ecstasy of Folly: Prophecy and Authority in Early Christianity.* Cambridge, Mass.: Harvard Theological Studies, 2003.

Nourbese Philip, Marlene. "Dis Place—The Space Between." In *A Genealogy of Resistance and Other Essays,* 74–112. Toronto: Mercury Press, 1998.

———. *A Genealogy of Resistance and Other Essays.* Toronto: Mercury Press, 1997.

O'Connor, Flannery. *The Complete Stories.* New York: Farrar, Straus, and Giroux, 1971.

Oliver, Paul. *Blues Fell This Morning: Meaning in the Blues.* New York: Cambridge University Press, 1990.

Olupona, Jacob K. *African Religions: A Very Short Introduction.* Oxford: Oxford University Press, 2014.

———. "To Praise and Reprimand: Ancestors and Spirituality in African Societies and Cultures." In *Ancestors and Post-Contact Religion: Roots, Ruptures and Modernity's Memories,* edited by Steven J. Friesen, 49–63. Cambridge, Mass.: Harvard University Press, 2001.

Ong, Aihwa. *Spirits of Resistance and Capitalist Discipline: Factory Women in Malaysia.* 2nd ed. Albany: SUNY Press, 2010.

Otto, Rudolf. *The Idea of the Holy: An Inquiry into the Non-Rational Factor in the Idea of the Divine and its Relation to the Rational.* Translated by John W. Harvey. New York: Oxford University Press, 1958.

OutKast. "Chonkyfire." *Aquemini.* LaFace Records, 73008–26053-2, compact disc.

Oyĕwùmí, Oyèrónkẹ́. *The Invention of Women: Making an African Sense of Western Gender Discourses.* Minneapolis: University of Minnesota Press, 1997.

———. "Visualizing the Body." In *The African Philosophy Reader,* edited by P. H. Coetzee, 456–86. London: Routledge, 2003.

Painter, Nell Irvin. "Soul Murder and Slavery: Toward a Fully Loaded Cost Accounting." In *U. S. History as Women's History: New Feminist Essays,* edited by Linda Kerber, Alice Kessler-Harris, and Kathryn Kish Sklar, 125–46. Chapel Hill: University of North Carolina Press, 1995.

Paredes, Julieta. *Hilando Fino: Desde el feminismo comunitario.* La Paz: Comunidad Mujeres Creando Comunidad, 2010.

Parramore, Thomas C. "Covenant in Jerusalem." In *Nat Turner: A Slave Rebellion in History and Memory,* edited by Kenneth S. Greenberg, 58–78. Oxford: Oxford University Press, 2003.

p'Bitek, Okot. *Decolonizing African Religions: A Short History of African Religions in Western Scholarship.* New York: Diasporic African Press, 2011.

Pennington, James. *The Fugitive Blacksmith.* 1849; 1850; Kitrinos Publishers, 2015. Kindle.

Phelan, Peggy. *Unmarked: The Politics of Performance.* New York: Routledge, 1993.

Pius XII. *Mystici corporis Christi.* Encyclical letter. Vatican website. June 29, 1943. http://w2.vatican.va/content/pius-xii/en/encyclicals/documents/hf_p-xii_enc_29061943_mystici-corporis-christi.html.

Pope Paul VI. *Lumen gentium.* Encyclical letter. Vatican website. November 21, 1964. http://www.vatican.va/archive/hist_councils/ii_vatican_council/documents/vat-ii_const_19641121_lumen-gentium_en.html.

Poussaint, Alvin F. "*The Confessions of Nat Turner* and the Dilemma of William Styron." In *William Styron's Nat Turner: Ten Black Writers Respond,* edited by John Henrik Clarke, 17–22. Boston: Beacon Press, 1968.

Prevot, Andrew. "Hearing the Cries of Crucified Peoples: Ignacio Ellacuría and James Cone." In *Witnessing: Prophecy, Politics, and Wisdom,* edited by Maria Clara Bingemer and Peter Casarella, 45–59. Maryknoll, N.Y.: Orbis, 2014.

Price, Charles Reavies. "'Cleave to the Black': Expressions of Ethiopianism in Jamaica." *New West Indian Guide* 77, no. 1/2 (2003): 31–64.

Prince and the Revolution. *I Would Die 4 U.* Warner Brothers Records, 1984. Audio recording.

Proctor, Brittnay. "'They Say I'm Different': Theories of Black Gender and the Grammatologies of Funk." PhD diss., Northwestern University, 2018.

Puar, Jasbir. *Terrorist Assemblages: Homonationalism in Queer Times.* Durham, N.C.: Duke University Press, 2007.

Quijano, Aníbal. "Colonialidad del poder y clasificación social." *Journal of World-Systems Research* 6, no. 2 (Summer/Fall 2000): 342–86.

———. "Coloniality and Modernity/Rationality." *Cultural Studies* 21, no. 2–3 (March/May 2007): 168–78.

———. "Coloniality of Power, Eurocentrism, and Latin America." *Nepantla: Views from South* 1, no. 3 (2000): 533–80.

———. "Coloniality of Power, Eurocentrism and Social Classification." In *Coloniality at Large: Latin America and the Postcolonial Debate*, 182–87. Durham, N.C.: Duke University Press, 2008.

Rabaka, Reiland. *Hip Hop's Inheritance: From the Harlem Renaissance to the Hip Hop Feminist Movement.* Lanham, Md.: Lexington Books, 2011.

Raboteau, Albert J. *Canaan Land: A Religious History of African Americans.* New York: Oxford University Press, 2001.

———. *A Fire in the Bones.* Boston: Beacon Press, 1996.

———. *Slave Religion: The "Invisible Institution" in the Antebellum South.* New York: Oxford University Press, 2004.

Rahner, Karl. "Anonymous Christianity and the Missionary Task of the Church." In *Theological Investigations*, vol. 12, translated by David Bourke, 161–78. New York: Seabury, 1974.

Rayan, Samuel. "Decolonization of Theology." *JNANADEEPA* 1, no. 2 (July 1998): http://sedosmission.org/old/eng/Rayan.html.

Reid-Bowen, Paul. "Vital New Matters: The Speculative Turn in the Study of Religion and Gender." *Religion and Gender* 1, no. 1 (2011): 44–65.

Reinhardt, Mark. *Who Speaks for Margaret Garner?* Minneapolis: University of Minnesota Press, 2010.

Richardson, Matt. *The Queer Limit of Black Memory: Black Lesbian Literature and Irresolution.* Columbus: Ohio State University Press, 2013.

Rickford, Russell, and John Rickford. *Spoken Soul: The Story of Black English.* New York: John Wiley & Sons, 2000.

Rivera, Mayra. *Poetics of the Flesh.* Durham, N.C.: Duke University Press, 2015.

Roberts, Neil. "Sylvia Wynter's Hedgehogs: The Challenge for Intellectuals to Create New 'Forms of Life' in Pursuit of Freedom." In *After Man,*

towards the Human: Critical Essays on Sylvia Wynter, edited by Anthony
Bogues, 157–89. Kingston, Jamaica: Ian Randle Publishers, 2006.

Robertson-Pearce, Pamela. "Jackie Kay." *In Person: 30 Poets.* London:
Bloodaxe Books, 2008, DVD.

Rodgers, Daniel T. *Age of Fracture.* Cambridge, Mass.: Belknap Press of
Harvard University Press, 2011.

Roelofs, Monique. "Racialization as an Aesthetic Production: What Does
the Aesthetic Do for Whiteness and Blackness and Vice Versa." In *White
on White, Black on Black,* edited by George Yancy, 83–124. Lanham, Md.:
Rowman & Littlefield, 2005.

Rose, Wendy. *Going to War with All My Relations: New and Selected Poems.*
Flagstaff, Ariz.: Entrada, 1993.

Royster, Francesca. *Sounding Like a No-No: Queer Sounds and Eccentric Acts in
the Post-Soul Era.* Ann Arbor: University of Michigan Press, 2013.

Russell, Heather. *Legba's Crossing: Narratology in the African Atlantic.* Athens:
University of Georgia Press, 2009.

Ryan, Judylyn S. *Spirituality as Ideology in Black Women's Film and Literature.*
Charlottesville: University of Virginia Press, 2005.

Sandoval, Chela. *Methodology of the Oppressed.* Minneapolis: University of
Minnesota Press, 2000.

Santos-Febres, Mayra. *Sirena: A Novel.* Basingstoke, England: Macmillan,
2000.

———. *Sobre piel y papel.* San Juan: Ediciones Callejon Incorporated,
2000.

Sarig, Roni. *Third Coast: OutKast, Timbaland, and How Hip-Hop Became a
Southern Thing.* Boston: Da Capo Press, 2007.

Schillebeeckx, Edward. *Christ: The Experience of Jesus as Lord.* Translated by
John Bowden. New York: Crossroad, 1981.

Scott, David. "The Re-Enchantment of Humanism: An Interview with
Sylvia Wynter." *Small Axe* 8 (September 2000): 119–207.

Senghor, Léopold Sédar. "The Spirit of Civilization, or the Laws of African
Negro Culture." *Presence Africaine* 8–10 (1956): 51–67.

Seuro Elliott, Mary Jane. "Postcolonial Experience in a Domestic Context:
Commodified Subjectivity in Toni Morrison's *Beloved.*" *Meleus* 25, no. 3–4
(Autumn–Winter 2010): 181–202.

Seyler, Frédéric. *"Barbarie ou culture": L'éthique de l'affectivité dans la phénoménologie de Michel Henry.* Paris: Editions Kimé, 2010.

Simpson, Leanne Betasamosake. *Islands of Decolonial Love: Stories & Songs.*
Winnipeg: Arp Books, 2015.

Smith, Andrea. *Conquest: Sexual Violence and American Indian Genocide.*
Durham, N.C.: Duke University Press, 2015.

Smith, J. T. "Funny Paper." "Fool's Blues." *Complete Recorded Works in Chronological Order (1930–1931)*. Document Records (2), BDCD-6016, 1991, compact disc.

Smith, Valerie. "Neo-Slave Narratives." In *The Cambridge Companion to the African American Slave Narrative*, edited by Audrey Fisch, 168–86. Cambridge: Cambridge University Press, 2007.

Snorton, C. Riley. *Nobody Is Supposed to Know: Black Sexuality on the Down Low*. Minneapolis: University of Minnesota Press, 2014.

Sobchack, Vivian. *Carnal Thoughts: Embodiment and Moving Image Culture*. Berkeley: University of California Press, 2004.

Soto, Sandra K. *Reading Chican@ Like a Queer: The De-Mastery of Desire*. Austin: University of Texas Press, 2015.

Soyinka, Wole. *Myth, Literature and the African World*. Cambridge: Cambridge University Press, 1976.

Spencer, Jon Michael. *Blues and Evil*. Knoxville: University of Tennessee Press, 1993.

Spillers, Hortense J. "The Idea of Black Culture." *CR: The New Centennial Review* 6, no. 3 (2006): 7–28.

———. "Interstices: A Small Drama of Words." In *Black, White, and in Color: Essays on American Literature and Culture*, 152–75. Chicago: University of Chicago Press, 2003.

———. "Mama's Baby, Papa's Maybe: An American Grammar Book." In *Black, White, and in Color: Essays on American Literature and Culture*, 203–29. Chicago: University of Chicago Press, 2003.

Spillers, Hortense J., Saidiya Hartman, Farah Jasmine Griffin, Shelly Eversley, and Jennifer L. Morgan. "'Whatcha Gonna Do?': Revisiting 'Mama's Baby, Papa's Maybe: An American Grammar Book': A Conversation with Hortense Spillers, Saidiya Hartman, Farah Jasmine Griffin, Shelly Eversley, & Jennifer L. Morgan." *Women's Studies Quarterly* 35, no. 1/2 (2007): 299–309.

Stepto, Robert B. "Intimate Things in Place: A Conversation with Toni Morrison." In *Conversations with Toni Morrison*, edited by Danille K. Taylor-Guthrie, 10–29. Jackson: University Press of Mississippi, 1994.

Stewart, Dianne. *Three Eyes for the Journey*. Oxford: Oxford University Press, 2005.

Stolle, Roger. *Hidden History of Mississippi Blues*. Charleston, S.C.: History Press, 2011.

Styron, William. *The Confessions of Nat Turner*. New York: Vintage International, 1992.

———. "Overcome." *New York Review of Books*, September 26, 1963.

Sun Ra. "Negroes Are Not Men." In Sun Ra, *The Wisdom of Sun-Ra: Sun Ra's Polemical Broadsheets and Streetcorner Leaflets*, edited by John Corbett. Chicago: White Walls Press, 2006.

———. *Sound Sun Pleasure!!* El Saturn Records, 1970. Audio recording.

TallBear, Kimberly. *Native American DNA: Tribal Belonging and the False Promise of Genetic Science*. Minneapolis: University of Minnesota Press, 2013.

Tate, Greg. "I'm White! On Michael Jackson." *Village Voice*, September 22, 1987, 15.

Taylor, Charles. *Modern Social Imaginaries*. Durham, N.C.: Duke University Press, 2004.

Thompson, Krista A. *Shine: The Visual Economy of Light in African Diasporic Aesthetic Practice*. Durham, N.C.: Duke University Press, 2015.

Thrasher, Steven. "A Black Body on Trial: The Conviction of HIV-Positive 'Tiger Mandingo.'" *BuzzFeed*, November 20, 2015, http://www.buzzfeed .com/steventhrasher/a-black-body-on-trial-the-conviction-of-hiv-positive -tiger-m.

Tonstad, Linn Marie. "Debt Time Is Straight Time." *Political Theology* 17, no. 5 (September 2016): 1–15.

———. "The Entrepreneur and the Big Drag: Risky Affirmation in Capital's Time." In *Sexual Disorientations: Queer Temporalities, Affects, Theologies*, edited by Kent Brintnall, Joseph Marchal, Stephen Moore, and Catherine Keller, 218–39. New York: Fordham University Press, 2018.

———. "The Limits of Inclusion: Queer Theology and Its Others." *Theology and Sexuality* 21, no. 1 (2015): 1–19.

———. "Sexual Difference and Trinitarian Death: Cross, Kenosis, and Hierarchy in the *Theo-Drama*." *Modern Theology* 26, no. 4 (October 2010): 603–31.

Townes, Emilie M. *Womanist Ethics and the Cultural Production of Evil*. New York: Palgrave Macmillan, 2006.

Tragle, Henry Irving. *The Southampton Slave Revolt of 1831: A Compilation of Source Material*. Amherst: University of Massachusetts Press, 1971.

Trouillot, Michel-Rolph. *Silencing the Past: Power and the Production of History*. Boston: Beacon Press, 1995.

Turner, Denys. *Julian of Norwich: Theologian*. New Haven, Conn.: Yale University Press, 2011.

Turner, Victor. *The Forest of Symbols: Aspects of Ndembu Ritual*. Ithaca, N.Y.: Cornell University Press, 1967.

United States Department of Labor. *The Negro Family: The Case for National Action*. Washington, D.C.: U.S. Government Printing Office, 1965.

Uzukwu, Elochukwu. *God, Spirit, and Human Wholeness: Appropriating Faith and Culture in West African Style.* Eugene, Ore.: Wipf and Stock Publishers, 2012.

Vallega, Alejandro A. *Latin American Philosophy from Identity to Radical Exteriority.* Bloomington: Indiana University Press, 2014.

van der Tuin, Iris. "Deflationary Logic: Response to Sara Ahmed's 'Imaginary Prohibitions: Some Preliminary Remarks on the Founding Gestures of the "New Materialism."'" *European Journal of Women's Studies* 15, no. 4 (2008): 411–16.

Vasko, Elizabeth T. "The Difference Gender Makes: Nuptiality, Analogy, and the Limits of Appropriating Hans Urs von Balthasar's Theology in the Context of Sexual Violence." *Journal of Religion* 94, no. 4 (October 2014): 504–28.

Viramontes, Helena María. *Their Dogs Came with Them: A Novel.* New York: Simon and Schuster, 2007.

Viriasova, Inna. "Unpolitical Life: Michel Henry and the Real Limits of Biopolitics." *Diacritics* 42, no. 3 (2014): 84–113.

von Balthasar, Hans Urs. *Theo-Drama: Theological Dramatic Theory*, vol. 5, *The Last Act.* Translated by Graham Harrison. San Francisco: Ignatius, 1998.

Walcott, Rinaldo. "The Problem of the Human: Black Ontologies and 'the Coloniality of Our Being.'" In *Postcoloniality—Decoloniality—Black Critique: Joints and Fissures*, edited by Sabine Broeck and Carsten Junker. New York: Campus Verlag, 2014.

Walker King, Debra. *African Americans and the Culture of Pain.* Charlottesville: University of Virginia Press, 2008.

Wall, Cheryl A. "Passing for What? Aspects of Identity in Nella Larsen's Novels." *Black American Literature Forum* 20, no. 1/2 (1986): 97–111.

Wallace, Cynthia R. *Of Women Borne: A Literary Ethics of Suffering.* New York: Columbia University Press, 2016.

Walters, Delores M. "Introduction: Re(dis)covering and Recreating the Cultural Milieu of Margaret Garner." In *Gendered Resistance: Women, Slavery, and the Legacy of Margaret Garner*, edited by Mary E. Frederickson and Delores M. Walters, 1–22. Urbana-Champagne: University of Illinois Press, 2012.

Wartofsky, Mark W. *Feuerbach.* Cambridge: Cambridge University Press, 1977.

Washington, Joseph R. "Are American Negro Churches Christian?" *Theology Today* 20, no. 1 (April 1, 1963): 76–86.

WatchLOUD, "CRWN w/Elliott Wilson Ep. 13 Pt. 2 of 2: Big K.R.I.T." YouTube video, 30:03, October 8, 2014, https://www.youtube.com/watch?v=7YDEL7miJok.

Watson, Roxane. "The Native Baptist Church's Political Role in Jamaica: Alexander Bedward's Trial for Sedition." *Journal of Caribbean History* 42, no. 2 (2008): 231–54.

Weeks, Kathi. *The Problem with Work: Feminism, Marxism, Antiwork Politics, and Postwork Imaginaries*. Durham, N.C.: Duke University Press, 2011.

Weheliye, Alexander G. "'Feenin': Posthuman Voices in Contemporary Black Popular Music." *Social Text* 20, no. 2 (2002): 21–47.

———. *Habeas Viscus: Racializing Assemblages, Biopolitics, and Black Feminist Theories of the Human*. Durham, N.C.: Duke University Press, 2014.

Wekker, Gloria. *The Politics of Passion: Women's Sexual Culture in the Afro-Surinamese Diaspora*. New York: Columbia University Press, 2006.

Weldon Johnson, James. *Autobiography of an Ex-Colored Man*. Boston: Sherman, French, & Company, 1912.

West, Cornel. *Prophesy Deliverance! An Afro-American Revolutionary Christianity*. Louisville, Ky.: Westminster John Knox Press, 2002.

Wiegman, Robyn. *Object Lessons*. Durham, N.C.: Duke University Press, 2012.

Wilson Gilmore, Ruth. *Golden Gulag: Prisons, Surplus, Crisis, and Opposition in Globalizing California*. Berkeley: University of California Press, 2007.

Wimbush, Vincent L. *White Men's Magic: Scripturalization as Slavery*. Oxford: Oxford University Press, 2012.

Winddance Twine, France. *A White Side of Black Britain: Interracial Intimacy and Racial Literacy*. Durham, N.C.: Duke University Press, 2010.

Wiredu, Kwasi. "African Religions from a Philosophical Point of View." In *Blackwell Companion to Philosophy of Religion*, edited by Philip L. Quinn and Charles Taliaferro, 34–42. Malden, Mass.: Blackwell, 2000.

———. "Introduction: African Philosophy in Our Time." In *Blackwell Companion to African Philosophy*, edited by Kwasi Wiredu, 1–28. Malden, Mass.: Blackwell, 2006.

Woodard, Vincent. *The Delectable Negro: Human Consumption and Homoeroticism within U.S. Slave Culture*. Edited by Justin A. Joyce and Dwight A. McBride. New York: New York University Press, 2015.

Woods, Clyde Adrian. *Development Arrested: The Blues and Plantation Power in the Mississippi Delta*. Haymarket Series. New York: Verso, 1998.

Wynter, Sylvia. "1492: A New World View." In *Race, Discourse, and the Origin of the Americas: A New World View*, edited by Vera Lawrence Hyatt and Rex Nettleford, 5–57. Washington, D.C.: Smithsonian Institution Press, 1995.

———. "Beyond Miranda's Meanings: Un/silencing the 'Demonic Ground' of Caliban's 'Woman.'" In *Out of the Kumbla: Caribbean Women and*

Literature, edited by Carole B. Davies and Elaine S. Fido, 355–70. Trenton, N.J.: Africa World Press, 1990.

———. "Beyond the Categories of the Master Conception: The Counterdoctrine of the Jamesian Poiesis." In *C. L. R. James's Caribbean*, edited by Paget Henry and Paul Buhle. Durham, N.C.: Duke University Press, 1992.

———. "Beyond the Word of Man: Glissant and the New Discourse of the Antilles." *World Literature Today* 63, no. 4 (Autumn 1989): 637–48.

———. "Black Metamorphosis: New Natives in a New World." Unpublished manuscript.

———. "The Ceremony Must Be Found: After Humanism." *boundary 2* 12/13 (1984): 19–70.

———. "'Genital Mutilation' or 'Symbolic Birth'? Female Circumcision, Lost Origins, and the Aculturalism of Feminist/Western Thought." *Case Western Reserve Law Review* 47, no. 2 (1997): 501–52.

———. *The Hills of Hebron*. Kingston, Jamaica: Ian Randle Publishers, 2010.

———. "Human Being as Noun? Or *Being Human* as Praxis? Towards the Autopoetic Turn/Overturn: A Manifesto." *The Frantz Fanon Blog*, October 27, 2014, http://readingfanon.blogspot.be/2014/10/Sylvia-wynter -human-being-as-noun-or.html.

———. "On How We Mistook the Map for the Territory and Re-Imprisoned Ourselves in Our Unbearable Wrongness of Being, of Désêtre: Black Studies Toward the Human Project." In *Not Only the Master's Tools: African-American Studies in Theory and Practice*, edited by Lewis Ricardo Gordon and Jane Anna Gordon, 107–69. Boulder, Colo.: Paradigm, 2006.

———. "One Love—Rhetoric or Reality?—Aspects of Afro-Jamaicanism." *Caribbean Studies* 12, no. 3 (1972): 64–97.

———. "The Pope Must Have Been Drunk, the King of Castile a Madman: Culture as Actuality, and the Caribbean Rethinking of Modernity." In *The Reordering of Culture: Latin America, the Caribbean and Canada in the Hood*, edited by Alvina Ruprecht and Cecilia Taiana, 17–41. Ottawa: Carleton University Press, 1995.

———. "Sambos and Minstrels." *Social Text* 1 (1979): 149–56.

———. "Unsettling the Coloniality of Being/Power/Truth/Freedom: Towards the Human, after Man, Its Overrepresentation—An Argument." *CR: The New Centennial Review* 3, no. 3 (Fall 2003): 257–337.

Wynter, Sylvia, and Katherine McKittrick. "Unparalleled Catastrophe for Our Species? Or, To Give Humanness a Different Future: Conversations." In *Sylvia Wynter: On Being Human as Praxis*, edited by Katherine McKittrick, 9–89. Durham, N.C.: Duke University Press, 2015.

Yanuck, Julius. "The Garner Fugitive Slave Case." *Mississippi Valley Histori-cal Review* 40, no. 1 (June 1953): 47–66.

Zahan, Dominique. *The Religion, Spirituality and Thought of Traditional Africa*. Chicago: University of Chicago Press, 1970.

RUFUS BURNETT JR. is a native of Gulfport, Mississippi, and an assistant professor of systematic theology at Fordham University. He previously taught within the Africana Department and Balfour-Hesburgh Scholars Program at the University of Notre Dame. His area of study focuses on the sonic, spatial, and embodied realities of the Christian imagination. His latest book, *Decolonizing Revelation: A Spatial Reading of the Blues* (Fortress Academic, 2018), takes up these realities with regard to the American music genre known as the blues. Burnett's constructive approach to systematic theology looks to expose the theological insights of people groups that respond to domination through the creative use of cultural production.

M. SHAWN COPELAND is a professor of systematic theology at Boston College. An award-winning writer, Copeland is the author and/or editor of six books, including *Enfleshing Freedom: Body, Race, and Being* (Fortress Press, 2009) and *The Subversive Power of Love: The Vision of Henriette Delille* (Paulist Press, 2009), and more than 125 articles, book chapters, reviews, and blog entries on spirituality, theological anthropology, political theology, social suffering, gender, and race.

JOSEPH DREXLER-DREIS is an assistant professor of theology at Xavier University of Louisiana. He is the author if *Decolonial Love: Salvation in Colonial Modernity* (Fordham University Press, 2018).

YOMAIRA C. FIGUEROA is an assistant professor of Afro-diaspora studies in the Department of English at Michigan State University. Written through the lens of decoloniality, women of color feminisms, and feminist philosophy, her forthcoming book, *Decolonizing Diasporas: Radical Mappings of Afro-Atlantic Literature* (Northwestern University Press, 2020), examines the textual, historical, and political relations between diasporic/exilic Puerto Rican, Cuban, Dominican, and Equatoguinean poetics. Her published work can be found in *Hypatia: A Journal of Feminist Philosophy*, *Decolonization: Indigeneity, Education & Society*, *CENTRO: Journal of the Center for Puerto Rican Studies*, and *SX Salon*. A scholar and organizer, she is a founder of the MSU Womxn of Color Initiative and of the collaborative hurricane recovery project #ProyectoPalabrasPR.

PATRICE HAYNES is a senior lecturer in philosophy at Liverpool Hope University. She publishes in the areas of continental philosophy of religion and feminist philosophy. She is currently working on her second monograph on the topic of decolonizing philosophy of religion specifically in light of African indigenous religions and philosophies.

KRISTIEN JUSTAERT wrote a doctoral dissertation on the concept of transcendence within immanence in the work of Heidegger, Derrida, and Deleuze ("Transcendentie in immanentie. Goddelijke hoogtes en laagtes met Heidegger, Deleuze en Derrida," Garant, 2010). Since then, her research interests have been situated within liberation philosophies and theologies, feminist and queer theories and theologies, and new materialist theories. She wrote *Theology after Deleuze* (Continuum, 2012) as well as several articles on Deleuze and theology. Currently, she is the director of a Belgian environmental nonprofit organization.

XHERCIS MÉNDEZ is an assistant professor in women and gender studies at California State University, Fullerton. She is a transdisciplinary scholar-activist whose research focuses on developing decolonial feminist methodologies and practices for building toward transformative justice and expanding our liberatory imaginations. She is the founder of the Transformative Justice Speaker Series and Initiative at Michigan State University and a co-organizer of the collaborative hurricane recovery project #ProyectoPalabrasPR. Her published work includes "Notes toward a Decolonial Feminist Methodology: Revisiting the Race/Gender Matrix" (*Trans-Scripts*, 2015), "Which Black Lives Matter?: Gender, State-Sanctioned Violence and 'My Brother's Keeper'" (*Radical History Review*, 2016), and her forthcoming article "Decolonial Feminist Movidas: A Caribeña Rethinks 'Privilege,' the Wages of Gender, and Building Complex Coalitions." She is currently working on her book project entitled *Decolonizing Feminist Methodologies from the Dark Side*.

ANDREW PREVOT is an associate professor of systematic theology at Boston College. He is the author of *Theology and Race: Black and Womanist Traditions in the United States* (Brill, forthcoming) and *Thinking Prayer: Theology and Spirituality amid the Crises of Modernity* (Notre Dame University Press, 2015). He is the coeditor of *Anti-Blackness and Christian Ethics* (Orbis, 2017). He has published articles on various aspects of spiritual, philosophical, and political theology in journals such as *Horizons, Pro Ecclesia, Spiritus, Heythrop, Tijdschrift voor Theologie, Transversalités, Political Theology,* and the *Journal of Feminist Studies in Religion.*

MAYRA RIVERA is a professor of religion and Latinx studies at Harvard University. Rivera works at the intersections between continental philosophy of religion, literature, and theories of coloniality, race, and gender—with particular attention to Caribbean postcolonial thought. Her research explores the relationship between discursive and material dimensions in shaping human embodiment. Her most recent book, *Poetics of the Flesh* (Duke University Press, 2015), analyzes theological, philosophical, and political descriptions of flesh as metaphors for understanding how social discourses materialize in human bodies. Rivera is currently developing a project that explores narratives of catastrophe in twentieth century Caribbean writing.

LINN MARIE TONSTAD is an associate professor of systematic theology at Yale Divinity School. Her interests include theology, queer and feminist theory, and theory and method in religious studies. She is the author of two books, *God and Difference: The Trinity, Sexuality, and the Transformation of Finitude* (Routledge, 2016) and *Queer Theology: Beyond Apologetics* (Cascade, 2018).

ALEXANDER G. WEHELIYE is a professor of African American studies at Northwestern University, where he teaches black literature and culture, critical theory, social technologies, and popular culture. He is the author of *Phonographies: Grooves in Sonic Afro-Modernity* (Duke University Press, 2005) and *Habeas Viscus: Racializing Assemblages, Biopolitics, and Black Feminist Theories of the Human* (Duke University Press, 2014). Currently, he is working on two projects. The first, *Feenin: R & B's Technologies of Humanity*, offers a critical history of the intimate relationship between R & B music and technology since the late 1970s. The second, *Black Life/SchwarzSein*, situates Blackness as an ungendered ontology of unbelonging.

CPSIA information can be obtained
at www.ICGtesting.com
Printed in the USA
LVHW111908291019
635711LV00003B/307/P